Spelling? Capitalization? Hyphenation? Titles?
Symbols? Usage? Possessives? Numerals? Punctuation?
Pluralization? Abbreviations? Proper Nouns?

21st CENTURY MANUAL OF STYLE

From the prestigious Princeton Language Institute and the renowned lexicographer Barbara Ann Kipfer, Ph.D., comes this remarkably accessible reference for people who need fast, definitive answers to questions about style and usage. Whether you're a journalist who relies on a style manual daily or a first-time user, this authoritative, easy-to-understand handbook will relieve the agonizing process of deciphering the dense guides currently available—and leave you with more time to do what you need to do . . . *write.*

—21ST—
CENTURY
MANUAL
OF STYLE

21ST CENTURY MANUAL OF STYLE

EDITED BY

THE PRINCETON LANGUAGE INSTITUTE

□

Barbara Ann Kipfer, Ph.D.,

HEAD LEXICOGRAPHER

□

PRODUCED BY THE PHILIP LIEF GROUP, INC.

A LAUREL BOOK
Published by
Dell Publishing
a division of
Bantam Doubleday Dell Publishing Group, Inc.
1540 Broadway
New York, New York 10036

Published by arrangement with The Philip Lief Group, Inc.
6 West 20th Street
New York, New York 10011

ISBN: 0-440-22074-2

Printed in the United States of America

Published simultaneously in Canada

May 1995

10 9 8 7 6 5 4 3 2 1

OPM

CONTENTS

Introduction/How to Use   ix

Part One **FORM: FROM A TO Z**
Abbreviation, Capitalization, Compounding, Hyphenation,
Pluralization, Punctuation, Variants   1

Part Two **DESCRIPTION**
Academic Degrees and Titles   259
Addresses   260
Aircraft Names   260
Arabic Numerals   261
Automobiles   261
Cabinet of the United States   261
Companies   261
Courtesy Titles   268
Formal Titles   268
Fraternal Organizations   269
Geographic Terms   269
Government Organizations   279
Historical Events and Periods   284
Labor Organizations   285
Languages   287
Military Titles and Organizations   288
Nobility Titles   290

Organizational and Team Names   291
Organizational Titles   295
Personal Names   296
Proper Nouns and Their Derivatives   297
Religious Concepts, Titles, and Organizations   297
Religious Writings   301
Roman Numerals   302
Titles of Works   303
Trademarks and Trade Names   303
Vehicle Names   306

Part Three   RULES OF PUNCTUATION

Appendices

1. Abbreviations   319
2. Affixes: Prefixes and Suffixes   324
3. Animals: Group and Young Names   338
4. Months and Days: Abbreviations   339
5. Nations of the World: With Capital, Resident Name   339
6. Official Forms of Address for Letter Writing   342
7. States and Territories Information: Standard and Two-Letter
   Postal Abbreviations, Capital, Resident Name   344
8. Weights and Measures   346

Proofreader's Signs and Symbols

350

INTRODUCTION

WHAT IS STYLE?

American English is rich and varied. Given the breadth and magnitude of the language, writers often encounter instances of ambiguity when they attempt to express themselves in writing.

Fortunately, a few systems of composition can help to ensure that what is written will be understood. When ideas are transferred from the mind to paper, the rules of grammar first order a writer's thoughts. Efforts to convey the proper meaning are then fine-tuned by paying close attention to *stylistic* considerations. In writing, *style* refers to the customary practices of spelling, punctuation, capitalization, abbreviation, and typography. The manner in which these elements of style are employed throughout your prose subtly directs the form and appearance of the completed written piece. Therefore, style considerations greatly impact upon the tone and character of your writing, exercising a profound influence over how your meaning will be received by your reader. The more rigidly a standard of style is observed, the more coherently and exactly your intentions will be translated into text. The less uniformly style standards are respected, the less precise and accurate your writing inherently will become.

Whether composing a novel, a business letter, or a term paper, strive for good style by adhering to a set of guidelines that are consistent, appropriate to the nature of the text, and likely to be familiar to your readership.

WHY YOU NEED THE *21ST CENTURY MANUAL OF STYLE*

The *21st Century Manual of Style,* arranged in a convenient dictionary format, breathes new relevance and flexibility into the classic style guide—making it a vital new interpretation perfectly suited to contemporary writers of all kinds, at all levels of ability.

Traditionally, style manuals have appealed to a narrow group of users, made up primarily of journalists, publishing professionals, and serious writers and academics. Characterized by labyrinthine explanations of style points, and often eccentrically organized, these manuals render a search for a simple rule extremely frustrating to the user who does not have enough time or interest to wade through copious pages of arcane prose for help in making a fast style decision.

With the *21st Century Manual of Style*, it is no longer necessary to decipher a complex structure like that of confusing style tomes. By blending the fundamental content of a traditional style manual with the ease and simplicity of a dictionary format, "21st-century" users can now resolve any common style question by simply looking up the troublesome word or problem alphabetically, and noting the answer. This vastly limits the amount of time and attention directed away from the writing process.

Both efficient and comprehensive, the *21st Century Manual of Style* gives users the advantage in easily determining the proper styling for everything from Baltimore Oriole to Beaufort scale to BLT. An indispensible companion to the dictionary, thesaurus, and grammar handbook, this "21st-century" compendium rolls their essentials all into one and adds to the mix an expansive representation of proper nouns and popular factual information—from the signs of the Zodiac to the names and terms of Supreme Court Justices. Careful attention has been given to select factual entries that provide answers to the questions writers most commonly ask; questions that can waste precious writing time spent poring over encyclopedias, almanacs, and other reference works for a simple name or date.

MATTERS OF STYLE

Style is fluid, as is language. A style manual must reflect contemporary linguistic transformation in order to be relevant—if language changes, a good style manual must recognize those shifts and incorporate them. The *21st Century Manual of Style* presents in one volume, an all-new, authoritative lexical compilation of cutting-edge information and insight regarding all aspects and details of style that are of practical interest to "21st-century" writers.

This computer-age style manual tells whether your software is *user friendly* or *user-friendly*. Gender-sensitive entries respect the movement toward equality of the sexes in the words we choose, and list the preferred forms of address acceptable for women and men today. Abreast of the changing face of the world, the *21st Century Manual of Style* includes up-to-the-minute names and spellings of post-Soviet republics and Eastern European nations.

Entries consisting of new words and advice about their proper spelling and usage (information that is not yet available in dictionaries) incorporate terms entering the popular culture through business, science, technology, politics, environmentalism, and the arts—from *greenhouse gasses* to *Twelve Step* to *glasnost* to *virtual reality*, and scores more. Hundreds of the most popular trademarks, the most prominent companies and corporations, current place names, titles and common abbreviations may be accessed by users in seconds.

The *21st Century Manual of Style* distills and prioritizes a myriad of contemporary style concerns to produce the innovative style sourcebook writers must have to keep up with the latest developments in a fast-changing world of sound bites.

STATE-OF-THE-ART STYLE

The widespread use of personal computers and laser printers has brought publishing capabilities into millions of homes and offices. While technological advances do permit laypeople to output polished documents, the computer has yet to supplant the style sensibility of its user.

The ability to manipulate factors like font and type create a number of interesting style questions. When are titles set off in quotes? When putting a resume together, should text be italicized or underscored? What is boldface used for? If you are printing a business report, a flier, your curriculum vitae, or a thesis from a personal computer, you'll find you can no longer hide behind the stylistic ambiguities a typed or written draft previously afforded you. Your approach to style must be as meticulous, demanding, and current as that of a publishing professional.

When producing a typeset page, matters of style become glaringly obvious; the *21st Century Manual of Style* is designed to help make writers compatible with their computers, enabling desktoppers to produce high-quality style-conscious documents.

21ST-CENTURY STYLE

Today's users will appreciate the easy access to a wealth of pertinent, timely information and strategies for styling their writing, all stored and presented in a convenient dictionary format. Traditional style manuals must give way to the *21st Century Manual of Style*—a new reference standard compiled with the contemporary writer's style needs and concerns in mind.

HOW TO USE

The *21st Century Manual of Style* is organized for maximum ease of use and optimum efficiency. It is divided into three parts: Part One, "Form: From A to Z," is a dictionary of words and terms that are often styled incorrectly, along with at-a-glance guidelines for their proper styling; Part Two, "Description," is a catalogue of thousands of Proper Nouns and the rules of style that govern them; and Part Three, "Rules of Punctuation," gives users a brief overview and refresher of the essentials.

PART ONE
FORM: FROM A TO Z

Entries in this comprehensive dictionary of style appear in boldface and usually consist of the troublesome word or phrase alone. In traditional style manuals, users are often forced to read the rules regarding abbreviation, capitalization, compounding, hyphenization, pluralization, punctuation, and variants and then interpret the few examples that are given with those rules to arrive at the proper styling for the word or term they want to apply in their own writing. Now, "21st-century" users simply have to look up the word or phrase as an entry in the *21st Century Manual of Style* to find its correct styling. If more information about styling is necessary, a brief further explanation accompanies the boldfaced entry.

Entries provide all the style answers, at your fingertips from A to Z. Users find, for example:

- **CPU** is the abbreviation for *central processing unit*;
- **Earth** is capitalized when referring to the planet and lowercased to signify "dirt" or "ground;"
- **fiber optics** is two words as a noun, and hyphenated as an adjective;
- compounds ending in **-holder** are usually one word, as in *mortgageholder*;
- **insure** and **ensure**, words easily confused with each other, are cross-referenced and defined;
- **Mother's Day** is capitalized and is the second Sunday in May;
- the plural of **parenthesis** is spelled **parentheses**;
- **résumé** is accented in this preferred manner, but **resume** or **resumé** are also acceptable;
- **souvenir**, a frequently misspelled word, is correctly spelled;
- **translucent** and **transparent**, two words commonly misused, are cross-referenced and defined;
- **vein, vane,** and **vain**, homonyms, are also cross-referenced and defined;
- compounds beginning with **zyg-, zygo-,** meaning to yoke or pair, are written as one word: *zygomorphic*.

Users will also find entries in Part One that pertain to general style considerations, like the styling of medical terms or scientific terms. These entries are invaluable when a governing style decision must be made, or a rule of internal consistency determined—answering questions like:

Are names of computer languages written as all capitals?
When are Latin names and expressions italicized?
How are meteorological terms styled?

Whether you are looking for a specific word or phrase, or an overarching rule to apply, Part One, "Form: From A to Z" gives concise, immediate gratification on all matters of style.

PART TWO
DESCRIPTION

"Description" will answer users' questions regarding the styling of Proper Nouns. Nouns are divided by category—from "Academic Degrees and Titles," "Geographic Terms," and "Languages" to "Roman Numerals," "Titles of Works," and "Trademarks and Trade Names." See the table of contents for a complete category listing.

Each category begins with general guidelines outlining any special styling requirements that are specific to it. These rules are followed by a complete alphabetical selection of hundreds of correctly styled Proper Nouns in common usage within that individual category.

For example, users may find enough information by simply looking up the general guidelines that apply to "Government Organizations" in order to solve a particular style predicament. Or they may continue to look through the listing of Proper Nouns to find the precise styling for *Joint Chiefs of Staff, Library of Congress, National Park Service* or whatever government-related group is sought.

The *21st Century Manual of Style* contains more Proper Nouns in current usage from more categories than any other style manual. Its extensive wide-ranging listings make it an indispensible desk reference for writers.

PART THREE
RULES OF PUNCTUATION

When all that's needed to resolve a tricky issue is the proper way to punctuate, users can get quick and relevant advice from consulting this brief condensation of the fundamentals. The ''Rules of Punctuation'' forms a convenient primer on how to use all of the major punctuation marks—from apostrophes to slashes, how to divide words, and how to use numbers in text.

The *21st Century Manual of Style* gives users grammar-at-a-glance—as much as they need or want to know, in clear straightforward language.

APPENDICES

Eight invaluable appendices consisting of commonly accessed information—like ''Official Forms of Address'' and ''Weights and Measures''—are grouped together at the back of the manual. The *21st Century Manual of Style* closes with a complete bibliography of related reference works, and a comprehensive set of proofreader's signs and symbols.

Use the *21st Century Manual of Style* to save invaluable time and effort as you endeavor to make ''style'' an inconspicuous component of your writing. Such an achievement will free those who read your work to concentrate on its substance, rather than its form.

1

FORM:
FROM A TO Z

a Article used before consonant or consonant sounds (e.g., *a car, a historical fact*).

Å *or* **A** Abbreviations for *angstrom unit*.

abacus; *pl.,* **abaci** *or* **abacuses**

abbé French clerical title.

abbr. *or* **abbrev.** Abbreviations for *abbreviated, abbreviation*.

abbreviation If an abbreviation is commonly pronounced as a word, the periods in between are usually omitted (e.g., *AWOL*).

When an abbreviation stands for one word (e.g., *TV*), periods are always omitted.

When an abbreviation begins with a capital letter but the rest is lowercase (e.g., *Eng.*) there is a period after the abbreviation.

Contracted abbreviations do not end with a period (e.g., *sec'y*).

abbreviation, capitalization Abbreviations are capitalized if the letters represent proper nouns or adjectives (e.g., *NBA*).

Abbreviations are usually capitalized if they represent the initial letters of the words from which they are being formed (e.g., *CPA, MVP*).

Abbreviations pronounced as words are capitalized (e.g., *OPEC, BASIC*).

abbreviation, plurals Abbreviations of single words are pluralized by adding *s* before the period (e.g., *adjs.*).

Abbreviations of compounds are pluralized by adding *'s* after the final period (e.g., *Ph.D.'s*).

Abbreviations written without punctuation are pluralized by adding *s* (e.g., *VDTs*).

Lowercase single-letter abbreviations are pluralized by doubling the letter (e.g., *pp. 48–50*).

Plurals of units of measure are the same as the singular (e.g., *4 in.*).

abbreviation, possessives The possessive is formed as if the abbreviation were written out: the singular adds *'s* (e.g., *IBM's employees*); the plural adds the apostrophe only (e.g., *Smith Bros.' products*).

ABC; *pl.,* **ABC's** *or* **ABCs**

abettor *or* **abetter**

abhorrent, abhorrible

abide, abode *or* **abided**

ab init. Abbreviation for *ab initio*, "from the beginning."

abjure To renounce, disavow. (Compare **adjure**.)

abl. Abbreviation for *ablative case*.

able-bodied *or* **ablebodied**

A-bomb

Aboriginal, Aborigine Refers to the indigenous people of Australia when capitalized.

aboriginal An adjective meaning first, indigenous.

aborigine; *pl.,* **aboriginals** *or* **aborigines** Any of the first or earliest known inhabitants of a region.

about-face As noun and verb.

aboveboard As adjective and adverb.

abr. Abbreviation for *abridged, abridgment, abridger.*

abridgment *or* **abridgement**

abscess

abscission

absence

absentminded *or* **absent-minded**

absinthe *or* **absinth**

absorb To take in or suck in. (Compare **adsorb**.)

abstract Do not capitalize, even if written with number, letter, or date.

abysmal

AC Abbreviation for *alternating current.*

A/C Abbreviation for *air-conditioning*

academy Capitalize if part of proper noun.

a cappella *or* **a capella**

acc. Abbreviation for *accusative case.*

accede To yield or consent. (Compare **exceed**.)

accent marks A mark used to show the placing or kind of emphasis on a letter or syllable of a word. They include acute (á), grave (è), and circumflex (ô) accents. Marks may be omitted in commonly used English words borrowed from foreign languages, like *resume, cafe.* (See also **diacritical marks**.)

accept To take or receive. (Compare **except**.)

accepter *or* **acceptor**

account payable; *pl.,* **accounts payable**

account receivable; *pl.,* **accounts receivable**

accountable Use with *to* or *for.*

accoutre *or* **accouter, accoutres** *or* **accouters, accoutring** *or* **accoutering, accoutrement** *or* **accouterment**

acct. Abbreviation for *account.*

accursed *or* **accurst**

accuse Use with *of,* not *with.*

acetic Acidy or vinegary. (Compare **ascetic**.)

Achilles' heel *or* **Achilles heel**

acknowledgment *or* **acknowledgement**

acre-foot

acre-inch

across-the-board

act Capitalize when part of the name of a piece of legislation: *Freedom of Information Act.*

act of God

acting Always lowercase, but with titles, use as follows: *the acting chair, Samuel Withers* or *acting Chair Samuel Withers.*

activate To start or make happen. (Compare **actuate**.)

actuate To incite or move to action. (Compare **activate**.)

A.D. Abbreviation for *anno Domini,* "in the year of the lord." It is printed before the date (e.g., *A.D. 1066*) and the typeface is often small capitals.

Adams, Abigail (1744–1818) American writer.

Adams, Ansel Easton (1902–1984). American photographer.

Adam's apple

Adams, Henry Brooks (1838–1918) Historian.

adapt To make fit or to fit in. (Compare **adopt**.)

adapt. Abbreviation for *adaptation* or *adapted*.

adapted Use with *to, for,* or *from.*

adapter *or* **adaptor**

addable *or* **addible**

Addison's disease A disease caused by failure of the adrenal glands.

addnl. Abbreviation for *additional.*

add-on Hyphenate as noun.

à deux

adherent, adherence

ad hoc Adjective or adverb, literally meaning ''for this'' (i.e., for a particular end or purpose).

adieu; *pl.,* **adieus** *or* **adieux**

ad inf. Abbreviation for *ad infinitum,* ''to infinity.''

adj. Abbreviation for *adjective.*

adjacent Use with *to.*

adjure To implore, ask earnestly. (Compare **abjure**.)

adjuster *or* **adjustor**

adjutant general; *pl.,* **adjutants general** Capitalize as formal title preceding name.

ad-lib To improvise.

adm., admin. Abbreviation for *administration, administrator, administrative.*

administration Usually lowercase. Capitalize when referring to the federal government under a specific president (e.g., *the Carter Administration*).

administrator Capitalize as formal title preceding name.

ad nauseam

adopt To take by choice or voluntarily. (Compare **adapt**.)

Amendments, ordinances, resolutions, and rules are *adopted* or *approved.* (Compare **approve, enact, pass.**)

adopted Adjective referring to the person or thing chosen or accepted (e.g., *the adopted child, the adopted legislation*).

adoptive Adjective referring to the ones that adopt (e.g., *the adoptive parents*).

Adrenalin Capitalize as the name of the synthetic drug. (Compare **adrenaline** as the name of the hormone and in figurative use.)

adsorb To condense on a surface of a solid or liquid. (Compare **absorb**.)

adv. Abbreviation for *adverb.*

advent Capitalize the religious season. Lowercase to mean coming, arrival.

adverse Unfavorable, hostile, contrary, opposing. (Compare **averse**.)

advice Recommendation or counsel. (Compare **advise**.)

advise To recommend or give counsel. (Compare **advice**.)

adviser *or* **advisor**

advisory

adz *or* **adze**

aegis (Not *egis.*) Protection or sponsorship. Usually used in the construction *under the aegis of.*

aerate

aerator

aerial

aerobics

aeronautics

aerospace

aesthetic *or* **esthetic**

AF Abbreviation for *audio frequency*.

affect To influence, produce a result, or change. (Compare **effect**.)

afferent Conducting toward or inward. Used especially in relation to the brain or spinal cord. (Compare **efferent**.)

affidavit

affinity Use with *between* or *with* because mutuality is meant.

afflict To cause distress or pain, often in an emotional sense. (Compare **inflict**.)

Afghan hound

aficionado

AFL Abbreviation for *American Football League*.

A-flat

AFL-CIO Abbreviation for *American Federation of Labor and Congress of Industrial Organizations*.

aforementioned

aforesaid

aforethought

afoul Use with *of*.

A-frame

African American Hyphenate when used as an adjective.

African violet

after When used to form a noun (e.g., *aftereffect*), usually no hyphen is used. As part of an adjective (e.g., *after-hours*), usually hyphenate.

after-shave

afterward *or* **afterwards**

again and again As adverb.

age Capitalize if naming a period in history or culture (e.g., *Stone Age, Gilded Age*) but not as a general reference to a more recent period of time (e.g., *space age, age of steam*).

age, aging *or* **ageing**

age-group

agency Capitalize if part of proper noun: *Central Intelligence Agency*.

agenda A list. Plural, *agendas*. (Compare **agendum**.)

agendum An item on a list. Plural, *agenda*; also *agendums* (items on an agenda). (Compare **agenda**.)

Agent Orange

agent provocateur; *pl.*, **agents provocateurs**

agnostic One who is unsure of the existence of a higher being or god. (Compare **atheist**.)

agreeable Use with *to*.

agreement Capitalize if part of proper noun.

agric. Abbreviation for *agricultural, agriculture*.

aha As interjection.

ahold As noun.

aid Assistance or to assist. (Compare **aide**.)

aide A person who gives assistance. (Compare **aid**.)

aide-de-camp; *pl.*, **aides-de-camp**

aide-mémoire Same as both singular and plural noun. Means a memory aid.

AIDS Abbreviation for *acquired immunodeficiency syndrome*.

air- Most compounds beginning with *air* are spelled closed: *airdate, airport*. Exceptions that take a hyphen include: *air-condition, air-cool, air-dry*. Exceptions that are written as

6

separate words include: *air bag, air base, air force* (capitalized as part of proper name), *air mattress, air raid, air pocket, air pressure, air time*.

airline Capitalize if part of proper noun.

airport Capitalize if part of proper noun.

a.k.a. Abbreviation for *also known as*.

AL Abbreviation for *American League* (baseball).

à la *or* **a la** French, meaning "in the manner of."

à la carte *or* **a la carte**

à la king

à la mode *or* **a la mode**

albacore; *pl.,* **albacore** *or* **albacores**

albatross; *pl.,* **albatross** *or* **albatrosses**

albeit Means "although it be" or "even though."

albino; *pl.,* **albinos**

albumen The white of an egg. (Compare **albumin**.)

albumin The protein contained in an egg and other tissues and fluids. (Compare **albumen**.)

Alcott, Louisa May (1832–1888) American writer. Author of *Little Women*.

al dente

alfresco

alga; *pl.,* **algae**

Alger, Horatio (1832–1899) American clergyman and author of popular books for boys.

ALGOL *or* **Algol** A language for programming a computer.

algorithm

alien Use with *to*.

alienable Transferable.

alight, alighted *or* **alit**

A-line

alkali; *pl.,* **alkalies** *or* **alkalis**

all- Most words beginning with the prefix *all* are hyphenated (e.g., *all-American, all-embracing, all-important, all-night, all-star*).

all fours As noun.

all get-out As noun.

Allied Governments

Allied Nations

Allied Powers

allies Capitalize if referring to the United States and its Allies during world wars.

all-or-nothing

allot, allotted, allotting; allotment

all out As adverb.

all-out As adjective.

all over As adverb.

all ready Prepared or in place. (Compare **already**.)

all right Do not use *alright*.

all-time *or* **all time** Hyphenate as a modifier before the noun; leave open when used after the noun.

all together Collectively, as a group, all in one place. (Compare **altogether**.)

all told As adverb.

allude To hint or refer to without specific mention. (Compare **elude, illude, refer**.)

allusion A hint, an indirect reference. (Compare **illusion**.)

alma mater; *pl.,* **alma maters**

almighty As adjective and adverb. Capitalize when used as name for supreme deity (e.g., *the Almighty*).

alms Singular and plural spelling.

aloof Use with *from.*

already Before, previous. (Compare **all ready**.)

also-ran; *pl.,* **also-rans**

altar A platform or table used in religious services. (Compare **alter**.)

alter To change. (Compare **altar**.)

alternately Every other, or by turns. (Compare **alternatively**.)

alternative Usually a choice between two things, though not wrong to use when referring to more than two choices.

alternatively In a manner that may be chosen, or by selecting between two or more things. (Compare **alternately**.)

alto; *pl.,* **altos**

altogether Completely, wholly, entirely. (Compare **all together**.)

alumnus; *pl.,* **alumni** Graduate(s).

Alzheimer's disease

a.m. *or* **A.M.** Abbreviation for *ante meridiem,* "before noon." The typeface is often small capitals.

amanuensis; *pl.,* **amanuenses**

ambassador Capitalize when used as formal title preceding a name.

ambience *or* **ambiance**

ambient Surrounding.

ambulant Moving around, itinerant. (Compare **ambulatory**.)

ambulatory Able to walk. (Compare **ambulant**.)

amend To improve or correct. Used in a variety of contexts. (Compare **emend**).

amendment Capitalize if referring to the amendments of the U.S. Constitution (e.g., *The Fifth Amendment*).

Amer. Abbreviation for *American, America.*

American cheese

American plan Hotel or inn service that includes a meal (or meals) as part of the daily rate. (Compare **European plan**.)

amiable Friendly, good-natured in disposition. (Compare **amicable**.)

amicable Friendly, peaceful in sociability. (Compare **amiable**.)

amid *or* **amidst**

amino Relating to acid in protein. (Compare **ammino**.)

Amish

ammino Relating to a molecule of ammonia. (Compare **amino**.)

amnesia; amnesiac *or* **amnesic**

amniocentesis; *pl.,* **amniocenteses**

amoeba; *pl.,* **amoebas** *or* **amoebae**

amok *or* **amuck**

amoral Having no moral standard or principle. (Compare **immoral**.)

amorous *or* **amative** Loving, disposed to loving.

amour

amour propre Self-esteem.

amp Shortened version of *amperage, ampere,* or *amplifier.*

ampersand This element of punctuation (&) replaces the word *and* when a shorter form is desirable. It should not be used in proper nouns, titles, document titles, or addresses unless it is part of the legal name. In abbreviations, often the spacing is omitted around the ampersand (e.g., *R&D*).

amphitheater *or* **amphitheatre**

ampoule or **ampule** or **ampul**

an Article used before a word beginning with a vowel or vowel sounds (e.g., *an apple, an heir*).

anal. Abbreviation for *analogous, analogy; analysis, analytic, analyze.*

analog, analogy, analogous

analysis; *pl.,* **analyses**

analyst A person who studies something in detail. (Compare **annalist**.)

anat. Abbreviation for *anatomic, anatomical, anatomy.*

anathema

anatomical or **anatomic**

anchor A radio or TV newscaster.

anchovy; *pl.,* **anchovies** or **anchovys**

ancien régime The old order, a system or rule no longer in effect.

ancillary Something that is not primary, that is secondary or extra.

anemia or **anaemia; anemic** or **anaemic**

anesthesia or **anaesthesia; anesthetic** or **anaesthetic**

aneurysm

angelfish

angel food cake

angelic or **angelical**

angel-hair pasta

Anglice or **anglice** Adverb meaning in an anglicized manner.

anglicize Always lowercase.

Anglo- A combining form meaning English. Hyphenated except for *Anglomania, Anglophile, Anglophobia.*

angora Lowercase; refers to the hair of an Angora rabbit or Angora goat (note capitalization).

angry Use with *at* or *with*.

anima Psychological term referring to the individual's inner self. (Compare **animus**.)

animal names Common and domestic names of animals are usually lowercased, though proper nouns and adjectives are capitalized (e.g., *Cooper's hawk, Irish setter*). Many animal names have a plural form that can be the same as the singular or can also take a suffix (e.g. *buffalo*; pl., *buffalo* or *buffalos*); others always add *s* to create the plural (e.g., *cat*; pl., *cats*); some always have identical singular and plural forms (e.g., *moose*; pl., *moose*).

animus Refers to a person's disposition. (Compare **anima**.)

anise

ankh

annalist A person who records historical detail. (Compare **analyst**.)

anno Domini Usually abbreviated, as *A.D.* (see entry).

annoyed Use with *by, at,* or *with*.

annul, annulled, annulling; annulment

anoint

anon. Abbreviation for *anonymous, anonymously.*

anorexia nervosa

antarctic Capitalize if part of proper noun (e.g., *Antarctic Circle*).

ante- This prefix means before. Compounds with *ante-* are formed without a hyphen unless the second part of the compound starts with a capital letter or an *e* (e.g., *antebellum, antecedent, antediluvian*).

ante meridiem *or* **a.m.** *or* **A.M.**

antenna; *pl.*, **antennas** (electrical) *or* **antennae** (zoology)

Anthony, Susan Brownell (1820–1906) American reformer and women's suffragist.

anti- This prefix means against. Compounds with *anti-* are written as one word unless second part is a proper noun (e.g., *anti-American*) or begins with an *i* (e.g., *anti-institution*).

antipathy Use with *to, toward,* or *against.*

antithesis; *pl.*, **antitheses**

any When used with *one, thing, way,* or similar references, to single out a particular person or thing, the words are written separated by a space. When used in an indefinite sense, compounds with *any* are closed up (e.g., *anybody, anyone, anything, anyway, anywhere*).

A-OK

A1

aorta; *pl.*, **aortas** *or* **aortae**

Apache; *pl.*, **Apache** *or* **Apaches**

apart Use with *from.*

aperçu; *pl.*, **aperçus**

aperitif

aphrodisiac *or* **aphrodisiacal**

apiary A home for bees. (Compare **aviary**.)

apostasy; *pl.*, **apostasies**

a posteriori

Apostle's Creed

apothegm A short, instructive saying.

appall *or* **appal**

Appaloosa horse

apparatus; *pl.*, **apparatuses** *or* **apparatus**

appendix; *pl.*, **appendixes** *or* **appendices** Capitalize if part of document title or in reference to specific document part. Abbreviation is *app., apps.*

appliqué

apprise To inform. (Compare **apprize**.)

apprize To assign a value. (Compare **apprise**.)

approve Amendments, ordinances, resolutions, and rules are *approved* or *adopted*. (Compare **adopt, enact, pass**.)

approx. Abbreviation for *approximate, approximately.*

appt. Abbreviation for *appoint, appointed, appointment.*

APR Abbreviation for *annual percentage rate.*

après French, meaning "after." Usually used in combination and hyphenated.

April fool As noun.

April Fools' Day The first day of April.

a priori

apt. Abbreviation for *apartment.*

aquarium; *pl.*, **aquariums** *or* **aquaria**

Aquarius (see **Zodiac Signs**).

aqua vitae

aqueduct

Arabic numerals The figures used to represent numbers (that is, 1, 2, 3, etc.).

arbiter A person chosen to judge something. (Compare **arbitrator**.)

arbitrageur or **arbitrager**

arbitrate To judge in a legal context.

arbitrator A person chosen to judge something in a legal context. (Compare **arbiter**.)

arc A curve. (Compare **ark**.)

arch- This prefix primarily means chief or principal (e.g., **archduke**), but can be defined as meaning extreme in a pejorative sense (e.g., **archconservative**). Compounds with **arch-** are spelled as one word.

arch. The abbreviation for archaic.

archaeology or **archeology**; **archaeologist** or **archeologist**; **archaeological** or **archeological**

archetype; **archetypal** or **archetypical**

archipelago; *pl.*, **archipelagoes** or **archipelagos**

arctic Capitalize if part of proper noun (e.g., *Arctic Ocean*).

areola; *pl.*, **areolae** or **areolas**

argyle or **argyll**

Aries (see **Zodiac Signs**).

arise, arose

Aristotle (384–322 B.C.) Greek philosopher.

arith. Abbreviation for *arithmetic, arithmetical.*

arithmetic or **arithmetical**. As adjective.

ark A large boat. (Compare **arc**.)

ARM Abbreviation for *adjustable rate mortgage.* Spell out in text on first reference.

arm- Most compounds are one word (e.g., *armpit, armchair*.)

armadillo; *pl.*, **armadillos**

arm and a leg As noun, meaning a high price.

armful; *pl.*, **armfuls**

armoire

arm's length

arm-twisting

army Capitalize if part of proper noun as official name (e.g., *the U.S. Army*), otherwise, lowercase (e.g., *the American army*).

around-the-clock

arouse To get someone's attention or interest.

arrant Extreme, outright. (Compare **errant**.)

arrester or **arrestor**

arrive Use *at* or *with*.

arroyo; *pl.*, **arroyos**

art, works of (See Part 2, **Titles of works**.)

art deco or **Art Deco**

artesian well

arthritis; *pl.*, **arthritides**

article Capitalize the word *article* only if part of document title or in reference to specific document part. Abbreviation is *art.*; pl. *arts*. (See also Part 2, **Titles of works**.)

art nouveau or **Art Nouveau**

ASAP Abbreviation for *as soon as possible.*

ascend To go up.

ascendable or **ascendible**

ascendance or **ascendence**

ascent To rise or climb (verb) or a rise or climb (noun). (Compare **assent**.)

ascetic Austere or strict. (Compare **acetic**.)

ASCII Abbreviation for *American*

Standard Code for Information Interchange.

A-sharp

ashtray

Asian; *pl.*, **Asians**

askance *or* **askant**

asphyxia

aspirin; *pl.*, **aspirin** *or* **aspirins**

assay To examine, test. (Compare **essay**.)

assemblage A grouping, gathering together. (Compare **assembly**.)

assembly A formal group or gathering. (Compare **assemblage**.) Capitalize if part of proper noun.

assembly line

assemblyperson Capitalize only if part of a formal title preceding a name.

assent To agree or say yes (verb) and agreement (noun). (Compare **ascent**.)

assentor *or* **assenter**

assistant Capitalize only if part of a formal title preceding a name.

assoc. Abbreviation for *associate, associated, association*.

associate Capitalize if part of formal title.

association Capitalize if part of proper noun (e.g., *Parent-Teacher Association*). Abbreviation is *assn.* or *assoc.*

asst. Abbreviation for *assistant*.

assume To take for granted.

assure To give certainty or convince.

astrol. Abbreviation for *astrology, astrologer*.

astrological signs

astron. Abbreviation for *astronomy, astronomer*.

astronomical *or* **astronomic**

asymmetrical *or* **asymmetric**

atelier

atheist One who does not believe in a higher being or god. (Compare **agnostic**.)

atheistic *or* **atheistical**

athenaeum *or* **atheneum**

at-home As a modifier before the noun (e.g., *at-home card*).

at large Do not hyphenate, and capitalize only if part of the name of a specific person in a government position: *Joan Syms, Ambassador at Large*.

atlas; *pl.*, **atlases**

ATM Abbreviation for *automated* (or *automatic*) *teller machine*.

atm. Abbreviation for *atmosphere, atmospheric*.

atrium; *pl.*, **atria** *or* **atriums**

attaché

attn. Abbreviation for *attention*.

attorney Capitalize only when used as part of officeholder's formal title preceding name (e.g., *The plea bargain was arranged by District Attorney Constance Richards*; but *the attorney handled the settlement*). The abbreviation is *atty.*

attorney-at-law; *pl.*, **attorneys-at-law**

attorney general; *pl.*, **attorneys general** *or* **attorney generals** Capitalize if part of formal title, preceding name. Abbreviation is *atty. gen.*.

attorney's fees

attract; attractable; attractor

attribute; attributable; attributive

au courant

Auden, Wystan Hugh (1907–1973) American poet.

audio Usually spelled closed, without a hyphen, when used as a prefix (e.g., *audiofrequency, audiotape, audiovisual*).

auger A tool for drilling. (Compare **augur**.)

aught Nil, zero. (Compare **ought**.)

au gratin

augur To predict. (Compare **auger**.)

au jus

auld lang syne

au naturel

au pair A noun (French) meaning a young person who lives and works in a foreign home (as a housekeeper or child-care provider) in exchange for board and the opportunity to learn the family's language.

aural By ear. (Compare **oral**.)

au revoir

aurora; *pl.*, **auroras** *or* **aurorae**

aurora australis

aurora borealis

Austen, Jane (1775–1817) British novelist. Author of *Pride and Prejudice*.

authentic; authentically

autism

auto. Abbreviation for *automatic*.

autobiographical *or* **autobiographic**

autogiro *or* **autogyro**

automatic pilot *or* **autopilot**

automatically

auxiliary The abbreviation is *aux.* or *auxil.*

avant-garde

avenge To get back at for a wrong or injury on behalf of another. (Compare **revenge**.)

avenue Capitalize when used as part of address. The abbreviation is *ave.* or *av.*

average The sum of numbers divided by the quantity of numbers added together. The abbreviation is *avg.*

averse Not inclined to, unwilling, disapproving. (Compare **adverse**.)

aviary A home for birds. (Compare **apiary**.)

aviator

avocado; *pl.*, **avocados**

avocation A hobby, interest. (Compare **vocation**.)

award A prize or gift. Capitalize if part of proper noun.

-away Compounds ending with **-away** are usually written as one word, without a hyphen (e.g., *thataway*).

awe-inspired

awestruck *or* **awestricken**

awhile An adverb meaning briefly, for a short period of time. (Compare **a while**.)

a while A short period of time. (Compare **awhile**.)

AWOL Abbreviation for absent without leave.

ax *or* **axe**

axis; *pl.*, **axes**

b. Abbreviation for *born*.

baby, babies; babied, babying

baby-sit, baby-sat, baby-sitting; baby-sitter

baby talk

baccalaureate

baccarat

bacchanalia

back- Compounds beginning with *back* are usually spelled as one word (e.g., *backyard*). Exceptions include *back burner, back court, back matter, back nine, back order, back room, back street, back talk.*

back and forth

backbite, backbit, backbitten, backbiting

back-formation

backhand *or* **backhanded** As adverb.

back-to-back

backup As noun.

backward *or* **backwards** Only *backward* may be used as an adjective to modify a following noun.

bacterium; *pl.,* **bacteria**

bad, worse, worst

bad-mouth

bail Money given as security for an accused criminal. (Compare **bale.**)

bailiwick

bailout As noun.

bait and switch

baited Ready with food or other lure: *the baited hook.* (Compare **bated.**)

bal. *or* **blc.** Abbreviation for *balance.*

bald-faced *or* **baldfaced** Obvious or open in manner. (Compare **bold-faced.**)

bale A bundle of material: *a bale of hay.* (Compare **bail.**)

balky, balkier, balkiest

ball- Compounds are spelled as one word unless second part begins with an *l* (e.g., *ballpark*).

ball-and-socket

ball bearing

ball of fire

ball of wax

baloney Nonsense, nonsensical talk. (Compare **bologna.**)

Baltimore oriole The bird.

bamboo, bamboos

band Capitalize if part of proper noun.

Band-Aid Trademark for a type of adhesive bandage.

bandanna *or* **bandana**

bandeau; *pl.,* **bandeaux**

band saw

bang-up As adjective

banjo; *pl.,* **banjos** *or* **banjoes**

bank Capitalize if part of proper noun.

bank note

bankroll

bank shot

banquet A meal laid out on a table. (Compare **banquette.**)

banquette A long bench or walkway. (Compare **banquet.**)

bantamweight

bar- Compounds are usually spelled as one word: *barfly.*

barbecue, barbecues, barbecued, barbecuing

barbed wire, barbwire
barbershop
barbiturate
bar car
bar chart
bare bones
bare, bares, bared, baring Means to expose, reveal. (Compare **bear**.)
bare- Compounds are usually spelled as one word (e.g., *bareback, barefaced, barefoot, bareheaded*). Exceptions include *bare-handed, bare-legged*.
barege A type of sheer fabric.
bar mitzvah, bar mitzvahed, bar mitzvahing An initiatory ceremony for Jewish boys. (Compare **bas mitzvah**.)
barn dance
Barnes, Djuna (1892–1982) American writer and painter. Author of *Nightwood*.
barnstorm
barnyard
barracuda; *pl.*, **barracuda** *or* **barracudas**
barrelful; *pl.*, **barrelfuls** *or* **barrelsful**
bartender
basal Forming or related to the base. (Compare **basic**.)
base- Compounds are usually formed as one word. Exceptions include *base angle, base hit, base on balls, base path, base pay, base runner*.
basic Fundamental, essential. (Compare **basal**.)
BASIC Abbreviation for *Beginner's All-purpose Symbolic Instruction Code*, a computer language.
basis; *pl.*, **bases**
basketball
basket case
basket weave
bas mitzvah An initiatory ceremony for Jewish girls. (Compare **bar mitzvah**.)
bas-relief
bass; *pl.*, **bass** *or* **basses**
basset hound
bateau; *pl.*, **bateaux**
bated Waiting, on hold. (Compare **baited**.)
bath- Compounds are usually one word. Exceptions include *bath chair, bath mat, bath towel, bath salts*.
bathing suit
battle- Compounds are usually one word. Exceptions include *battle cruiser, battle cry, battle fatigue, battle group, battle jacket, battle royal, battle star, battle station*.
battle-ax
baud; *pl.*, **baud** *or* **bauds**
Baudelaire, Charles-Pierre (1821–1867) French Symbolist poet.
bay Capitalize if part of proper noun (e.g., *Chesapeake Bay*).
bay leaf
bay window
bazaar A market or fair. (Compare **bizarre**.)
B.C. Abbreviation for *before Christ*. It is printed following the year. The typeface is often small capitals.
B complex As noun. Hyphenate as adjective.

bd. ft. Abbreviation for *board foot*, used in measuring lumber.

bdrm. Abbreviation for *bedroom*.

beach Sandy land near body of water. (Compare **beech**.)

beach ball

beach buggy

beachcomber

beach grass

be-all and end-all

beanbag

beanpole

beanstalk

bear, bears, bore, borne, bearing To suffer, to transport, or to give birth. (Compare **bare**.)

bear hug

béarnaise sauce

bearskin

beat, beaten *or* **beat**

beatify

beat-up As adjective.

beau; *pl.,* **beaux**

Beaufort scale

beau ideal; *pl.,* **beau ideals**

beau monde; *pl.,* **beau mondes** *or* **beaux mondes**

beauty shop

Beauvoire, Simone Bertrand de (1908–1986) French writer and political activist. Author of *The Second Sex.*

beaux arts

béchamel sauce

beck and call

bed- Compounds are usually written as one word. Exceptions include *bed board, bed check, bed jacket, bed linen, bed rest, bed table.*

bed-and-breakfast *or* **B&B**

bedside manner

bedtime story

bed-wetting

beech A type of hardwood tree. (Compare **beach**.)

beef; *pl.,* **beefs** *or* **beeves**

beefcake

beefsteak

beef Stroganoff

beef Wellington

beehive

Beethoven, Ludwig Van (1770–1827) German composer.

bef. Abbreviation for *before*.

beforehand

beg. Abbreviation for *begin* or *beginning*.

beget, begotten *or* **begot**

begin, began, begun

behind-the-scenes

behold, beholds, beheld

behoove *or* **behove**

bel. Abbreviation for *below*.

belie, belying

belief; *pl.,* **beliefs**

bell-bottoms Singular noun. As an adjective, *bell-bottom*.

belles lettres

bellwether

belly button

belly dance

belly flop

belly laugh

belt Capitalize if part of proper noun (e.g., *Sun Belt, Bible Belt*).

belt-tightening

beltway Capitalize if part of proper noun.

benchmark A point of reference or a standard by which other things are measured. (Compare **bench mark**.)

bench mark Mark on object that serves as a reference. (Compare **benchmark**.)

benchwarmer

beneficent or **beneficial** Producing good; conducive.

benefit, benefited or **benefitted**

berceuse; pl., **berceuses**

bereave, bereft or **bereaved**

Berlioz, Louis-Hector (1803–1869) French composer.

Bermuda bag

Bermuda grass

Bermuda shorts

Bernini, Giovanni Lorenzo (1598–1680) Italian Baroque sculptor, architect, and painter. Works included *Ecstasy of St. Teresa.*

-berry Compounds ending in **-berry** are usually written as one word.

berth A resting place or space on a mode of transportation. (Compare **birth**.)

beseech, besought or **beseeched**

beside Next or adjacent to, at the side of. (Compare **besides**.)

besides In addition to. (Compare **beside**.)

best man Traditional. Use *best honor attendant.*

best; pl., **best**

best- Compound adjectives formed with *best-* are written with a hyphen when they appear before the noun they modify (e.g., *best-selling book*).

bestride, bestrode, bestridden or **bestrid** or **bestrode**

best-seller

bet., btwn. Abbreviation for *between.*

betake, betook, betaken

beta particle

beta ray

beta wave

bête noire; pl., **bêtes noires**

bêtise; pl., **bêtises**

better, best Comparative and superlative forms of *good.*

better- Compound adjectives formed with *better-* are written with a hyphen when they appear before the noun they modify (e.g., *better-dressed brother*).

better-off Always takes a hyphen.

bettor or **better**

betwixt and between

BeV or **bev** Abbreviations for *billion electron volts.*

bev. Abbreviation for *beverage.*

bevel, beveled or **bevelled**

B-flat

bi- Compounds of this prefix, which means two, are spelled as one word: *bicentennial, bifocals.*

biannual or **semiannual** Twice a year. (Compare **biennial**.)

bias, biased/biassed

bib and tucker

Bibb lettuce

Bible Capitalize when referring to the religious text (but do not set off with quotation marks or italics) and lowercase when referring to authority (*The dictionary is an editor's bible.*)

   The books of the Bible are usually spelled out, but may be abbreviated when also giving chapter and verse references. (See Part 2, **Religious writings**.)

The abbreviation is *Bib*.

bibliog. *or* **bibl.** Abbreviation for *bibliography, bibliographical, bibliographer.*

bicolored *or* **bicolor**

bid, bade *or* **bid**

bide, bode *or* **bided**

biennial Every two years. (Compare **biannual**.)

big, bigger, biggest

big- Compounds are usually spelled as one word. Exceptions include *big band, big bang, big business, big deal, big game, big gun, big house, big league, big name, big shot, big stick, big time, big toe, big top, big wheel.*

bijou; *pl.,* **bijous** *or* **bijoux**

bil Abbreviation for *billion.*

bill of fare; *pl.,* **bills of fare**

bi-level

bill Do not capitalize except for *Bill of Rights*, the historic document.

billet-doux; *pl.,* **billets-doux**

bimonthy Every other month.

bind, bound

bio- Compounds are written as one word.

bio. Abbreviation for *biography.*

biog. Abbreviation for *biography, biographical, biographer.*

biol. Abbreviation for *biology, biological/biologic, biologist.*

bird- Compounds usually spelled as one word. Exceptions include *bird dog, bird song.*

-bird Compounds ending in **-bird** are usually written as one word.

bird-dog As verb.

bird's nest

bird's-eye

bird-watch As verb.

birth The event of becoming alive. (Compare **berth**.)

birth date

birthday

birthmark

birthplace

bison; *pl.,* **bison**

bite, bitten *or* **bit**

bitter end

bitter-ender

biweekly Every other week. (Compare **semiweekly**.)

bizarre Strange, very unusual. (Compare **bazaar**.)

bkgd. Abbreviation for background.

black A dark-skinned person, especially of African descent.

black- Compounds written as one word include *blackball, blackberry, blackbird, blackboard, blackguard, blackhead, blackjack, blacklist, blackmail, blackout* (noun), *blacksmith, blacktop.*

black-and-blue

black-and-white As adjective.

black and white *or* **B&W** As noun.

black-eyed

Black Hawk (1767–1838) American Indian leader.

black-market As verb.

black marketer *or* **black marketeer**

black-tie As adjective.

Blake, William (1757–1827) British poet, artist, and mystic.

blasé

blast-off As noun.

bleary-eyed

bleed, bled

blessed *or* **blest**

blindman's bluff

blindside   As verb.

blintze *or* **blintz**

bloc   A group of people or nations acting in common. But *block grant* is the term for a federal award of money for a project.

block and tackle

blockbuster

blockhead

blockhouse

blond

blood-   Compounds that are one word include *bloodbath, bloodcurdling, bloodhound, bloodletting, bloodline, bloodmobile, bloodred, bloodshed, bloodshot, bloodstain, bloodstream, bloodthirsty.*

blood-alcohol level

-blossom   Compounds ending in *-blossom* are usually written as one word.

blow, blew, blown

blow-by-blow

blow-dry

blowout   As noun.

blowsy *or* **blowzy**

BLT   Abbreviation for *bacon, lettuce, and tomato sandwich.*

blue-   Compounds are open except for *bluebeard, blueberry, bluebird, bluebonnet, bluegrass, bluenose, blueprint.* Hyphenated compounds are those in which blue is a modifier (e.g., *blue-eyed, blue-sky, blue-collar*).

bluing *or* **blueing**

B'nai B'rith

-board   Compounds ending in

-board are usually written as one word.

board game

boardinghouse

boarding school

boardwalk

-boat   Compounds ending in *-boat* are usually written as one word.

boat people

boat race

bobby pin

bobby socks *or* **bobby sox**

bobby-soxer

bobwhite

boccie *or* **bocci**   Preferred Italian is *bocce.*

bodybuilding, bodybuilder

bodyguard

bodysurf

bodywork

bogey, bogeyed

boiler room

boldface   As noun.

boldface   Set in heavy type.

bold-faced   Brave in manner. (Compare **bald-faced**.)

bollix   Use with *up*.

bologna   Sausage or luncheon meat. (Compare **baloney**.)

bombproof

bombshell

bona fide   As adjective.

bona fides   As noun. Sincerity, good faith.

bonbon

bond paper

bond servant

bone china

boned   With bones removed.

bone-dry

bongo; *pl.,* bongo *or* **bongos**

bonhomie

19

bon mot; *pl.*, bons mots *or* bon mots

bon ton

bonus; *pl.*, bonuses

bon vivant; *pl.*, bons vivants *or* bon vivants

bon voyage

bony *or* boney, bonier, boniest

boo-boo; *pl.*, boo-boos

boob tube

booby hatch

booby prize

booby trap

boogie *or* boogy, boogies, boogying

boogie-woogie

book titles   (See Part 2, **Titles of works**.)

book-   Compounds written as two words include *book club, book value, book learning, book jacket, book match, book review, book trade, book dealer.*

-book   Compounds ending in *-book* are usually written as one word.

bookkeeping, bookkeeper

Boolean

boomtown

boondocks

booster shot

boot camp

bootee *or* bootie   An ankle-height shoe or sock, usually an infant's. (Compare **booty**.)

boot tree

booty; *pl.*, booties   Spoils stolen, or a prize. (Compare **bootee**.)

Bordeaux; *pl.*, Bordeaux

bordelaise sauce

bordello; *pl.*, bordellos

borderline

Borges, Jorge Louis   (1899–1986) Renowned Argentinian author.

born   Brought into life through the birth process. (Compare **borne**.)

born-again

borne   Carried into a place or endured. (Compare **born**.)

borough   Capitalize if part of proper noun (e.g., *the Borough of Queens*).

Botticelli, Sandro   (1445–1510) Italian painter. Works include the *Primavera* and *Birth of Venus*.

bottle-feed, bottle-fed

bottle green

bottleneck

bottomland

bottom-line   As adjective.

bottom line   As noun.

bouffant

bough   The branch of a tree or bush. (Compare **bow**.)

bouillabaisse

bouillon   Clear soup. (Compare **bullion**.)

boulder

-bound   Compounds ending in this suffix are written as one word when used to indicate the process of achieving an end or a destination, unless the first part is a proper noun (e.g., *northbound, Chicago-bound*). When used to describe a state of fastening or attachment, compounds ending in *-bound* are usually written as one word (e.g., *unbound*).

boundary

bounteous

bountiful

bouquet garni; *pl.*, bouquets garnis

bourgeois   As adjective.

bourgeois; *pl.*, bourgeois   A

middle-class person. (Compare **bourgeoisie**.)

bourgeoisie The middle class. (Compare **bourgeois**.)

boutique

boutonniere

bow Means to bend the head or body in respect or submission. (Compare **bough**.)

Bowen, Elizabeth Dorothea Cole (1899–1973) Irish novelist and story writer.

bow saw

bow tie

bowwow

box- Compounds written as two words include *box camera, box elder, box kite, box lunch, box office* (adjective is *box-office*), *box pleat, box score, box seat, box spring* (noun).

-box Compounds ending in *-box* are usually written as one word (e.g., *toolbox*).

box-spring mattress

Boy Scout

bp Abbreviation for *boiling point*.

B picture

braggadocio

braggart

braille Often capitalized.

brain- Compounds written as one word include *brainchild, brainpower, brainsick, brainstorm, brainteaser, brainwash.*

-brained Compounds ending in *-brained* are usually written as one word (e.g., *scatterbrained*).

brake To slow down to stop (as verb) or device for slowing and

stopping (as noun). (Compare **break**.)

Brancusi, Constantin (1876–1957) Rumanian sculptor.

brand name

brand-new

Braque, Georges (1882–1963) French Fauve painter. With Picasso, he pioneered the Cubist style.

brassbound

brasserie A French restaurant. (Compare **brassiere, brazier**.)

brassiere A woman's undergarment. (Compare **brasserie, brazier**.)

bravado; *pl.,* **bravadoes**

bravo; *pl.,* **bravos**

brazen-faced

brazenness

brazier A brassworker, a metal pan filled with coals (used for heating), or a grill-like cooking utensil. (Compare **brasserie, brassiere**.)

breach To break (as verb) or a break or gap (as noun). (Compare **breech**.)

bread-and-butter As adjective.

bread and butter As noun.

breadline *or* **bread line**

break, broke To separate or fracture (as verb) or an interruption or a fracture (as noun). (Compare **brake**.)

break-even As adjective.

break-in As noun.

breaking and entering

breaking point

breakthrough

breakwater

21

breast-feed, breast-fed

breath The air one takes in and out in the act of respiration. (Compare **breathe**.)

breathe Drawing air in and out, respiring.

Brecht, Bertoldt (1898–1956) German playwright and poet.

breech Buttocks or pants (breeches). (Compare **breach**.)

breed, bred

breeding ground

breezeway

brewer's yeast

bric-a-brac; *pl.,* **bric-a-brac**

brick; *pl.,* **bricks** or **brick**

bridal Concerning marriage. (Compare **bridle**.)

bridegroom Traditional. Use *groom*.

bridesmaid Traditional. Use *honor attendant*.

bridge Capitalize if part of proper noun

bridgeable

bridle Gear for a horse (noun) or to put such equipment on a horse (verb). (Compare **bridal**.)

briefcase

brier

brigadier general; *pl.,* **brigadier generals**

bring, brought

briquette or **briquet**

British Pertaining to or native to Great Britain. (Compare **Briton, Britisher, English**.)

Britisher Used informally to designate a native of Great Britain (Compare **Briton, British, English**.)

Briton; *pl.,* **Britons** A person

native (or natives) to Britain. (Compare **British, Britisher, English**.)

bro., bros. Abbreviation for *brother, brothers.*

broach To address an issue, subject. (Compare **brooch**.)

broadax

broadcast, broadcast or **broadcasted**

broad jump

broad-minded

broken-down

broken-field

brokenhearted

bronco; *pl.,* **broncos**

Brontë, Charlotte (1816–1855) English novelist. Author of *Wuthering Heights*. Sister of Emily.

Brontë, Emily Jane (1818–1848) English novelist. Author of *Jane Eyre*. Sister of Charlotte.

Bronx cheer

Bronze Age

brooch A necklace or ornament. (Compare **broach**.)

brother; *pl.,* **brothers** or **brethren**

brother-in-law; *pl.,* **brothers-in-law**

brouhaha

brown-bagging; brown-bag; brown bagger

brown Betty

brown-eyed

brownie point Often capitalized *Brownie*.

Browning, Elizabeth Barrett (1806–1861) English poet. Spouse of Robert.

Browning, Robert (1812–1889) English poet. Spouse of Elizabeth.

brownnose
brownout
brunet *or* brunette Brown-haired, or a brown-haired person.
Brunswick stew
brushfire
brush-off As noun.
brusque
brussels sprout; *pl.*, brussels sprouts
bsmt. Abbreviation for *basement*.
bu. Abbreviation for *bushel*.
bubble gum
buccaneer
buck; *pl.*, bucks *or* buck A male deer. Also used as slang meaning ''money'' or ''a dollar.''
buckaroo *or* buckeroo; *pl.*, buckaroos *or* buckeroos
bucketful; *pl.*, bucketfuls *or* bucketsful
bucket seat
Buddha
Buddhist
buddy system
buffalo; *pl.*, buffalo *or* buffaloes
-bug Compounds ending in -*bug* are usually written as one word (e.g., shutterbug).
bugaboo; *pl.*, bugaboos
bug-eyed
build, built
building Capitalize if part of proper noun. The abbreviation is *bldg*.
building block
buildup As noun.
built-in As adjective.
built-up As adjective.
bulkhead
bulldog
bulletin Capitalize if part of

document title. The abbreviation is *bull.; pl.*, bulls.
bullion A piece of gold or silver. (Compare bouillon.)
bull pen
bull session
bull's-eye; *pl.*, bull's-eyes
bullterrier
bulwark
bumblebee
bumper-to-bumper
bunion Swelling on a big toe.
bunk bed
bunkhouse
Bunsen burner *or* bunsen burner
buoy
buoyant; buoyance *or* buoyancy
bur *or* burr Prickly seed of a bush.
bureau; *pl.*, bureaus *or* bureaux Capitalize if part of proper noun. Lowercase for corporate subdivisions (e.g., *the Los Angeles bureau of NBC*).
burgeon
burglar
burgundy Often capitalized.
Burke, Edmund (1729–1797) British statesman.
burn, burned *or* burnt
burned-out *or* burnt-out
burnout
Burroughs, William Seward (1855–1898) American inventor of the adding machine.
burst, burst *or* bursted
bus, buses, bused, busing Transporting by large vehicle with professional driver. (Compare buss.)
bus; *pl.*, buses As noun.
-bush Compounds ending in -*bush*

are usually written as one word
(e.g., *sugarbush*).

bush jacket

bush-league   As adjective.

bush-leaguer

bush league   As noun.

bushwhack

businessperson

buss, busses, bussed, bussing   To
kiss. (Compare **bus**.)

bust, busted *or* bust

busybody

busywork

butter bean

butter clam

butter dish

butter knife

button-down

buttonhole

buy, bought

bwd. *or* back.   Abbreviation for
backward.

bx.   Abbreviation for *box*.

by-and-by   As noun.

by and by   As adverb.

by and large   As adverb.

bye-bye *or* by-by

by-election

by-product

Byron, Lord George Gordon
(1788–1824) English Romantic
poet.

by the way

Byzantine

C

c A *c* at the end of a word changes to *ck* when adding endings like *-ed*, *-er*, *-ing*, or *-y* (e.g., *picnic*, *picnicking*).

c Abbreviation for *curie* or *cubic*.

c. Abbreviation for *copyright*.

C. Abbreviation for *Celsius*, *centigrade*.

ca. or c. Abbreviation for *circa*, meaning "about" (e.g., *ca. 1991*).

cabana

cabaret

cabbie or cabby; *pl.*, **cabbies**

cabdriver

cabinet Capitalize if part of proper noun or if referring to a specific high-ranking body (e.g., *the president's Cabinet*). (See Part 2, **Cabinet**, for a listing of the departments of the Cabinet of the United States.)

cabstand

cacciatore

cache A hiding place or hidden supply. (Compare **cash**.)

cachet

cacophonous

cactus; *pl.*, **cacti** or **cactuses**

caddie A helper on the golf course. (Compare **caddy**.)

caddy A serving tray or small container. (Compare **caddie**.)

cadre

Caesar, Julius (100–44 B.C.) Roman general and statesman.

caesura; *pl.*, **caesuras**

café or cafe

cafeteria

caffeine

cagey

caisson

cajole

cake mix

cal. Abbreviation for *calorie*.

Cal. Abbreviation for *large calorie*.

calc. Abbreviation for *calculate*, *calculates*, *calculated*, *calculating*.

calculus; *pl.*, **calculi** or **calculuses**

caldron or cauldron

calendar A system of days of a year. (Compare **calender**.)

calender A machine for producing paper in sheets. (Compare **calendar**.)

calf; *pl.*, **calves**

calfskin

caliber

calico; *pl.*, **calicoes** or **calicos**

caliper or calliper

calisthenics

calix; *pl.*, **calices**

call- Compounds are generally spelled as one word. Exceptions include *call girl*, *call letters*, *call number*, *call slip*.

calliope A keyboard instrument.

Calliope The Greek muse.

callous Insensitive. (Compare **callus**.)

call-up or callup

callus; *pl.*, **calluses** A hard blister on the skin. (Compare **callous**.)

calumniate

calvary A crucifixion or suffering. (Compare **cavalry**.)

calyx; *pl.*, **calyxes** or **calyces**

camaraderie

camel's-hair As adjective.

camel hair *or* **camel's hair** As noun.

Camembert

cameo; *pl.*, **cameos**

camouflage

campaign

campfire

campground

campsite

Camus, Albert (1913–1960) French existentialist novelist, essayist, and playwright. Author of *The Stranger*.

can, could

can. *or* **canc.** Abbreviation for *canceled*.

canal Capitalize if part of proper noun: *the Erie Canal*.

canapé An appetizer. (Compare **canopy**.)

canard

cancan

cancel, canceled *or* **cancelled**

cancer Lowercase when referring to illness, unless specific emphasis is intended. Uppercase as the fourth sign of Zodiac. (see **Zodiac Signs**).

candelabra *or* **candelabrum;** *pl.*, **candelabras**

candidacy *or* **candidature**

candlelight

candy; *pl.*, **candy** *or* **candies**

canister *or* **cannister**

canker sore

cannon; *pl.*, **cannons** *or* **cannon** A large weapon. (Compare **canon**.)

cannonade

cannot *or* **can't**

canoe, canoed, canoeing

canon An established rule or body of works. (Compare **cannon**.)

can opener

canopy An overhanging covering, as for a door or window. (Compare **canapé**.)

cantaloupe, cantaloup, canteloupe, *or* **canteloup** Takes same form in plural.

canto; *pl.*, **cantos**

canvas Heavy cloth. (Compare **canvass**.)

canvass To question or solicit. (Compare **canvas**.)

cape Capitalize if part of proper noun (e.g., *Cape May, New Jersey*).

capful; *pl.*, **capfuls**

capital A city that is a government seat. (Compare **capitol**.)

capitalization Many words and phrases are listed separately in this manual. If there is no specific entry here, consult a dictionary. As a rule, capitalize common nouns such as *battle, bank, canal* only if part of a proper noun.

capitol The main building in a city that is a government seat. Capitalize when referring to state and national government seats and the building in Washington, D.C. (Compare **capital**.)

caprice; capricious

Capricorn (see **Zodiac Signs**).

caps. Abbreviation for *capitals*.

capt. Abbreviation for *captain*.

carabao; *pl.*, **carabao** *or* **carabaos**

carafe

caramel

carat A unit of weight for precious

stones. (Compare caret, carrot, karat.)

Caravaggio, Michelangelo (1573–1610) Italian painter whose paintings exhibit the technique of dramatic shadows known as chiaroscuro. Works included *Supper at Emmaus* and the *Crucifixion of St. Peter*.

carburetor

carcass

carcinoma; *pl.*, carcinomas *or* carcinomata

cardamom

card-carrying

cardsharper *or* cardsharp

careen To zig-zag in movement. (Compare career.)

career To move straight ahead at top speed. (Compare careen.)

carefree

caret The proofreading mark (^) indicating insertion. (Compare carat, carrot, karat.)

caretaker

carfare

cargo; *pl.*, cargoes *or* cargos

Caribbean

caribou; *pl.*, caribou *or* caribous

caries; *pl.*, caries

carillon

carload

carmaker

carnauba wax

carny; *pl.*, carnies

carousal A rousing, often drunken, social time. (Compare carousel.)

carousel A merry-go-round ride. (Compare carousal.)

carrot The orange root vegetable. (Compare carat, caret, karat.)

carry- Compounds are usually spelled as one word (e.g., *carryall*.)

carrying-on; *pl.*, carryings-on

carryout As both noun and adjective.

carry-over *or* carryover

carsick

carte blanche; *pl.*, cartes blanches

cartouche *or* cartouch

car wash *or* carwash

case history

casein

case in point

case study

casework

cash Money. (Compare cache.)

cash-and-carry

cash flow

cashier

cashmere

casino; *pl.*, casinos

cassette

cast To throw, or to assign a role in a theater production. (Compare caste.)

castaway

caste Strictly defined social position, division. (Compare cast.)

caster A rolling device on furniture or holder for bottles. (Compare castor.)

cast-iron As adjective.

castoff As noun.

castoff *or* cast-off As adjective.

castor An oil used as medicine. (Compare caster.)

casual Informal, unimportant. (Compare causal.)

casualty; *pl.*, casualties

CAT Abbreviation for

computerized axial tomography (e.g., *CAT scan*).

catalog *or* catalogue

catalysis; *pl.*, catalyses

cat-and-mouse As adjective.

catastrophe; *pl.*, catastrophes

catbird seat

catcall

catch, caught

catchall

catch-as-catch-can

catchphrase

catch-22

catch-up As noun or adjective.

catchword

catechism

catechist

catechize

catechumen

cater-cornered *or* catercorner *or* cater-corner *or* catty-cornered *or* kitty-cornered

caterpillar

caterwaul

catharsis; *pl.*, catharses

Cather, Willa Sibert (1873–1947) American novelist. Author of *Death Comes to the Archbishop*.

cathode ray

catholic Capitalize when related to religion; lowercase to mean universal.

catnap

cat-o'-nine-tails

cat's-eye

cat's-paw

catsup *or* ketchup

cattle call

CATV Abbreviation for *community antenna television*.

catwalk

Caucasian

cauliflower

caulk *or* calk

causal Having a reason or producing an effect. (Compare **casual**.)

cause célèbre

causerie

cauterize

cavalry Military on horseback. (Compare **calvary**.)

caveat A warning.

caveat emptor

cave dweller *or* cavedweller

cave-in As noun.

caviar

cavil, caviled *or* cavilled

cayenne pepper

CBer One who uses a citizens' band (CB) radio.

cc. *or* cc Abbreviation for *copies, copies to; cubic centimeter(s)*.

CDT Abbreviation for *central daylight time*.

cease and desist

cease-fire

cecum; *pl.*, ceca

cede Give in.

-cede Words with this ending include *accede, antecede, concede, intercede, precede, recede, secede*. (Compare **-ceed**.)

cedilla

-ceed Words with this ending include *exceed, proceed, succeed*. (Compare **-cede**.)

ceiling

celebrant The person who officiates in a religious ceremony. (Compare **celebrator**.)

celebrator A person who has fun socially. (Compare **celebrant**.)

cellar

cello; *pl.*, cellos

cellist

cellophane

cellulite

Celsius The abbreviation is *Cel.* or *Cels.*

cement Powdered rock that can be mixed with water to make a binding element. (Compare concrete.)

cemetery Capitalize only if part of proper noun.

censer A container for burning incense. (Compare censor, censure.)

censor To suppress as immoral, objectionable. (Compare censer, censure.)

censure To condemn, criticize harshly. (Compare censer, censor.)

cent A monetary unit or coin. (Compare scent.)

centenary

centennial

center Capitalize only if part of proper noun (e.g., *Javitz Center*).

center field

centerfold

centerpiece

centipede

cento; *pl.*, centones *or* centos

Central America

central standard time *or* central time The abbreviation is *CST.*

century Lowercase; spell out the preceding ordinal if less than 10 (e.g., *second century*).

CEO Abbreviation for *chief executive officer.*

cereal Breakfast foods made of grain. (Compare serial.)

ceremonial Formal, ritual. (Compare ceremonious.)

ceremonious Punctilious, devoted to detail. (Compare ceremonial.)

cert. Abbreviation for *certificate, certification, certified, certify.*

certainty Something that is actually sure. (Compare certitude.)

certiorari

certitude Belief in the certainty of something. (Compare certainty.)

Cervantes, Miguel de (1547–1616) Spanish novelist. Author of *Don Quixote.*

cesarean section *or* cesarian section *or* Caesarian section *or* Cesarean section *or* C section.

cession Yielding to another. (Compare session.)

Cézanne, Paul (1839–1906) French Impressionist painter.

cf. Abbreviation meaning *compare, confer.*

cg Abbreviation for *centigram.*

c.g. Abbreviation for *center of gravity.*

cgs Abbreviation for *centimeter-gram-second*

Chablis or chablis A type of white wine.

cha-cha

chafe To rub or irritate. (Compare chaff.)

chaff To tease; or, the husks of grain separated in threshing. (Compare chafe.)

chafing dish

Chagall, Marc (1889–1985) Russian-born Abstract Expressionist painter.

chagrin

chain-smoke

chain-smoker

chair or chairperson Capitalize only if part of formal title.

chair lift

chaise longue; pl., chaise longues or chaises longues

chalkboard

challis; pl., challises

chameleon

chamois; pl., chamois or chamoix

chamomile or camomile

champagne

chancellery or chancellory

chancellor

chancre; chancrous

chancy

chandelier

changeover

change-up

channel Capitalize only as part of proper noun (e.g., *Channel 3* or *the English Channel*).

channel, channeled or channelled

chanteuse; pl., chanteuses

Chantilly lace

chaos

chapeau; pl., chapeaus or chapeaux

chaperon

chapfallen

chaplain Capitalize only if part of formal title.

Chaplin, Charlie (1889–1977) Silent film comedian and actor.

chaps or chaparajos or chaparejos

chapter Capitalize in reference to specific document part (e.g., Chapter 22). The abbreviation is *chap.* or *ch.*; pl., *chaps.* or *chs.* (See also Part 2, **Titles of works**.)

character

charbroil

chardonnay

charge d'affaires; pl., charges d'affaires Capitalize only if part of formal title.

charisma

charlatan

chart Capitalize only in reference to specific document part.

charted Planned out with a map. (Compare **chartered**.)

charter Capitalize only if part of proper noun.

chartered Rented for transportation. (Compare **charted**.)

chartreuse

chasm

chassis; pl., chassis

chaste

chateau or château; pl., chateaus, châteaus, chateaux, or châteaux

chattel

Chaucer, Geoffrey (1342–1400) English writer. Author of *The Canterbury Tales*.

chauffeur

chautauqua (Often capitalized.)

chauvinism

cheapskate

check- Compounds with *check-* are usually spelled as one word (e.g., *checkmark, checkbook, checklist, checkpoint, checkroom*).

checkerboard

check-in As noun.

checkout As noun.

checkup As noun.

cheddar or Cheddar

cheekbone

cheerleader

cheese Lowercase after capitalized

specific name (e.g., Swiss cheese).

cheeseburger

cheesecake

cheesecloth

cheetah

chef; *pl.,* **chefs**

chef d'oeuvre; *pl.,* **chefs d'oeuvre**

chemical elements and compounds Names of chemical elements and compounds are lowercased when written out (e.g., *aluminum, sodium bisulfate*). Chemical symbols are capitalized and unpunctuated.

The number of atoms is subscripted and to the right of a chemical symbol (e.g., CO_2). The mass number is superscripted and to the left of a chemical symbol (e.g., ^{51}Cr).

chemise

chenille

cherry bomb

cherub; *pl.,* **cherubs**

chervil

chesterfield A type of overcoat or a type of davenport.

chevron

Cheyenne

Chianti

chiaroscuro; *pl.,* **chiaroscuros**

chic Elegant, stylish. (Compare **sheikh**.)

chicanery

chichi

chickenhearted

chicken pox

chick-pea

chicory *or* **chickory**

chide, chid *or* **chidden** *or* **chided**

chief; *pl.,* **chiefs** Capitalize only if part of formal title.

chief justice Capitalize only if part of formal title (e.g., Chief Justice Susan Stein).

chief of staff; *pl.,* **chiefs of staff** Capitalize only if part of formal title.

chieftain

chiffon

chignon

Chihuahua

chilblain

chili; *pl.,* **chilies**

chili con carne

chimerical *or* **chimeric**

chimney; *pl.,* **chimneys**

chinchilla

chino; *pl.,* **chinos**

chintzy

Chippendale

chiropractor

chisel, chiseled *or* **chiselled**

chitchat

chivalrous

chlorophyll

chockablock

chock-full *or* **chockful**

chocolate

chocolaty *or* **chocolatey**

choke chain

cholera

cholesterol

choose, chose

Chopin, Frederic (1810–1849) Polish composer and pianist.

Chopin, Kate (1851–1904) American novelist and story writer. Author of *The Awakening*.

chopstick

chop suey

choral Relating to song. (Compare **chorale, coral, corral**.)

chorale *or* **choral** A hymn or poem that is sung. (Compare **choral, coral, corral**.)

chord A group of musical notes played together.

chorea; choreic

chow chow A breed of dog.

chow mein

Christian name A given name (first name) that is also a name found in the Christian Bible.

chrome

chuck wagon *or* **chuckwagon**

chugalug

church Capitalize only if part of proper noun.

churchgoer

Churchill, Sir Winston Leonard Spencer (1874–1965) British statesman.

church key

church school

chute A passage downward; descent or fall.

chutney; *pl.,* **chutneys**

chutzpah

ciao

cicada; *pl.,* **cicadas** *or* **cicadae**

cicatrix; *pl.,* **cicatrices**

cigarette

cilium; *pl.,* **cilia**

cinema verité

cipher

circa The abbreviation is *ca.* or *c.*

circadian

circle Capitalize only if part of proper noun or address.

cirrhosis; *pl.,* **cirrhoses**

cirrus; *pl.,* **cirri**

cite To refer to or extract a quote from. (Compare **site**.)

citizen A person with full legal rights either by birth or naturalization.

citizens band *or* **CB**

citrus; *pl.,* **citrus** *or* **citruses**

city Capitalize only if part of proper noun or title (e.g., *Panama City*).

city-born

city-bred

city-state

citywide

civic-minded

civil Capitalize only if part of proper noun.

civilly

Civil War

civvy *or* **civie;** *pl.,* **civvies** *or* **civies**

-clad Compounds are hyphenated, except for *ironclad*.

clairvoyance

clambake

clamor

clamshell

clandestine

clapboard

claque People hired to applaud a performance.

claqueur Person within a claque.

claret

class act

class action

class-conscious

classic Something that meets a standard of excellence and is memorable. (Compare **classical**.)

classical Concerning literature, art, architecture, or music of earlier periods that conforms to certain established standards. (Compare **classic**.)

claw-footed

clean-cut

cleanhanded

clean-shaven or **clean-shaved**

cleanup As noun.

clear-cut

clear-eyed

clearheaded

clearinghouse

clear-sighted

cleave, cleaved or **cleft** or **cloven** To divide, split, or sever.

clench To hold fast with a body part. (Compare **clinch**.)

clew A lower corner on a sail, or the metal grommet at that corner. (Compare **clue**.)

cliché or **cliche**

client A person who hires a business consultant or other contractor for help, services.

clientele

cliff dweller or **cliffdweller**

cliff-hanger or **cliffhanger**

climacteric Relating to a critical point or stage in time. (Compare **climactic, climatic**.)

climactic Relating to a climax or ending. (Compare **climacteric, climatic**.)

climatic Relating to the weather of a region. (Compare **climacteric, climactic**.)

climb Ascent to a higher place. (Compare **clime**.)

clime A region, often in regard to weather. (Compare **climb**.)

clinch To hold fast or to gain a victory. (Compare **clench**.)

cling, clung

clinician

clipboard

clip-clop

clip joint

clip-on As adjective.

clipsheet

clique; cliquey or **cliquy; cliquish**

cloak-and-dagger

cloakroom

clock radio

clock tower

cloisonné

close- Compounds that are open include *close call, close corporation, close order, close quarters, close shave*. Compounds that are hyphenated include *close-cropped, close-grained, close-knit, close-shaven*. Compounds that are one word include *closefisted, closeminded, closemouthed, closedown, closeout*.

closed-captioned

closed-circuit

closed-door

closed shop

close-up As noun.

close up As adverb.

closure The act of closing or a part that closes. (Compare **cloture**.)

clothes closet

cloture The parliamentary procedure for ending a debate. (Compare **closure**.)

cloudburst

cloud nine

cloverleaf

club- Compounds that are open include *club car, club chair, club sandwich, club soda, club steak, club coupe*.

clue A piece of evidence, information. (Compare **clew**.)

cm Abbreviation for *centimeter*.

cml. Abbreviation for *commercial*.

co- Compounds formed with this prefix, which means together with, are formed as one word. Exceptions include when joining words beginning with "o," and words describing status or occupation: (e.g., *coaxial, cobelligerent*, but *co-op, co-opt, co-owner, co-worker, co-pilot, co-author, co-star*).

c/o Abbreviation for *care of*.

coadjutor

coal- Most compounds are open, including *coal gas, coal oil, coal tar, coal seam*.

coalesce; coalescent; coalescence

coarse Rough.

coast Capitalize if referring to major region of a country (e.g., *the West Coast*). Lowercase shorelines and smaller regions (e.g. *the Maine coast, Atlantic coast*).

coast guard Capitalize when referring to a specific one: *the U.S. Coast Guard*.

coastline

coast-to-coast

coatdress

coat hanger

coat of arms

coatrack

coatroom

coattails

coat tree

COBOL Abbreviation for *Common Business-Oriented Language*.

cobweb

cocaine

coccyx; *pl.*, **coccyges**

cocker spaniel

cockeyed

cocksure

coconut

cocoon

COD *or* **c.o.d.** *or* **C.O.D.** Abbreviation for *cash on delivery*.

code Capitalize only if part of legal document title or in reference to specific legal document part.

codeine

codex; *pl.*, **codices**

codicil

cod-liver oil

coerce; coercion

C. of C. Abbreviation for *chamber of commerce*.

coffee- Compounds that are written open include *coffee break, coffee cake, coffee klatch, coffee maker, coffee mill, coffee room, coffee shop, coffee table, coffee cup*.

coffeepot

coffee-table book

cog. Abbreviation for *cognate*.

cognizable *or* **cognoscible**

cognoscente; *pl.*, **cognoscenti**

coiffeur A male hairstylist. (Compare **coiffure**.)

coiffeuse A female hairstylist.

coiffure Styled hair. (Compare **coiffeur**.)

coincidentally *or* **coincidently**

coin-operated

col A pass through a mountain.

COLA Abbreviation for *cost of living adjustment*.

colander A kitchen utensil for sifting.

cold-blooded

coldhearted

cold-shoulder As verb.

cold-water As adjective.

Coleridge, Samuel Taylor
(1772–1834) English poet.
Author of "Kubla Khan" and
"Rime of the Ancient
Mariner."

coleslaw

colic; colicky

coliseum

collage A picture made of a variety
of materials.

collateral

collectible As noun.

collectible *or* **collectable** As
adjective.

collector's item

college Capitalize only if part of
proper noun.

colloq. Abbreviation for
colloquial, colloquialism.

colloquial

colloquium; *pl.*, colloquiums

colloquy; *pl.*, colloquies

cologne

colonel

colonies Capitalize only when
referring to one or more of the
original thirteen territories of the
United States.

colonnade

color-blind

color blindness

colorfast

color guard

colossal

Colosseum The building in Rome,
Italy.

Columbus, Christopher
(1451–1506) Spanish explorer.
Credited as the discoverer of
America.

column Abbreviation is *col.*; *pl.*,
cols.

coma A state of unconsciousness.

combo; *pl.*, combos

comeback As noun.

comedian A humorous performer.

comedown As noun.

come-hither

come-on; *pl.*, come-ons As noun.

comeuppance

coming-of-age

comity A friendly atmosphere;
courtesy.

commander Capitalize only if part
of a formal title preceding a
name. The abbreviation is *Cmdr.*
or *Cdr.* or *comdr.*

**commander in chief; *pl.*,
commanders in chief** Capitalize
only if part of formal title
preceding a name.

commando; *pl.*, commandos *or*
commandoes

comme il faut

commensurable Having a common
measure; easily figured. (Compare
commensurate.)

commensurate Being equal in
measure to something else.
(Compare **commensurable.**)

commingle

comminute

commiserate Use with *with.*

commission Capitalize only if part
of proper noun.

commissioner Capitalize only if
part of a formal title preceding a
name.

committee Capitalize only if part
of proper noun.

committeeperson Capitalize only if part of a formal title preceding a name.

common-law marriage

Common Market Refers to the European Economic Community (EEC).

commonplace

commonsense As adjective.

common sense As noun.

commonwealth Capitalize only if part of proper noun (e.g., *The British Commonwealth*).

communicable Transmittable. (Compare **communicative**.)

communicative Expressive, responsive. (Compare **communicable**.)

communiqué

communist Capitalize if part of proper noun (e.g., *the Communist party*).

comp. Abbreviation for *compiler, compiled by*.

compact disc or **CD**

company Capitalize only if part of proper noun. The abbreviation as part of proper noun is *Co.*; *pl.*, *Cos*.

compar. Abbreviation for *comparative*.

comparable Suitable or useful for seeing differences and similarities. (Compare **comparative**.)

comparative A relative degree of difference or similarity. (Compare **comparable**.)

compared Use with *to* when asserting that something is qualitatively similar to another. Use *with* when giving specific examples to illustrate similarities and/or differences.

comparison shop

compendious Briefly treating a subject.

compendium; *pl.*, **compendiums** or **compendia**

complacent Not concerned, self-satisfied. (Compare **complaisant**.)

complaisant Eager or inclined to please. (Compare **complacent**.)

complement Something that completes, improves, or pairs well with something else. (Compare **compliment**.)

complementary Completing or improving. (Compare **complimentary**.)

-complexioned or **-complected**

compliment A comment of respect or admiration, or to express praise. (Compare **complement**.)

complimentary Respectful or admiring in comment. (Compare **complementary**.)

comply Use with *with*.

compose To create, put together.

compote

compounds, plural To pluralize compounds composed of two nouns, generally just add *s* or *es* (e.g., *cloakroom, cloakrooms*).

For compound nouns that are composed of words that are not nouns, add *s* to the end (e.g., *come-on; pl., come-ons*).

Compounds in the form of noun-preposition-noun are usually pluralized by adding *s* to the first noun (e.g., *brother-in-law; pl., brothers-in-law*).

For compounds that are in the

form of noun-adjective or noun-adverb, add *s* to the noun (e.g., *father-to-be*; pl., *fathers-to-be* and *looker-on*; pl., *lookers-on*). If the adjective in such a compound is often a noun itself, the compound may have more than one plural form (e.g., *attorney general*; pl., *attorneys general* or *attorney generals*).

comprise   To be made up of parts; consist of. (Compare **constitute**.)

comptroller *or* **controller**   Capitalize only if part of formal title.

compulsive   Obsessive. (Compare **compulsory**.)

compulsory   Required or enforced. (Compare **compulsive**.)

comrade

Comsat   The brand name of a communications satellite.

con.   Abbreviation for *contra*, "against."

con amore

con anima

concave   Hollow or curved inward. (Compare **convex**.)

conceit

conceive

concerto; pl., **concertos** *or* **concerti**

concessionaire

conch; pl., **conchs** *or* **conches**

concierge; pl., **concierges**

concomitant

concordat   Compact, agreement (often between church and state).

concrete   Hardened material made from cement, water, and gravel. (Compare **cement**.)

concur, concurred

condemn   To criticize as very bad. (Compare **contemn**.)

condensable *or* **condensible**

condign   Appropriate.

conducive   Use with *to*.

confectioner's sugar

confectionery   As noun.

confederacy,
confederate   Capitalize if referring to the American South during the Civil War.

confer, conferred

conference   Capitalize only if part of proper noun.

confess   Use with *to*.

confidant   A person in whom one confides. (Compare **confident**.)

confident   Sure, certain. (Compare **confidant, confidante**.)

confiscable *or* **confiscatable**

conflict of interest

conform   Use with *to* or *with*.

confrere

Confucius   (551–479 B.C.) Chinese philosopher. Also, K'ung Ch'iu.

congé

congeries; pl., **congeries**

congress   Capitalize only if part of proper noun, (e.g., U.S. Congress.) Individual members of congresses are referred to as representatives. Lowercase unless referring to a specific member of a congress: *Representative Joe Moakley of the U.S. Congress.*

congressional   Capitalize only if part of proper noun or document title.

conj.   Abbreviation for *conjunction, conjugation*.

conjurer *or* **conjuror**

connectable *or* connectible

connector *or* connecter

connoisseur

connote To imply. (Compare denote.)

conqueror

consanguine; consanguineous

conscience

conscientious

conscionable

conscious

-conscious Compounds are hyphenated except for *unconscious*.

consciousness-raising

consensus

conservative Tending to be cautious, moderate in beliefs, views.

consignable; consignor

consol. Abbreviation for *consolidated*.

consommé

consortium; *pl.*, consortia *or* consortiums

conspectus; *pl.*, conspectuses

constitute To establish, form. (Compare comprise.)

constitution Capitalize only if part of a document title: *The United States Constitution*.

constr. Abbreviation for *construction*.

consul A foreign representative. (Compare consulate.) Capitalize if part of a formal title preceding a name.

consulate The residence of a foreign representative. (Compare consul.) Capitalize only when used as part of proper noun.

consul general; *pl.*, consuls general

consumer price index Capitalize in reference to the U.S. index (abbreviated *CPI*) issued by the Labor Department.

cont. *or* contd. *or* cont'd Abbreviations for *continued*.

contact lens

contagious Medically communicable through contact.

contagium; *pl.*, contagia

contemn To scorn or treat as being very bad. (Compare condemn.)

contemporaneous

contemptible Low and provoking scorn. (Compare contemptuous.)

contemptuous Feeling or expressing scorn. (Compare contemptible.)

continent May be capitalized in reference to specific body of land. *The Continent* means Europe.

Continental Army

Continental Congress

Continental Divide

continental shelf

continental slope

continual Prolonged in succession, recurrence. (Compare continuous.)

continuous Uninterrupted in flow or extent. (Compare continual.)

continuum; *pl.*, continua *or* continuums

contr. Abbreviation for *contraction*.

Contra; *pl.*, Contras Nicaraguan rebel fighter(s).

contractions Abbreviations that are contractions do not have a period at the end (e.g., *sec'y*, *int'l*).

contralto; *pl.*, contraltos

contretemp; *pl.,* **contretemps**

control, controlled

contumacy Stubbornness. (Compare **contumely**.)

contumely Rude, haughty language. (Compare **contumacy**.)

convener *or* **convenor**

convention Capitalize only if part of a proper noun (e.g., *the 1992 Democratic Convention*).

conversable Sociable, friendly to talk with.

conversant Able to talk knowledgeably.

convex Rounded or curved outward. (Compare **concave**.)

convince Use with *of* or *that*.

cookie *or* **cooky;** *pl.,* **cookies**

cookout

coolheaded

coolly

cooped-up

Cooper, James Fenimore (1789–1851) American author.

cooperate

cooperative; co-op

coordinate

copacetic *or* **copesetic**

cop-out As noun.

cop out As verb.

copr. Abbreviation for *copyright*.

copyediting

copy editor

coq au vin

coquet *or* **coquette;** *pl.,* **coquets** *or* **coquettes, coquetted,**

coral The plant or the color. (Compare **choral, chorale, corral**.)

cordon bleu

cordovan Capitalize when an inhabitant of Cordoba, Spain, is meant.

corduroy

cordwood

core The center or the integral part. (Compare **corps**.)

corespondent *or* **co-respondent** A joint defendant, esp. a person charged with adultery in a divorce case. (Compare **correspondent**.)

corgi; *pl.,* **corgis**

corkboard

corkscrew

corn- Compounds written open include *corn bread, corn chip, corn flour, corn pone, corn silk, corn sugar, corn syrup*.

Corn Belt

corned beef

cornerstone

corn-fed

cornfield

cornflakes

cornrow

corporal Bodily (as in punishment). (Compare **corporeal**.)

corporeal Physical, tangible in nature. (Compare **corporal**.)

corporation *or* **corp.** Capitalize only if part of proper noun.

corps de ballet; *pl.,* **corps de ballet**

corps A group that acts in unison. Captalize if part of proper noun. Possessive form is *corps'*. (Compare **core, corpse**.)

corpse A dead body. (Compare **corps**.)

corpus delicti; *pl.,* **corpora delicti**

corral An enclosure for animals.

(Compare **choral, chorale, coral**.)

correspondent A person who reports or writes letters. (Compare **corespondent**.)

corrigendum; *pl.,* **corrigenda**

corroborate

corrugated

corrupter *or* **corruptor**

cortege *or* **cortège**

cortex; *pl.,* **cortices** *or* **cortexes**

coruscate

cost-effective

cost of living As noun.

coterie

cotillion

Cotton Belt

cotton candy

cotton gin

cotton-picking As adjective.

coulee A stream of molten lava.

council A legislative body. (Compare **counsel**.) Capitalize if part of proper noun.

councillor *or* **councilor** A member of legislative body. (Compare **counseler**.)

counsel A lawyer. (Compare **council**.)

counsel, counseled *or* **counselled**

counselor *or* **counsellor** A lawyer, adviser, or supervisor. (Compare **councillor**.)

counselor-at-law; *pl.,* **counselors-at-law**

countdown As noun.

counter- Compounds are spelled as one word (e.g., *counterweight*).

counter check A check available at a bank for the use of depositors making a withdrawal.

counterfeiter

country-born

country-bred

country club

county Capitalize only if part of proper noun or in a formal title preceding a name (e.g., *McKean County, Pennsylvania; County Commissioner Susan Costello*).

county seat

coup; *pl.,* **coups**

coup de grace; *pl.,* **coups de grace**

coup d'etat; *pl.,* **coups d'etat**

coupé *or* **coupe**

coupon

court Capitalize only if part of proper noun, address, or formal title (e.g., *County Court Judge Christopher Carveth*). Abbreviation is *ct.*

courtesan

courthouse

court-martial; *pl.,* **courts-martial**

court-martialed *or* **court-martialled** As verb.

courtroom

courtyard

cousin-german; *pl.,* **cousins-german**

coverall *or* **coveralls**

cover-up As noun.

covey; *pl.,* **coveys**

cow's milk

cow town

coxcomb

coyote; *pl.,* **coyotes** *or* **coyote**

cp. *or* **cf.** Abbreviation for *compare*.

C.P. Abbreviation for Communist party.

CPA Abbreviation for *certified public accountant*.

CPM Abbreviation for *cycles per minute.*

CPR Abbreviation for *cardiopulmonary resuscitation.*

CPS Abbreviation for *cycles per second* or *characters per second.*

CPU Abbreviation for *central processing unit.*

crabgrass

crabmeat

cracker-barrel

crackerjack

crack-up or **crackup** As noun.

-craft Compounds ending in *-craft* are usually written as one word.

cranium; *pl.,* **craniums** or **crania**

crankcase

crankshaft

crapshoot; crapshooter

crash-dive As verb.

crash dive As noun.

crash helmet

crash pad

crash-land As verb.

crash landing As noun.

crawfish or **crayfish**

crawl space

crazy bone

Crazy Horse (1842–1877) American Sioux Indian chief.

crazy quilt

creak A squeaky sound. (Compare **creek.**)

cream cheese

cream puff

cream soda

crèche

credible Believable. (Compare **creditable, credulous.**)

creditable Worthy of belief. (Compare **credible, credulous.**)

credo; *pl.,* **credos**

credulous Ready to believe. (Compare **credible, creditable.**)

creek A stream or small river. (Compare **creak.**)

creep, crept

crème or **creme**

crème de cacao

crème de la crème

crème de menthe

crenellate or **crenelate**

crepe or **crêpe**

crepe de chine

crepe paper

crepe suzette; *pl.,* **crepes suzette** or **crepe suzettes**

crescendo; *pl.,* **crescendos** or **crescendoes**

crescent

crestfallen

crevasse A deep crack in the land. (Compare **crevice.**)

crevice A small crack. (Compare **crevasse.**)

crew cut

crew neck

crew sock

crib, cribbed

crisis; *pl.,* **crises**

crisscross

criterion; *pl.,* **criteria**

critique

crocus; *pl.,* **crocuses**

croquet A lawn game in which mallets are used to drive a ball through a series of hoops placed in the ground. (Compare **croquette.**)

croquette A small, round patty of fried minced meat, chicken or vegetable. (Compare **croquet.**)

cross- Compounds that are hyphenated include *cross-check,* *cross-country, cross-cultural, cross-examine, cross-examination, cross-eye, cross-eyed, cross-legged, cross-grained, cross-index, cross-link, cross-pollinate, cross-purpose, cross-question, cross-reaction, cross-refer, cross-reference, cross-stitch.* Open compounds include *cross fire, cross section, cross talk.*

crossbreed, crossbred

croup; croupy

crouton

crowbar

crow's-foot; *pl.*, **crow's-feet**

crow's nest

CRT Abbreviation for *cathode-ray tube*

crucible

crudités

cruel, crueler *or* **crueller** *or* **more cruel**

cruise missile

crustacean

crux; *pl.*, **cruxes** *or* **cruces**

crybaby

crystal ball

crystal-clear

crystalline

crystallize *or* **crystalize**

C-sharp

cu. ft. Abbreviation for *cubic foot.*

cu. in. Abbreviation for *cubic inch.*

cubbyhole

cube steak

Cub Scout

cuckoo clock

cudgel, cudgeled *or* **cudgelled**

cue ball

cue, cuing *or* **cueing**

cuff link

cuisine

cul-de-sac; *pl.*, **culs-de-sac** *or* **cul-de-sacs**

cum laude

cummerbund

cummings, ee (1894–1962) Edward Estlin. American writer of experimental prose and poetry. Works include *The Enormous Room.*

cuneiform

cupboard

cupcake

cupful; *pl.*, **cupfuls** *or* **cupsful**

cure-all

Curie, Marie (1867–1934) Polish physical chemist. Pioneer researcher of radioactivity. Discovered polonium and radium.

curio; *pl.*, **curios**

curlicue

curmudgeon

currant A berry-like fruit. (Compare **current**.)

current Flow. (Compare **currant**.)

curriculum; *pl.*, **curricula** *or* **curriculums**

curriculum vitae; *pl.*, **curricula vitae**

curtsy *or* **curtsey, curtsied** *or* **curtseyed**

curvaceous *or* **curvacious**

curveball

custom-built

customer A person who does business at a store, bank, or other establishment for goods and services.

customhouse *or* **customshouse**

custom-made

customs Capitalize only if part of

proper noun (e.g., *the U.S. Customs Service*).

customs official

custom-tailored

cut-and-dried

cutaway

cutback

cutdown

cut glass As noun.

cut-in As noun or adjective.

cutoff *or* **cut-off**

cutout As noun.

cut-rate

cutthroat

cutting board

cutup As noun.

CV Abbreviation for *curriculum vitae*.

cwt. Abbreviation for *hundredweight*.

cyclopedia The British spelling is *cyclopaedia*.

cylindrical *or* **cylindric**

cymbal A musical instrument. (Compare **symbol**.)

cynic A person who is critical of widely-held societal beliefs, and is given to fault finding and sarcasm.

cynosure

cyst

czar The emperor of Russia until the Bolshevik Revolution of 1917. The adjective is *czarist*.

d. Abbreviation for *died*.

'd A contraction meaning *had* or *would* (e.g., *I'd, they'd*).

DOA Abbreviation for *dead on arrival*.

d.b.a. *or* **d/b/a** Abbreviation for *doing business as*.

DA *or* **D.A.** *or* **dist. atty.** Abbreviation for *district attorney*. Capitalize *Dist. Atty.* if used as a formal title preceding a name.

dachshund; *pl.,* **dachshunds**

Dacron

dado; *pl.,* **dadoes**

daffodil

dahlia

daiquiri

Dairy Belt

dairy A manufacturer of milk products (as noun); having to do with milk or milk products (as adjective): *dairy goat, dairy farm*. (Compare **diary**.)

dais; *pl.,* **daises**

dalliance

Dalmatian

dam Capitalize only if part of proper noun.

damage Destruction caused by someone or something. (Compare **damages**.)

damages A monetary award as compensation to a defendant in a court case. (Compare **damage**.)

damask

dammed Plugged up, blocked. (Compare **damned**.)

damned, damnedest *or*

damndest Detestable, condemned. (Compare **dammed**.)

damning Causing condemnation or disdain.

dance hall

dandelion

Danish pastry *or* **Danish**

dappled *or* **dapple** As adjective.

daredevil

daredevilry *or* **daredeviltry**

daresay

Dark Ages

dark horse

darkroom

Darwin, Charles Robert (1809–1882) English naturalist. Originated theory of evolution/ natural selection.

dashboard

dat. Abbreviation for *dative*.

data Plural form of *datum*, but used as singular or plural.

data-base As adjective.

data base As noun.

datable *or* **dateable** That which may be assigned a date.

data processing As noun.

data processing As adjective.

data processor

dateline The place of origin typed at beginning of news story. (Compare **date line**.)

date line A hypothetical line along 180th meridian. (Compare **dateline**.)

datum, *pl.,* **data**

daughter-in-law; *pl.,* **daughters-in-law**

davenport A couch or small writing desk.

daybed

daybreak

day-care
daydream
day in, day out
day laborer
daylight saving time *or* daylight-saving time *or* daylight time
daylong
day nursery
dayroom
day school
daytime
day-to-day
d.b.a. *or* **d/b/a** Abbreviation for *doing business as*.
DC Abbreviation for *direct current*.
D day *or* **D-day**
DDT Abbreviation for *dichlorodiphenyltrichloroethane*, an insecticide.
de- Prefix meaning away from, down, or reverse. Hyphenate the prefix when second word begins with *e*, as in *de-escalate* or *de-emphasize*, or when the open version appears strange to the eye (e.g. *deink* should be *de-ink*).
dead As noun in both plural and singular.
dead- Compounds are often written as one word, including *deadbeat*, *deadeye*, *deadfall*, *deadline*, *deadlock*, *deadlight*, *deadpan*, *deadweight*, *deadwood*.
dead center
dead end As noun.
dead-end As verb or adjective.
dead heat
dead letter
dead load
dead-on
dead set

deaf-mute; deaf-muteness
deal, dealt
dean Capitalize only if part of formal title preceding a name.
dean's list
dearth
deathbed
death benefit
deathblow
death-defying
death's-head
deathwatch
debonair
debone *or* **bone** To remove bones.
debris
debt
debtor
debug
debut
debutant A person making a first appearance.
debutante *or* **deb** Traditional term for a young woman making first formal social appearance.
deca- *or* **deka-** *or* **dek-** Multiplied by ten. (Compare **deci-**.)
decades Four-digit decades are written numerically (e.g., *1980s*). Two-digit references can be spelled out (e.g., *the eighties*) or written numerically with or without an apostrophe preceding and an *s* after (e.g., *'80s* or *80s*).
decaffeinated
decal
Decalogue *or* **decalogue** Capitalized, this refers to the Ten Commandments. Lowercase, means basic rules.
decathlon
deceased As noun in both plural and singular.

decent Proper, suitable (Compare **descent**.)

deci- One-tenth. (Compare **deca-**.)

decibel or **db** or **dB**

decidua; pl., **deciduae**

decimate Literally, "to kill every tenth person" or to destroy a large proportion of something.

deck chair

deckhand

deckhouse

declarant A foreign person who states desire for citizenship. (Compare **declarer**.)

Declaration of Independence

declarer A person who makes a statement, especially a card player calling trump. (Compare **declarant**.)

déclassé

décolletage Low-cut clothing. (Compare **decolleté**.)

decolleté Attired in strapless or low-cut clothing. (Compare **décolletage**.)

decor or **décor**

decoration Capitalize the names of decorations, medals, or awards given by a government (e.g., *Purple Heart*).

decorative Ornamental. (Compare **decorous**.)

decorous Good, correct, honorable. (Compare **decorative**.)

decoupage or **découpage**

decrepit

decrescendo; pl., **decrescendos**

decry To voice strong disapproval. (Compare **descry**.)

deduce To figure out, infer. (Compare **deduct, educe**.)

deducible Possible to be understood. (Compare **deductible**.)

deduct To subtract, take away. (Compare **deduce**.)

deductible Possible as a subtraction. (Compare **deducible**.)

deduction An inference, understanding by general principle.

deep- Compounds beginning with *deep-* are often hyphenated, as in *deep-dish pie, deep-freeze, deep-fry, deep-sea, deep-seated, deep-set*.

Compounds written as two words include *deep fat, deep freeze, deep fryer, deep six (noun), deep space, deep structure*.

-deep Compounds ending in *-deep* are usually hyphenated (e.g., *knee-deep*).

Deep South

deer; pl., **deer** or **deers**

deerskin

def. Abbreviation for *definite, definition*.

de facto in reality; actually.

defective Having imperfections. (Compare **deficient**.)

defer To allow someone else to go ahead.

deferential or **deferent**

deferrable

deficient Lacking. (Compare **defective**.)

definite Certain, precise, decided. (Compare **definitive**.)

definitive Complete, perfect, final. (Compare **definite**.)

Defoe, Daniel (1660–1731) English journalist and novelist.

46

Degas, Edgar (1834–1917) French
  Impressionist painter.
degree-day
dehydr- *and* **dehydro-** Compounds
  are written as one word (e.g.,
  dehydrator).
de-ice To melt frozen material.
deign
deity; *pl.,* **deities**
déjà vu
de jure By right.
delay To postpone the start or
  continuation of something.
delegate Capitalize only if part of
  a formal title preceding a name.
delegate at large
delft *or* **delftware**
delicatessen *or* **deli**
delicious Capitalized when
  referring to the variety of apple.
delinquent
deliquesce; deliquescent
delirium tremens *or* **Delirium
  Tremens** *or* **d.t.'s** *or* **DTs**
delta Capitalize if part of proper
  noun (e.g., *the Mississippi River
  Delta*).
delusion A mental state based on
  false belief.
delusive *or* **delusory**
deluxe
demagogue *or* **demagog**
demagoguery *or* **demagogy**
demarche
demeanor
demi- A prefix meaning half, or
  less than usual in size or power.
  Compounds with "**demi-**" are
  formed as one word: *demigod,
  demijohn.*
demitasse
democracy

Democrat A member of the
  political party. Lowercase to
  indicate a believer in government
  of social equality.
démodé *or* **demoded**
demographics As noun.
demonic *or* **demoniac**
demonstration *or* **demo**
demur, demurred To object or
  hesitate to do something.
  (Compare **demure**.)
demure Quiet and modest.
  (Compare **demur**.)
dengue
denizen
denote To signify, indicate.
  (Compare **connote**.)
denouement *or* **dénouement**
dentifrice
denunciation
department Capitalize if part of
  proper noun (e.g., *U.S. State
  Department*).
dependence *or* **dependance**
dependency
dependent *or* **dependant**
depilate; depilatory
deposit slip
depositary A person who holds a
  valuable for someone. (Compare
  depository.)
depository A person or place for
  holding valuables. (Compare
  depositary.)
depot Capitalize if part of proper
  noun.
deprecate To mildly disapprove.
  (Compare **depreciate**.)
depreciate To lower in value or
  believe to have lower value.
  (Compare **deprecate**.)
dept. Abbreviation for *department*.

depth charge

depth perception

deputy Capitalize if part of formal title preceding a name.

derby; *pl.,* **derbies** A horse race. Capitalize if part of proper noun (e.g., *Kentucky Derby*).

derby hat *or* **derby**

de rigueur Proper, suitable for the occasion.

derisive Scornful. (Compare **derisory**.)

derisory Ridiculous. (Compare **derisive**.)

deriv. Abbreviation for *derivative*.

dermat-, dermato- Words formed with this prefix, which means skin, are not hyphenated (e.g., *dermatitis*).

dernier cri The latest thing.

derriere *or* **derrière**

Descartes, René (1596–1650) French mathematician and philosopher.

descendant *or* **descendent**

descent Derivation, or moving downward. (Compare **decent**.)

descry To discover, detect. (Compare **decry**.)

desecrater *or* **desecrator**

desert Desolate, arid geographical region. (Compare **desserts**, **dessert**.)

deshabille *or* **dishabille**

desideratum; *pl.,* **desiderata**

-designate Compounds ending in *-designate* are usually hyphenated.

desirable Wished for. (Compare **desirous**.)

desirous Wishful in thinking. (Compare **desirable**.)

desktop

desperado; *pl.,* **desperadoes**

desperate Without hope and very anxious; filled with despair.

dessert A course consisting of sweetened food that follows a meal. (Compare **desert**, **desserts**.)

dessert fork

dessert knife

dessert wine

desserts A reward or punishment that is fairly deserved. (Compared **desert**, **dessert**.)

dessertspoon

desuetude The state of being no longer in use (e.g., *The once-familiar custom had fallen into desuetude*).

desultory

détente

determiner *or* **determinator**

detonatable *or* **detonable**

detritus; *pl.,* **detritus**

deuces wild

deus ex machina

deutero- A prefix meaning second or secondary. Words formed with this prefix are not hyphenated.

Deuteronomy

deutschemark *or* **Deutsche mark** *or* **DM** A unit of German currency.

device A mechanical thing. (Compare **devise**.)

devil Lowercase unless referring to the devil of the Bible, Satan.

devil's advocate

devil's food cake

devil-may-care

devilry *or* **deviltry**

devise To formulate, invent. (Compare **device**.)

deviser A person who invents, formulates. (Compare **devisor**.)

devisor A person who leaves property in a will. (Compare **deviser**.)

devoir Duty. (Compare **devour**.)

devotee

devour To eat voraciously. (Compare **devoir**.)

dewdrop

dewfall

dew point

dexterous or **dextrous**

dextr-, dextro- A prefix meaning toward or on the right-hand side. Words formed with this prefix are not hyphenated.

dharma

di- Words formed with this prefix, which means "two of" or "double," are not hyphenated: *diatomic*.

dia-, di- Words formed with these prefixes, which mean "through" or "across," are not hyphenated: *diaphonic*.

diabolic or **diabolical**

diacritical or **diacritic**

diacritical marks Marks, including accent marks, added to a letter or symbol to show its pronunciation or to otherwise distinguish it. They include the diaeresis or umlaut (ü), tilde (ñ), cedilla (ç), macron (ē), and breve (ĕ). Marks may be omitted only in commonly used English words borrowed from foreign languages like *smorgasbord, facade*. (See also **accent marks**.)

diaeresis or **dieresis**; *pl.*, **diaereses** or **diereses**

diag. Abbreviation for *diagonal; diagram*.

diagnosis; *pl.*, **diagnoses**

diagnostic or **diagnostical**

diagram, diagramed or **diagrammed**

dial, dialed or **dialled**

dial. Abbreviation for *dialect, dialectical*.

dialectical or **dialectic** or **dialectal**

dialogue or **dialog**

dial tone

dialysis; *pl.*, **dialyses**

diam. or **dia.** Abbreviation for *diameter*.

diametric or **diametrical**

diamond in the rough

diaper

diaphragm

diarrhea

diary A personal journal. (Compare **dairy**.)

dichotomy

Dickens, Charles (1812–1870) English novelist. Author of *Great Expectations* and *A Tale of Two Cities*.

dickey or **dicky** or **dickie**; *pl.*, **dickeys** or **dickies**

Dickinson, Emily (1830–1886) American poet.

dict. Abbreviation for *dictionary*.

Dictaphone A trademark name for a machine that records spoken words and plays them back for the purpose of typing transcripts and other documents.

dictum; *pl.*, **dicta** or **dictums**

did not or **didn't**

dido; *pl.*, **didoes**

die; *pl.*, **dice** or **dies**

die-cast

die-cut

diehard   As noun.

die-hard   As adjective.

diesel engine

diesel-electric

dietitian or dietician

diff. or dif.   Abbreviation for *difference, different.*

differentia; *pl.,* differentiae

dig, dug

dilapidated

dilatory

dilemma

dilettante; *pl.,* dilettantes *or* dilettanti

dill pickle

dillydally

diluter *or* dilutor

diluvial *or* diluvian

dim.   Abbreviation for *diminutive; diminished; dimension.*

diminuendo; *pl.,* diminuendos

dimwit

dim-witted

diner-out; *pl.,* diners-out

Diners Club

Dinesen, Isak   (1885–1962) Danish author. Wrote *Out of Africa.*

dinette

ding-a-ling

dingbat

dingdong

dinghy; *pl.,* dinghies

dining car

dining hall

dining room

dinner-   Compounds formed with *dinner* that are written as two words include *dinner bell, dinner dance, dinner jacket, dinner hour.*

dinnertime

dinnerware

dinosaur

diphtheria

diphthong   A vowel combination within a single syllable that indicates a speech sound that glides from one vowel to a second vowel sound, as in the *oy* of the word *joy.* The adjective is *diphthongal.*

diploma   The abbreviation is *dipl.* or *dpl.* or *dip.*

diplomat   A person representing a country in foreign affairs. (Compare **diplomate.**) Do not capitalize.

diplomate   A person who passes professional schooling and exams. (Compare **diplomat.**)

dipstick

diptych

dir.   Abbreviation for *director.*

directions   Do not capitalize a word indicating direction or position if it is not a proper noun; capitalize only if a term denotes a definite region, locality, or geographical feature (e.g., *the East,* but *eastern*).

director   Capitalize if part of formal title preceding a name.

director's chair

dirigible

dirndl

dirt bike

dirt-cheap

dirt-poor

dirt road

dirty pool

dirty trick

dirty word

dirty work

dis-   Words beginning with the

prefix *dis-*, which means "not," "opposite," or "excluding," are usually spelled without a hyphen (e.g., *disadvantageous*).

disassociate *or* **dissociate**

disaster area

disastrous

disbar, disbarred

disbeliever A person who refuses to hold something as true. (Compare **unbeliever**.)

discernible *or* **discernable**

disciple

disc jockey *or* **disk jockey** *or* **deejay** *or* **DJ**

discombobulate

discomfit To frustrate. (Compare **discomfort**.)

discomfiture

discomfort To make uneasy, not comfortable. (Compare **discomfit**.)

discontent *or* **discontented**

discotheque *or* **disco**

discount store

discover To find something that already exists.

discreet Careful, prudent, secretive. (Compare **discrete**.)

discrete Individually distinct. (Compare **discreet**.)

discus; *pl.,* **discuses**

discussable *or* **discussible**

disease Capitalize only a proper name in the name of a disease (e.g., *Alzheimer's disease, German measles, Parkinson's disease*; but *measles, heart disease*).

disenthrall *or* **disenthral**

dish- Compounds formed with *dish-* as one word include

dishcloth, dishpan, dishrack, dishrag, dishboard, dishwasher, dishwater, dishware, dishwashing.

dishabille *or* **deshabille**

dishevel, disheveled *or* **dishevelled**

dish towel

disinterested Not prejudiced or biased. (Compare **uninterested**.)

disk *or* **disc** Short form for *diskette*.

diskette *or* **floppy disk** A thin plate covered with magnetic material used for recording and storing computer data.

dislikable *or* **dislikeable**

dislodgment *or* **dislodgement**

disorient *or* **disorientate**

disparate Distinct, separate. (Compare **divers, diverse**.)

dispel, dispelled

disproved *or* **disproven**

dissect

dissemble

disseminate

dissent A difference of opinion (as noun) or to voice disagreement with the majority (as verb).

dissertation The abbreviation is *diss.* (e.g., *Ph.D. diss.*). (See also Part 2, **Titles of works**.)

dist. Abbreviation for *district*.

distaff; *pl.,* **distaffs**

distend To stretch, extend, expand.

distension *or* **distention**

distill *or* **distil, distilled**

distinct Separate, notable.

distinctive Stylishly different.

distingué

distrait Absent-minded. (Compare **distraught**.)

distraught Very upset. (Compare *distrait*.)

district Capitalize only if part of proper noun: *District of Columbia*.

district attorney; *pl.*, district attorneys Capitalize only if part of formal title preceding a name (e.g., *District Attorney Peter Stinton*).

ditchdigger

ditto mark

ditty bag

diurnal Happening daily or occurring or active during the day. (Compare *nocturnal*.)

div. Abbreviation for *division* or *divorced*.

dive, dived *or* **dove**

dive-bomb

divers Several, various. (Compare *disparate*, *diverse*.)

diverse Differing, unlike. (Compare *disparate*, *divers*.)

divide Capitalize only if part of proper noun (e.g., *the Continental Divide*).

divine Capitalize when used in the theological sense referring to a supreme being (e.g., *Divine Host*).

diving board

D-major

do; *pl.*, dos *or* **do's**

do. Abbreviation for *ditto*, "the same."

Doberman pinscher

docile

dock- Compounds are written as one word (e.g., *dockside*).

docket

doctor *or* **Dr.**

doctrinaire Dogmatic, dictatorial. (Compare *doctrinal*.)

doctrinal Having to do with principles, beliefs. (Compare *doctrinaire*.)

doctrine Government policy, principle, or position. Capitalized only as part of the formal name of a specific statement of government policy (e.g., *Monroe Doctrine*).

docudrama

document title (See Part 2, **Titles of works**.)

dodo; *pl.*, dodoes *or* **dodos**

doe; *pl.*, does *or* **doe**

-doer Compounds with *-doer* are usually written as one word (e.g., *evildoer*).

does not *or* **doesn't**

dog- Compounds formed with *dog-* that are two words include *dog paddle* (noun), *dog show*, *dog tag*, *dog biscuit*, *dog collar*, *dog days*.

dog and pony show

dogcatcher

dog-eared

dogface

dogfight

doggerel

doggie bag *or* **doggy bag**

doggone *or* **doggoned**

doggy *or* **doggie; *pl.*, doggies**

dogmatic *or* **dogmatical**

do-gooder

dogsled

dog-tired

doily; *pl.*, doilies

do-it-yourself

dolce vita

dollar sign

dollhouse

dolman sleeve

domicile

dominion Capitalize only if part of proper noun (e.g., *Dominion of Canada*).

domino; *pl.,* **dominoes** or **dominos**

doneness

donnée; *pl.,* **données**

Donne, John (1572–1631) British Metaphysical poet.

donnybrook

donor or **donator**

do not or **don't**

do-nothing

doohickey

doomsday

door- Compound words formed with *door-* are usually written as one word. Exceptions includes *door lock, door key, door chain,* and *door prize.*

do-or-die

door prize

door-to-door

dopey or **dopy**

Doppler effect

dory A type of small boat.

do's-and-don'ts

do-si-do; *pl.,* **do-si-dos**

dossier

Dostoyevsky, Fyodor (1821–1881) Russian novelist. Author of *Crime and Punishment* and *The Brothers Karamazov.*

dotted swiss

double- Compounds formed with *double-* are often hyphenated: *double-barrel, double-breasted, double-check* (verb), *double-chinned, double-cross* (verb), *double-dealer, double-dealing, double-deck, double-decker,* *double-digit, double-edged, double-faced, double-jointed, double-park, double-quick, double-ring, double-space, double-talk, double-team, double-time* (verb). Most others are written as two words.

double entendre; *pl.,* **double entendres** A word or phrase having two intended meanings.

doubleheader

double knit

doublespeak

doublethink

double take

double-talk

double time As noun.

doughnut or **donut**

doughty Fearless, valiant. (Compare **dowdy**.)

Douglass, Frederick (1817–1895) American abolitionist.

dour Humorless, grim.

dovetail

Dow-Jones average

dowdy Frumpy or old-fashioned. (Compare **doughty**.)

dowel A small wooden rod or stick used for connecting.

down- Many compounds beginning with *down-* are written as one word, including *downfield, downgrade, downhill, downplay, downright, downshift, downside, downsized, downstairs, downfall, downtrodden.*

-down Compounds (nouns, adjectives) with this ending are usually written as one word (e.g., *shakedown*).

down-and-out

down-easter or **Down-Easter**

down-home
downlink
download
down payment
downsize
Down's syndrome *or* mongolism
down-the-line
down-to-earth
down under   As adverb.
Down Under   The region including
   Australia and New Zealand.
downward *or* downwards
doxology
doyen
Doyle, Sir Arthur Conan
   (1858–1930) British author of *The
   Adventures of Sherlock Holmes.*
doz.   The abbreviation for *dozen*
DPAHC   Abbreviation for *durable
   power of attorney for health care.*
drachma; *pl.,* drachmas *or*
   drachmai *or* drachmae   A unit
   of Greek currency.
draft age
draft beer
draftee
dragonfly
drag race
drainpipe
dramatis personae   Latin, meaning
   the cast of characters.
drape; drapable *or* drapeable
draw, drew
drawing board
drawing room
drawstring
dream, dreamed *or* dreamt
dreamworld
dress circle
dressing room
dressing-down
dressmaker

dress rehearsal
dress shield
dress shirt
dress uniform
dried-up
drier *or* dryer   Appliance for
   taking wetness out of clothing.
driftwood
drink, drunk *or* drank
drip-dry
drive, drove
drive-in   As both adjective and
   noun
drivel, driveled *or* drivelled
drive shaft
driver's license
driver's seat
drivetrain
driveway
driving range
drop-   Compounds formed with
   drop- spelled as two words
   include *drop cloth, drop curtain,
   drop front, drop leaf, drop pass,
   drop seat, drop shot.*
drop-dead   As adjective.
drop-in   As noun.
dropkick   As noun.
drop-kick   As verb.
drop-off   As noun.
dropout   As noun.
drought
drudgery; *pl.,* drudgeries
drugstore
druid *or* Druid
drum major
drunk   As noun.
drunken *or* drunk   As adjective.
   Drunken is the modifier used
   before a noun.
drunkenness
dry-   Compounds formed with *dry-*

that are hyphenated include *dry-clean*, *dry-dock* (verb), *dry-eyed*, *dry-nurse* (verb), *dry-rot* (verb).

dry-cleanable

dry cleaning

dry dock   As noun.

dry-dock As verb.

dry mop

dry rot

dry sink

drywall

dual   Double, two. (Compare **duel**.)

dual-purpose

Du Bois, W. E. B.   (1868–1963) American educator. Creator of NAACP.

duck call

duckfooted

duckpond

duck soup

duckwalk

dudgeon

due process

duel   A formal contest between two people. (Compare **dual**.)

dueled *or* **duelled**

duet

duffel bag

duffle coat *or* **duffel coat**

du jour   French, literally "of the day" or "today's" (e.g., *soup du jour*).

dull-witted

dully   In a bland manner. (Compare **duly**.)

duly   In a proper manner. (Compare **dully**.)

Dumas, Alexandre, père   (1802–1870) French author.

dumbbell

dumbfound *or* **dumfound**

dumbwaiter

dumdum   A type of bullet. (Compare **dum-dum**.)

dum-dum   A stupid person.

dump truck

Duncan, Isadora   (1878–1927) American avante-garde dancer.

dunk shot

duo; *pl.,* **duos**

duo-   Words formed with the combining form *duo-* (meaning "two") are written as one word.

dupl. *or* **dup.**   Abbreviation for *duplicate*.

duplex

dust bowl

dust devil

dust jacket

dust mop

dust storm

Dutch elm disease

Dutch oven

dutch treat As adverb.

Dutch treat   As noun.

duteous   Obedient. (Compare **dutiable, dutiful**.)

dutiable   Responsible. (Compare **duteous, dutiful**.)

dutiful   Motivated to be responsible. (Compare **duteous, dutiable**)

duty-free

dwell, dwelt *or* **dwelled**

DWI   Abbreviation for *driving while intoxicated*.

DUI   Abbreviation for *driving under the influence* (of alcohol or another substance that causes impairment).

dye, dyeing   To change the color of something.

dyed-in-the-wool
dyestuff
dynamo; *pl.,* **dynamos**
dynasty
dys- Abnormal or malfunctioning.

Words formed with this prefix are not hyphenated (e.g., *dyslexia, dyspepsia*).
dysentery
dysfunction *or* **disfunction**

ea. Abbreviation for *each*.

eagle eye

Eakins, Thomas (1844–1916) American realist painter.

ear- Most compound words formed with *ear-* are written as one word (e.g., *earmark*).

Earhart, Amelia (1897–1937) American aviator.

early bird

earned run average *or* **ERA**

Earth Capitalize when referred to as astronomical body, lowercase as ground/dirt.

earth- Most compound words formed with *earth-* are written as one word: *earthworm*.

earthly Associated with physical life. (Compare **earthy**.)

earth science

earthy Simple or natural. (Compare **earthly**.)

easel

east, eastern Capitalize if naming a specific part of a geographic entity rather than a general direction (e.g., *Middle East, Eastern Hemisphere*).

Easter, Eastertide

Easterner A person who lives in or is from the eastern United States.

eastward As adjective, adverb, noun.

eastwards As adverb.

easygoing

easy mark

eat, ate, eaten

eatery A place to eat, a restaurant.

eau de cologne; *pl.,* **eaux de cologne**

eau-de-vie; *pl.,* **eaux-de-vie**

eavesdrop

ebb tide

ebullient; ebullience

eccentric

ecclesiastical *or* **ecclesiastic**

echelon

echo; *pl.,* **echoes**

éclair

éclat

eclectic

economic Concerning finance. (Compare **economical**.)

economical Careful with money; a good bargain; thrifty. (Compare **economic**.)

eco-rich

ecru

ecstatic

ect-, ecto- Combining form meaning "outside, external" (e.g., *ectopic pregnancy*).

-ectomy Suffix meaning "surgical procedure."

eczema

ed.; *pl.,* **eds.** Abbreviation for *editor/edition*; plural, *editors/editions*.

Edam cheese

eddy; *pl.,* **eddies**

edelweiss

edema; *pl.,* **edemas** *or* **edemata**

edematous

Eden

edgeways *or* **edgewise**

Edison, Thomas Alva (1847–1931) American inventor of telegraph, phonograph, and electric lamp.

editor in chief   Capitalize if part of formal title preceding a name.

EDT *or* **E.D.T.** *or* **e.d.t.**   Abbreviation for *eastern daylight time*.

educable   Capable of being taught. (Compare **educated**.)

educated   Learned, knowledgeable. (Compare **educable**.)

educe   To figure out, deduce. (Compare **deduce**.)

EEG   Abbreviation for *electroencephalogram* or *electroencephalograph*.

eerie *or* **eery**

effect   As a noun, means the result of influence or an accomplishment.

effect   As a verb, means to bring about, cause, accomplish. (Compare **affect**.)

effective   Having an impact. (Compare **effectual**.)

effectual   Producing the desired impact. (Compare **effective**.)

efferent   Conducting from or outward. Used especially in relation to body parts or organs. (Compare **afferent**.)

effete

efficacious   Having the power to produce a desired impact. (Compare **efficient**.)

efficient   Productive of desired effect without waste. (Compare **efficacious**.)

effluent   Moving away from, flowing out.

effluvium; *pl.,* **effluvia**

e.g.   Abbreviation meaning *exempli gratia,* "for example." Always preceeded by a comma.

égalité   French, meaning "equality."

eggbeater

egg cream

eggcup

egghead

eggnog

eggplant

egg roll

eggs Benedict

eggshell

egomaniac

egotism *or* **egoism**

egotist *or* **egoist**

egotistical *or* **egotistic**

ego trip   As noun.

egret   A heron.

ei *and* **ie**   *I* before *e*, except after *c* or when sounded like *ay* as in *neighbor* and *weigh*.

eiderdown

Eiffel, Alexandre-Gustave   (1832–1923) French engineer. Designed framework for the Statue of Liberty and the Eiffel tower.

eight ball

eighth

eighty

Einstein, Albert   (1879–1955) American physicist, developed theory of relativity.

either-or   As adjective (e.g., *an either-or proposition*).

ejection seat

eke, eking

EKG   Abbreviation for *electrocardiogram* or *electrocardiograph*.

elbow grease

elbowroom

elder, eldest

elec. *or* **elect.** Abbreviation for *electric, electrical, electrician, electricity, electrified.*

-elect Compounds ending in *-elect,* which indicates a person who has been elected but has not officially taken office, are hyphenated (e.g., *governor-elect*).

Election Day *or* **election day**

elective Optional.

electoral college

electric *or* **electrical**

electro- Compounds with *electro-* are written as one word, except for combinations that would double the *o* (e.g., *electrolysis,* but *electro-optics, electro-osmosis*).

electronic Using or working with electrons, particles with negative electricity. (Compare **electronics**.)

electronic mail *or* **e-mail** A computerized communication system with an extensive network.

electronics The branch of physics that is involved with electrons and electronic devices. (Compare **electronic**.)

electroshock therapy

elegy A mournful poem, often for a dead person. (Compare **eulogy**.)

elemental Primal, integral. (Compare **elementary**.)

elementary Basic, introductory, fundamental. (Compare **elemental**.)

elevated railroad *or* **elevated railway** *or* **el**

eleventh hour Near the end; with little time left.

elf; *pl.,* **elves**

elhi Concerning grades 1 through 12, that is, *e*lementary school through *hi*gh school.

elicit To draw out, derive.

Eliot, T. S. (1888–1965) British poet and critic. Author of *The Waste Land*.

elite

ellipse Oval or closed plane figure.

ellipsoid *or* **ellipsoidal**

elopement

elude To escape, avoid. (Compare **illude**.)

eluvial

Emancipation Proclamation

embargo; *pl.,* **embargoes**

embark

embarrass

embassy; *pl.,* **embassies** Capitalize if part of proper noun.

embed

emblematic *or* **emblematical**

embryo; *pl.,* **embryos**

embryo sac

emend To improve or correct. Usually used in reference to a document or text (Compare **amend**).

emerge To rise out of something.

emeritus; *pl.,* **emeriti**

Emerson, Ralph Waldo (1803–1882) American Transcendental essayist and poet.

emery board

emetic

emigrant A person who leaves a country to settle elsewhere. (Compare **emigré, immigrant**.)

emigré *or* **émigré** A person who leaves a country for political reasons. (Compare **emigrant, immigrant**.)

eminent domain

eminent Outstanding, prominent, important. (Compare **immanent, imminent**.)

emissary

Emmy; *pl.,* **Emmys**

emollient Soothing, something that soothes. (Compare **emolument**.)

emolument Compensation, perks from employment. (Compare **emollient**.)

emote

empathic *or* **empathetic**

emperor Capitalize as formal title preceding a name.

emphasis; *pl.,* **emphases**

emphysema

empirical *or* **empiric**

employee

emporium; *pl.,* **emporiums** *or* **emporia**

emprise

empty; *pl.,* **empties** As noun.

empty-handed

empty-headed

empyrean

emulsifiable *or* **emulsible**

enact Laws are *enacted.* (Compare **adopt, approve, pass**.)

enamel, enameled *or* **enamelled**

enamelware

enamor

en brochette

enceinte

encephalitis

encephalogram

enchilada

encircle

enclave

encore

ency. *or* **encyc.** Abbreviation for *encyclopedia.*

encyclopedia The British spelling is *encyclopaedia.*

end line

end point

end run

end table

end zone

end-all

endemic Local, native. (Compare **epidemic**.)

endgame

endmost

endo- Compounds with *endo-,* which means within or inner, are written as one word (e.g., *endocrine*).

endpaper

endways *or* **endwise**

enema; *pl.,* **enemas** *or* **enemata**

enervate To unnerve, make lose momentum. (Compare **innervate**.)

enfant terrible; *pl.,* **enfants terribles**

enfold

eng. *or* **engin.** Abbreviation for *engineering.*

Eng. Abbreviation for *English.*

engine A device that develops its own power. (Compare **motor**.)

English As noun, people native to England. (Compare **Briton, British, Britisher**.)

English muffin

engr. Abbreviation for *engineer.*

enigmatic *or* **enigmatical**

enjoin

en masse As a group.

enmesh

enmity

ennui

enroll *or* **enrol**

en route On the way.

enscounce

ensemble

ensign

ensure To make certain; guarantee. (Compare **insure**.)

entente

entero- Compounds formed with *entero-*, which means intestine, are written as one word (e.g., *enterotoxemia*).

enthrall *or* **enthral**

entitled Designated, given a right.

entomology Means the study of insects. (Compare **etiology**, **etymology**.)

entourage

entranceway

entreé *or* **entree**

entrepôt

entrepreneur

entry word *or* **headword**

enumerable

enumerate

enunciate To say clearly or make explicit.

envelop As verb.

envelope As noun.

environ To surround. (Compare **environs**.)

environs One's location, surrounding. (Compare **environ**.)

envisage To regard in a certain way. (Compare **envision**.)

envision To formulate in one's mind, to mentally picture. (Compare **envisage**.)

envoi Explanatory remarks for a poem or other piece of literature. (Compare **envoy**.)

envoy A delegate, representative. (Compare **envoi**.)

EOF Abbreviation for *end of file*.

eon *or* **aeon**

EPA Abbreviation for *Environmental Protection Agency*. Use in text only after full name has been used on first reference.

epaulet *or* **epaulette**

épée

epexegesis; *pl.*, **epexegeses**

ephemeral

ephemeron; *pl.*, **ephemera**

epi- Compounds with *epi-*, which can mean on, over, outside, besides or among, are written as one word (e.g., *epicenter*, *epidermis*).

epidemic Rampant as a condition. (Compare **endemic**.)

epigean *or* **epigeic** *or* **epigeous**

epilepsy

epilogue *or* **epilog**

episcopal Of or governed by bishops. Capitalize as the religious denomination.

episodic *or* **episodical**

epitaph The inscription on a grave. (Compare **epithet**.)

epithet A word or phrase characterizing someone or something. (Compare **epitaph**.)

epitome A short summary.

eponym A person for whom something is named (e.g., *The eponymous hero of the book* is *Huckleberry Finn*.)

Epsom salts *or* **Epsom salt**

eqpt. *or* **equip.** *or* **equipt.** *or* **eq.** Abbreviations for *equipment*.

equal, equaled *or* **equalled**

equal-opportunity employer

Equal Rights Amendment *or* **ERA** A proposed amendment to the U.S. Constitution outlawing discrimination on the basis of sex.

equal sign

equator

equerry; *pl.,* **equerries**

equestrian A person who rides horses.

equi- Compounds with *equi-*, which means equal, are written as one word (e.g., *equidistant, equilateral*).

equilibrium; *pl.,* **equilibriums** or **equilibria**

equiv. Abbreviation for *equivalent, equivalency.*

equivocal Questionable, undecided.

ergo Therefore.

ergonomics *or* **human engineering** Study of the interaction between humans and their tools and environment and the enhancing of that interaction by design and arrangement.

erodible *or* **erosible**

erogenous Sexually sensitive.

erotic

eroticize

errant Wayward, wandering. (Compare **arrant**.)

erratic Ever-changing, not reliable.

erratum; *pl.,* **errata** *Errata* is the common form.

erroneous Wrong.

ersatz

erstwhile At one time (in the past).

eruption A burst outward. (Compare **irruption**.)

escape artist

escape mechanism

escapee *or* **escaper**

escargot An edible variety of snail. (Compare **escarole**.)

escarole The herb endive. (Compare **escargot**.)

eschew

escutcheon

Eskimo; *pl.,* **Eskimos**

esoteric Understood by a special few; private. (Compare **exoteric**.)

esoterica Things that are esoteric.

esp Abbreviation for *espressivo*, "with expression."

ESP Abbreviation for *extrasensory perception.*

esp. Abbreviation for *especial, especially.*

espadrille

especial, especially Synonyms for *special, specially.*

Esperanto

espionage

esplanade

espresso; *pl.,* **espressos**

esprit de corps French; team spirit.

Esq. Abbreviation for *esquire*, used after the last name of lawyers, architects, court clerks, and justices of the peace.

essay To try out, attempt. (Compare **assay**.)

essence The spirit of something. (Compare **essential**.)

essential Absolutely necessary. (Compare **essence**.)

EST *or* **E.S.T.** *or* **e.s.t.** Abbreviation for *eastern standard time.*

est. *or* **estab.** Abbreviations for *establish, establishment.*

est. *or* **estd.**   Abbreviations for *estimated*.

establishment   Capitalize when referring to a preeminent group or a bureaucracy.

est'd   Contraction for *established*.

esthete; esthetic; esthetician; estheticism; esthetics   Variants of words formed with *aesthet-*.

estivate   To spend the summer. (Compare **hibernate**.)

estrus *or* **estrum**

ET *or* **E.T.** *or* **e.t.**   Abbreviation for *eastern time*.

et al.   Abbreviation for *et alii* or *et aliae* or *et alia*, meaning "and others."

et cetera *or* **etc.**   Meaning "and so forth." *Etcetera* is the noun.

et seq.   Abbreviation for *et sequentia*, "and the following."

ETA   Abbreviation for *estimated time of arrival*.

étagère *or* **etagere**

ether   The strong liquid used as anesthetic.

ethic   A specific set of moral principles. (Compare **ethics**.)

ethical *or* **ethic; ethically**

ethics   Moral principles generally. (Compare **ethics**.)

ethyl alcohol

ethylene glycol

etiology   The study of the causes of disease. (Compare **entomology, etymology**.)

etiquette

Eton collar

Eton jacket

étude

etymology   The study of word history. Abbreviation is *ety*. (Compare **entymology, etiology**.)

etymon

eucalyptus; *pl.,* **eucalyptuses**

Eucharist

euchre

euclidean *or* **euclidian**

eugenics   The study of improving the human species through control of hereditary factors.

eulogy   A speech given in honor of a dead person. (Compare **elegy**.)

eunuch

euphemism   A less direct word substituting for a word considered offensive or upsetting. (Compare **euphuism**.)

euphony   Pleasing sound.

euphuism   Elegant literary style or artificial elegance in language use. (Compare **euphemism**.)

Eurasian   A person of European and Asian descent.

eureka

Eurodollar

European plan   Hotel or inn service that does not include a meal (or meals) in the daily rate. (Compare **American plan**.)

eurythmic *or* **eurhythmic**

eustachian tube

euthanasia

evacuee

Evangelical

evaporated milk

eve   Capitalize if part of proper noun (e.g., *All Hallows' Eve*).

even break

evenhanded

even keel

even money   As noun.

evenness

even-numbered

evensong

even-steven

even-tempered

eventide

ever- Compounds formed with *ever-* are hyphenated if used to describe a noun (e.g., *an ever-vigilant mother*).

everglade

evergreen

everyday Usual, ordinary. (Compare **every day**.)

every day Happening daily. (Compare **everyday**.)

everyone A pronoun meaning people as a whole. (Compare **every one**.)

every one Each and every person involved. (Compare **everyone**.)

every so often Now and then.

every time

every which way

evil; eviler *or* **eviller**

evildoer

evildoing

evil eye

evil-minded

ewe A female sheep.

ex- Compounds formed with *ex-* are hyphenated if referring to a former role or position (e.g., *ex-husband, ex-president*).

ex.; *pl.,* **exx.** Abbreviations for *example, examples.*

exactor *or* **exacter**

exalt To praise. (Compare **exult**.)

examination *or* **exam**

exc. Abbreviation for *except, excepted, exception.*

Excalibur

exceed To go beyond a boundary or surpass. (Compare **accede**.)

exceedingly To an extreme degree. (Compare **excessively**.)

excel, excelled

excellence Superiority. (Compare **excellency**.)

excellency Dignitary. (Compare **excellence**.) Capitalize if part of formal title preceding name (e.g., *Her Excellency Queen Elizabeth*).

excelsior

except To exclude. (Compare **accept**.)

exceptionable Objectionable. (Compare **exceptional**.)

exceptional Superior. (Compare **exceptionable**.)

excerpt; excerpter *or* **excerptor**

excessively Too much. (Compare **exceedingly**.)

exchange rate

exchange student

excise tax

excl. Abbreviation for *exclude, excluding,* or *exclusive.*

excogitate To think about deeply.

excommunicate

excoriate

excrement

excrescence

exculpate To clear of blame.

exec Slang for *executive.*

execrable Horrible.

executioner

executor

exegesis; *pl.,* **exegeses**

exemplum; *pl.,* **exempla**

exeunt In theatrical terminology, a direction to leave the stage.

exhausting Tiring, wearing. (Compare **exhaustive**.)

exhaustive Thorough, complete. (Compare **exhausting**.)

exhibit Capitalize if part of document title or in reference to specific document part (e.g., *the lawyer presented Exhibit A*).

exhilarate To excite, raise spirits.

existential Concerning the experience of being. (Compare **experiential**.)

ex libris

exo- Compounds beginning with the prefix *exo-*, which means outside or outer part, are written as one word (e.g., *exoskeleton, exosphere*).

exodus Capitalize when naming the book of the Bible.

ex officio

exorcise *or* **exorcize** To remove an evil spirit.

exoteric Understood by many. (Compare **esoteric**.)

exotic Dramatically foreign, different.

exotica Things that are exotic.

expandable *or* **expansible**

expatiate To wander, do something at will. (Compare **expatriate**.)

expatriate To be banished or to withdraw from one's native country; or one who does so. (Compare **expatiate**.)

expect To believe something will happen.

expectancy *or* **expectance**

expediency *or* **expedience**

expediter *or* **expeditor**

expel, expelled

expense account

experiential Coming from

participation in or perception of existence as a being. (Compare **existential**.)

expiate To make amends.

explainable *or* **explicable**

expletive An exclamatory word or phrase.

explicit Distinctly expressed.

exploitive *or* **exploitative**

exposé *or* **expose** A revelation of facts.

exposition *or* **expo**

ex post facto

expropriate To take over property or deprive of possession.

extant In existence.

extemporaneous

extempore Adverb

extemporize

extendable *or* **extendible** *or* **extensible**

extended Prolonged, elongated. (Compare **extensive**.)

extended family

extension cord

extensive A great deal; large, broad. (Compare **extended**.)

extenuate To make light of, mitigate.

extol *or* **extoll**

extortioner *or* **extorter**

extra- Compounds formed with *extra-* are often one word (e.g., *extramural, extraordinary, extraterrestrial*) except for some double adjectives such as *extra-fine, extra-large, extra-wide*.

extra-base hit

extra point

extrasensory perception *or* **ESP**

extravaganza

extrinsic Not part of, originating elsewhere. (Compare **intrinsic**.)

extrovert *or* **extravert**

exult To be joyful. (Compare **exalt**.)

eye- Many compounds beginning with *eye-* are written as one word, including *eyeball, eyebrow, eyecup, eyelash, eyeliner, eyeshade, eyesore, eyespot, eyestrain, eyewash*.

eye bank
eye-catching
eye chart
eye contact
eye-opening
eyelet
eye shadow
eyetooth
eyewitness

F

f., *pl.*, **ff.** Abbreviations for *and the following one/page*; *and the following ones/pages*.

FAA Abbreviation for *Federal Aviation Administration*. Spell out on first reference in text.

fabricate To construct, invent.

facade

face card

facecloth

-faced Compounds ending in *-faced* are usually hyphenated (e.g., *two-faced*).

facedown

face-lift

face-off

face-saving

face-to-face

face up Use with *to*.

face value

faceted *or* **facetted**

facetious

facial

facilitate To make easier to do, accomplish. (Compare **felicitate**.)

facsimile *or* **fax**

facsimile machine *or* **fax machine**

fact-finding

fact finder

fact of life

factional Concerning a group. (Compare **factitious**.)

factitious Artificial, sham. (Compare **factional**.)

factotum; *pl.*, **factotums**

faculty; *pl.*, **faculties** Ability, power. (Compare **faculty; faculty**.)

faculty; *pl.*, **faculty** The teaching staff in an educational institution. (Compare **faculty; faculties**.)

fadeaway

fade-out

Fahrenheit Abbreviations are *F.*, *Fah.*, *Fahr.*

faience *or* **faïence** Italian; a type of glazed earthenware.

fail-safe

faille French; a type of silk or rayon fabric.

faineant *or* **fainéant** Idle, lazy. (Compare **faint, feint**.)

faint To lose consciousness. (Compare **faineant, feint**.)

fainthearted

fairground

fair-minded

fair play

fair shake

fair trade

fairway

fair-weather

fairyland

fairy tale As noun.

fairy-tale As adjective.

fait accompli; *pl.*, **faits accomplis** French; literally, "accomplished fact," a deed that is already done and often not reversible.

faithful; *pl.*, **faithful** *or* **faithfuls**

faith healing; faith healer

faker A person who pretends. (Compare **fakir**.)

fakir A wonderworker or impostor. (Compare **faker**.)

fall Lowercase as the season.

fall, fell, fallen

fallback As noun.

falling-out; *pl.*, **fallings-out** *or* **falling-outs**

fallopian tube

fallout As noun.

falsetto; *pl.,* **falsettos**

fanatic *or* **fanatical** As adjective.

fan belt

fancy-free

fandango; *pl.,* **fandangos**

fan letter

fan mail

fantasia *or* **fantasie** An unrestricted musical or literary composition.

fantastic *or* **fantastical**

far, farther, farthest, farthermost Refers to physical distance. (Compare **far, further**.)

far, further, furthest, furthermost Indicates continuing or adding in degree, manner, or time. (Compare **far, farther**.)

far and away

far and wide

faraway

far cry

fare The cost of transportation.

Far East

fare-thee-well

farfetched Unlikely, hard to believe.

far-flung

far-gone

farinaceous

farm- Most compounds formed with **farm-** are written as one word (e.g., *farmhouse, farmhand*).

farm-bred

far-off

far-out

farrago; *pl.,* **farragoes** Hodgepodge.

far-reaching

farseeing

far side

farsighted; farsightedness

Far West The Western region of the United States.

fasc. Abbreviation for *fascicle*.

fascicle *or* **fascicule** *or* **fasciculus**

fascism; fascist

fashion plate

fast and loose

fastback

fastball

fast-break As verb.

fast break As noun.

fastener

fast-food As adjective.

fast-talk

fat cat

fat-free

father Capitalize only in direct address (when used as a name) or if part of formal title preceding a name.

Father Christmas Variant of *Santa Claus*.

father-in-law; *pl.,* **fathers-in-law**

Father's Day

fathom

fatigue

fatuous

faucet

Faulkner, William (1897–1962) American novelist. Author of *The Sound and the Fury*.

faultfinding

faun A mythological figure. (Compare **fawn**.)

fauna; *pl.,* **faunas** *or* **faunae**

faux pas; *pl.,* **faux pas** French; literally, "false step," a social blunder.

fawn A young deer. (Compare **faun**.)

faze To disconcert, disturb. (Compare **phase**.)

FBI Abbreviation for *Federal Bureau of Investigation*. Spell out on first reference in text.

FCC Abbreviation for *Federal Communications Commission*. Spell out on first reference in text.

FDA Abbreviation for *Food and Drug Administration*. Spell out on first reference in text.

fealty

feather bed As noun.

featherbed As adjective or verb.

-feathered Compounds ending in *-feathered* are usually hyphenated (e.g., *gray-feathered*).

featherweight

-featured Compounds ending in *-featured* are usually hyphenated (e.g., *under-featured*).

febrile Feverish.

February *or* **Feb.**

fed up

federal Capitalize only if part of proper noun, formal title, or address: *Federal Bureau of Investigation*.

federation Capitalize only if part of proper noun: *Federation of American Scientists*.

feed, fed

feedback

feel, felt

feign To pretend.

feint To lure, deceive. (Compare **faineant, faint**.)

feisty

felicitate To congratulate. (Compare **facilitate**.)

feline Having to do with cats, or catlike.

fellow; fellowship Capitalize only if part of a proper noun.

fem. *or* **f.** Abbreviation for *female* or *feminine*.

feminine Having characteristics considered female.

femur; *pl.,* **femurs** *or* **femora**

fencepost

fender bender

fenestrate

ferment *or* **foment** These words have a shared sense, meaning "to incite or agitate."

Ferris wheel

ferrule A cap on a stick or cane. (Compare **ferule**.)

ferryboat

ferule A stick used for punishment. (Compare **ferrule**.)

fervent Hot or intense. (Compare **fervid**.)

fervid Extremely hot or intense. (Compare **fervent**.)

festal Concerning a festival. (Compare **festive**.)

festive Happy, rejoicing. (Compare **festal**.)

feta cheese

fete *or* **fête**

fetid Rank in smell.

fetish

fettuccine

fettuccine Alfredo

fever blister

fever pitch

few, fewer, fewest Refers to number of individual items. (Compare **less**.)

fey

fez; *pl.,* **fezzes** *or* **fezes**

fiancé A man engaged to be married. (Compare **fiancée**.)

fiancée A woman engaged to be married. (Compare **fiancé**.)

fiasco; *pl.*, **fiascoes** *or* **fiaschi**

fiber *or* **fibre**

fiberboard *or* **fibreboard**

fiberglass

fiber-optic As adjective.

fiber optics As noun.

fibr-, fibro- A combining form meaning fibrous in matter or structure. Compounds of *fibr-* or *fibro-* are written as one word (e.g., *fibrositis, fibrovascular*).

fibula; *pl.*, **fibulae** *or* **fibulas**

fiche; *pl.*, **fiche** *or* **fiches** Short form for *microfiche*.

fictional Not true. (Compare **factitious, fictitious**.)

fictitious Imaginary, hypothetical. (Compare **factitious, fictional**.)

fictitious Imaginary, hypothetical.

fiddle-faddle

fiddlesticks

-field Compounds ending in *-field* are usually written as one word (e.g., *hayfield, ballfield*).

field event

field house

fielder's choice

fieldstone

field-test As verb.

field test As noun.

fieldwork

fiend A dastardly person.

fife; *pl.*, **fifes**

fifth column

fifth wheel Something extra or unnecessary.

fifty-fifty

fig leaf

fig. Abbreviation for *figure*.

fight, fought

figuratively In a representative or analogous sense. (Compare **literally, virtually**.)

figure eight

figurehead A symbolic leader with little real power.

figure of speech

figure skating

filch To steal, take unfairly.

filet mignon; *pl.*, **filets mignons**

filibuster

filigree

Filipino; *pl.*, **Filipinos** Inhabitant(s) of the Philippines.

fill-in As noun.

filler-in; *pl.*, **fillers-in**

fillet A thin piece of material or slice of meat or fish with bones removed.

fillet of sole

fillip

filmmaker

filmstrip

filterable *or* **filtrable**

filter paper

filter tip

fin de siècle French; literally "end of the century." Usually used in English in references concerning the close of the 19th century.

finable Able to be charged a fine.

finale

finally Ending, at the close. (Compare **finely**.)

financier

find, found

fine art

finely Extremely well or minutely. (Compare **finally**.)

70

fine print

fines herbes

finespun

finesse

fine-tooth comb

fine-tune

finger- Compounds written as one word include *fingerboard*, *fingernail*, *fingerprint*, *fingertip*.

finger bowl

finger painting

finicky *or* **finical** *or* **finicking**

finish line

finishing school

finnan haddie Smoked haddock.

fire- Compounds formed with *fire-* that are written as two words include *fire ant*, *fire brigade*, *fire department*, *fire drill*, *fire engine*, *fire escape*, *fire extinguisher*, *fire fighter*, *fire hall*, *fire irons*, *fire sale*, *fire screen*, *fire station*, *fire tower*, *fire truck*, *fire wall*.

Most other compounds are written as one word (e.g., *firebomb*, *firebrand*, *firecracker*, *firefly*, *firewood*).

firearm; *pl.,* **firearms**

fire-eating

fire-stop

firing line

firing pin

firing squad

firm A partnership. *Firm* is not synonymous with *corporation*.

first- Most compounds with *first-* are written as two words.

first aid

firstborn

first-class As adjective and adverb.

first-degree burn

first-degree murder

First Family, First Lady Not official appellations, but uppercase before a proper name: *First Lady Jacqueline Kennedy*. Lowercase when a socially prominent family or woman is meant (e.g., *The Lowells were one of Boston's first families*.)

firsthand

first-rate

first-string

First World War *or* **World War I** *or* **WWI**

fiscal Concerning a budget or form of accounting.

fish; *pl.,* **fish** *or* **fishes**

-fish Compounds ending in *-fish* are usually written as one word (e.g., *cuttlefish*).

fish-and-chips

fishbowl

fishhook

fishmonger

fishnet

fishpond

fish stick

fishtail

fistfight

fistful

fisticuffs A fistfight.

fit, fitted *or* **fit**

fitful Irregular, restless.

fitted *or* **fit** As adjective.

Fitzgerald, F. Scott (1896–1940) American writer. Author of *The Great Gatsby*.

five-and-ten

five-star

fjord *or* **fiord**

flaccid Not firm.

flack A press agent. (Compare **flak**.)

flacon A small ornamental bottle. (Compare **flagon**.)

Flag Day June 14th.

flagellate

flag football

flagitious Scandalous.

flagon A large vessel for wine. (Compare **flacon**.)

flagpole

flagrante delicto Latin; in the act of committing a crime or misdeed.

flagship

flag-waving

flail To swing arms wildly. (Compare **flay**.)

flair Flashy style; talent. (Compare **flare**.)

flak Kidding or criticism. (Compare **flack**.)

flaky *or* **flakey**

flambé, flambés, flambéed, flambéing

flambeau; *pl.,* **flambeaux** *or* **flambeaus**

flamboyant

flamenco; *pl.,* **flamencos**

flameproof

flamethrower

flamingo; *pl.,* **flamingos** *or* **flamingoes**

flammable *or* **inflammable** Both mean capable of catching on fire.

flannelette Lightweight flannel.

flapjack

flare A flame or an outburst. (Compare **flair**.)

flare-up As noun.

flashback

flashbulb

flash card

flash flood

flash-forward

flash in the pan

flashlight

flash point

-flat Hyphenated with musical note.

flatbed

flatboat

flat-bottomed

flatfoot

flat-footed

flatland

flat-out As adjective.

flat out As adverb.

flattop

flatware

Flaubert, Gustave (1821–1880) Founder and master of Realist school of French literature. Author of *Madame Bovary*.

flaunt To show off. (Compare **flout**.)

flay To criticize harshly or lash. (Compare **flail**.)

fleabag

fleabite; flea-bitten

flea-bitten

flea collar

flea market

fledgling

flee, fled

fleet Capitalize if part of proper noun.

fleet-footed

fleshpot

fleur-de-lis *or* **fleur-de-lys;** *pl.,* **fleurs-de-lis** *or* **fleur-de-lis** *or* **fleurs-de-lys** *or* **fleur-de-lys**

flexion *or* **flection**

flexor A muscle that controls an extremity.

flextime *or* **flexitime**

flick A movie (slang).

flier or **flyer**

flight-test As verb.

flimflam

fling, flung

flip side

flip-flop

floatage or **flotage**

floating-point As adjective.

flood- Many compounds beginning with *flood-* are written as one word (e.g., *floodgate, floodlight*).

flood tide

floorboard

floor-length

floorwalker

flophouse

floppy disk

flora; *pl.,* **floras** or **florae**

florescent Flourishing, blooming. (Compare **fluorescent**.)

Florida Keys

florist

flotation or **floatation**

flotsam

flounder As verb, means to struggle or be clumsy. (Compare **founder**.)

flounder; *pl.,* **flounder** or **flounders**

flout To mock or scorn. (Compare **flaunt**.)

flowchart

-flower Compounds ending in *-flower* are usually written as one word (e.g., *sunflower*).

flowerbed

flowerpot

flower people

flow sheet

flu A virus; short for *influenza*. (Compare **flue**.)

flue A channel, pipe, chimney. (Compare **flu**.)

fluky or **flukey**

flunky or **flunkey;** *pl.,* **flunkies** or **flunkeys**

fluor-, fluoro- Compounds of this combining form, which means fluorine or fluorescence, are written as one word: *fluorocarbon*.

fluorescent Artificially lit; emitting radiation. (Compare **florescent**.)

flutist or **flautist**

flutter kick

flutterboard

fly; *pl.,* **flies**

fly, flies, flew, flown

-fly Compounds ending in *-fly* are usually written as one word (e.g., *barfly, mayfly, housefly*).

flyaway

flyby; *pl.,* **flybys**

fly-by-night

flycatcher

fly-fishing

flyover As noun.

flypaper

flyspeck

flyswatter

flyweight

flywheel

FM Abbreviation for *frequency modulation*, a radio term.

foam rubber

focal point

focus; *pl.,* **foci** or **focuses**

focus, focused or **focussed**

fogbound

foghorn

fogy or **fogey;** *pl.,* **fogies** or **fogeys**

foible

foie gras French; the fattened liver of an animal served as a pâté.

-fold Compounds ending in *-fold*

are usually written as one word (e.g., *twofold, manifold*).

foldaway

folderol *or* **falderal** A nonsense or trivial item.

foldout As noun

foliage

folio; *pl.,* **folios**

folk; *pl.,* **folk** *or* **folks**

folk dance

folklore

folk medicine

folksinger

folk song

folktale

follow-through As noun.

follow-up As adjective, noun.

folly; *pl.,* **follies**

fondue

fontanel *or* **fontanelle**

foodstuff

foolhardy

foolproof

fool's gold

fool's paradise

foot; *pl.,* **feet**

foot-and-mouth disease

foot-dragging

footlocker

footnote

foot-pound The abbreviation is *ft-lb.*

foot-pound-second

footprint

footrest

foot soldier

forasmuch as

forbear, forbears, forbore, forborne To hold back, abstain, be patient. (Compare **forebear.**)

forbid, forbade *or* **forbad**

forceful Having effect. (Compare **forcible.**)

force of habit

force-out As noun.

forceps

forcible By force. (Compare **forceful.**)

fore-and-aft As adjective.

fore and aft As adverb.

forebear An ancestor. (Compare **forbear.**)

foreboding

forecast, forecast *or* **forecasted**

foreclose

forefinger

forego, foregoes, forewent, foregone To go before, to precede. (Compare **forgo.**)

foregone conclusion

foreground

forehand

forehead

foreign-born

foreign words and phrases Many foreign words or phrases, particularly Latin and French, are pluralized according to the rules of the original language. Some also have an English plural (e.g., *focus; pl.,* **foci** *or* *focuses*).

foremost

forename *or* **first name**

forensic medicine

foreplay

foresaid

foresee, foresaw, foreseen

foreshadow

foresight

forest Capitalize if part of proper noun (e.g., *Allegheny National Forest*).

forest ranger

74

forestall

foretaste

foretell, foretold

forethought

foreword An introduction, preface. (Compare **froward**.)

forfend

forgather or **foregather**

forget, forgot, forgotten or **forgot**

forget-me-not; pl., **forget-me-nots**

forgettable

forgive, forgave, forgiven

forgo, forgoes, forwent, forgone To relinquish, renounce. (Compare **forego**.)

forklift

forlorn

form letter

formally In a structured, methodical manner.

formal title A designation of a position in an organization or government, capitalized when used officially to identify a person (e.g., *Senator George Mitchell*), lowercased when used as a description (e.g., *the senator from Indiana*).

formerly Previously.

formfitting

Formica

formula; pl., **formulas** or **formulae**

forsake, forsook, forsaken

forswear, forswore, forsworn

forsythia

forte Strong point.

forth Forward. (Compare **fourth**.)

forthcoming

forthright

forthwith

fortissimo; pl., **fortissimos** or **fortissimi**

fortnight Two weeks. Singular in construction.

FORTRAN or **Fortran** *Formula translation*, a computer-programming language.

fortuitous Lucky, happening by chance.

fortune cookie

fortune hunter

fortune-teller

forty winks A brief sleep, a nap.

forum; pl., **forums** or **fora**

forward-looking

forward pass

foul Bad or dirty. (Compare **fowl**.)

foul ball

foul line

foulmouthed

foul play

foul tip

foul-up As noun.

foundation Capitalize if part of proper noun (e.g., *The MacArthur Foundation*).

founder To fail or sink. (Compare **flounder**.)

foundry

fountain pen

fountainhead

four-bagger

four-flush

4-H

four-in-hand

four-letter word

four of a kind

four-poster

fourscore

four-star

four-wheel

fourth A quarter of something or the number four in order. (Compare **forth**.)

Fourth of July *or* **Independence Day**

fowl Poultry, bird. (Compare *foul.*)

fox; *pl.,* **foxes** *or* **fox**

foxhole

foxhound

fox terrier

fox-trot

fr. Abbreviation for *from.*

fracas; *pl.,* **fracases**

fractious

framable *or* **frameable**

frame of reference

frame-up As noun.

framework

franc A unit of French currency.

franchise; franchiser, franchisee, franchisor

Franciscan

frangible

Frankenstein

frankfurter

frankincense

Franklin, Benjamin (1706–1790) American statesman, scientist, and philosopher. One of the drafters and signers of the Declaration of Independence.

Franklin stove

frantically *or* **franticly**

frappé *or* **frappe**

fraternity *or* **frat**

freaked-out

freak of nature

freak show

free agent

free and easy

freebie *or* **freebee**

free enterprise

free-for-all

freehand As adjective, adverb.

free hand As noun.

free kick

free lance As noun.

free-lance As adjective, verb.

free-lancer

free-living

free market

free rein

free ride

freestanding

freestyle

freethinker

free thought

free throw

free trade

free verse

freeway

freewheel

free will As noun.

free world Democratic society, governments.

freeze, froze

freeze-dry; freeze-dried

freeze-frame

french curve *or* **French curve**

French dressing

french fry *or* **French fry**

french-fried *or* **French-fried**

French- Compounds beginning with *French-* are usually two words, with *French* capitalized (e.g., *French doors, French horn*).

Freon Trademark for a type of gas or liquid used as an aerosol propellant and as a refrigerant.

freq. Abbreviation for *frequent, frequency, frequently.*

fresco; *pl.,* **frescoes**

Freud, Sigmund (1856–1939) Austrian neurologist and founder of psychoanalysis.

Freudian slip To misspeak in a manner that reveals unconscious desires.

friable Crumbly. (Compare **fryable**.)

friar

fricassee

friedcake

frieze A decorative band or line.

frijole; *pl.,* **frijoles**

fringe benefit

Frisbee

frog kick

frontcourt

front-end

frontier

frontispiece

frontline As adjective.

front-page As adjective, verb.

front-runner As noun.

frontward *or* **frontwards**

frostbite, frostbitten

froufrou As noun.

froward Disobedient. (Compare **foreword**.)

frowsy *or* **frowzy**

frozen food

fruitcake

fruit fly

fruition

fryable Capable of being fried. (Compare **friable**.)

fryer

frying pan

F-sharp

f-stop

fuchsia

fuel, fueled *or* **fuelled**

fugacious

fugue

führer *or* **fuehrer** German; a leader or a tyrant.

-ful The plural form is *-fuls* for words with this ending, although some can also take a form where the *s* precedes *ful* (e.g., *tablespoonful*, but pl., *tablespoonfuls* or *tablespoonsful*).

fulcrum; *pl.,* **fulcrums** *or* **fulcra**

fulfill *or* **fulfil**

full house

full moon

full- Com:pounds that are hyphenated include *full-blooded*, *full-blown*, *full-bodied*, *full-dress*, *full-fledged*, *full-length*, *full-out*, *full-scale*, *full-service*, *full-size*, *full-time* (adjective).

fullback

fuller's earth

fulsome excessive, overdone.

fun and games

fun house

fund-raiser; fund-raising

funereal

fungus; *pl.,* **fungi** *or* **funguses**

fungal *or* **fungous**

funlover

funloving

funnel, funneled *or* **funnelled**

funny; *pl.,* **funnies**

fur coat

furbelow

furlough A leave of absence from work or military duty.

furtherance

furthermore

fuselage
fusillade
fussbudget
fut. Abbreviation for *future*.
futz

f.v. Abbreviation for *folio verso*, "on the back of the page" or "on the back page of."
FYI Abbreviation for *for your information*.

G

gabardine

gabfest

gable roof

gadabout

gadfly

gadget; gadgetry

gadzooks

gaffe A blunder.

gaga

gaiety

gainsay, gainsaid

gait A manner of walking, moving. (Compare **gate**.)

gala Festive.

galact-, galacto- Compounds using this combining form, meaning milk or milky, are written as one word.

Galilean

Galileo (1564–1642) Italian mathematician, astronomer, and physicist. Pioneered the use of the telescope to observe the skies.

gallbladder

galley proof

gallimaufry A hodgepodge.

gallivant *or* galavant

gallon *or* gal.

gallows humor

gallows; *pl.*, gallows *or* gallowses

gallstone

Gallup Poll

galore Plentiful (e.g., *entertainment galore*).

galosh *or* galoshe; *pl.*, galoshes

galumph

gambit A calculated move. (Compare **gamble, gambol**.)

gamble To take a chance; wager. (Compare **gambit, gambol**.)

gambol, gamboled *or* gambolled To skip, leap. (Compare **gambit, gamble**.)

gambrel roof

gamekeeper

game plan

gamma ray

gamut Entire range. (Compare **gantlet**.)

gamy *or* gamey

Gandhi, Mahatma (1869–1948) Indian nationalist and spiritual leader who fought to free India from British colonization.

gangbusters

ganglion; *pl.*, ganglia *or* ganglions

gangplank

gangrel A vagrant.

gangrene; gangrenous

gangway

gantlet The switching area on railroad tracks. (Compare **gamut**.)

gauntlet

garage sale

garbage can

garbage truck

garbanzo bean

garden apartment

Garden of Eden

garden-variety Ordinary, run-of-the-mill.

gargantuan Colossal in size.

gargoyle

garlicky

garrote *or* garotte An instrument for strangulation.

garrulous Talkative.

garter belt

garter snake

gas; *pl.*, gases *or* gasses

gasbag

gas chamber

gaseous

gas-guzzling

gaslight

gas mask

gasoline

gas-operated

gas station

gastronomy   The art of eating in an aesthetically satisfying way.

gate   Opening, entrance. (Compare gait.)

gate-crasher

gatekeeper

gateleg table

gauche   Crude, awkward. (Compare gaucherie.)

gaucherie   Crude behavior. (Compare gauche.)

gaucho; pl., gauchos

gaudy

gauge

Gaulle, Charles de   (1890–1970) French soldier and statesman.

gaunt

gauss; pl., gauss or gausses

gauze; gauzy

gavel, gaveled or gavelled

gawky

gazelle; pl., gazelles or gazelle

gazette

gazetteer

gazpacho soup

G clef

gearbox

gearshift

gee-whiz

Geiger counter or Geiger-Müller counter   An instrument for detecting radiation.

geisha; pl., geisha or geishas

gel   Means to become like jelly.

gelatin or gelatine

Gemini   (see Zodiac Signs).

gemstone

genealogy   The study or history of family ancestry.

generalissimo; pl., generalissimos   In foreign usage, the commander in chief of the armed forces. Capitalize only if part of formal title preceding name.

general manager or GM

general practitioner or GP

general store

genesis; pl., geneses

Genet, Jean   (1910–1986) French writer who expressed his anti-bourgeois morality in his poems, novels, and plays.

Genghis Khan   (c.1162–1227) Mongol conqueror.

genie; pl., genies or genii

genitalia or genitals

genius; pl., geniuses or genii

genre   Type, category.

genteel; gentility

gentile   Christian, non-Jewish.

gentry; pl., gentries

genus; pl., genera

geo-   Compounds formed with geo-, which means earth, are written as one word (e.g., geomorphology).

geog.   Abbreviation for geography and its derivatives.

geographic or geographical

geographic terms   Capitalize the following and similar words if part of a proper noun: archipelago, area, arroyo, bank, bar, basin, bay, bayou, beach, bench, bend, bluff, bog, borough, branch, brook, butte, canal, *canyon, cape, cascade, cave, cavern, channel, cove, crater, creek, crossroads, cutoff, dam, delta, desert, divide, dome, dune, escarpment, estuary, falls, fault, flat(s), ford, forest, gap, geyser, glacier, glacis, glen, gorge, gulch, gulf, harbor, head, hill, hollow, inlet, island, isle, islet, lagoon, lake, landing, ledge, lowland, marsh, mesa, mound, mount, mountain, narrows, neck, notch, oasis, ocean, palisades, park, pass, passage, peak, peninsula, plain, plateau, point, pond, pool, port, prairie, range, rapids, ravine, reef, reservoir, ridge, river, rock, run, sea, seaway, shoal, sound, spring, strait, stream, summit, swamp, thoroughfare, trench, valley, volcano, waterway, woods.*

geol. Abbreviation for *geology* and its derivatives.

geologic *or* **geological**

geom. Abbreviation for *geometry* and its derivatives.

geometric *or* **geometrical**

georgette *or* **georgette crepe**

ger. Abbreviation for *gerund*.

geranium

gerbil

germ warfare

German measles

germane Relevant.

germfree

germproof

gerrymander

Gershwin, George (1898–1937) American composer. Composed *Rhapsody in Blue*, as well as the scores for many Broadway musical comedies.

Gestalt psychology

gestapo; *pl.*, **gestapos**

gesundheit

get, got *or* **gotten**

getable Reachable, accessible.

getaway As noun.

get-together As noun.

getup As noun.

get-up-and-go

geyser

ghastly

gherkin

ghetto; *pl.*, **ghettos** *or* **ghettoes**

ghostwrite, ghostwrote

ghoul

GI; *pl.*, **GI's** *or* **GIs**

gibberish

gibe *or* **jibe** To taunt, tease. (Compare **jib, jibe.**)

gift certificate

gift of gab

giftware

gift wrap

gigolo; *pl.*, **gigolos**

Gila monster

gild To cover with gold or other material. (Compare **guild.**)

Gilman, Charlotte P. (1860–1935) American feminist and writer. Author of "The Yellow Wall-Paper."

gilt Gold, or other, covering; money. (Compare **guilt.**)

gilt-edged *or* **gilt-edge**

gimlet

gimmick

gimmickry

gimp Plastic string for braiding.

gin and tonic

gingerbread

gingerroot
gingersnap
gingham
gingivitis   Inflammation of the
  gums.
gin rummy
giraffe; *pl.*, giraffes *or* giraffe
Girl Scout
gist
give, gave
give-and-take
giveaway   As noun.
given name   A person's first name.
gizmo *or* gismo; *pl.*, gizmos *or*
  gismos   A gadget.
gizzard
glacé   French; glazed.
glacier; glacial
glad rags   Dressy, festive clothing.
glad-hand   As verb.
glad hand   As noun.
gladiolus; *pl.*, gladiolus *or*
  gladioluses
glamour *or* glamor
glasnost
glassblowing
glasshouse
glassmaker
glassware
glasswork
Glauber's salt *or* Glauber salt *or*
  Glauber's salts
glaucoma
glazier   One who sets glass.
glee club
glen plaid
glimpse   A brief look at something.
glitz
globe-trotter
glockenspiel   A percussion
  instrument with flat metal bars set

in a frame and played with small
  hammers.
gloss-, glosso-   Compounds of this
  combining form, which means of
  words or language, are written as
  one word: *glossographer*.
glossary   Abbreviations are *gloss.*,
  glos., *gl.*
glossy; *pl.*, glossies
glower   To frown at.
glowworm
glue, gluing *or* glueing
glycerin *or* glycerine
glyph
G-major
G-minor
gnarled *or* gnarly
gnash
gnat
gnaw
gneiss
gnome
Gnostic
gnu; gnu *or* gnus
go, goes, went, gone, going
go-ahead
goalie
goalkeeper
goalpost
goaltender
go-around *or* go-round   As noun.
goatee   A small, pointed beard.
gobbledygook *or*
  gobbledegook   Indecipherable
  language.
go-between; *pl.*, go-betweens
go-cart
go-getter
go-go
god   Capitalize when used as a
  name for the one god of a
  monotheistic religion.

god- Compounds formed with *god-* are usually written as one word: *goddaughter*.

god-awful

goddamned or **goddamn** or **goddam** As adjective.

goddess

God-fearing

godforsaken

God-given

Godiva

godsend

Godspeed

-goer Compounds ending in *-goer* are usually written as one word (e.g., *theatergoer*).

Goethe, Johann Wolfgang von (1749–1832) German poet. Author of *Faust*.

gofer A helper who runs errands. (Compare **gopher**.)

going-over; *pl.*, **goings-over**

goings-on

goiter

gold coast or **Gold Coast**

gold digger

golden mean

golden retriever

golden rule or **Golden Rule**

gold-filled

goldfinch

goldfish bowl

gold leaf

gold-plated

gonorrhea A sexually transmitted disease.

good, better, best

good-bye or **good-by** or **goodbye**

good day

good-for-nothing

Good Friday

good-hearted

good-humored

good-looking

good morning

good-natured

good-neighbor As adjective.

good night

Good Samaritan

goodwill

goody-goody

gooey

goof-off

goose; *pl.*, **geese**

goose bumps or **goose pimples**

gooseneck

goose step As noun.

goose-step As verb.

gopher Means the burrowing rodent. (Compare **gofer**.)

Gordian knot A complex and seemingly unsolvable problem.

gorgeous

Gorgonzola cheese

gorilla An ape, or an ugly, violent person. (Compare **guerrilla**.)

gormandize To eat greedily.

gospel Capitalize when referring to one or all of the Books of Matthew, Mark, Luke, and John of the New Testament of the Bible.

gospeler or **gospeller**

gossamer

Gothic novel or **gothic novel**

gothic type or **gothic typeface**

gouache French; a painter's method using opaque watercolor.

Gouda cheese

goulash

gourd

gourmand A person who likes to eat, drink. (Compare **gourmet**.)

gourmet A person who cultivates

knowledge of food. (Compare **gourmand**.)

government Always lowercase.

governor *or* **gov.** Capitalize only if part of formal title preceding a name: *Governor Mario Cuomo.*

grab bag

grace note A small ornament or embellishment

grade, -grader Hyphenate forms like *third-grader* and *fourth-grade homework.* But write: *The student is in first grade.*

grade point average *or* **GPA**

grade school

graffiti *Graffito* is the singular noun, but *graffiti* is the form in usage.

graham cracker

graham flour

gram

grammar school

gram-negative, gram-positive

granary A storehouse for grain.

grand- Compounds describing family relationships are written as one word (e.g., *grandfather*). Other compounds using *grand* as an adjective are written as two words (e.g., *grand duke*).

grande dame; *pl.,* **grandes dames** *or* **grande dames** French; literally "great lady;" traditionally, an older woman of great ability, fame, or fortune.

grandeur

grand finale

grandiloquent

grand jury

grand mal seizure A severe epileptic seizure.

grand master

grand prix; *pl.,* **grand prix**

grand-slam As adjective.

grand slam As noun.

grand tour

granny *or* **grannie;** *pl.,* **grannies**

granola

grant-in-aid; *pl.,* **grants-in-aid** A type of public subsidy.

granular

grapefruit

grape juice

grapevine

graph Capitalize only if part of document title or in reference to a specific document part.

graphic arts

grapho- Compounds formed with *grapho-*, which means writing or drawing, are written as one word.

graph paper

grass roots Social or political organization that originates at the local level.

grasshopper

grassland

grater A cooking utensil for grinding.

gratin French; covered with a crust or with cheese. Usually used with *au* (e.g., *potatoes au gratin*).

gratiné *or* **gratineé**

gratis Free.

gratuitous Unwarranted or free.

gratuity A tip.

gravamen, *pl.,* **gravamens** *or* **gravamina** The main element or basis of a grievance.

grave accent

gravedigger

graven image

gravestone

graveyard shift

gravity; *pl.*, **gravities**
gravy; *pl.*, **gravies**
gravy train
gray matter   Slang for brains.
gray
gray-haired
greasepaint
greasy spoon   A small, cheap, and dirty restaurant or diner.
great-   Hyphenate all family compounds (e.g., *great-aunt*).
Great Britain   England, Scotland, and Wales.
greatcoat
Great Dane
Great Depression
greater   Capitalize *greater* when referring to a major metropolitan area.
greathearted
Great Lakes
Greeley, Horace   (1811–1872) American journalist and political leader. Co-founded *The New Yorker*.
Green   Capitalize when referring to the environmental movement.
greenback
greenbelt
green-eyed
greengrocer
greenhorn
greenhouse
Greenhouse effect
greenhouse gasses
green onion
green pepper
greenroom
greens fee
green thumb
Greenwich time
greeting card

greyhound
griddle cake   A pancake.
gridiron   A football field.
grief
grievance
grievous   Horrible, painful, serious.
griffin *or* griffon
grill   A stove for cooking. (Compare **grille**.)
grille   An ornamental grating. (Compare **grill**.)
grillwork
grimace
grind, ground
grindstone
gringo; *pl.*, **gringos**
grip   To hold fast. (Compare **gripe**, **grippe**.)
gripe   To complain, harangue. (Compare **grip**, **grippe**.)
grippe   Flu virus. (Compare **grip**, **gripe**.)
grisly   Gruesome, horrible. (Compare **grizzly**.)
gristle
gristmill
grizzly   Gray. (Compare **grisly**.)
grocer
grocery store
groomsman   Traditional. Use *honor attendant*.
grosgrain
gross national product *or* GNP
grotesque
grotto; *pl.*, **grottoes** *or* **grottos**
ground-   Most compounds formed with *ground-* are written as two words.
Groundhog Day
groundout   As noun.
groundsheet
groundskeeper

groundwater
groundwork
groupie
groupthink
grouse; *pl.,* grouse *or* grouses
grovel, groveled *or* grovelled
grow, grew
-grower Compounds ending in
    -grower are usually written as one
    word (e.g., *applegrower*).
growing pains
grown-up
grubstake
grueling *or* gruelling
gruesome
grungy
Gruyère cheese
G-sharp
guanaco; *pl.,* guanacos *or*
    guanaco A camel-like animal
    native to South America.
guarantee *or*
    guaranty Abbreviations are
    guar. or *gu.*
guaranteed Abbreviations are
    guar., gu., gtd., grd.
guarantor Abbreviation is *guar.*
guard Capitalize if part of proper
    noun.
guardhouse
guardian
guardrail
gubernatorial Concerning a
    governor (e.g., *The guber-
    natorial election*).
guerrilla *or* guerilla A soldier
    engaged in unorthodox warfare.
    (Compare **gorilla**.)
guesstimate An estimate arrived at
    by surmising rather than by
    analyzing hard data.
guesswork

guest A person who is entertained
    at the home of another, a visitor;
    or, a paying customer in a hotel,
    club, etc.
guesthouse
guestroom
guidebook
guided missile As noun.
guided-missile As adjective.
guideline
guidepost
guide word
guild An association. (Compare
    gild.)
guile; guileless
guillotine
guilt A feeling arising from self-
    reproach or remorse. (Compare
    gilt.)
guinea pig
guise Outward style, a costume, or
    a misleading appearance.
guitar
gulf Capitalize if part of proper
    noun (e.g., *the Persian Gulf, the
    Gulf of Mexico*).
gumbo
gumboil
gumdrop
gumption Spunk, sensible self-
    motivation.
gumshoe A detective.
gun- Compounds written as one
    word include *gunfight, gunfire,
    gunpoint, gunboat, gunflint,
    gunlock, gunmetal, gunplay,
    gunpowder, gunrunner, gunship,
    gunslinger, gunshot, gunsmith.*
gung ho
gunk
gunnysack
gun-shy

gun room

gunwale *or* **gunnel**

guppy; *pl.,* **guppies**

gurney; *pl.,* **gurneys**

guru; *pl.,* **gurus**

gussy up

gusto; *pl.,* **gustoes**

guttersnipe   A person of extremely low social or economic status.

guttural

gymn-, gymno-   Compounds of this combining form, which means stripped or bare, are written as one word: *gymnosophist.*

gymnasium *or* **gym;** *pl.,* **gymnasiums** *or* **gymnasia**

gynec-, gyneco-   Compounds of this combining form, which means woman, are written as one word (e.g., *gynecology*).

gypsy; *pl.,* **gypsies**

gypsy moth

gyrate

gyro horizon

gyroscope

ha-ha

habeas corpus

haberdasher; haberdashery

habile Skillful. (Compare habiliment.)

habiliment Clothing, equipment for an occasion. (Compare habile.)

habitué French; one who frequents a certain place or a particular type of place.

hacienda Spanish; a plantation, or the plantationhouse.

hackneyed Overused, stale, clichéd.

hack saw

hackwork

had not or hadn't

haiku; pl., haiku

hail To yell for. (Compare hale.)

Hail Mary

hailstone

hailstorm

hair- Compounds written as one word include hairbreadth, hairbrush, haircut, hairdresser, hairpiece, hairpin, hairstyle, hairdressing, hairline, hairsplitter, hairstyling, hairstylist.

hair ball

hairdo; pl., hairdos

hair follicle

hair-raising

hair shirt

hair-trigger As adjective, meaning responsive to the slightest stimulus.

halcyon days A time of happiness, peace, or prosperity.

hale To compel to go somewhere; or, sound in body, hearty. (Compare hail.)

half; pl., halves

half, halves As verb.

half- Compounds are usually hyphenated (e.g., half-mast, half-staff, half-truth, half-wit).

Compounds written as two words include half boot, half brother, half cock, half hitch, half hour, half line, half nelson, half note, half past, half pay, half rest, half sister, half step, half title, half volley.

half-and-half

halfback

half-breed; half-bred

half-cocked

halfhearted

halftime

halftone

halfway

halitosis Bad breath.

hallelujah

Halley's comet

hallmark

Hall of Fame

Halloween

halls of ivy

hallucinate

hallway

halo; pl., halos or haloes

halogen

halvah or halva A Middle Eastern confection made of crushed sesame seeds and honey.

halyard

hamburger

ham-handed or ham-fisted

hamlet A small village. (Compare Hamlet.)

Hamlet The Danish prince, subject of Shakespeare's play. (Compare **hamlet**.)

hammer and sickle

hammerhead

hammertoe

hammer throw

hamstring, hamstrung Crippled.

hand and foot

handbag

handbook Abbreviations are *hdbk.* or *handbk.* or *hndbk.*

hand copy

handcuff

hand-feed, hand-fed

handful; *pl.,* **handfuls** *or* **handsful**

handgrip

handgun

hand-holding

handicap

handicraft

hand in glove *or* **hand and glove**

hand in hand

handkerchief; *pl.,* **handkerchiefs** *or* **handkerchieves**

handlebar

handmade

hand-me-down; *pl.,* **hand-me-downs**

hand mower

hand organ

handout As noun.

hand over fist Quickly and in large volumes (e.g., *to make money hand over fist*).

handpick

hand puppet

handrail

handsaw

handsel A present given for good luck, as on New Year's.

handshake

hands-off

handsome Good-looking. (Compare **hansom**.)

hand-tailored

hand-to-hand As adjective.

hand-to-mouth With no surplus money or food (e.g., *living hand to mouth*).

hand truck

handwriting

hang, hung *or* **hanged**

hangar A building for airplane storage. (Compare **hanger**.)

hangdog

hanged Suspended by the neck to die. (Compare **hung**.)

hanger An instrument for hanging items such as clothing. (Compare **hangar**.)

hanger-on; *pl.,* **hangers-on**

hang glider

hangman

hangnail

hangout As noun.

hangover

hang-up As noun.

hankie *or* **hanky;** *pl.,* **hankies**

hanky-panky

hansom Transportation by taxi. (Compare **handsome**.)

Hanukkah *or* **Chanukah**

haphazard

happenstance *or* **happenchance**

happy hour

happy hunting ground

happy-go-lucky

hara-kiri Japanese; a ritual suicide.

harangue

harass; harassment

harbinger

harbormaster

hard-and-fast
hardball
hard-bitten
hardboard
hard-boil
hardbound
hard copy
hard-core   As adjective.
hardcover book *or* hardback book
hard-earned
hardhanded
hardheaded
hard-hearted
hard-hitting
hard-line
hardliner
hardly
hard-nosed
hard-of-hearing
hard-pressed
hard-shell
hardstand
hard-surface
hardtack
hardtop
hardware   Tools or fittings made
   of metal, or the physical
   components of a computer.
   (Compare **software**.)
   Abbreviations are *hdwe.* or *hdw.*
   or *hdwre.* or *hrdwre.*
hardwood
hardworking
hare; *pl.,* hare *or* hares
harebrained
Hare Krishna
harelip
harem pants
harlequin
harmonica
harmony; *pl.,* harmonies
harness racing

harpsichord
harried *or* harassed
hart   An older male deer.
hartebeest
harum-scarum
harvester
harvest moon   The full moon that
   occurs around the time of the
   September equinox.
harvesttime
has-been   A person whose success
   has passed or declined.
hash browns *or* hash brown
   potatoes *or* hashed brown
   potatoes *or* hashed browns
hashish
hash mark
has not *or* hasn't
hassock
hasten
hasty pudding
hatband
hatbox
hatchback
hatcheck
hatchet job
hateful
hatha-yoga
hat in hand
hat tree
hat trick
hausfrau   German; a housewife.
haute *or* haut   French; classy,
   sophisticated, fashionable.
haute couture   French; high
   fashion.
haute cuisine   French; artful
   cooking.
haut monde *or* haute
   monde   French; high society.
hauteur
have-not

haversack
havoc
Hawaiian
Hawthorne, Nathaniel
(1804–1864) American
writer. Wrote *The Scarlet
Letter*.
hay fever
hay wagon
haywire
hazelnut
Hazlitt, William (1778–1830)
English writer and drama critic.
Author of *The Characters of
Shakespeare's Plays*.
H-bomb or **hydrogen bomb**
head- Most compounds are written
as one word (e.g., *headache,
headband, headfirst, headgear,
headrest, headstrong,
headwaiter*).
head and shoulders
head cold
-headed Compounds ending in
-headed are usually written as one
word (e.g., *levelheaded*).
head-hunter
head louse
head-on
head over heels
headquarters Capitalize if part of
proper noun or address. The
abbreviation is *hdqrs.* or *HQ.*
head start
heads up As interjection.
heads-up As adjective.
head-to-head
head wind
health insurance
health maintenance organization
or **HMO**
healthful or healthy

hear, heard
hearing aid
hearken or harken
hearsay evidence
hearse
heart- Many compounds are
written as one word (e.g.,
*heartache, heartburn,
heartwarming*).
heart attack
heart block
heart condition
heart disease
-hearted Compounds ending in
-hearted are usually written as one
word (e.g., *kindhearted*).
heart failure
hearth
heart-to-heart
heat exhaustion
heat lightning
heat rash
heatstroke
heat wave
heathen; *pl.*, heathens or heathen
heave, heaved or hove
heave-ho
heaven Capitalize when referring
to a place rather than as a
concept.
heaven-sent
heaven's sake
heavy-duty
heavy-handed
heavyhearted
heavy hitter
heavy metal
heavyset
heavyweight
hebetudinous Lethargic.
hectare
hedgehog

91

hedonistic
hee-haw
heel-and-toe
Hegel, Georg (1770–1831)
German Idealist philosopher.
Author of *Die Phanomenologie
des Geistes.*
hegemony
hegira *or* **hejira** Lowercase when
describing a journey taken to
escape a situation. Capitalize
when referring to Muhammad's
flight from Mecca.
heifer
heigh-ho
height; heighten
Heimlich maneuver
heinous
heir apparent; *pl.,* **heirs apparent**
heir presumptive; *pl.,* **heirs
presumptive**
heist A holdup or theft.
helicopter
helix; *pl.,* **helices** *or* **helixes**
hell-bent
hellfire
hellhole
hellhound
hellion
hello; *pl.,* **hellos**
hell or high water
hell-raiser
helluva
helpmate
helter-skelter Scattered,
scrambled, hurried, and confused.
hem-, hemo-, hemat-, hemato-
Compounds of this combining
form, which means blood, are
written as one word (e.g.,
*hemoglobin, hematinic,
hematogenesis*).

hematoma; *pl.,* **hematomas** *or*
hematomata
hemi- Compounds formed with
hemi-, which means half, are
written as one word.
Hemingway, Ernest (1899–1961)
American writer. Author of *The
Sun Also Rises.*
hemisphere Capitalize when
referring to a specific hemisphere.
hemispheric *or* **hemispherical**
hemline
hemoglobin
hemorrhage
hemorrhoid
henceforth From now on.
henhouse
henna A reddish dye.
hepat-, hepato- Compounds of
this combining form, which means
liver, are written as one word:
hepatic.
hepatitis
heptagon A seven-sided figure.
herbaceous
herbicide
herculean task
Herculean Capitalize when
referring to the mythical Greek
hero.
here- Compounds indicating a
relative position and spelled as
one word include *hereabouts,
hereabout, hereafter, hereby,
herein, hereinabove, hereinafter,
hereinbefore, hereinbelow, hereof,
hereon, hereto, heretofore,
hereunder, hereunto, hereupon,
herewith.*
here and now
here and there
hereditary

heresy; *pl.*, heresies
herky-jerky
hermetic *or* hermetical
hermit crab
hero; *pl.*, heroes *or* heros
heroic *or* heroical
heroin   The narcotic drug.
hero-worship
herpes simplex
herpes virus
herringbone
hesitance *or* hesitancy
heter-, hetero-   Compounds of this
   combining form, which means
   other or another, are written as
   one word (e.g., *heterogeneity,
   heterosexual*).
heterogenous *or* heterogeneous
hew, hewed *or* hewn   To split or
   fashion with, or as if with, an ax.
   (Compare **hue**.)
hexa-, hex-   Compounds of this
   combining form, which means
   six, are written as one word (e.g.,
   hexagon).
heyday
hiatus; *pl.*, hiatuses
Hiawatha
hibernate   To spend the winter.
   (Compare **estivate**.)
hibachi
hibiscus
hiccup *or* hiccough
hickey; *pl.*, hickeys
hickory; *pl.*, hickories
hide, hid, hidden *or* hid
hide-and-seek
hideaway
hidebound
hideous
hideout
hie, hying *or* hieing

hierarchical *or* hierarchic
hieroglyphic *or* hierglyphical
hi-fi *or* high fidelity
high-   Compounds that are
   hyphenated include *high-and-
   mighty, high-class, high-count,
   high-energy, high-flown, high-
   flying, high-grade, high-handed,
   high-hat* (adjective), *high-level,
   high-minded, high-pitched, high-
   power, high-powered, high-
   pressure, high-priced, high-rise,
   high-sounding, high-speed, high-
   spirited, high-strung, high-
   tension, high-water* (adjective).
      Compounds that are written as
   two words include *high beam,
   high chair, high comedy, high
   fashion, high frequency, high
   gear, high horse, high jump, high
   noon, high place, high roller,
   high schooler, high sea(s), high
   style, high tea, high technology,
   high tech* (noun), *high tide, high
   treason.*
high and dry
high blood pressure
High Church
High Court   Variant for *Supreme
   Court* (of the United States).
higher learning
higher-up; *pl.*, higher-ups
highfalutin
highlight, highlighted
high mass *or* High Mass   Use with
   sing or celebrate.
high school   Capitalize if part of
   proper noun. Abbreviation is *H.S.*
high-tech   As adjective.
hightail
highway   Capitalize only if part of

93

proper noun. Abbreviations are *hwy.* or *hgwy.*

hijack; hijacker

hijinks *or* **high jinks**

hillside

hilltop

hinder; hindrance

hindmost

hindquarter

Hindu

hinterland

hip *or* **hep** Slang for "in" or "with it."

hipbone

hip joint

hippie; *pl.,* **hippies**

hippo *or* **hippopotamus;** *pl.,* **hippos** *or* **hippopotamuses** *or* **hippopotami**

Hippocratic oath

hireling

Hispanic

hist-, histo- Compounds beginning with this combining form, which refers to tissue, are written as one word: *histone, histoplasmosis.*

hist. Abbreviation for *history, historical, historian.*

historic Very important, or historical.

histrionics

hit-and-miss

hit-and-run

hitchhiker

Hitler, Adolf (1889–1945) German leader of the Nazi party who ordered the creation of concentration and extermination camps to imprison and murder Jews and political enemies; brought on World War II. Author of *Mein Kampf.*

hit list

hit-or-miss

hit parade

HIV Abbreviation for *human immunodeficiency virus.*

hives A rash.

HMO Abbreviation for *health maintenance organization.*

ho-hum As adjective

hoagie *or* **hoagy;** *pl.,* **hoagies**

hoard To hold on to greedily, stash a large amount of something. (Compare **horde**.)

hoarse Scratchy in sound.

hoary Aged; white or gray with age.

hobby; *pl.,* **hobbies**

hobbyhorse

hobnob, hobnobbed

hobo; *pl.,* **hoboes** *or* **hobos**

Hobson's choice A choice of taking what is offered or nothing at all because no alternative exists.

hocus, hocussed *or* **hocused**

hocus-pocus

hodgepodge

Hodgkin's disease

hoedown A square dance or barn party.

hog-tie

hogwash

hog-wild

hoi polloi The general population.

hoity-toity

hokey Corny, or contrived.

hokum

hol-, holo- Compounds beginning with this combining form, which means complete or total, are written as one word (e.g., *holocaust, hologram*).

hold, held

hold- Compounds written as one word include *holdall, holdfast, holdout* (noun), *holdover* (noun), *holdup* (noun).

-holder Compounds ending in *-holder* are usually written as one word (e.g., *mortgageholder*).

holding company

holding pattern

hole An opening, gap.

hole in one

hole-in-the-wall; *pl.,* **holes-in-the-wall**

holey Having openings, gaps. (Compare **holy, wholly.**)

holidays Those to capitalize include *April Fools' Day, Arbor Day, Armed Forces Day, Christmas Day, Christmas Eve, Columbus Day, Father's Day, Flag Day, Fourth of July, Halloween, Hanukkah, Inauguration Day, Independence Day, Labor Day, Lincoln's Birthday, Memorial Day, Mother's Day, New Year's Day, New Year's Eve, Rosh Hashanah, Thanksgiving Day, V-J Day, Veterans Day, Washington's Birthday, Yom Kippur.*

hollandaise sauce

holland fabric *or* **Holland fabric**

holler

Hollywood bed

Holmes, Oliver Wendall (1841–1935) American jurist. Author of *The Common Law.*

holstein

holy Religious in nature. (Compare **holey, wholly.**)

Holy Communion

Holy Ghost

Holy Spirit

homage

home- Many compounds formed with *home-* are written as one word (e.g., *hometown, homework*).

home brew

home economics

home fries

home front

home plate

home port

home rule

home run

home stand

home truth

Homer (9th–8th? century B.C.) Greek poet. Author of the *Iliad* and the *Odyssey.*

homeward *or* **homewards**

homey Comfortable, like home.

homicide A legal term; killing.

homily; *pl.,* **homilies**

homo-, homeo-, homoi-, homoio- Compounds beginning with these combining forms, which mean like or similar, are written as one word (e.g., *homeopathy, homograph, homologous, homonym*).

Homo sapiens

homogeneity

homogeneous *or* **homogenous**

homology; *pl.,* **homologies**

homosexual

honcho; *pl.,* **honchos**

honeybee

honeycomb

honeydew melon

honeyed *or* **honied**

honeymoon

95

honeysuckle

honorable   When used before a name of a person of high legal or governmental office, it may either be written out or abbreviated as *Hon.*, preceded by the word *the* (e.g., *The Hon. Samuel Collier* or *The Honorable Sarah Olmstead*).

honorarium; *pl.*, honorariums

hoodlum

hoodwink

hoof; *pl.*, hooves *or* hoofs

hoof-and-mouth disease

hook-and-ladder truck

hook, line, and sinker

hookup   As noun.

hooky *or* hookey

hoopla

Hoosier   Nickname for a native or resident of the State of Indiana.

hootenanny   A gathering for singing folk songs.

hop, skip, and a jump   Not far.

hope chest

hopscotch

horde   A large group of people or animals. (Compare **hoard**.)

horehound

hornbook

hornet's nest

horn-rims

hornswoggle

horny

horoscope

horror-struck

hors d'oeuvre; *pl.*, hors d'oeuvres *or* hors d'oeuvre   French; appetizers.

horse-and-buggy

horse chestnut

horsefeathers

horsehair

horseplay

horsepower *or* HP

horseradish

horse sense

horseshoe

horse show

horse trade

horsey *or* horsy

hosanna *or* hosannah

hosiery *or* hose *or* stockings *or* nylons

hospice

hospital   Capitalize only if part of proper noun: *Massachusetts General Hospital*. Abbreviation is *hosp.*

hostel   A cheap lodging for travelers. (Compare **hostile**.)

hostelry; *pl.*, hostelries   Lodging.

hostile   Mean, unfriendly. (Compare **hostel**.)

hot air

hot-blooded

hotbed

hotcake

hotdog   As verb.

hot dog   As noun, interjection.

hotelier

hot flash

hotfoot

hothead

hothouse

hot line

hot pot

hot potato

hot pursuit

hot rod

hot seat

hotshot

hot spring

hot tub

hot water

houndstooth *or* **hound's-tooth**
hourglass
hour-long
house- Most compounds formed
with *house-* are written as one
word (e.g., *houseboat,
housecleaning, housecoat,
houseguest, household,
housekeeper, housepainter,
housewares*).

Those written as two words
include *house arrest, house call,
house cat, house detective, house
of cards, house organ, house
party, house physician, house
rule, house seat, house sitter,
house trailer*.
-house Compounds ending in
-house are usually written as one
word (e.g., *outhouse*).
house-poor
house-proud
house-raising
house-to-house
housebreak, housebroke
housing development
housing project
howbeit Nevertheless.
howdy An informal greeting.
Howells, William Dean
(1837–1920) American man of
letters. Author of *A Chance
Acquaintance*.
howitzer
how-to
hr. *or* **h.** Abbreviation for *hour*.
hubbub
hubcap
hubris Unwarranted pridefulness.
hue A shade of a color. (Compare
hew.)
hue and cry

hula
hullabaloo; *pl.,* **hullabaloos**
human Concerning the human
race. (Compare **humane**.)
humane Compassionate,
considerate. (Compare **human**.)
human nature
humble pie
humbug
humdinger
humdrum Boring, ordinary.
Hume, David (1711–1776)
Scottish philosopher and historian.
Author of *A Treatise of Human
Nature*.
humerus; *pl.,* **humeri**
humidor
humility The state of being
humble.
humongous Huge, tremendous.
humpback; humpbacked
Humpty-Dumpty
hundred
hung Suspended from something.
(Compare **hanged**.)
hunger strike
hung jury A jury that cannot reach
a verdict.
hung up
hunky-dory
hunt-and-peck Typing by
searching out keys one at a time.
hunter
hurly-burly
hurrah *or* **hurray**
hurricane Capitalize the name of a
specific storm (e.g., *Hurricane
Diane*).
hurry-up As adjective.
hush-hush
hush puppy
hussar

huzzah or **huzza** A shout or cheer to express gratification or approval.

hyacinth

hydr-, hydro- Compounds of this combining form, which means water, are written as one word (e.g., *hydrate, hydrogen, hydroplane*).

hydrangea

hyena

hygiene; hygienic; hygienically

hymn; hymnal Capitalize only if part of proper noun.

hype

hyped-up

hyper- Compounds formed with *hyper-* are written as one word.

hyperbola; *pl.*, **hyperbolas** or **hyperbolae**

hyperbole

hyperbolic or **hyperbolical**

hypercritical Extremely fault-finding. (Compare **hypocritical**.)

hypnosis; *pl.*, **hypnoses**

hypnotism

hypo-, hyp- Compounds of this combining form, meaning under, beneath, or below, are written as one word (e.g., *hypochondria*).

hypocritical Pretending to be what one is not. (Compare **hypercritical**.)

hypodermic needle

hypotenuse or **hypothenuse**

hypothesis; *pl.*, **hypotheses**

hyster-, hystero- Compounds of this combining form, which means uterus or hysteria, are written as one word (e.g., *hysterectomy*).

hysterical or **hysteric**

I

iamb *or* **iambus;** *pl.,* **iambs** *or* **iambuses**

I beam

ibex; *pl.,* **ibex** *or* **ibexes**

ibid. *or* **ib.** Latin; abbreviation for *ibidem,* "in the same place."

Ibsen, Henrik (1828–1906) Norwegian poet and dramatist. Author of *A Doll's House.*

ice- Compounds written hyphenated include *ice-cold, ice-cream* (adjective), *ice-skate* (verb).

  Those written as one word include *iceberg, iceboat, icebox, icebound, icebreaker, icefall, icehouse.*

  Those written as two words include *ice age, ice bag, ice cap, ice field, ice storm, ice water, ice cream* (noun), *ice hockey, ice pick, ice show, ice skater, ice pack, ice cap, iced tea, ice floe, ice milk.*

Ice Age *or* **ice age**

iceberg lettuce

icicle

iconoclast Someone who rejects religion or government or other established institutions.

id. *or* **idem** Latin; the same, from something previously written.

ID card *or* **identification card** *or* **identity card**

Idaho potato

idée fixe; *pl.,* **idées fixes** French; literally, "a fixed idea," an obsession.

identical *or* **identic**

identity crisis

ideology *or* **idealogy**

idiom An expression whose meaning is different from the literal definitions of its parts (e.g., *kick the bucket* means "to die").

idiosyncrasy An individual peculiarity.

idle Not occupied. (Compare **idol, idyll.**)

idol Someone who is worshiped. (Compare **idle, idyll.**)

idolater *or* **idolator**

idyll *or* **idyl** A pastoral scene. (Compare **idle, idol.**)

i.e. Latin; abbreviation for *id est,* "that is."

-ie- Write *i* before *e* except after *c,* or when sounded like *ay,* as in *neighbor* and *weigh.* Exceptions include *either, height, leisure, neither, seize, sleight,* and *weird.*

IFR Abbreviation for *instrument flight rules.*

igloo; *pl.,* **igloos**

igneous

ignis fatuus; *pl.,* **ignis fatui** Latin; an illusory goal or hope.

ignitable *or* **ignitible**

igniter *or* **ignitor**

ignominious; ignominy

ignoramus A stupid, ignorant person.

iguana

ill, worse, worst

ill- Many compounds formed with *ill-*are hyphenated, including *ill-advised, ill-bred, ill-fated, ill-favored, ill-gotten, ill-humored, ill-mannered, ill-natured, ill-tempered, ill-treat* (verb), *ill-use* (verb).

ill at ease

illegal

ill health

illicit   Immoral and illegal.

illiterate

illus. *or* illust. *or* ill. *or*
   il.   Abbreviations for *illustrated,
   illustration, illustrator*.

illusion   A false mental image or
   intellectual deception. (Compare
   allusion.)

illusory *or* illusive   Unreal,
   deceptive.

illustrious

ill will

ILS   Abbreviation for *instrument
   landing system*.

imagery   A mental picture.

imaginable   Possible to be
   conceived.

imaginary   Made-up, not real.

imaginative   Creative.

imbecile *or* imbecilic

imbroglio; *pl.,* imbroglios

imit.   Abbreviation for *imitation,
   imitative*.

Immaculate Conception

immanent   Existing, intrinsic,
   inherent. (Compare **eminent,
   imminent**.)

immaterial   Not important.

immigrant   A person who enters a
   country to settle there. (Compare
   emigrant, emigré.)

imminent   Threatening, about to
   happen. (Compare **eminent,
   immanent**.)

immiscible   Not mixable.
   (Compare **impartible**.)

immoral   Evil, unethical.
   (Compare **amoral**.)

immortal   Incapable of dying.

immovable

immune   Not susceptible; exempt.

immutable

impartible   Unable to be divided.
   (Compare **immiscible**.)

impassable   Blocked, not
   travelable. (Compare **impassible,
   impassive**.)

impasse

impassible   Emotionally restrained
   or incapable of feeling pain.
   (Compare **impassable,
   impassive**.)

impassive   Unfeeling,
   expressionless. (Compare
   impassable, impassible.)

impatience   Restlessness.
   (Compare **impatiens**.)

impatiens   The flower. (Compare
   impatience.)

impecunious   Consistently in a
   state of pennilessness.

impedimenta   Equipment.

impel, impelled

impeller *or* impellor

imper.   Abbreviation for
   imperative.

imperceptible *or* imperceivable

imperiled *or* imperilled

impermeable

impersonate

impetigo

impetus; *pl.,* impetuses

impious   Irreverent, disrespectful.

implacable

implicit   Implied but not expressed,
   outright.

imply   To suggest. (Compare
   infer.)

import   As a noun, implies
   signification, meaning (e.g., *The
   action today carries import for the
   future*).

100

importune

impostor *or* **imposter**

impr. *or* **imp.** Abbreviations for *improved, improvement.*

impracticable Not possible to do. (Compare **impractical**.)

impractical Foolish or inefficient in approach.

impregnable

impresario; *pl.,* **impresarios**

Impressionist *or* **impressionist**

imprimatur Approval, permission, license. (Compare **imprimis**.)

imprimis Latin; in the first place, among the first things. Used to introduce a list. (Compare **imprimatur**.)

impromptu Without preparation, improvised.

improvident

improvise

improviser *or* **improvisor**

imprudent Lacking discretion. (Compare **impudent**.)

impudent Cocky, brash. (Compare **imprudent**.)

impugn

impuissant French, literally, "without power," helpless, weak.

in Function word indicating location, position.

in- There is no hyphen in words formed with *in-* as a prefix meaning "not."

-in Compounds ending with *-in* are hyphenated (e.g., *sit-in*).

in absentia Latin; "in absence."

inapt Not suitable. (Compare **inept, unapt**.)

inasmuch as

inaugurate

Inauguration Day January 20 after a U.S. presidential election.

in-between As adjective or noun.

in between As adverb or preposition.

inborn

inbound

inbred; inbreeding

Inc. Abbreviation for *incorporated*. Do not use a comma before *Inc.* unless the punctuation is part of the company's formal name.

inch-deep

inchoate Just started, imperfectly formed.

incisor A cutting tooth.

incl. Abbreviation for *inclusive; including, includes.*

include To take in as part of a whole. The words *comprise, compose,* and *constitute* are used when a full list of items making up the whole are given.

includable *or* **includible**

incognito; *pl.,* **incognitos**

income tax

incommensurate Not adequate, out of proportion.

incommunicado Out of contact, deprived of communication.

incongruent *or* **incongruous**

incongruity *or* **incongruence**

inconsequential *or* **inconsequent**

incontrovertible Unquestionable.

inconvenience *or* **inconveniency**

incorporated *or* **inc.** Capitalize if part of proper noun. (See also **Inc.**)

incorporeal Having no physical form.

incredible Hard to believe.
(Compare **incredulous**.)

incredulous Unbelieving,
skeptical. (Compare **incredible**.)

incubus; *pl.,* **incubi** *or* **incubuses**

inculcate To teach by repetition.

incunabulum; *pl.,* **incunabula**

incurable Not able to be cured.

indentation A notch, recess, or
dent in something solid. (Compare
indention.)

indention A blank in typewritten
work made by spacing in from the
left. (Compare **indentation**.)

in-depth

index; *pl.,* **indexes** *or* **indices**

index finger The forefinger or
pointing finger.

india ink *or* **India ink**

Indian A native of India. Always
capitalize.

Indian corn

Indian pudding

Indian summer

india rubber

indic. *or* **ind.** Abbreviation for
indicative; indicated, indicator.

indicia Distinctive marks.

indict To charge with a crime;
accuse. (Compare **indite**.)

indifferent Not having an opinion
one way or another.

indigent Very poor, destitute.

indigo; *pl.,* **indigos** *or* **indigoes** A
deep blue dye, or the plant that
produces it.

indiscreet Not careful or prudent.
(Compare **indiscrete**.)

indiscrete Not separated into parts.
(Compare **indiscreet**.)

indistinct Blurred, dim. (Compare
indistinctive.)

indistinctive Not having distinct
qualities. (Compare **indistinct**.)

indite To make up, compose in
writing. (Compare **indict**.)

indiv. Abbreviation for *individual.*

Indo-European

indolent; indolence

indoor As adjective.

induction An inference,
understanding from particular
circumstance.

indurate Hardened, physically or
mentally. (Compare **obdurate**.)

indus. *or* **ind.** Abbreviation for
industry, industrial.

industrial arts

industrial engineering

inedible Unfit to be eaten.

ineffaceable *or* **ineradicable**

ineffective *or* **ineffectual** *or*
inefficacious Not giving desired
result. (Compare **inefficient**.)

inefficient Wasteful in execution.
(Compare **ineffective**.)

inept Lacking, not capable.
(Compare **inapt, unapt**.)

inequity Unfairness. (Compare
iniquity.)

inexpediency *or* **inexpedience**

infamous Notorious, of very bad
reputation.

infant A child one year old or
younger.

infarction Diseased tissue.
(Compare **infraction**.)

infectious Disease-related and
communicable through
microorganisms.

infer To draw a conclusion.
(Compare **imply**.)

inferable *or* **inferrible**

inferiority complex

infidel A person who does not believe in a god or religion.

infield

infielder

infighting

infin. Abbreviation for *infinitive*.

inflict To cause distress or pain, often in a physical sense. (Compare **afflict**.)

in-flight

informant A person who discloses information sought by another. (Compare **informer**.)

information *or* **info**

informer A person who discloses something about another. (Compare **informant**.)

infraction A violation of a law, rule. (Compare **infarction**.)

infrared

infrastructure

ingenious Clever, thoughtful. (Compare **ingenuous**.)

ingenue *or* **ingénue**

ingenuity Cleverness, thoughtfulness. (Compare **ingenuousness**.)

ingenuous Natural, innocent. (Compare **ingenious**.)

ingenuousness Naturalness, innocence. (Compare **ingenuity**.)

inglenook

ingrained

ingratiate

in-group

inherent Part of character, nature; intrinsic. (Compare **inherit**.)

inherit To come into possession of something through another's death. (Compare **inherent**.)

in-house

inhuman Savage, brutal.

iniquity Wickedness, sin. (Compare **inequity**.)

initial, initialed *or* **initialled**

inkblot test

in lieu of Instead of.

in memoriam In memory of.

in-law Plurals of words with this ending (e.g., *daughter-in-law*) are made on the first word (e.g., *daughters-in-law*).

inmost *or* **innermost**

innards

inner city As noun.

inner-city As adjective.

inner space

inner tube

innervate To give momentum to. (Compare **enervate**.)

innkeeper

innocuous Harmless.

innuendo; *pl.,* **innuendos** *or* **innuendoes**

inpatient A person staying at a hospital for treatment.

input, inputted *or* **input**

in re *or* **re** Concerning, in the matter of, regarding.

inroad

ins and outs

in-service

inset, inset *or* **insetted**

inside out

inside track

insight

insignia *or* **insigne;** *pl.,* **insignia** *or* **insignias**

insofar as

insole *or* **innersole**

insomnia

insomniac As adjective and noun.

insomuch as

insouciant; insouciance

inspector general Capitalize only if part of a formal title preceding a name. The abbreviation is *Insp. Gen.* or *IG*.

inspissated Thickened.

installment *or* **instalment**

instant replay

instill *or* **instil**

institute Capitalize only if part of proper noun: *the Brookings Institute*.

instr. *or* **inst.** Abbreviation for *instrument, instrumental; instruction, instructor*.

insure To protect, make secure. (Compare **ensure**.)

intake

intelligentsia The knowledgeable elite.

intense Extreme, severe. (Compare **intensive**.)

intensive Highly concentrated, done with force. (Compare **intense**.)

inter- Compounds formed with *inter-*, which means between or among, are written as one word unless the second word is a proper noun (e.g., *intercollegiate, interdepartmental, interdependent, intergovernmental, interplanetary, interracial, interscholastic*.)

intercession Intervention. (Compare **intersession**.)

interj. Abbreviation for *interjection*.

interment Burial. (Compare **internment**.)

interminable Seeming never to end.

internal-combustion engine

international date line

International Phonetic Alphabet *or* **IPA**

International Scientific Vocabulary *or* **ISV**

internment Holding during wartime. (Compare **interment**.)

interpellate To question formally. (Compare **interpolate**.)

Interpol *or* **International Criminal Police Organization**

interpolate To insert estimated number values. (Compare **interpellate**.)

interpretative *or* **interpretive**

interregnum; *pl.*, **interregnums** *or* **interregna**

interrobang A punctuation mark that is combination of explanation point and question mark (?).

intersession Period between academic terms. (Compare **intercession**.)

interstate Between states. Capitalize if part of proper noun. (Compare **intrastate**.)

interstice; *pl.*, **interstices**

intervenor *or* **intervener**

interweave, interwove *or* **interweaved**

intestacy The fact of dying without a will.

intl. *or* **intnl.** *or* **int.** Abbreviation for *international*.

into A function word indicating entry, introduction, motion.

in toto Entirely.

intr. Abbreviation for *introduced, introducing, introduction, introductory*.

intra- Compounds formed with *intra-*, which means within or inside of, are written as one word unless the second word begins with an *a* (e.g., *intra-arterial*, but *intramural*).

intrans. *or* **intr.** Abbreviation for *intransitive*.

intrastate Within a state. (Compare **interstate**.)

intrauterine device *or* **IUD** A device inserted in the uterus as a contraceptive.

intriguer *or* **intrigant** *or* **intriguant**

intrinsic *or* **intrinsical** An essential part of, originating from within. (Compare **extrinsic**.)

intro- Compounds formed with *intro-*, which means into, within, or inwards, are written as one word.

introduction *or* **intro** The abbreviation is *intr.* or *introd.*

introvert

inundate To flood or overwhelm.

inure To become used to something unpleasant (e.g., *The football players were inured to pain*).

inv. Abbreviation for *invented, invention, inventor.*

invaluable Precious, priceless.

inveigh To complain harshly. (Compare **inveigle**.)

inveigle To lure, seduce. (Compare **inveigh**.)

invent To think up, create something new.

inward *or* **inwards**

I/O Abbreviation for *input/output.*

ion

IOU; *pl.,* **IOUs** Abbreviation for *I owe you* in an informal written statement of debt.

ipecac

ipse dixit Latin; literally, "he himself said it," an unproved assertion. (Compare **ipso facto**.)

ipso facto Latin; literally, "by the fact itself," by the nature of something. (Compare **ipse dixit**.)

IQ *or* **I.Q.** *or* **intelligence quotient**

ir- Prefix often used before words beginning with *r*, meaning "non-" or "un-".

irascible

iridescent Rainbowlike.

iris; *pl.,* **irises** *or* **irides**

Irish coffee

Irish potato

Irish setter

Irish stew

ironclad

Iron Curtain *or* **iron curtain**

ironfisted

iron hand

ironhanded

ironside

irons in the fire

ironwork

irradicable Unable to be wiped out or destroyed.

irrefragable *or* **irrefutable**

irreg. *or* **irr.** Abbreviation for *irregular.*

irreligous Indifferent or hostile toward religion.

irreparable Not fixable or retrievable.

irruption A burst inward. (Compare **eruption**.)

IRS Abbreviation for *Internal Revenue Service*. In most cases, use in text only after the full name has been used.

Irving, Washington (1783–1859)

American author. Wrote the "Legend of Sleepy Hollow."

is-, iso- Compounds beginning with these forms, which mean "equal" or "uniform," are written as one word: *isotope*.

island Capitalize if part of proper noun (e.g., *Staten Island*).

island-hop

isle Island.

is not *or* **isn't**

isosceles

isthmus

Italian dressing

italics with possessives The *'s* to make an italicized word possessive is usually written in roman typeface as in "*Life*'s The Year in Pictures issue."

iterate *or* **reiterate** To say or do again. (Compare **itinerant**.)

itin. Abbreviation for *itinerary*.

itinerancy *or* **itineracy**

itinerant Traveling. (Compare **iterate**.)

itinerary

its A possessive pronoun (e.g., *The bottle is missing its lid*). Does not take an apostrophe.

it's A contraction of *it is*.

itty-bitty *or* **itsy-bitsy**

IV Abbreviation for *intravenous, intravenously*.

ivory-tower As adjective.

ivory tower As noun.

ivy; *pl.,* **ivies**

Ivy League

jabot
jackal
jackanapes
Jack Frost
jackhammer
jack-in-the-box
jack-in-the-pulpit; *pl.*, jack-in-the-pulpits *or* jacks-in-the-pulpit
jackknife
jack-o'-lantern
jackpot
jackrabbit
jacquard
jaguar
jai alai
jail A local facility for confinement of lawbreakers or people awaiting trial. (Compare **prison**.)
jailbait
jailbreak
jailer *or* jailor
jalapeño
jalopy; *pl.*, jalopies
jalousie A type of slatted window covering. (Compare **jealousy**.)
Jamaica ginger
Jamaica rum
jamb The posts or frame around an opening such as a door.
jamboree
James, Henry (1843–1916) American novelist. Author of *The Bostonians*.
James, William (1842–1910) American psychologist and one of the founders of pragmatic philosophy.
jam-pack
jam session An informal, improvised performance by a group of musicians.

Jane Doe/John Doe A name given to a woman or man whose actual name is not known (as used in hospitals or in court proceedings).
japan black
Japan wax
jardiniere
jargon An expression or body of language that is either strange and obscure or special to a domain or occupation.
jaundice
java Coffee (named after the Indonesian island where coffee beans are grown).
jawbone
jawbreaker
jaybird
jaywalker A pedestrian who crosses a street carelessly or without obeying traffic rules.
jct. *or* jctn. *or* junc. Abbreviation for *junction*.
jealousy The quality or condition of being resentfully envious. (Compare **jalousie**.)
jeep Capitalize if referring to the trademarked vehicle. Otherwise it refers to the general-purpose Army vehicle.
Jehovah's Witness
jejune
Jekyll and Hyde A personality split between good and evil.
Jell-O A trademark name for flavored gelatin.
jelly bean
jellyfish
jelly roll

jeopardy

jerry-build To rig together quickly and cheaply.

jersey; *pl.*, **jerseys**

jersey cow

jet lag

jet-propelled

jet propulsion

jetsam

jet set

jet-setter

jet stream

jettison

Jew A believer in Judaism, or a descendent of the Hebrew people.

JHS Abbreviation for *junior high school*.

jib A sail (noun); to cause to sail or shift (verb); or to balk (verb). (Compare **gibe, jibe**.)

jibe To agree, coincide. (Compare **gibe, jib**.)

jiffy

jigsaw puzzle

jinx

job action

job-hopping

job lot

jock itch

jockstrap

jocular

jocund

jodphur

John Hancock *or* **John Henry** A signature.

johnnycake

Johnson, Samuel (1709–1784) English writer, lexicographer, and critic.

joie de vivre French; literally "joy of living." Pleasure in being alive.

jonquil

jostle

joule A unit of energy storage measure.

joyride

joystick

judge Capitalize only if part of formal title preceding a name: Judge Leslie Fields.

judgeship

judgmatic *or* **judgmatical**

judgment *or* **judgement**

Judgment Day

jujitsu *or* **jujutsu** Japanese; an art of weaponless self-defense.

jukebox

julep

julienne

jumbo; *pl.*, **jumbos**

jumbo jet

jump-off As noun.

jumpsuit

june bug *or* **June bug**

Jung, Carl Gustav (1875–1961) Swiss psychologist and psychiatrist.

jungle gym

junior *or* **jr.** Capitalize when part of proper noun. A comma may be used before the designation when it follows a surname (e.g., *Hank Williams, Jr.*).

junketeer *or* **junketer**

junkie *or* **junky;** *pl.*, **junkies**

junk mail

junkyard

junta

junto; *pl.*, **juntos**

jurisprudence

juror

justice of the peace Capitalize only as a formal title preceding a name: *Justice of the Peace Hopkins*.

jury-rig To set up a makeshift arrangement.

juvenile delinquent A young person who habitually engages in antisocial or illegal behavior.

kabob *or* **kebab** *or* **kebob**

kaffeeklatsch German; a get-together for drinking coffee and sharing gossip.

Kafka, Franz (1883–1924) German writer.

kaleidoscope

kamikaze

Kandinsky, Wassily (1866–1944) Russian nonfigurative painter. Author of *Uber das Geistige in der Kunst.*

Kant, Immanuel (1724–1804) German philosopher. Author of *Critique of Pure Reason.*

kapok

kaput *or* **kaputt**

karat The unit of measure indicating gold content of alloyed gold objects. (Compare **carat, caret, carrot.**)

karate A Japanese art of self-defense.

katydid

kayak

kayo *or* **KO, kayoed** *or* **KO'd**

Keats, John (1795–1821) English poet. Author of *Endymion.*

keep, kept

-keeper, -keeping Compounds formed with these endings are usually written as one word (e.g., *innkeeper, beekeeping*).

keepsake

keeshond; *pl.,* **keeshonden**

Keller, Helen (1880–1968) American author and lecturer on the blind. She, herself, was left blind, deaf, and mute by illness at a young age.

kelly green

Kelvin scale A scale that measures extreme cold, on which absolute zero is approximately −273°C.

kempt Nicely kept (e.g., *a kempt hairstyle*).

kennel, kenneled *or* **kennelled**

kerchief; *pl.,* **kerchiefs** *or* **kerchieves**

kernel

kerosene

Kerouac, John (1922–1969) American Beat novelist. Author of *On the Road.*

ketchup *or* **catsup**

kettledrum

kettle of fish

keyboard

keyhole

keynote

keypunch

key ring

keystone

keystroke

key word

KGB The intelligence agency of the former Soviet Union (analogous to the **CIA**).

khaki

Khrushchev, Nikita (1894–1971) Soviet Communist politician.

kibosh A stop to something, usually used in the construction *put the kibosh on.*

kickoff As noun.

kickstand

kid glove

kidnap, kidnapped *or* **kidnaped**

kidney stone

kid stuff

kielbasa; *pl.,* **kielbasas** *or* **kielbasi**

Kierkegaard, Søren (1813–1855)

Danish founder of existentialist philosophy.

killjoy

kilogram *or* **kg**

kilohertz *or* **kHz**

kilometer *or* **km**

kilowatt *or* **kw** *or* **kW**

kilowatt-hour *or* **kwh** *or* **kWh**

kimono; *pl.,* **kimonos**

kindergarten

kindhearted

kindred

kinesiology

kinetic energy

king Capitalize only if part of formal title preceding a name: *King Henry VIII*.

King, Jr., Martin Luther (1929–1968) American clergyman and civil rights leader.

kingdom come The next world.

king-size *or* **king-sized** Larger than the usual standard.

kiosk

Kipling, Rudyard (1865–1936) English writer. Author of *The Jungle Book*.

kiss-off As noun. Slang term meaning an abrupt dismissal.

kitchenette

kitty-corner

Klee, Paul (1879–1940) Swiss painter and co-founder of the German abstract group *Blaue Reiter*.

Kleenex A trademark name for tissues.

kleptomaniac

klieg lights

klutz; klutzy

knack

knapsack

knave; knavish; knavery

knead

kneecap

knee-deep

knee-high

knee-jerk As adjective.

knee jerk As noun.

kneel, knelt *or* **kneeled**

kneepad

knickerbockers

knickknack

knife, knived

knife; *pl.,* **knives**

knight-errant; *pl.,* **knights-errant**

knit, knit *or* **knitted**

knob

knock

knockabout As adjective or noun.

knockdown As adjective or noun.

knock-down-and-drag-out *or* **knock-down-drag-out**

knock-kneed

knockoff As noun. Slang term meaning a copy or imitation, especially a copy of something more expensive.

knockout As adjective or noun.

knockwurst *or* **knackwurst** A type of sausage.

knoll

knothole

know, knew, known

know-how

know-it-all

knowledgeable

know-nothing An ignorant person.

Know-Nothing Capitalize as the secret U.S. political party of the 1850s whose attitude was hostile to Roman Catholics, immigrants, and foreign influence as perceived threats.

knucklebone

knucklehead

koala

kohlrabi; *pl.*, **kohlrabies** A type of cabbage.

Koran *or* **Qur'an** The sacred scripture of Islam.

kosher Sanctioned by Jewish law; used generally to mean appropriate or proper.

kowtow To demonstrate extreme deference.

kraft paper An especially strong paper.

K ration

kraut Short form for *sauerkraut*.

Kriss Kringle Santa Claus.

krypton

kudos Public honor.

Ku Klux Klan *or* **KKK** A secret organization whose membership is understood to be limited to American-born white Christians who espouse white supremacy.

kumquat

kvetch Yiddish; to gripe.

KWIC Abbreviation meaning *keyword in context*.

kyrie A prayer beginning with the words "Lord, have mercy."

L

l., ll. Abbreviation for *line, lines*.

label, labeled *or* **labelled**

labellum; *pl.,* **labella**

labium; *pl.,* **labia**

laboratory *or* **lab** Capitalize only if part of proper noun.

Labor Day

labor-intensive

laborsaving

Labrador retriever

labyrinth

labyrinthine *or* **labyrinthian**

lacework

lachrymal *or* **lacrimal** Related to the tear ducts.

lachrymose Sorrowful, weepy.

lackadaisical Dispirited or unconcerned.

lackey; *pl.,* **lackeys**

lackluster

laconic Habitually terse in speech.

lacquer

lacrosse

lacuna; *pl.,* **lacunae** *or* **lacunas** A void.

ladder-back

ladder truck

lade, laded *or* **laden**

la-di-da *or* **la-de-da**

ladybug

ladyfinger

lady-in-waiting; *pl.,* **ladies-in-waiting**

Laetrile *or* **laetrile** A drug used in cancer therapy.

lager

lagoon A small lake or pond near a large body of water. (Compare **laguna**.)

laguna A small lake or pond. (Compare **lagoon**.)

laid-back

laissez-faire

lake Capitalize if part of proper noun. Abbreviation is *L*.

lakefront

lakeshore

lama A monk practicing Mahayana Buddhism. (Compare **llama**.)

lamasery; *pl.,* **lamaseries**

lambaste *or* **lambast**

lambent

lamé Shiny, metallic material.

lamebrain *or* **lamebrained** As adjective.

lame duck As noun.

lame-duck As adjective.

lamella; *pl.,* **lamellae** *or* **lamellas**

Lamentations

lamina; *pl.,* **laminae** *or* **laminas**

lampblack

lamplight

lampoonery Ridiculing.

lamppost

lampshade

LAN Abbreviation for *local area network*.

lance corporal

land- Many compounds formed with *land-* are spelled as one word (e.g., *landfill, landlocked, landlubber, landmark, landowner, landscaper, landslide*).

-land Compounds ending in *-land* are written as one word (e.g., *homeland*).

land grant

land office As noun.

land-office As adjective.

land-poor

lane Capitalize only if part of

proper noun. Abbreviations are *La.* or *In.*

lang. Abbreviation for *language*.

languid An adjective meaning weak, sluggish. (Compare **languor, languorous**.)

languish To decrease in health and vitality.

languor A noun meaning weakness, sluggishness. (Compare **languid, languorous**.)

languorous Inducing or producing weakness, sluggishness. (Compare **languid, languor**.)

lanolin

lanyard

Lao-Tsu (6th century B.C.) Chinese founder of Taoist philosophy.

lap belt

lapdog

lapelled *or* **lapeled** As adjective.

lapidary Related to stones, especially in terms of cutting, engraving, or sculpting.

lap robe

lapis lazuli

larceny; *pl.,* **larcenies** Theft of personal property.

lares and penates Household items.

largehearted

large-minded

large-print

largess *or* **largesse**

largo A musical direction to play in an expansive, stately manner.

lariat

larkspur

larva; *pl.,* **larvae** *or* **larvas**

laryngitis

larynx; *pl.,* **larynges** *or* **larynxes**

lasagna *or* **lasagne**

lascivious

laser

lasso; *pl.,* **lassos** *or* **lassoes**

last-ditch As adjective.

last hurrah

last straw

Last Supper

last word

Lat. *or* **L.** Abbreviation for *Latin*.

latchkey

latecomer

latent Dormant, hidden, not obvious. (Compare **manifest**.)

latex; *pl.,* **latices** *or* **latexes**

lath; *pl.,* **laths** *or* **lath** A thin piece of wood used as building material. (Compare **lathe**.)

lathe Means to cut with a rotating machine. (Compare **lath**.)

Latin abbreviations Abbreviations of Latin words and phrases are punctuated, lowercased, and usually not italicized.

Latin American

latitude Latitude, described by parallels, is written out in text (e.g., *45 degrees 45 minutes north latitude* or *45th parallel north*), and abbreviated in tables (e.g., *lat. 45-45N*). (See also **longitude**.)

latter The second of two things, or the last in a series.

Latter-day Saint *or* **Mormon**

latticework

laudable Praiseworthy. (Compare **laudatory**.)

laudatory Expressing praise. (Compare **laudable**.)

laughing gas

laughingstock

launchpad
launch vehicle
launderette
laundry room
laureate Noun or adjective describing the recipient of honor, from Latin meaning "crowned with laurel."
lavaliere or lavalliere
lavatory
lavender
law-abiding
lawbreaking; lawbreaker
lawmaking; lawmaker
lawn mower
laws The official names of laws and bylaws are written out on the first mention and may be abbreviated in subsequent references.
lawsuit
laxative
lay, laid
layabout As noun.
layaway As noun or adjective.
layette
layoff As noun.
layout As noun.
layover As noun.
layperson
lay-up As noun.
lazybones
lb or lb. Abbreviation for libra "pound."
LCD Abbreviation for liquid crystal display.
lead, led
lead glass
lead-in As noun or adjective.
leading edge
leadoff As adjective or noun.
lead-pipe As adjective.

lead poisoning
lead time
lead-up As adjective or noun.
leaf; pl., leaves or leafs
leaflet
league Capitalize only if part of proper noun (e.g., an American League team).
leak Drippage, escape. (Compare leek.)
lean, leaned or leant
lean-to; pl., lean-tos
leap, leapt or leaped
leapfrog
leap year
learn, learned or learnt
leaseholder
least common denominator
leastwise or leastways
leathery
leave, left
lo and behold
leavening
leave-taking
lecherous
lecithin
lectern A reading stand from which a person speaks to a congregation.
lecture or speech titles (See Part 2, Titles of works.)
LED Abbreviation for light-emitting diode.
ledger
Lee, Robert E. (1807–1870) Confederate General. Served as military adviser to Jefferson Davis at outbreak of the Civil War.
leek An onionlike vegetable. (Compare leak.)
leeward
leeway

left field; left fielder
left-hand; left-hander
leftover   As adjective or noun.
left wing   As noun.
left-wing   As adjective.
left-winger
lefty; *pl.*, lefties
legacy; *pl.*, legacies
legalese
legatee   The person to whom
   property is left through a will.
   (Compare legator.)
legator   The person who writes a
   will. (Compare legatee.)
legerdemain   Adroitness, trickery,
   sleight of hand.
Legionnaire's disease
legislate   Abbreviation for this and
   variants is *legis.* or *leg.*
legitimate *or* legit
legitimate *or* legitimize *or*
   legitimatize   As verb.
leg-pull
legroom
legume
legwork
leisure
leitmotiv *or* leitmotif   A dominant
   theme, as in a long piece of music
   or a novel.
lemma; *pl.*, lemmas *or* lemmata
lemon yellow
lemonade
lend, lent
lend-lease
length; *pl.*, lengths
lengthwise *or* lengthways
lenient
Lenin, V. I.   (1870–1924) Russian
   Communist leader.
lens *or* lense; *pl.*, lenses

lentil   The leguminous plant or its
   seed.
Leo   (see Zodiac Signs).
Leonardo da Vinci   (1452–1519)
   Italian painter, sculptor, architect,
   and scientist. Painted the *Mona
   Lisa* and *Last Supper*.
leopard
leotard
leper
leprechaun   From Irish folklore; a
   type of elf.
leprosy
lesbian
lèse-majesté *or* lese
   majesty   French; an offense
   against an established power.
lesion
less   Refers to quantity or degree of
   a bulk amount or a whole.
   (Compare few.)
less-, lesser-   Compounds are
   hyphenated before a noun but
   written as two words if they fall
   after it (e.g., *a less-worn rug, a
   lesser-known writer*, but *the rug
   was less worn, the writer was
   lesser known*).
-less   Compounds ending in *-less*
   are written as one word unless the
   combination would result in a
   double *l* (e.g., *model-less*, but
   cheerless).
lessee   The person renting a
   property. (Compare lessor.)
lessor   The person renting out
   property. (Compare lessee.)
letdown   As noun
let's *or* let us
letter carrier
letterhead
letter-perfect

letterpress

letters Plurals of letters used as nouns are usually formed by adding an apostrophe and *s*, though sometimes the plural of capital letters is formed by adding *s* alone, depending on which form causes the least confusion in context (e.g., *p's and q's*, but *ABC's or ABCs*).

lettuce

letup As noun.

leuk-, leuko-, leuc-, leuco- Compounds of this combining form, which means white or colorless, are written as one word (e.g., *leukemia*.)

leukocyte *or* **leucocyte**

levee A reception for a person of honor or an embankment against river flooding. (Compare **levy**.)

level, leveled *or* **levelled**

levelheaded

Levi's Trade name for a type of denim jeans.

levity Lightness, frivolity.

levy A tax, imposition. (Compare **levee**.)

lewd

Lewis and Clarke

Lewis, Sinclair (1885–1951) American novelist. Author of *Babbit*.

lexicography Dictionary making.

lexicon; *pl.,* **lexica** *or* **lexicons**

LF Abbreviation for *low frequency*.

lg., L, lge., lrg. Abbreviations for *large*.

Lhasa apso; *pl.,* **Lhasa apsos**

liable

liaison

lib. Abbreviation for *library, librarian*.

libel A published defamatory statement. (Compare **slander**.)

libeled *or* **libelled**

liberal arts

liberal-minded

libertarian A person who advocates free will, liberty. (Compare **libertine**.)

libertine A person unconcerned with morals. (Compare **libertarian**.)

Liberty Bell

libidinous

libido; *pl.,* **libidos**

Libra (see **Zodiac Signs**).

library Capitalize only if part of a proper noun (e.g., the *New York Public Library*, but *the local library*).

Library of Congress The abbreviation is *LC*.

libretto; *pl.,* **librettos** *or* **libretti** Also called *the book;* the text for an opera or musical.

lic. Abbreviation for *license, licensed*.

license plate

licentious Lacking restraint.

lichen

licit Legal or permissible.

lickerish Greedy, desirous, or lecherous. (Compare **licorice**.)

lickety-split Quickly.

licorice *or* **liquorice** A root from which candy is made. (Compare **lickerish**.)

lie, lay, lain To position horizontally, exist, extend. (Compare **lie, lied**.)

lie, lied To tell a falsehood. (Compare **lie, lay**.)

Liederkranz cheese

lien A legal interest in or hold on personal property for its value against debt. (Compare **lieu**.)

lieu Place. Chiefly used as in **lieu of**. (Compare **lien**.)

lieutenant or **lt.** or **lieut.** Capitalize only if used as formal title preceding a name.

lieutenant governor or **lt. gov.** Capitalize only if used as formal title preceding a name.

life; pl., lives

life- Compounds formed with *life-* that are written as one word include *lifeblood, lifeguard, lifeline, lifesaver, lifesaving, lifetime, lifework.*
   Compounds that are hyphenated include *life-giving, life-size* or *life-sized, life-support.*

life-and-death or **life-or-death**

life history

life insurance

life jacket or **life vest**

lifelong For the entire time of one's existence. (Compare **livelong**.)

life of Riley An easy, carefree life.

life preserver

Life Savers Trademark name for a type of candy.

life span The duration of existence of a living creature.

life-style or **lifestyle**

lift-off As noun.

light, lighted or **lit**

-light Compounds ending in *-light* are written as one word (e.g., *sunlight*).

light bulb

light-footed

light-handed

light-headed

lighthearted

light heavyweight

lighthouse

light meter

lightening Making less in weight, burden. (Compare **lightning**.)

lighter-than-air

lightfaced

lightning An electrical discharge in the air. (Compare **lightening**.)

lightplane

lightship

lights-out

lightweight

light-year

likable or **likeable**

-like Compounds ending in *-like* are written as one word unless the *l* is doubled or tripled or the resulting combination appears strange to the eye (e.g., *girl-like, cell-like, haiku-like,* but *childlike*).

likelihood

like-minded

likewise

lilliputian or **Lilliputian** Miniature, very small.

lily-livered

lily of the valley

lily-white

lima bean

limb An appendage, such as an arm or a leg or a branch of a tree. (Compare **limn**.)

Limburger cheese

limelight

limerick

limited-access highway

limn To outline, describe.
(Compare **limb**.)

Limoges

limousine A large automobile driven by a chauffeur.

limpid Clear, untroubled.

linage Number of lines printed. (Compare **lineage**.)

linchpin A fastening element; something that holds everything else together.

Lincoln's Birthday

Lindbergh, Charles A.
(1902–1974) American aviator who completed first solo nonstop transatlantic flight.

-line Compounds ending in *-line* are written as one word (e.g., *online*).

lineage Descent, ancestry. (Compare **linage**.)

lineament Outline or distinguishing feature. (Compare **liniment**.)

linebacker

lineup As noun.

ling. Abbreviation for *linguistic, linguistics*.

lingerie

lingo; *pl.*, **lingoes** Jargon, slang, or unfamiliar or individualized vocabulary.

lingua franca; *pl.*, **lingua francas** *or* **linguae francae** A common language.

linguine

linguistic *or* **linguistical**

liniment A medicinal cream. (Compare **lineament**.)

linkup As noun.

linoleum

Linotype

lion; *pl.*, **lions** *or* **lion**

lionhearted

lion's share

lip-read

lipreading

lip service

lipstick

lip sync As noun.

lip-synch *or* **lip-sync** As verb.

liq. Abbreviation for *liquid*.

liquefy *or* **liquify**

liqueur A sweetened liquor. (Compare **liquor**.)

liquor A strong (usually distilled) alcoholic beverage. (Compare **liqueur**.)

lissome *or* **lissom**

list price

listener-in; *pl.*, **listeners-in**

lit. Abbreviation for *literal, literally; literary, literature*.

litany; *pl.*, **litanies**

liter *or* **litre** The abbreviation is *l* or *L* or *lit*.

literal In the exact sense. (Compare **littoral**.)

literally Means actually, exactly. (Compare **figuratively, virtually**.)

literate A person who can read and write. (Compare **literati, literatim**.)

literati Educated people as a group. (Compare **literate, literatim**.)

literatim Letter for letter. (Compare **literate, literati**.)

lith-, litho- Compounds of this combining form, which means stone, are written as one word (e.g., *lithograph*).

lithe *or* **lithesome** Flexible.

litigant

litmus paper
litterateur
litterbag
litterbug
little, less, least   As adverb.
little, littler or less or lesser, littlest
   or least   As adjective.
   Concerning size, duration, or
   importance.
little-   Compounds are hyphenated
   before a noun but written as two
   words if they fall after it (e.g., *a
   little-known desire*, but *the desire
   was little known*).
little by little
littoral   Concerning the seashore.
   (Compare literal.)
livable or liveable
live-in   As adjective or noun.
livelihood
livelong   Whole. (Compare
   lifelong.)
live oak
liverwurst
livery; pl., liveries
livestock
live wire
livid
living room   As noun.
living-room   As adjective.
Livingston, Stanley   (1905–1986)
   American physicist. Co-developed
   the atom-smashing device called
   the cyclotron.
llama   The camel-like pack animal
   native to South America.
   (Compare lama.)
-load   Compounds ending in *-load*
   are written as one word (e.g.,
   workload).
loaf; pl., loaves
loafer

loan shark
loan-sharking
loanword
loath or loathe   As adjective:
   unwilling, reluctant. (Compare
   loathe.)
loathe   As verb: to hate. (Compare
   loath.)
lobbyist or lobbyer
lobotomy
lobster pot
loc.   Abbreviation for *locative;
   location*.
local or localite   As noun.
locale   The site of particular event,
   action; neighborhood. (Compare
   location.)
locater or locator
location or locality   General
   position, place. (Compare locale.)
loc. cit.   Abbreviation for *loco
   citato*, "in the place cited."
lock, stock, and
   barrel   Completely (e.g., *They
   outfitted the fishing camp lock,
   stock, and barrel with salvaged
   material*).
lockbox
locked-in   As adjective.
locker-room   As adjective.
locker room   As noun.
lockjaw
locknut
lockout   As noun.
lockstep
lockup   As noun.
loco   Spanish; crazy.
locum tenens; pl., locum
   tenentes   Latin; literally, "(one)
   holding the place," a temporary
   substitute.
locus; pl., loci

lode A deposit of metal, ore.
lodestar
lodestone
lodgment *or* **lodgement**
log Abbreviation for *logarithm*.
log-, logo- Compounds of this combining form, which means word or speech, are written as one word (e.g., *logarithm*).
logbook
loggerhead(s)
loggia; *pl.,* **loggias** *or* **loggie** Italian; a covered balcony overlooking a courtyard or (in a theater) a stage.
logistics The details of doing something.
logjam
logo; *pl.,* **logos**
log on As verb. **log-on** *or* **logon** As noun.
logroll Trading votes for favors in politics.
loincloth
lollipop *or* **lollypop**
lollygag *or* **lallygag**
London broil
loneliness
long-ago As adjective.
long ago As noun.
long-awaited
longbow
long-distance As adjective or adverb.
long distance As noun.
long-drawn-out
longevity
Longfellow, Henry Wadsworth (1807–1882) American poet. Author of *Tales of a Wayside Inn.*

long-hair *or* **long-haired** As adjective.
longhand
longhorn
longitude Longitude, described by meridians, is written out in text (e.g., *45 degrees 45 minutes west longitude* or *45th meridian west*), and abbreviated in tables (e.g., *long. 45-45W*). (See also **latitude**.)
long-lived
long-playing
long-range
long shot
long-sought
long-standing *or* **longtime**
long-suffering
long suit
long-term
longtime As adjective.
longueur; *pl.,* **longueurs**
long view
long-winded
loofah *or* **luffa** A sponge made from the fruit of a loofah plant.
look-alike
looker-on; *pl.,* **lookers-on**
look-in As noun.
looking glass
lookout As noun.
look-see
lookup As noun.
loony *or* **looney**
loony bin
loophole
loose *or* **loosen** To make less tight. (Compare **lose**.)
loose end
loose-jointed
loose-leaf
lopsided

log. Abbreviation for *loquitur*, "he/she speaks."

loquacious Talkative

LORAN *or* **loran** Abbreviation for *long-range navigation*.

Lord's Prayer

lose, lost To fail to keep possession. (Compare **loose**.)

lothario *or* **Lothario** A seducer of women.

Lou Gehrig's disease

loudmouth

loudspeaker

lounge lizard

loungewear

louse; *pl.,* **lice**

louver *or* **louvre**

lovable *or* **loveable**

love affair

lovebird

love-in

lovelorn

lovemaking

lovers' lane

love seat

lovesick

lowborn

lowboy

lowbred

lowbrow

lowdown As noun.

low-down As adjective.

low-end As adjective.

lower class As noun.

lower-class As adjective.

lowercase

lowest common denominator

low-grade

low-key *or* **low-keyed**

lowland *or* **lowlands**

low-level

lowlife; *pl.,* **lowlifes** *or* **lowlives**

low-life As adjective.

low-lying

low-pressure

low-spirited

lox; *pl.,* **lox** *or* **loxes**

lozenge

LP A long-playing record.

LPG Abbreviation for *liquefied petroleum gas*.

LSD Lysergic acid diethylamide, a psychedelic drug.

ltd. *or* **Ltd.** *or* **lim.** Abbreviation for *limited*. Do not use a comma before *Ltd.* unless the punctuation is part of the company's formal name.

luau

lubricious Lecherous. (Compare **lugubrious**.)

lucent Glowing, very clear. (Compare **lycid**.)

lucid Transparent, lighted, clear. (Compare **lucent**.)

Lucite A brand name for a transparent plastic.

lucre

lugubrious Mournful, dismal. (Compare **lubricious**.)

lukewarm

lullaby; *pl.,* **lullabies**

lulu

lumbar Relating to vertebrae. (Compare **lumber**.)

lumber Building material milled from logs. (Compare **lumbar**.)

lumberjack

lumberyard

luminary

luminescent

lunacy

lunar

lunch counter

luncheonette
lunchroom
lunchtime
lupine
luscious
luster *or* lustre
Luther, Martin (1483–1546)
German founder of the
Reformation and Protestantism.
luxuriant Profuse, fertile, lush.
(Compare **luxurious**.)

luxurious Very pleasurable,
satisfying; self-indulgent.
(Compare **luxuriant**.)
lyceum
lye A harsh chemical.
lynch
lynx; *pl.,* **lynx** *or* **lynxes**
lyonnaise
lyricist A person who writes
musical lyrics.

M

macabre

macadamia nut

macadamize

macaroni

macaroon

Mace As noun. A trademark name for a chemical compound packaged in aerosol containers that combines nerve gas and tear gas to temporarily stun assailants.

mace As verb.

machete

Machiavellian

machinable or machineable

machine-gun As adjective or verb.

machine gun As noun.

machine-readable

machine shop

machine tool

machismo

Mach number

mackerel; pl., mackerel or mackerels

mackintosh or macintosh The waterproof coat or fabric. (Compare McIntosh.)

macr-, macro- Compounds of this combining form, which means long, large, or enlarged, are written as one word (e.g., macrobiotic).

macramé or macrame

macro; pl., macros

macron A bar over a letter to show long-vowel pronunciation.

madam or ma'am

madame; pl., mesdames or madames Capitalize if used preceding a name. Abbreviation is Mme. or Mdme.; pl., Mmes.

madcap

Madeira wine

madeleine

mademoiselle; pl., mademoiselles or mesdemoiselles Capitalize if used preceding a name. Abbreviation is Mlle.; pl., Mlles.

made-to-order

made-up As adjective.

madhouse

Madison Avenue

madras

maelstrom

maestro; pl., maestros or maestri

Mafia

mafioso; pl., mafiosi

magenta

maggot

magic or magical

magistrate Capitalize only if part of formal title preceding a name.

Magna Charta or Magna Carta

magna cum laude Latin; with great distinction, an honor at graduation distinguishing an academic degree.

magnate A very powerful person. (Compare magnet.)

magnesia

magnet An iron alloy that attracts metals. (Compare magnate.)

magneto; pl., magnetos

magniloquent

magnolia

magnum A large wine or champagne bottle.

magnum opus Latin; an artist or writer's greatest work.

magpie

maharaja or maharajah Hindu; a prince ranking above a raja.

maharani *or* **maharanee** Hindu; a princess ranking above a rani.

maharishi Hindu; a mystical teacher, sage, and poet.

mah-jongg

mahogany

maid of honor Traditional. Use *best honor attendant.*

mailbag

mailbox

mail drop

maillot

mail order As noun.

mail-order As adjective.

mainframe

mainland

mainline As adjective or verb.

main line As noun.

mainstay

mainstream

Main Street

maître d' *or* **maitre d'**; *pl.,* **maître d's** *or* **maitre d's** Anglicized short form for *maître d'hôtel.*

maître d'hôtel; *pl.,* **maîtres d'hôtel** French; headwaiter.

maize Corn. (Compare **maze**.)

majolica *or* **maiolica**

major Capitalize only if part of formal title preceding a name. Abbreviation is *Maj.*

major general; *pl.,* **major generals** Capitalize only if part of formal title preceding a name. Abbreviation is *Maj. Gen.*

majordomo; *pl.,* **majordomos**

majority More than half of an amount, number. (Compare **plurality**.)

majority leader Capitalize only if part of formal title preceding

name: *Majority Leader Steven Hanley.*

major-league As adjective.

major league As noun.

major-medical

make, made; makable *or* **makeable**

make-believe

make-do

make-or-break

make-over As noun.

-maker, -making Compounds formed with these endings are written as one word (e.g., *policymaker*).

makeready

makeshift

makeup As noun.

mal- Bad, abnormal, or inadequate. Compounds in which *mal-* is a prefix are written as one word (e.g., *maladjusted, maladroit, malapportioned*).

malaise

malaprop *or* **malapropian**

malapropism

malarkey

Malcolm X (1925–1965) African-American spiritual and political leader. Formed religious group called Muslim Mosque and preached black separatism, nationalism, and pride in race.

mal de mer Seasickness.

malevolent

malice

malign To speak ill of.

malignancy *or* **malignance**

malignant Cancerous or with tumor.

mallard; *pl.,* **mallard** *or* **mallards**

malleable

malodorous Very bad smelling or very improper.

malted milk

malt liquor

mama *or* **mamma**

mammary gland

mammogram

managing editor

mañana Spanish; tomorrow.

mandamus; *pl.,* **mandamuses**

mandarin collar

mandarin orange

mandibular *or* **mandibulate**

mandola A small mandolin. (Compare **mandolin**.)

mandolin *or* **mandoline** A string instrument of lute family. (Compare **mandola**.)

mandrel *or* **mandril**

manege *or* **manège** French; the training of a horse.

Manet, Edouard (1832–1883) French painter and forerunner of Impressionism. Painter of *Dejeuner sur l'herbe*. See *Monet, Claude*.

maneuverable

mango; *pl.,* **mangoes** *or* **mangos**

manhattan A cocktail made with vermouth, whiskey, and (sometimes) bitters.

mania Excitement, a craze over something.

-mania Compounds ending in *-mania* are written as one word (e.g., *erotomania*).

maniacal *or* **maniac**

manic-depressive

manicotto; *pl.,* **manicotti**

manifest Obvious, apparent from the surface. (Compare **latent**.)

manifest destiny *or* **Manifest Destiny**

manifesto; *pl.,* **manifestos** *or* **manifestoes**

manila *or* **manilla**

manila paper *or* **Manila paper**

manipulable *or* **manipulatable**

Mann, Thomas (1875–1955) German writer. Author of *Doktor Faustus*.

mannequin *or* **manikin** *or* **mannikin**

manqué Frustrated.

manslaughter Killing without expressed or deliberate malice.

mansuetude Gentleness.

mantel *or* **mantelpiece** A shelf above a fireplace. (Compare **mantle**.)

mantilla

mantis; *pl.,* **mantises** *or* **mantes**

mantle A cape, cloak. (Compare **mantel**.)

manual

manuf. Abbreviation for *manufacture, manufacturing*.

manufacture To construct using labor, machinery.

manumit

manure

manuscript

Manx cat

many, more, most

many-sided

Mao Tse-Tung (1893–1976) Chinese Marxist. Developer of Chinese Communist party and leader of the 1966 Cultural Revolution.

Maoist

maple sugar

maple syrup

mapmaker
marabou *or* marabout
maraschino *or* Maraschino
marathoner
marble cake
marbling *or* marbleizing
Mardi Gras
marg. Abbreviation for *marginal;
margin.*
margarine
marginalia
margarita
marijuana
marinade; marinate
Marine Corps *or* the
Marines Capitalize if referring
to the specific branch of the
United States armed forces.
marital Concerning marriage.
(Compare **martial**.)
markdown As noun.
marketplace
market research *or* marketing
research
market value
markup As noun.
marmalade
marquee A canopy or tent.
(Compare **marquise**.)
marquise A gem cutting.
(Compare **marquee**.)
marsala *or* Marsala
marshal *or* marshall
marshland
marshmallow
marsupial
marten A weasel-like animal.
(Compare **martin**.)
martial Concerning war, military.
(Compare **marital**.)
martian *or* Martian

martin A swallow. (Compare
marten.)
martinet
martini
Martin Luther King Day
martyr
marveled *or* marvelled
marvelous *or* marvellous
Marx, Karl (1818–1883) German
political philosopher. Author of
Das Kapital and *The Communist
Manifesto.*
Marxist
marzipan
masc. *or* m. Abbreviations for
masculine.
mascara
masochism
mason jar
Mason-Dixon line
masquerade *or* masque *or* mask
massacre
masseur, masseuse
mass medium; *pl.*, mass media
mass-produce
mastectomy; *pl.*,
mastectomies Operation(s) to
remove a (usually cancerous)
breast.
masterful Authoritative,
overpowering. (Compare
masterly.)
master key
masterly Knowledgeable, skillful.
(Compare **masterful**.)
mastermind
master of ceremonies *or* emcee *or*
MC
masterpiece *or* masterwork
master plan
masterstroke
masthead

mastiff A breed of dog.

mat or matt or matte Dull, not glossy or shiny.

matchbook

matchbox

matchmaker

match play

match point

matchstick

-mate Compounds ending in -mate are written as one word (e.g., soulmate).

materia medica Latin; literally, "medical matter," the study of drugs and remedies.

matériel or materiel Supplies for an organization.

math. Abbreviation for mathematics, mathematical.

mathematical or mathematic

mathematician

mathematics or math

matinee or matinée

matinee idol

matriarch Mother, female head of group.

matrix; pl., matrices or matrixes

matter of course

matter-of-fact

mature

matutinal

matzo or matzoh; pl., matzoth or matzos or matzohs

matzo ball

maudlin

maul To beat up.

maunder To grumble, mumble. (Compare meander.)

Maundy Thursday or Holy Thursday The Thursday before Easter.

mausoleum; pl., mausoleums or mausolea

mauve

maven or mavin

mawkish

maximum; pl., maxima or maximums

may, might

mayapple

maybe

Mayday A distress signal. (Compare May Day.)

May Day Celebration on the first day of May. (Compare Mayday.)

mayhem

mayonnaise

mayor Capitalize only if part of formal title preceding name: Mayor Jane M. Byrne.

maypole

maze A winding path or puzzle. (Compare maize.)

McIntosh A variety of red apple; also a brand name of a computer. (Compare mackintosh.)

M.D. Abbreviation for medical doctor.

M-day or mobilization day

mea culpa Latin; literally, "through my fault," acknowledgment that oneself is to blame.

Mead, Margaret (1901–1978) American anthropologist and writer.

meadowland

meadowlark

meager or meagre

meal ticket

mealtime

mealybug

mealymouthed

mean The sum of a series of numbers divided by the count of those numbers. (Compare **median**.)

mean, meant

meander To wander. (Compare **maunder**.)

mean-spirited

meantime

meanwhile

measurable *or* **mensurable**

measures Weights and measures may be abbreviated when used with numbers designating units (e.g., *2 lbs., 1 tbsp*). If the number is written out, the unit of measure is written out (e.g., *four cups, ten miles*).

Abbreviations for metric units are usually not punctuated (e.g., *10 km*); standard units are usually punctuated (e.g., *10 mi.*).

See Appendix 8, **Weights and measures**.

meat-and-potatoes As adjective.

meat and potatoes As noun.

meatball

meat loaf

mech. Abbreviation for *mechanic, mechanics, mechanical, mechanism, mechanized*.

mechanical drawing *or* **mechanical**

med. Abbreviation for *medium; medical; median*.

medal An emblem, usually a piece of metal, made to commemorate some event, or awarded for some distinguished action. Capitalize if part of proper noun or as name of specific honor: *Medal for Achievement*. (Compare **meddle**.)

medalist *or* **medallist**

Medal of Honor

meddle To interfere. (Compare **medal**.)

Medfly *or* **Mediterranean fruit fly**

medi-, medio- Compounds of this combining form, which means middle, are written as one word (e.g., *mediacy*).

median The number exactly in the middle of a series of values; that is, the number having an equal number of values on either side. (Compare **mean**.)

median strip

mediate To listen to arguments of two parties and offer reason and counsel from a more neutral standpoint.

medic

Medicaid *or* **medicaid**

medical terms Names of diseases, conditions, symptoms, tests, and so forth are lowercase except for any proper nouns contained in a name.

Organisms described by their Latin names follow the guidelines under **scientific terms**. Drug names are lowercase; trade or brand names are capitalized.

Medicare *or* **medicare**

medicinal *or* **medicinable**

medico; *pl.*, medicos

medico- Compounds formed with *medico-* are written as one word.

medieval *or* **mediaeval**

mediocre

Mediterranean

medium; *pl.*, mediums *or* media

medium-size *or* **medium-sized**

medulla oblongata; *pl.*, medulla

oblongatas *or* **medullae oblongatae**

meet, met

meetinghouse

meeting of minds

mega-, meg- Compounds of this combining form, which means large or great, or a million, are written as one word (e.g., *megascopic, megabucks*).

megabyte *or* **MB**

megahertz *or* **MHz**

megal-, megalo- Compounds of this combining form, which means large, great, or powerful, are written as one word (e.g., *megalomania*).

megalith

megalomaniac *or* **megalomaniacal** *or* **megalomanic**

megalopolis *or* **megapolis**

meiosis

Meir, Golda (1898–1978) Israeli politician who helped form the Labor party and eventually served as prime minister of the country.

melancholia

mélange French; a hodgepodge.

melba toast

melee *or* **mêlée** A brawl.

meliorate Variant for *ameliorate*.

melodious *or* **melodic**

melting point *or* **mp** *or* **MP**

melting pot

Melville, Herman (1819–1891) American writer. Author of *Moby Dick*.

membranous

memento; *pl.*, **mementos** *or* **mementoes**

memo; *pl.*, **memos** Short form of *memorandum*.

memorabilia

memorandum; *pl.*, **memorandums** *or* **memoranda**

Memorial Day *or* **Decoration Day**

memory lane

ménage à trois French; literally, "a household for three," a domestic arrangement of three people who are sexually involved with each other.

menagerie

Mencken, H. L. (1880–1956) American journalist and writer.

mendacity Deceptiveness, lying. (Compare **mendicancy**.)

mendicancy *or* **mendicity** Begging. (Compare **mendacity**.)

meningitis

menopause

Menorah A nine-branched candelabrum used during Hanukah.

menstruate

mentor

menu; *pl.*, **menus**

meow

mephitic

mercenary

merchant marine

merchant ship

merciful

mercurial

Mercurochrome

mercy killing *or* **euthanasia**

meretricious

meridian

meringue

merino; *pl.*, **merinos**

merit system

merry-go-round

merrymaker

mes-, meso- Compounds of this

combining form, which means in
the middle, are written as one
word: *mesolithic*.

mesalliance; *pl.*, mesalliances

mesmerize

mesquite A type of wood.

mess hall

messiah Capitalize when referring
to a religious figure.

mess kit

mestizo; *pl.*, mestizos Spanish; a
person of mixed European and
Native American ancestry.

meta-, met- Compounds of this
combining form, which means
changed in position or form, or
altered, are written as one word
(e.g., *metacarpal, metalanguage,
metaphysics*).

metaled *or* metalled

metalware

metalwork

metamorphose

**metamorphosis; *pl.*,
metamorphoses**

metaph. *or* met. Abbreviations for
*metaphor, metaphorical;
metaphysics, metaphysical*.

metaphor A comparison or
expression made in figurative
language, describing one thing in
terms of another. (Compare
simile.)

metaphoric *or* metaphorical

metastasis; *pl.*, metastases

metastasize

mete To dole out.

meteor. *or* meteorol.
Abbreviations for *meteorology,
meteorological*.

meter *or* m.

methadone *or* methadon

methinks, methought

methodical *or* methodic

métier *or* metier French; talent,
vocation.

métis *or* Métis French; a person of
mixed French-Canadian and
Native American ancestry.

metonymy

me-too

metr-, metro- Compounds of this
combining form, which means
measure, are written as one word
(e.g., *metronome, metropolitan*).

metric *or* metrical

-metric, -metrical Compounds
formed with these endings are
written as one word (e.g.,
isometric).

mettalize *or* metalize

mettle Vigor, spirit.

mew

mewl To cry weakly.

mezzanine

mezzo-soprano

mezzotint

mfd. Abbreviation for
manufactured.

mfg. Abbreviation for
manufacturing.

mfr. Abbreviation for
manufacture, manufacturer.

mgr. Abbreviation for *manager*.

MIA Abbreviation for *missing in
action*.

miasma; *pl.*, miasmas *or* miasmata

Michelangelo Buonarroti
(1475–1564) Italian Renaissance
and mannerist sculptor, painter,
architect, and poet. Painted
the ceiling of the Sistine
Chapel.

Mickey Mouse

micr-, micro- Compounds of this combining form, which means little or minute, are written as one word (e.g., *microchip, microcomputer, microcosm, microeconomics, microorganism*).

microbiological *or* **microbiologic**

microfiche; *pl.*, **microfiche** *or* **microfiches**

microphone *or* **mike**

microscopic *or* **microscopical**

microwave oven

mid- Compounds formed with *mid-* are usually written as one word, except when the second word is a proper noun or is a figure (e.g., *midair, midday, midline, midpoint, midsection, midsize, midterm, midtown, midway*, but *mid-Victorian*).

mid. Abbreviation for *middle*.

Middle Ages

middle ear

Middle East *or* **Mideast**

middle ground

middle management

middle name

middle school

middle-aged

middle-American As adjective.

Middle American As noun.

middle-class

middle-of-the-road As adjective.

middle of the road As noun.

middleweight

mid-life

midnight Twelve A.M. (Compare **noon**.)

midriff

Midwest *or* **Middle West**

midwife

mien One's personality, demeanor.

mignon Filet mignon, a choice loin cut of beef.

migraine

mil One one-thousandth of an inch. (Compare **mill**.)

mil. *or* **mill.** Abbreviations for *million*.

mildew

mile *or* **mi.**

mileage

milestone

miliaria A skin inflammation resulting from inflammation of the sweat glands, as from exposure to heat.

milieu; *pl.*, **milieus** *or* **milieux** French; setting, surroundings, environment.

militancy *or* **militance**

military academy Capitalize only if part of proper noun.

military *or* **militaries**

militate To carry weight, have an effect.

militia

milk-and-water

milk glass

milk shake *or* **milkshake**

milkweed

Milky Way

mill One one-thousandth of a dollar (0.1 cents, or $0.001). (Compare **mil**.)

-mill Compounds ending in *-mill* are written as one word (e.g., *lumbermill*).

Mill, John Stuart (1806–1873) English philosopher and economist.

Millay, Edna St. Vincent (1892–1950) American poet and

dramatist. Author of *The Harp Weaver and Other Poems*.

millenary A group of one thousand. (Compare **millinery**.)

millennia *or* **millenniums**

Miller, Henry (1891–1980) American autobiographical writer. Author of *The Tropic of Cancer*.

milli- Compounds formed with *milli-*, which means a one-thousandth part of, are written as one word.

milligram *or* **mg** *or* **mgm** *or* **mgrm**

milliliter *or* **ml**

millimeter *or* **mm**

millinery Women's hats. (Compare **millenary**.)

millionaire

millpond

millstone

millstream

millwork

Milton, John (1608–1674) English poet. Author of *Paradise Lost*.

milquetoast

mimeograph

mimosa

min. Abbreviation for *minute*.

minable *or* **mineable**

minaret A narrow tower.

mincemeat

mince pie

mind-blowing

mind-boggling

-minded Compounds ending in *-minded* are written as one word (e.g., *strongminded*).

mind reader

mind reading

mind-set

mind's eye

mineral oil

mineral water

minestrone

mini- Compounds formed with *mini-*, which means very small or very short, are written as one word (e.g., *minibike, minicar, minicomputer, miniseries, miniskirt*).

miniature

miniature schnauzer

minimize

minimum; *pl.,* **minima** *or* **minimums**

minimum wage

mink; *pl.,* **mink** *or* **minks**

minority; *pl.,* **minorities**

minor-league As adjective.

minor league As noun.

mint julep

minuet

minuscule *or* **miniscule**

minus sign

minute, minuter, minutest

minute hand

minuteman; *pl.,* **minutemen**

minute steak

minutia; *pl.,* **minutiae**

MIPS Abbreviation for *million instructions per second*.

miracle drug

mirage An optical illusion.

mirror image

mirth

mis- When this prefix is used to mean "bad or wrong," "opposite," "not," or "unfavorable," compounds are written as one word (e.g., *misappropriate, misbegotten, miscast, misfit, misguidance, mislay, mislead, mispronounce, misquote, misread, misshapen,*

misspend, misstate, misstep,
misthink, misunderstand, misuse).
misanthrope
misc. Abbreviation for
miscellaneous, miscellany.
miscarriage
miscellanea
miscellaneous
miscellany; *pl.,* miscellanies
mischief
mischievous
miscible Able to be mixed.
miscreant Unbelieving, or
criminal.
misdeal, misdealt
misdemeanor
misdo, misdoes, misdid, misdone
mise-en-scène; *pl.,* mise-en-
scènes French; a film director.
miser A stingy person.
mishmash
misnomer
missile An exploding weapon.
(Compare missive.)
missing link
Mississippi
missive A letter of communication.
(Compare missile.)
misspelled *or* misspelt
mistake, mistook
mistletoe
mistral
misty-eyed
miter *or* mitre
miter box
miter square
mitigate To soften, alleviate.
mitosis; *pl.,* mitoses
mitt
mixed-up
mixture
mix-up As noun.

m.m. Abbreviation for *mutatis
mutandis,* "necessary changes
being made," substituting new
terms.
mnemonic A memory aid.
moat A water-filled ditch
surrounding something. (Compare
mote.)
mobile
moccasin
mocha
mock-heroic
mockingbird
mock-up As noun.
mod. Abbreviation for *moderate;
modify, modified, modification;
modern.*
modeled *or* modelled
modem Modulator/demodulator, a
device that allows a computer user
to send computer data over
telephone lines.
moderate
modicum
modular
modus operandi; *pl.,* modi
operandi Abbreviation is *M.O.*
modus vivendi; *pl.,* modi vivendi
mogul
mohair The hair of an Angora
goat, considered a precious fiber,
or a fabric or yarn made from this
hair.
moiety; *pl.,* moieties One of two
equal parts.
moiré *or* moire French; a wavy
pattern on cloth.
moisten
molar
molasses
molding *or* moulding
moldy

134

molehill
molestation
mollify
mollusk *or* mollusc
Molotov cocktail A homemade hand grenade made from a bottle filled with gasoline and a strip of cloth as a wick for igniting it.
molt
mol. wt. Abbreviation for *molecular weight*.
moment of truth
momentum; *pl.,* **momenta** *or* **momentums**
mommy; *pl.,* **mommies**
mon-, mono- Compounds of this combining form, which means one, are written as one word (e.g., *monosyllable, monotone*).
monarchical *or* **monarchic** *or* **monarchal** *or* **monarchial**
monastery; *pl.,* **monasteries**
Monet, Claude (1840–1926) Premier French Impressionist painter. Works include the water lily and Rouen cathedral series. See *Manet, Edouard.*
monetary Concerning money supply.
money; the plural moneys *or* **monies** Means sums of money and are terms now used chiefly in law.
moneybags
money changer
moneyed *or* monied
money-maker
money market
money order
-monger Compounds ending in *-monger* are written as one word (e.g., *rumormonger*).

Mongoloid
mongoose; *pl.,* **mongooses** *or* **mongeese**
mongrel
moniker *or* monicker
monkey; *pl.,* **monkeys**
monkey bars
monkey business
monkeypod
monkeyshines
monkey wrench
monochromatic
monocle
monogamous *or* monogamic
monologue
mononucleosis *or* mono
monosodium glutamate *or* MSG
Monotype
Monroe Doctrine
monsieur; *pl.,* **messieurs** Capitalize if part of formal title preceding a name.
monsignor; *pl.,* **monsignors** *or* **monsignori** Capitalize if part of formal title. Abbreviation is *Msgr.*
monsoon
montage
Montaigne, Michel Eyquem de (1533–1592) French essayist.
Monterey Jack
Montezuma's revenge Traveler's diarrhea.
month; *pl.,* **months** Abbreviation is *mo.; pl., mos.*
monument Capitalize only if part of proper noun (e.g., *The Washington Monument*).
mooch To get something for free by stealing, begging, or cajoling (e.g., *to mooch a ride*).
moola *or* **moolah** Slang for "money."

moon May be capitalized when referring to Earth's satellite.

moonbeam

moonlight, moonlighted As verb.

moonlit As adjective.

moonshine

moon shot *or* **moon shoot**

moonstruck

moony

moose; *pl.,* **moose**

mop To clean a floor with a long-handled absorbent tool. (Compare **mope**.)

mope To be gloomy, apathetic, dispirited. (Compare **mop**.)

moped

moppet

moraine

moral A lesson to be learned. (Compare **morale**.)

morale Mental state, spirit. (Compare **moral**.)

morass A swamp.

moratorium; *pl.,* **moratoriums** *or* **moratoria**

mordant Biting, incisive.

more and more

more or less

moreover

morgue

moribund

Mornay sauce

morning-after As adjective.

morning sickness

morose Sullen, depressed.

morpheme A linguistic unit. (Compare **morphine**.)

morphine A narcotic drug. (Compare **morpheme**.)

morphology

morris chair A large easy chair

with removable cushions and an adjustable back.

Morse code

morsel

mortal sin

mortarboard

mortgagee

mortgagor *or* **mortgager**

mortise *or* **mortice**

mortuary

mosaic

mosey, moseyed

Moslem *or* **Muslim** An adherent of Islam.

mosque

mosquito; *pl.,* **mosquitoes** *or* **mosquitos**

mosquito net

mossback

mot juste; *pl.,* **mots justes** French; the most suitable word or phrase.

mote A dot, speck. (Compare **moat**.)

moth; *pl.,* **moths**

mothball

moth-eaten

Mother Goose The fictitious author of a collection of traditional English nursery rhymes.

mother-in-law; *pl.,* **mothers-in-law**

mother-of-pearl *or* **nacre**

Mother Teresa

Mother's Day The second Sunday in May.

mothproof

motif Theme. (Compare **motive**.)

motile

motion picture

motion sickness

motive Reason, cause. (Compare motif.)

motley

motor A device that uses power from outside source. (Compare engine.)

motorbike

motorboat

motorcar

motorcycle

motor home

motor inn

motor lodge

motor scooter

motor vehicle

motto; pl., mottoes or mottos

mount, mountain Capitalize if part of proper noun (e.g., We climbed Porcupine Mountain). Abbreviation is Mt.

mountaineer

mountain lion

mountainside

mountain time or mountain standard time or MT or MST. Mountain daylight time is MDT.

mountaintop

mountebank A deceiving person.

Mountie or Mounty A member of the Royal Canadian Mounted Police.

mourning dove

mouse; pl., mice

mousetrap

mousse A creamy dessert; or, a foamy hair-styling product.

mousy or mousey

mouth; pl., mouths

-mouthed Compounds ending in -mouthed are written as one word (e.g., openmouthed).

mouthpiece

mouth-to-mouth

mouthwash

movable or moveable

moviegoer

moviemaker

movie titles (see Part 2, Titles of works.)

mow, mowed or mown

moxie Courage, spunk.

Mozart, Wolfgang Amadaeus (1756–1791) Austrian musician and composer. Composer of The Marriage of Figaro.

mozzarella

MP Abbreviation for military police, mounted police, or member of Parliament.

mpg or MPG Abbreviation for miles per gallon.

mph or MPH Abbreviation for miles per hour.

Mr., pl., Messrs. Courtesy title for a man, men.

Mrs., pl., Mrs. Traditional courtesy title for married woman, women. Ms. is now generally preferred.

MS or ms; pl., MSS or mss Abbreviations for manuscript; pl., manuscripts.

Ms. The courtesy title of preference for women, equivalent to Mr. for men.

msg. Abbreviation for message.

msgr. or msngr. Abbreviations for messenger.

msl or MSL Abbreviation for mean sea level.

much, more, most

much as

mucilaginous

muckamuck

muckraker

mucous Means slimy. (Compare **mucus**.)

mucous membrane *or* **mucosa**

mucus Slime from a gland. (Compare **mucous**.)

muddleheaded

mudguard

mudslinger

Muenster cheese

mufti Arabic; a judge who interprets the law of Islam; or, ordinary, civilian clothes (as opposed to a military uniform).

mug shot

mugwump

mukluk Eskimo; an Eskimo slipper or soft boot made from hide.

mulatto; *pl.,* **mulattoes** *or* **mulattos** A person whose racial ancestry includes both black and white.

mulberry

mulch A gardening technique that involves spreading a protective ground cover. (Compare **mulct**.)

mulct To fine or swindle. (Compare **mulch**.)

mullein *or* **mullen**

mulligan stew

mulligatawny

multi- Compounds formed with *multi-*, meaning many, are written as one word unless the second word is a proper noun or begins with *i* (e.g., *multi-industry*, but *multinational, multipurpose*).

multiculturalism

multifarious

multiple-choice

multiple personality

multiple sclerosis *or* MS

multiplex

mumbo jumbo

mummify

mumps

munchies

mundane

municipal

munificent

murky

murmur

Murphy bed

Murphy's Law

mus. Abbreviation for *museum; music, musical*.

muscadet *or* Muscadet

muscle-bound

muscular dystrophy

museum Capitalize only if part of proper noun: *Metropolitan Museum of Art*.

mushroom

musical chairs

music box

musician

musketeer

muskmelon

muskrat; *pl.,* **muskrat** *or* **muskrats**

Muslim *or* **Moslem** Adherents of the Islamic faith.

muslin

mussel The shellfish.

Mussolini, Benito (1883–1945) Italian dictator.

mustache *or* moustache

mustached *or* mustachioed

mutatis mutandis Latin; with the necessary changes having been made (as in drafts of a document).

mutt

mutual
mutually exclusive
muumuu
Muzak
muzzle
MVP   Abbreviation for *most
    valuable player*.
myopia
myriad

myrrh
myrtle
myself
mystic *or* mystical
mysticism
mystique
mythical *or* mythic
mythological *or* mythologic

N

n. Abbreviation for Latin *natus*, "born."

n.; *pl.,* **nn.** Abbreviation for *note; pl., notes.*

NA Abbreviation for *not applicable; not available.*

NAACP Abbreviation for *National Association for the Advancement of Colored People.*

Nabokov, Vladimir (1899–1977) American novelist. Author of *Lolita.*

nacho; *pl.,* **nachos**

nacre *or* **mother-of-pearl**

nadir

nagger *or* **nag**

nailbrush

nail file

naive *or* **naïve**

naïveté *or* **naiveté** *or* **naivete**

naked

namby-pamby

nameable *or* **namable**

name-calling

name-dropping

name of the game

nameplate

namesake

nanny goat

napalm

naphtha

napoleon

Napoleon Bonaparte (1769–1821) French Emperor.

naptime

narcissism

narcissus; *pl.,* **narcissi** *or* **narcissuses** *or* **narcissus**

narcotic

narrow-minded

narthex

NASA Abbreviation for *National Aeronautics and Space Administration.* Spell out on first reference in text.

nasal

nascency *or* **nascence**

nascent

nasturtium

nat. Abbreviation for *national; natural.*

natatorium

national Capitalize only if part of proper noun: *National Security Council.*

national anthem

nationality Capitalize the proper nouns describing nationalities, ethnic groups, or tribes (e.g., *Pakistanis, Jews, Sioux*).

nation-state

nationwide

Native American

NATO Abbreviation for *North Atlantic Treaty Organization.*

Naugahyde A brand name for a type of imitation leather.

naught *or* **nought** Nothing.

naughty

nausea

nauseating Causing sickness, disgust. (Compare **nauseous.**)

nauseous *or* **nauseated** Affected by sickness, disgust. (Compare **nauseating.**)

nautical mile

nautilus; *pl.,* **nautiluses** *or* **nautili**

Navaho *or* **Navajo;** *pl.,* **Navaho** *or* **Navahos** *or* **Navajo** *or* **Navajos**

naval Concerning ships, shipping, or navies. Capitalize if part of proper noun (e.g., *U.S. Naval Academy*).

navel *or* **belly button**

navel orange

navigable

navy; *pl.,* **navies** Capitalize only if part of proper noun or referring to specific organization.

navy blue

navy yard

Nazi

Nazism *or* **Naziism**

N.B. Abbreviation for Latin *nota bene,* "mark well" or "take careful note."

NBA Abbreviation for *National Basketball Association.*

NC Abbreviation for *no change; no charge.*

ne-, neo- Most compounds made from this combining form, which means new or different, are written as one word, unless second word is a proper noun (e.g., *neo-Nazi,* but *neologism*).

Neanderthal

Neapolitan ice cream

neap tide The tide with the smallest range, between the first- and third-quarter moons.

nearby

near-miss

nearsighted

nebbish

nebula; *pl.,* **nebulas** *or* **nebulae**

nebulous *or* **nebular**

neck and neck

neckerchief; *pl.,* **neckerchiefs** *or* **neckerchieves**

necklace

necktie

necr-, necro- Compounds made

with this combining form, which means death, corpse, or dead tissue, are written as one word (e.g., *necrology, necromancy, necrophilia*).

necropolis; *pl.,* **necropolises** *or* **necropoles** *or* **necropoleis**

nectarine

needlepoint

needlework

need not *or* **needn't**

ne'er-do-well

nefarious

neg. Abbreviation for *negative.*

negator *or* **negater**

negative feedback

negligee *or* **negligé**

neighborhood

nemesis; *pl.,* **nemeses**

neoclassic *or* **neoclassical**

neo-impressionism

neomycin

neon

neonate

neophyte A beginner.

nephew

nephr-, nephro- Compounds formed from this combining form, which means kidney, are written as one word: *nephrogenic.*

nepotism

nerd

nerve center

nerve-racking *or* **nerve-wracking**

nervous breakdown

nervous Nellie *or* **nervous Nelly;** *pl.,* **nervous Nellies**

nescient

Nesselrode

nest egg Money put in savings for future needs.

netherworld

nettlesome
networking
Neufchâtel cheese
neur-, neuro- Compounds formed from this combining form, which means of the nerves or nervous system, are written as one word (e.g., *neurologist, neuromuscular*).
neural arch
neuron
neurosis
neut. Abbreviation for *neuter; neutral*.
neuter
neutral
neutron bomb
never-ending
never-failing
nevermore
never-never land
nevertheless
New Age
newborn; *pl.,* **newborn** *or* **newborns**
newcomer
new deal *or* **New Deal**
New England
newfangled
new-fashioned
newfound
New Left
newlywed
new math
new moon
news- Compounds written as one word include *newsbreak, newscast, newscaster, newsdealer, newsletter, newsmagazine, newspaper, newsperson, newsprint, newsreader, newsreel,* *newsroom, newsstand, newsweekly, newswriting*.
news conference
newspeak
newt
New Testament
Newton, Sir Isaac (1642–1727) English physicist and mathematician. Initiated the study of universal gravity after seeing an apple fall in his garden.
new wave *or* **New Wave**
New World North and South America. (Compare **Old World**.)
New Year's Day
next-door As adjective.
next door As adverb.
next of kin
nexus; *pl.,* **nexuses** *or* **nexus**
niacin
nicety
niche
nickel *or* **nickle**
nickel-and-dime As adjective.
nickel and dime, nickeled and dimed, nickeling and diming *or* **nickel and diming**
nickeled *or* **nickelled**
nickelodeon
nicknack Variant for *knickknack*.
nickname
nicotine
niece
Nietzsche, Friedrich Wilhelm (1844–1900) German philosopher and poet.
niggardly Miserly.
niggler Someone who constantly gripes or finds fault over petty issues.
night and day
night blindness

nightcap
nightclothes
nightclub
night court
nightfall
nightgown
nighthawk
nightie or nighty; pl., nighties
night letter
nightlife
night-light
nightmare
night owl
night rider
nightshade
nightshirt
nightstand
nightstick
night table
nighttime
nihilist
nil Nothing, zero.
nimbostratus
nimbus; pl., **nimbi** or **nimbuses**
Nimrod
Nin, Anaïs (1903–1977) American
writer. Author of her lifelong
Diary and *Seduction of the
Minotaur.*
nincompoop
ninepin(s)
nineteen
ninety; pl., nineties
ninny; pl., ninnies
ninth
nirvana
nisi Latin; taking effect at a
specified time.
nitpicker
nitr-, nitro- Compounds formed
with this combining form, which
means containing nitrogen

compounds, are written as one
word.
nitric acid
nitroglycerin or nitroglycerine
nitty-gritty
nitwit
nix
n.m. or **n.mi.** Abbreviation for
nautical mile.
no.; pl., **nos.** Abbreviation for
number; pl., numbers.
no-account
Nobel prize or Nobel Prize
nobody; pl., nobodies
nocturnal Active or occurring
during the night or happening
nightly. (Compare **diurnal**.)
nocuous
nodule
nodus; pl., nodi
no-fault
noggin
no-good
no-hitter
no-holds-barred
noisemaker
nolo contendere Latin; a legal plea
of no contest.
nom de guerre; pl., **noms de
guerre** French; pseudonym.
nom de plume; pl., **noms de
plume** French; a pen name, a
writer's pseudonym.
nom. Abbreviation for *nominative.*
nomenclature
nominative case
non- Compounds formed with *non-*
are usually written as one word,
except when the second word is a
proper noun (e.g., *non-Christian,*
but *nonalcoholic, noncommittal,
nonconformist, nondescript,*

nonentity, nonevent, nonexistent, noninvolvement, nonnative, nonsmoker, nonstop, nonviolent).

nonage Youth.

nonce word

nonchalant

noncommissioned officer

non compos mentis Latin; literally "not having control of one's mind," mentally unsound.

nonesuch Peerless, without equal.

nonetheless

nonhero *or* **anti-hero**

no-no; *pl.,* **no-no's** *or* **no-nos**

non obs. Abbreviation for Latin; *non obstante,* "notwithstanding."

no-nonsense

nonpareil French; unparalleled, without equal. Also, a type of chocolate candy.

nonplus, nonplussed *or* **nonplused** To put in a quandary.

nonprofit *or* **not-for-profit**

nonresidence *or* **nonresidency**

non seq. Abbreviation for Latin, *non sequitur,* "it does not follow."

non sequitur

noon Twelve P.M. (Compare midnight.)

no one

noontime

no place

normalcy

northbound

northeast; northeasterly

northerly

north-northeast

north-northwest

north pole *or* **North Pole**

North Star

northward *or* **northwards**

northwest; northwesterly

Norway spruce

nosebleed

nosedive As noun.

nose-dive As verb.

nosegay

nose job

nosh

no-show

nostalgia

nosy *or* **nosey**

nota bene Latin; take note. The abbreviation is *N.B.*

notary public; *pl.,* **notaries public** *or* **notary publics**

notebook

notepad

notepaper

noteworthy

notwithstanding

nougat

nous A reason, purpose.

nouveau riche; *pl.,* **nouveaux riches** French; literally, "newly rich," a person who has suddenly risen in economic status.

nouvelle cuisine

novelette *or* **novella**

novitiate The state of being a novice, as in a convent.

Novocain *or* **Novocaine** A trademark name for procaine, a local anesthetic.

nowadays

now and then

noway *or* **noways**

nowhere

no-win

nth degree

nuance A subtle difference, a shade (as in meaning or color).

nucle-, nucleo- Compounds made from these combining forms, which mean nucleus or nuclear, are written as one word.

nuclear

nucleus; *pl.,* **nuclei** *or* **nucleuses**

nugatory

nuisance

nuke As noun or verb.

null and void

null-space

number one

number(s) The word *number* is abbreviated as *No.* when used with figures to indicate rank or rating. It is also abbreviated in tables and bibliographic matter (e.g., *Docket No. 053087*).

In ordinary text, if space and clarity permits, spell out whole numbers from one through ninety-nine, and any of these followed by *hundred, thousand, million,* etc. In other cases, use figures. This rule applies to both cardinal and ordinal numbers.

Plurals of numbers are formed by adding *s* alone (e.g., *1960s*).

The plural of a written-out number is also formed by adding *s* (e.g., *twos*).

Possessives are formed the same as if the number were written out: singulars add *s* (e.g., *1990's car of the year*), plurals add an apostrophe only (e.g., *the 1990s' most celebrated author*).

numerical *or* **numeric**

numero uno Number one.

numskull *or* **numbskull**

nunchaku Japanese; a type of weapon.

nursery rhyme

nursery school

nurse's aide

nursing home

nutcracker

nuthatch

nutmeg

nuts-and-bolts As adjective.

nuts and bolts As noun.

nutshell

nylon

nymph

oak; *pl.*, **oaks** or **oak**

oasis; *pl.*, **oases**

oath; *pl.*, **oaths**

ob. Abbreviation for Latin, *obiit*, "died."

obdurate Stubborn, hardened, unyielding. (Compare **indurate**.)

obeisant

obelisk

obese

obey

OB-GYN Abbreviation for *obstetrician-gynecologist* or *obstetrics-gynecology*.

obiter dictum; *pl.*, **obiter dicta** Latin; literally, "something said in passing," an insignificant comment.

obituary or **obit**

obj. Abbreviation for *object; objective; objection*.

objet d'art; *pl.*, **objets d'art** French; an object that is valuable for its artistry.

objurgate To criticize harshly.

obligated Having a moral or legal responsibility. (Compare **obliged**.)

obliged Indebted, bound to do a favor for. (Compare **obligated**.)

oblique

oblong

obloquy; *pl.*, **obloquies**

oboe; **oboist**

obs. Abbreviation for *obsolete; obscure*.

obscene

obsequious

observatory Capitalize only if part of proper noun.

obsessive-compulsive

obsolete; obsolescent; obsolescence

obstacle course

obstetric or obstetrical

obstreperous

occ. Abbreviation for *occasional, occasionally*.

occup. Abbreviation for *occupation, occupational*.

ocean Capitalize only if part of proper noun (e.g., *the Indian Ocean*, but *we took a swim in the ocean*).

oceanographic or oceanographical

ocher or ochre

o'clock According to the clock (e.g., *Six o'clock is our closing time*).

OCR Abbreviation for *optical character reader, optical character recognition*.

octavo; *pl.*, **octavos**

octopus; *pl.*, **octopuses** or **octopi**

OD, OD'd or **ODed** Variant for *overdose, overdosed*.

O/D Abbreviation for *overdraft, overdrawn*.

-odd Compounds ending in *-odd* are hyphenated (e.g., *twenty-odd*).

oddball

odd lot

odds and ends

odds-on

ode

odorous or odoriferous

odyssey; *pl.*, **odysseys**

Oedipus complex

OEM Abbreviation for *original equipment manufacturer*.

off. or **offic.** Abbreviation for *official*.

-off Compounds ending in *-off* are

written as one word (e.g.,
takeoff).

offal Waste, by-product.

off and on

offbeat

Off-Broadway As adjective and
adverb.

Off Broadway As noun.

off-chance

off-color *or* **off-colored**

offense *or* **offence**

offhand *or* **offhanded**

off-hour

office Capitalize only if part of
proper noun: *the Oval Office.*

officeholder

official Concerning an office;
authoritative. (Compare **officious**.)

officious Meddlesome, interfering.
(Compare **official**.)

off-key

off-limits

off-line

Off-Off-Broadway

off-peak

offprint

off-road vehicle

off-season

offscreen

offset

offshoot

offshore

offspring; *pl.,* **offspring** *or*
offsprings

offstage

off-the-cuff

off-the-record

off-the-shelf

off-the-wall

offtrack

off-white

off year

oftentimes *or* **ofttimes**

ogle

ogre

oh well

oilcan

oilcloth

oil color

oil field

oil paint

oil slick

oil well

OK *or* **okay**, **OKs** *or* **okays** As
noun.

OK *or* **okay**, **OK's** *or* **okays** As
verb.

O'Keefe, Georgia (1887–1986)
American abstract painter. Known
for floral forms, desert terrain,
and bleached animal skulls. Wife
of Alfred Stieglitz.

okeydoke *or* **okeydokey**

okra

-old Compounds with *-old*
designating age are hyphenated
(e.g., *five-year-old*).

old country A European
immigrant's country of origin.

older *or* **elder**

old-fashioned

old fogy

old-fogyish

old guard *or* **Old Guard**

old hand

old hat

old-line

old-school As adjective.

old school As noun.

old style As noun.

Old Testament

old-timer

old-world As adjective.

Old World Europe. (Compare New World.)

oleomargarine

olive branch Used figuratively to mean a gesture of peace.

olive drab

olla podrida; *pl.*, **olla podridas** *or* **ollas podridas** Spanish; a type of spicy stew. Also used generally to mean a hodgepodge.

Olympiad

Olympic Games

ombré French; colors that blend into each other from light to dark.

omelet *or* **omelette**

omni- Compounds formed with *omni-*, a combining form meaning all, are written as one word (e.g., *omnibus, omnifarious, omnipotent, omnipresent, omniscient*).

omnium-gatherum; *pl.*, **omnium-gatherums** Latin; a miscellaneous collection of people or things.

-on Compounds ending in *-on* are hyphenated (e.g., *hanger-on*).

on-again, off-again

on and off

once-over

one-handed

one-horse

one-on-one

one-piece

onerous Burdensome, troublesome.

oneself

one-shot

one-sided

one-step

onetime

one-track

one-two punch

one-up As verb.

one up As adjective.

one-way

ongoing

onionskin

on-line *or* **online**

onlooker

onomatopoeia Language (as a spoken word or expression) that sounds like what it describes (e.g., *fizz, choo-choo train*).

onrush

on-screen

onset

onshore

onside kick

on-site

onslaught

onstage

on-the-job

onus Burden, obligation.

onward *or* **onwards**

onyx

oodles

oompha *or* **oompah-pah**

oops

op. cit. Abbreviation for Latin, *opere citato*, "in the work cited," or *opus citatum*, "from the work cited." Used in scholarly writing.

OPEC Abbreviation for *Organization of Petroleum Exporting Countries*.

op-ed page The section of a newspaper where editorial comment, letters from readers, and opinion pieces appear.

open-air As adjective.

open air As noun.

open-and-shut

open bar

open-circuit

open-door As adjective.

open door As noun.

open-end

open-ended

open enrollment

openhanded

open-heart

open house

open-minded

openmouthed

open season

opera glass

opera house

opera titles (See Part 2, **Titles of works.**)

ophthalmologist *or* **oculist** A physician who specializes in diseases of the eye. (Compare **optician, optometrist.**)

opossum; *pl.,* **opossums** *or* **opossum**

Oppenheimer, J. Robert (1904–1967) American physicist. Developed the atomic bomb.

oppugn

optical *or* **optic**

optical illusion

optician A person who makes and deals with eye glasses and lenses. (Compare **ophthalmologist, optometrist.**)

optimum; *pl.,* **optima** *or* **optimums**

optimum *or* **optimal** As adjective.

optometrist An eye doctor who specializes in defects and refractory problems. (Compare **ophthalmologist, optician.**)

opus; *pl.,* **opera** *or* **opuses** A work, used to describe a musical composition.

OR Abbreviation for *operating room.*

oral By mouth or verbal. (Compare **aural.**)

orangeade

orange peel

orange pekoe

orangutan

order of business

ordinal number A number that indicates order in a sequence (e.g., *twelfth*).

ordinance A rule or regulation. (Compare **ordnance, ordonnance.**)

ordnance Military supplies. (Compare **ordinance, ordonnance.**)

ordonnance The proper or orderly arrangement of parts, as in a painting, literary material, etc. (Compare **ordinance, ordnance.**)

oregano

organ-, organo- Compounds are written as one word if the meaning is ''organic'' or concerning body organs.

organdy *or* **organdie**

organ-grinder

organism

organization Capitalize only if part of proper noun.

organza

orgy; *pl.,* **orgies**

orient *or* **orientate**

Orient Asia.

Oriental Pertaining to the Orient. When referring to a native of the Orient, use the term *Asian.*

Oriental rug

orienteering

origami

original sin

oriole (compare **aureole**)

Orlon A trademark name for a synthetic acrylic fiber resembling nylon.

ornith-, ornitho- Compounds of this combining form, which means bird, are written as one word: *ornithologist.*

orotund

orphan

orthodox According to prescribed form, traditional.

orthographic *or* **orthographical**

orthopedic *or* **orthopaedic**

oscillate

osmosis

ossify

oste-, osteo- Compounds of this combining form, which means bone or bones, are written as one word.

ostensible *or* **ostensive**

ostrich

OTC Abbreviation for *over-the-counter.*

otherworldly

otiose

ottoman

ought Should. (Compare **aught**.)

Ouija board

ourselves

ouster

out- Compounds formed with *out-* are usually written as one word (e.g., *outbreak, outdated*).

outage

out-and-out

outback

outbid, outbid *or* **outbidden**

outdoor *or* **outdoors**

outer space

outermost

outerwear

outfield

out-front

outhouse

out-of-bounds

out-of-court As adjective.

out-of-date

out-of-door *or* **out-of-doors**

out-of-pocket

out-of-print

out-of-the-way

out loud

outpatient

outpost

outrageous

outré French; outside the norm, bizarre, eccentric.

outshine, outshone *or* **outshined**

outsize *or* **outsized**

outward *or* **outwards**

outward-bound

ouzo

ovary; *pl.,* **ovaries**

ovenbaked

ovenproof

over *or* **o'er**

over- Many compounds formed with *over-* are written as one word (e.g., *override, overseas, overshirt*).

-over Compounds ending in *-over* are written as one word (e.g., *stopover*).

overalls

over and above

over and over

overbear, overborne *or* **overborn**

overleap, overleaped *or* **overleapt**

oversize *or* **oversized**

overt Obvious, manifest.

over-the-counter

over-the-hill

overture

overwrought

Ovid (43 B.C.–17 A.D.) Roman poet. Author of *Metamorphoses* and *Tristia*.

ovoid *or* **ovoidal**

ovum; *pl.,* **ova**

-owner Compounds ending in *-owner* are written as one word (e.g., *landowner*).

ox; *pl.,* **oxen** *or* **ox**

oxbow

oxford cloth

oxygen

oyster cracker

oz. Abbreviation for *ounce, ounces.*

P

p & h Abbreviation for *postage and handling*.

p's and q's

p.; *pl.,* **pp.** Abbreviation for *page; pl., pages.*

pabulum

pablum A brand name for a cereal food for infants. Derived from *pabulum*, and used interchangeably with it.

PAC Abbreviation for *political action committee*.

pace car

pacemaker

pacesetter

pachyderm

Pacific time *or* **PT**

pacifism *or* **pacificism**

pacifist *or* **pacificist** *or* **pacifistic**

package store

pack animal

packhorse

pack rat

pact Capitalize only if part of proper noun.

paddleball

paddle tennis

paddle wheel

paddy *or* **padi;** *pl.,* **paddies** *or* **padis**

paddy wagon

padre

paean A song of praise. (Compare **peon**.)

paella

pageantry

pagoda

Paine, Thomas (1737–1809) American political philosopher and writer. Author of *The Rights of Man*.

painkiller

painstaking

paintbrush

pair; *pl.,* **pairs** *or* **pair** Two of something. (Compare **pare**, **pear**.)

paisley

pajamas *or* **pajama**

palate The roof of the mouth, or sense of taste. (Compare **palette**, **pallet**, **pallette**.)

palatial Magnificent.

palaver

palazzo; *pl.,* **palazzi**

pale Very light in color.

pale-, paleo-, palae-, palaeo- Compounds of these combining forms, which mean ancient, prehistoric, or primitive, are written as one word (e.g., *paleontology*).

paleontological *or* **paleontologic**

palette A painter's board, or spectrum, range, especially of color. (Compare **palate**, **pallet**, **pallette**.)

palfrey; *pl.,* **palfreys**

palimony

palindrome Something that reads the same backward as forward (e.g., *1991*). (Compare **palinode**.)

palinode An ode or song. (Compare **palindrome**.)

palisade

pall A heavy covering, concealment.

palladium; *pl.,* **palladia**

pallbearer

pallet A movable platform, a small mattress, or a temporary bed.

(Compare **palate, palette, pallette**.)

pallette One of the pieces of a suit of armor. (Compare **palate, palette, pallet**.)

palliate

pallid Dull, pale. (Compare **pallor**.)

pall-mall A ball-and-mallet game. (Compare **pell-mell**.)

pallor Paleness. (Compare **pallid**.)

palmetto; *pl.*, **palmettos** *or* **palmettoes**

palmistry

palm oil

Palm Sunday

palomino; *pl.*, **palominos**

palooka An easily defeated boxer, or an oaf.

palpate To give medical exam by touch. (Compare **palpitate**.)

palpitate To beat, throb. (Compare **palpate**.)

palsy-walsy

paltry

pamphlet

panacea A cure-all, something that fixes anything.

panache Great style, flamboyance.

panama hat

Pan-American Involving all of both North and South America.

panatela A type of cigar.

pancake

Pan-Cake A brand name type of theatrical makeup.

pancreas

panda

pandemic Occurring over large area.

pandemonium

pander To stoop to gratify another.

Pandora's box A source of problems.

pandowdy; *pl.*, **pandowdies** A type of apple dessert.

pane Section of glass.

panegyric Elaborate praise.

panel, paneled *or* **panelled**

panel discussion

panfry

panhandler

panic button

panic-stricken

panne Heavy, lustrous velvet, silk, or satin.

pannier *or* **panier** One of a pair of bags or baskets strapped to a pack animal or to the rear wheels of a bicycle.

panoply; *pl.*, **panoplies**

panorama

pansy; *pl.*, **pansies**

pantaloon

pantheistic *or* **pantheistical**

pantheon

panther; *pl.*, **panthers** *or* **panther**

pantie *or* **panty**; *pl.*, **panties**

pantomime

pantsuit *or* **pants suit**

panty hose *or* **pantyhose**

papal Concerning the pope of the Roman Catholic church.

paparazzo; *pl.*, **paparazzi** Italian; a photographer who doggedly follows celebrities in order to take candid pictures of them.

papaw *or* **pawpaw**

papaya

paperback As noun.

paperback *or* **paperbound** *or* **paperbacked** As adjective.

paperboard
paper cutter
paperhanger
paper money
paper-thin
paper tiger   Something or someone that acts fierce or poses a threat but is actually ineffective or powerless.
paperweight
paperwork
papier-mâché
papilla; *pl.*, papillae
papoose
paprika
Pap smear *or* Pap test
papyrus; *pl.*, papyruses *or* papyri
par.   Abbreviation for *paragraph; parenthesis.*
para-, par-   Compounds of this combining form, which means beside or secondary, or a protection against, are written as one word (e.g., *parachute, paradigm, paradox, paragraph, paralegal, paranormal, paraphrase, paraplegia, paraprofessional, paratroops.*)
parable
parabola
paradisiacal *or* paradisiac *or* paradisaic *or* paradisaical   Heavenly.
paraffin
parakeet *or* parrakeet
parallel
parallelogram
paralysis; *pl.*, paralyses
paramedic *or* paramedical   As noun.
paramedical *or* paramedic   As adjective.

parameter   A set of properties; characteristic.
paranoia; paranoiac *or* paranoic
parapet
paraphernalia
parasitic *or* parasitical
parasol
parboil
parcel, parceled *or* parcelled
parcel post
Parcheesi
pare   To shave the outer covering off. (Compare **pair, pear.**)
paregoric
parenthesis; *pl.*, parentheses
parenthetic *or* parenthetical
parenthood
parent-teacher association *or* PTA
parent-teacher organization *or* PTO
paresis; *pl.*, pareses   Partial paralysis.
par excellence   French; literally, "by preeminence," the best thing of its kind, unequaled (e.g., *a teacher par excellence*).
parfait glass
pariah   An outcast.
parietal bone
pari-mutuel   A system of betting on races, or the machine that takes such bets.
paring knife
pari passu   Latin; side by side, stride for stride (e.g., *The two hurried along, pari passu*).
parishioner
parity; *pl.*, parities
park   Capitalize only if part of proper noun or address. Abbreviations are *Pk.* or *P.*
parka

parking lot

parking meter

Parkinson's disease

parkland

parkway Capitalize only if part of address. Abbreviation is *Pkwy*.

parlay To make into something better; exploit. (Compare **parley**.)

parley Conversation. (Compare **parlay**.)

parliament Capitalize if part of proper noun.

parlor car

parlor game

parlous Dangerous.

Parmesan cheese

parmigiana *or* **parmigiano**

parochial school

parodic *or* **parodistic**

parody; *pl.,* **parodies**

parol Word of mouth (e.g., *The news spread quickly by parol*). (Compare **parole**.)

parole The conditional release of a prisoner before his or her term expires. (Compare **parol**.)

paroxysm A sudden attack, action.

parquet, parqueted

parquetry; *pl.,* **parquetries**

parsimony

parsley

parsonage

part. Abbreviation for *participle*.

partake, partook

parterre The part of a theater floor that is under the rear balcony.

Parthenon The temple to Athena on the acropolis in Athens, Greece.

partiality

partible Able to be divided. (Compare **partitive**.)

particle physics

particleboard

parti-color *or* **parti-colored**

particularly

parting of the ways

partisan *or* **partizan**

partitive Dividing or denoting division. (Compare **partible**.)

partly *or* **partially**

part of speech

partridge; *pl.,* **partridge** *or* **partridges**

part-time *or* **PT**

parturient Bearing young.

partway

party line

PASCAL A computer programming language.

Pascal, Blaise (1623–1662) French scientist, mathematician, and philosopher.

pas de deux French; literally, "step for two," a dance for two performers, or more; generally, an intricate activity involving two people.

paseo; *pl.,* **paseos** Promenade.

pass Bills are *passed*. (See also **adopt, approve, enact**.)

pass-fail

passable Acceptable, okay. (Compare **passible**.)

passageway

passbook *or* **bankbook**

passed ball

passel A large group.

passenger

passerby; *pl.,* **passersby**

passible sensitive. (Compare **passable**.)

passim Latin; here and there.

passing shot

passionflower
passion fruit
passion play
passive resistance Noncooperation with government or authority.
passkey
Passover
passport
pass-through
password
pasta
pastel
pasteup
Pasteur, Louis (1882–1895) French chemist and microbiologist. Disproved the idea that minute organisms are produced through spontaneous generation.
pasteurize
pastiche or pasticcio A work that borrows from or imitates a number of disparate other works.
pastime Leisure activity.
pastoral
pastrami or pastromi
pastry; pl., pastries
patchouli or patchouly An East Indian shrubby mint that yields a fragrant essential oil used as a perfume.
patch test
patchwork
pate The head. (Compare pâté.)
pâté A meat paste served as a spread. (Compare pate.)
pâté de foie gras Goose liver pâté.
patella Kneecap.
patent leather
paternoster A prayer or incantation.
path; pl., paths

path-, patho- Compounds made up of this combining form, which refers to disease, are written as one word (e.g., pathogenic).
pathetic or pathetical
pathfinder
pathological or pathologic
pathos A pitiable quality or state.
pathway
patience Means the ability to bear events calmly.
patients Means people who contract a doctor for health-care services. (Compare patience.)
patina; pl., patinas or patinae
patio; pl., patios
patisserie
patois French; jargon, dialect.
patr-, patri-, patro- Compounds of these combining forms, which mean father, are written as one word (e.g., patrilineal).
patriarch Father, male head of group. (Compare patrician.)
patrician Aristocrat. (Compare patriarch.)
patronage
patron saint
patsy; pl., patsies
patty or pattie; patties
pattycake
paucity
pauperism
pave To cover with a smooth surface for traveling. (Compare pavé.)
pavé or pavéed or pavéd Closely set together, as with jewels. (Compare pave.)
pavilion
Pavlovian
pawnbroker

pawnshop
pay, paid
pay-as-you-go
payer *or* payor
payback
paycheck
payday
pay dirt
payed out   To slacken or allow to run out.
pay envelope
payload
payment
payoff   As adjective and noun.
payola   A bribe.
payout   As noun.
payroll
pay station
pay-TV *or* pay-cable *or* subscription TV
PBS   Abbreviation for *Public Broadcasting Service*.
PC   Abbreviation for *personal computer*.
PCB   Abbreviation for *polychlorinated biphenyl*.
pct. *or* **p.c.**   Abbreviations for *percent, percentage*.
P.D.   Abbreviation for *police department*.
PDT   Abbreviation for *Pacific Daylight Time*.
pea; *pl.*, peas *or* pease
Peace Corps
peacekeeping
peacemaker
peace offering
peace pipe
peace sign
peacetime
peach Melba
peacock, peahen, peafowl

pea green
pea jacket
peaked   Pale.
peanut oil
pear   The fruit. (Compare **pair, pare**.)
Pearl Harbor
pearl onion
pear-shaped
peasant
peashooter
pea soup
peat moss
peccadillo; *pl.*, peccadilloes *or* peccadillos   A slight sin.
pecking order *or* peck order
pectoral muscle
peculate   To embezzle.
pecuniary   Having to do with money.
ped-, pede-, pedi-   Compounds of these combining forms, which mean foot or feet, are written as one word (e.g., *pedicure*).
ped-, pedo-, paed-, paedo-   Compounds of these combining forms, which mean small, small animal or child, or ground, soil or earth, are written as one word (e.g., *pedology, pedodontics*).
pedagogical *or* pedagogic
pedagogue *or* pedagog
pedal, pedaled *or* pedalled   To operate by pressing on a lever with the foot. (Compare **peddle**.)
pedal pushers
peddle   To offer for sale. (Compare **pedal**.)
peddler *or* pedlar
pedestrian
pediatrician *or* pediatrist
pedigreed *or* pedigree

157

peekaboo

peel To cut or remove the skin from.

peephole

peep show

peer An equal. (Compare pier.)

peevish

peewee

pegboard

peg leg

peignoir

pejorative Open to negative or disparaging connotations.

Peking duck

Pekingese or Pekinese; pl., Pekingese or Pekinese

pekoe

pelerine

pelican

pell-mell Confused, disordered. (Compare pall-mall.)

pellucid Easy to understand, or accepting of light.

pelvis; pl., pelvises or pelves

penal code

penalty box

penance

penchant A strong inclination.

pencil, penciled or pencilled

pencil pusher

pendant Something that is hanging, or a supplementary thing. (Compare pendent.)

pendent Overhanging, in the state of being suspended or pending. (Compare pendant.)

pendulum

penetrating or penetrative or penetrant Pervading, acute.

penguin

penicillin

peninsula Capitalize only if part of proper noun (e.g., the Gaspé Peninsula in Quebec).

penis; pl., penes or penises

penitence Regret, sorrow. (Compare penitent.)

penitent or penitential Regretful, sorrowful. (Compare penitence.)

penitentiary Capitalize only if part of proper noun.

penknife

penlight

pen name or nom de plume

penniless

Pennsylvania Dutch

penny; pl., pennies or pence

penny-ante As adjective.

penny ante As noun.

penny arcade

penny-pinching

pen pal

penta-, pent- Compounds of this combining form, which means five, are written as one word (e.g., pentathlete).

pentagon Capitalize if referring to U.S. military leadership or headquarters.

Pentecost; Pentecostal

penthouse

pent-up

penuche or panocha or panoche A fudgelike confection.

penult or penultima The next to last in series.

penumbra; pl., penumbrae or penumbras

penurious Stingy, frugal.

peon A servant or a menial person. (Compare paean.)

peony; pl., peonies

people; pl., people

people mover

peoples Persons united in culture, tradition, beliefs, or other common factor.

peplum

pepper mill

pepper shaker

peppercorn

peppermint

pepperoni

peppertree

pep pill

pep talk

peradventure Maybe, possibly, by chance.

perambulate

per annum Every year.

percale

per capita Latin; literally, "by heads," for each individual.

percent or **per cent;** *pl.,* **percent** or **percents**

perchance

percolator

per contra On the other hand, by way of contrast.

percussion

per diem By the day (e.g., *She took the job on a per diem basis*).

perdu or **perdue** French; out of sight, in hiding, or concealed; or one who is lost, such as a soldier sent on a dangerous mission.

perdure To remain in existence. (Compare **perjure**.)

peregrination

peremptory Urgent, decisive or arrogant, haughty. (Compare **perfunctory, preemptory**.)

perennial Year after year, enduring.

perf. or **pf.** Abbreviation for *perfect*.

perfervid Very passionate. (Compare **perfidy**.)

perfidy Treachery. (Compare **perfervid**.)

perfunctory Lacking enthusiasm; mechanical. (Compare **peremptory, preemptory**.)

perh. Abbreviation for *perhaps*.

peridot

peril, periled or **perilled**

perimeter Boundary, outer limits, circumference.

periodic or **periodical**

periodic table

periodontal

period piece

peripatetic Constantly moving, itinerant.

periphery

periphrasis; *pl.,* **periphrases** The use of long words when shorter ones would do.

periscope

periwinkle

perjure To tell a falsehood despite taking an oath promising truthfulness. (Compare **perdure**.)

perm. Abbreviation for *permanent*.

permanence or **permanency**

permissive Optional, discretionary.

permutation A major change or ordered arrangement.

pernicious

perorate To make long speech.

peroxide

perp. Abbreviation for *perpendicular; perpetual*.

perpetrate To commit, carry out. (Compare **perpetuate**.)

perpetual calendar

perpetuate To cause to go on

indefinitely. (Compare
perpetrate.)

perquisite or **perk** An extra,
bonus.

pers. Abbreviation for *person,
personal*.

per se Latin; as such.

persecute To harass, annoy, or
punish unjustly.

Perseids

persiflage Foolish banter.

persimmon

persnickety or **pernickety**

-person Compounds ending in
-person are written as one word
(e.g., *spokesperson*).

persona; *pl.*, **personas** One's
social personality.

persona grata Latin; a person who
is acceptable or welcome.

personal effects

personal foul

persona non grata Latin; an
unwelcome person.

personnel Staff, a group of people
with the same employer.

perspective One's view, opinion,
mental approach.

perspicacious Keen, shrewd.

perspicuous Very clear, easily
understood.

persuadable or **persuasible**

pertinacious Stubborn, persistent.

pertinence or **pertinency**

pertussis Whooping cough.

perverted or **perverse**

pervious Accessible, permeable.

pestle

pesto

petaled or **petalled**

Peter Pan collar

petite bourgeoisie or **petit**

bourgeois French; the lower
middle class, shopkeepers and
tradespeople.

petit four; *pl.*, **petits fours** or **petit
fours** French; a small, square
frosting-covered confection.

petit point An embroidery stitch.

pet peeve

petri dish

petrochemical

petrodollars Foreign money made
by oil-rich countries through
export sales.

petrol Variant for gasoline, chiefly
British usage.

petroleum jelly or **petrolatum**

petticoat

pettifogger

petty officer

petulance or **petulancy**

petulant Rude, peevish.

pew The church furniture: a bench,
bank of seats. (Compare **phew**.)

pg. Abbreviation for *page*.

pH A measure used to indicate
acidity or alkalinity measure.

phalanx; *pl.*, **phalanxes** or
phalanges

phallus; *pl.*, **phalli** or **phalluses**

phantasm or **phantasma**

phantasmal or **phantasmic**

phantom

pharaoh

pharisaical or **pharisaic**

pharm. or **phar.** Abbreviations for
*pharmacy, pharmacist,
pharmaceutical*.

pharmacological or **pharmacologic**

pharmacopoeia or **pharmacopeia**

phase A transitory state or aspect.
(Compare **faze**.)

phaseout As noun.

Ph.D. Abbreviation for *Doctor of Philosophy*.

pheasant; *pl.*, **pheasant** *or* **pheasants**

phenomenon; *pl.*, **phenomena** *or* **phenomenons** *or* **phenom**

phew A sigh of relief. (Compare **pew**.)

Phi Beta Kappa A scholastic honor society.

phil-, philo- Compounds of this combining form, which means loving or liking, are written as one word (e.g., *philology, philosophize*).

phil. *or* **philos.** Abbreviations for *philosophy, philosopher, philosophical*.

philanderer

philanthropic *or* **philanthropical**

philharmonic *or* **symphony orchestra**

philippic A tirade.

Philippines

philistine A crass, materialistic, shallowly motivated person.

philodendron; *pl.*, **philodendrons** *or* **philodendra**

philosophical *or* **philosophic**

phlebitis

phlebotomy

phlegm A bodily secretion, mucus. (Compare **phloem**.)

phlegmatic Sluggish.

phloem Bodily tissue. (Compare **phlegm**.)

phlox; *pl.*, **phlox** *or* **phloxes**

phobia Excessive fear of something.

phoenix

phon-, phono- Compounds of this combining form, which means sound, tone, or speech, are written as one word (e.g., *phonograph, phonology*).

phone *or* **telephone**

phonemic *or* **phonematic**

phonetic *or* **phonetical**

phony *or* **phoney;** *pl.*, **phonies**

phooey

phosphorus

phot-, photo- Compounds are usually written as one word (e.g., *photocopy, photoelectric, photojournalism*).

phot. Abbreviation for *photograph, photographer, photography, photographic*.

photo finish

photog. Abbreviation for *photography, photographic*.

photograph *or* **photo**

photo-offset

photo-realism

photostat As verb.

Photostat As noun.

phrase book

phyllo *or* **fillo** Greek; a very thin pastry dough.

phylum; *pl.*, **phyla**

phys. ed. *or* **PE** *or* **phy. ed.** Abbreviations for *physical education*.

physi-, physio- Compounds of this combining form, which refers to nature or physicality, are written as one word: *physiology*.

physician

physique Bodily structure, condition.

phyt-, phyto- Compounds of this combining form, which refers to plants, are written as one word: *phytoxic*.

P.I. Abbreviation for *private investigator*.

piano; *pl.,* **pianos**

piazza; *pl.,* **piazzas** *or* **piazze** Porch.

picaresque Concerning rogues.

Picasso, Pablo (1881–1973) Spanish painter and sculptor. Along with Braque, founded Cubism.

picayune Trivial.

piccolo; *pl.,* **piccolos**

pick and choose

-picker, -picking Compounds ending in these are written as one word (e.g., *cherrypicker*).

pick-me-up

pickpocket

pickup As adjective and noun.

picnic, picnicked

picture-book As adjective.

picture book As noun.

picturesque

pidgin

Pidgin English

piebald Made of different parts, colors. (Compare **pied**.)

-piece Compounds ending in *-piece* are written as one word (e.g., *mantelpiece*).

piece by piece

pièce de résistance French; a showpiece item.

piece-dye

piecemeal

piece of cake

piece of eight

piecework

pie chart *or* **circle graph**

piecrust

pied Blotchy. (Compare **piebald**.)

pied-à-terre; *pl.,* **pieds-à-**terre French; a secondary residence.

pied piper

pie-eyed

pie-faced

pie in the sky

pier A docking place, wall. (Compare **peer**.)

pigeon-livered

pigeon-toed

pigeonhole

piggyback

pigheaded

pig iron

pig latin *or* **pig Latin**

pigpen

pigskin

pigsty

pigtail

pilaf *or* **pilaff** *or* **pilau** *or* **pilaw**

pileated A crested head on a bird, such as the pileated woodpecker.

pile driver

pile-driving

pileup As noun.

pilgrim Capitalize when referring to U.S. settlers of 1620.

pillbox

pillowcase *or* **pillow slip**

pillow sham

pilothouse

pilot-in-command; *pl.,* **pilots-in-command**

pilot light

pilsner *or* **pilsener**

pilule A tiny pill.

Pima cotton

pimento; *pl.,* **pimentos** *or* **pimento**

pimpernel

PIN Abbreviation for *personal identification number*.

piña colada

pinafore

piñata *or* pinata

pinball machine

pince-nez   Eyeglasses without temples, which are kept in place by a spring that grips the bridge of the nose.

pincer *or* pincher

pinch-hit   As verb.

pinch hit   As noun.

pin curl

pincushion

pineapple

pinecone

pine nut

Ping-Pong

pinhead

pinhole

pink-collar   As adjective.

pink elephants

pinkeye

pinkie *or* pinky

pinking shears

pink slip

pin money

pinnacle   The top, peak. (Compare pinochle.)

pinochle   The card game. (Compare pinnacle.)

Pinot grape

pinpoint

pinprick

pins and needles

pinsetter

pinstripe   As noun.

pin-striped

pinto; *pl.,* pintos *or* pintoes

pinto bean

pint-size *or* pint-sized

pinup   As adjective and noun.

pinwale

pinwheel

pious   Reverent.

pipe cleaner

pipe cutter

pipe dream

pipe fitter

pipeline

pipette *or* pipet   A little syringe-like tube used for dispensing fluids.

pipe wrench

piping hot

pip-squeak

piquancy *or* piquance

pique   A momentary feeling of irritation or resentment. (Compare piqué.)

piqué *or* pique   A strong, nubby fabric. (Compare pique.)

Pirandello, Luigi   (1867–1936) Italian novelist and dramatist. Developed the concept of "theater within the theater."

piranha

pirouette   To turn the body fully around.

pis aller; *pl.,* pis allers   French; literally, "to go worse," a last resort.

Pisces (see Zodiac Signs).

pistachio; *pl.,* pistachios

pistil   The reproductive part of a flower. (Compare pistol.)

pistol   A weapon. (Compare pistil.)

pistol-whip

pit-a-pat

pitch-black *or* pitch-dark

pitchfork

pitchout   As noun.

pitfall

pithy   Concise and having substance (e.g., *a pithy letter*).

pitter-patter

pituitary gland

pixel One of the tiny units or dots that combine to form a picture on a screen or monitor.

pixie *or* **pixy;** *pl.,* **pixies**

pixilated *or*
pixillated Unbalanced, of pixieish humor.

pizzazz *or* **pizazz**

pizzeria

pj's Shortened form for pajamas.

pkg. *or* **pkge.** Abbreviations for *package*.

pl. Abbreviation for *plural; place*.

PLC *or* **Plc.** *or* **p.l.c.** Abbreviation for *public limited company*.

PL/1 Abbreviated form for *programming language version 1*.

placate; placable *or* **placative** *or* **placatory**

place Capitalize only if part of address or proper noun.

placebo; *pl.,* **placebos**

placecard

placeholder

placekick

place mat

place-name

placenta; *pl.,* **placentas** *or* **placentae**

place setting

place value

placket

plagiarize

plainspoken

plaintiff The person who instigates a lawsuit. (Compare **plaintive**.)

plaintive Melancholy. (Compare **plaintiff**.)

plain weave As noun.

plain-woven

plaiting *or* **braiding**

plan-, plano- Compounds of this combining form, which refers to motion or flatness, are written as one word: *planography*.

planchette

-plane Compounds ending in *-plane* are written as one word (e.g., *biplane*).

planeload

planetarium; *pl.,* **planetariums** *or* **planetaria** Capitalize only if part of proper noun: *Hayden Planetarium*.

Planets *Mercury, Venus, Earth, Mars, Jupiter, Saturn, Uranus, Neptune, Pluto*.

plangent

planned parenthood

planter's punch

plant food

plant names Common or horticultural-variety names of plants are usually lowercased, though proper nouns and adjectives are capitalized (e.g., *Virginia creeper, Golden Delicious apple*). Some horticultural varieties are patented or registered as trademarks.

Scientific names of plants (that is, the Latin name indicating genus and species) are set italic, with the generic name capitalized and the specific name lowercased (e.g., *Acer rubrum*).

plaque

plasma

plaster cast

plaster of paris *or* **plaster of Paris**

plastic surgeon

plastic surgery

plateau; *pl.,* **plateaus** *or* **plateaux**

plateful; *pl.*, platefuls
plate glass
platelet
platen
plate rail
Plath, Sylvia (1932–1963) American poet. Author of *The Bell Jar*.
platinum
Plato (c.428–347 B.C.) Greek philosopher. Wrote *The Republic*, in which the philosophical ideals on the Western culture were discussed. (See **Socrates**.)
platonic
platterful
platypus; *pl.*, platypuses *or* platypi
plaudit
plausible
plausive Approving.
play- Compounds written as one word include *playact*, *playacting*, *playback* (noun), *playbill*, *playbook*, *playgoer*, *playground*, *playhouse*, *playland*, *playmaker*, *playmate*, *playpen*, *playroom*, *playsuit*, *plaything*, *playtime*, *playwear*, *playwright*.
play-action pass
play-by-play
player piano
playing card
playing field
play-off As noun
play therapy
play titles (See Part 2, **Titles of works**.)
plaza Capitalize only if part of address or proper noun.
plea bargaining As noun.
plea-bargaining As adjective and verb.

plead, pleaded *or* pled
pleasure principle
pleb *or* plebe; *pl.*, plebs *or* plebes A common person, a nobody.
plebeian
Pledge of Allegiance
pledger *or* pledgor
plenary Full, complete (often used in respect to participation, as in *a plenary vote was held*).
plenipotentiary
plenteous Fruitful, productive. (Compare **plentiful**.)
plentiful Abundant, giving a great supply. (Compare **plenteous**.)
plenum; *pl.*, plenums *or* plena
plethora
pleurisy
Plexiglas A trademark name for a lightweight, transparent, synthetic resin, used to make items such as lenses and windows.
pliable *or* pliant
plica; *pl.*, plicae
plicate As verb.
plié
pliers
plow *or* plough
plug-in As adjective and noun.
plug-ugly
plumage
plumb line
pluperfect
plurality The highest percentage in a contest between more than two candidates, which may be less than 50 percent. (Compare **majority**.)
plurals Plurals of common nouns are formed by adding *s* or *es*: *books, telephones, watches,*

classes. Words ending in *o* preceded by a vowel take the *s*: *portfolios, taboos*. Words ending in *o* preceded by a consonant take *es*: *heroes, tomatoes*. Words that end in *y* that are preceded by a vowel take the *s*: *pulleys, ways*. For words that end in *y* that are preceded by a consonant, the plural is formed by changing the *y* to *i* and adding *es*: *allies, babies*.

Examples of plurals and exceptions to these rules are listed throughout this section. Also, see individual entries (**abbreviations, compounds, plurals, numbers,** etc.) for more information on plurals.

plus; *pl.*, **pluses** *or* **plusses**
plus sign
plutonium
Plymouth Rock
p.m. *or* **P.M.** Abbreviation for *post meridiem*, "after noon." The typeface is often small capitals.
pneum-, pneumo- Compounds of this combining form, which means lung or lungs, are written as one word: *pneumectomy*.
pneumat-, pneumato- Compounds of this combining form, which means air, spirit, or breath, are written as one word: *pneumatic*.
pneumonia
PO Abbreviation for *purchase order* or *post office*.
pocketbook
pocket edition
pocketful; *pl.*, **pocketfuls**
pocketknife
pockmark
pocket money

pocket-size *or* **pocket-sized**
pocket veto
pococurante Lacking interest.
podium; *pl.*, **podiums** *or* **podia**
Podunk A small, unimportant, isolated town.
Poe, Edgar Allan (1809–1849) American poet and creator of the American Gothic tale. Author of *The Fall of the House of Usher* and "Annabel Lee."
poem titles (See Part 2, **Titles of works.**)
poetic *or* **poetical**
poetic justice
poetic license
poet laureate; *pl.*, **poets laureate** *or* **poet laureates**
pogo stick
poignant
poinsettia
point-blank
pointillism
pointillistic *or* **pointillist**
point of departure
point of no return
point of view
poison ivy
poison oak
poison-pen
poison sumac
poker face As noun.
poker-faced As adjective.
pokeweed *or* **pokeberry**
poky *or* **pokey**
polar bear
Polaris *or* **North Star** *or* **polestar**
Polaroid camera
polecat; *pl.*, **polecats** *or* **polecat**
polemic A vicious attack, dispute.
polemical *or* **polemic**
polenta

pole vault As noun.

pole-vault As verb.

policyholder

policymaker

policy-making

poliomyelitis or **polio**

polit. or **pol.** Abbreviations for *political*.

politburo The executive decision-making body of a Communist party.

politesse

politic Suave, shrewd. (Compare **political, politick**.)

political Concerned with government policy. (Compare **politic, politick**.)

political party Capitalize as a proper noun the name of the organization, but do not capitalize the word *party*. Capitalize the party designation for a member (e.g., *Republican party, Republican*).

politician or **politico**

politick To engage in political activity. (Compare **politic, political**.)

polity An organization, usually political.

polka dot

poll A vote, survey.

Pollock, Jackson (1912–1956) American Abstract Expressionist and Action painter.

Pollyanna A person who is relentlessly optimistic.

pollywog or **polliwog**

Polo, Marco (1254–1324) Venetian explorer who served on mission under Kublai Khan. *Il milione* is the story of his travels.

polo shirt

poltergeist A noisy ghost.

poltroon A coward.

poly- Compounds of this combining form, which means many, are written as one word (e.g., *polygamy, polyglot, polygraph, polynomial, polysemy, polysyllabic, polytechnic, polyunsaturated*).

polyester

polyglotism or **polyglottism** Fluency in many languages.

polyp

pomade

pomander

pomegranate

Pomeranian

pommel, pommeled or **pommelled**

pommel horse

pom-pom or **pompon** A fluffy ball on clothing.

pompadour

poncho; *pl.,* **ponchos**

ponderosa pine

ponderous Very heavy or lifeless.

pons; *pl.,* **pontes** Nerve fibers in the brain.

pontiff The Roman Catholic Pope.

pontoon boat

pony express

ponytail

pooh-bah or **poo-bah**

pooh-pooh or **pooh**

poolroom

poolside

pool table

poop deck

poor boy A submarine sandwich; or, a type of ribbed sweater.

poorhouse

poor-mouth As verb. To speak badly of.

pop. Abbreviation for *popular, popularly; population.*

pop artist A performer engaged in commercialized, popular entertainment.

popcorn

pope Capitalize when referring to the head of the Catholic church.

Pope, Alexander (1688–1744) English poet. Author of *Essay on Man.*

popgun

poplin

popover

poppy seed

Popsicle

population *or* **populace**

populous Crowded, inhabited by many people.

pop-up *or* **pop fly**

porcelain; procelaneous *or* **porcellaneous**

porcupine

pork chop

porkpie hat

pornography *or* **porn**

porpoise

porridge

port Capitalize only if part of proper noun.

portable *or* **portative**

porte cochère French; a roof over part of a driveway that shelters people as they get out of the car and walk to the house.

portend A verb. To signify, act as an omen. (Compare **portent, portentous.**)

portent A noun. An omen, a sign. (Compare **portend, portentous.**)

portentous Wondrous or ominous. (Compare **portend, portent.**)

porterhouse steak

portfolio; *pl.,* **portfolios**

porthole

portico; *pl.,* **porticoes** *or* **porticos**

portiere French; a curtain across a doorway.

portland cement

portmanteau; *pl.,* **portmanteaus** *or* **portmanteaux** French; a large travel bag.

Portuguese

pos. Abbreviation for *positive.*

poseur An insincere person.

positiveness *or* **positivity**

poss. *or* **pos.** Abbreviations for *possessive; possession.*

poss. Abbreviation for *possible, possibly.*

posse A group of people organized to do a search or assist in an arrest.

posslq Abbreviation for *person of the opposite sex sharing living quarters.*

post- Compounds are usually written as one word, in both the sense of "after" and in meanings referring to the U.S. mail service, except when the second word is a proper noun (e.g., *post-Freudian,* but *postcard, postdate, postdoctoral, postgraduate, postmark, postmortem, postoperative, postpaid, postpartum, postprandial*).

postage meter

postage-stamp As adjective.

postage stamp As noun.

poster paint *or* **poster color**

posthaste

posthumous

postlude

post meridiem *or* **p.m.** *or* **P.M.** *or* P.M.

postnasal drip

post-obit

post office *or* **P.O.** Capitalize if part of proper noun or address.

post office box *or* **P.O.B.** *or* **P.O. Box**

pot cheese Variant for cottage cheese.

potable Safe or acceptable for drinking.

potash

potassium

potato chip

potato; *pl.,* **potatoes**

potbellied stove *or* **potbelly stove**

potboiler

potency *or* **potence**

pother Commotion, confusion.

pot holder

pothole

pothook

potluck

potpie

potpourri

pot roast

potshot

potter's clay

potty-chair

pouilly-fuissé A dry, white wine.

pound; *pl.,* **pounds** *or* **pound**

pound cake

Pound, Ezra (1885–1972) American critic, editor, poet and leader of the Imagist movement. Author of *The Spirit of Romance*.

pound-foolish

pourboire French; a tip for a waiter.

pourparler French; conversation prior to getting the official discussion started.

pousse-café French; literally, "coffee chaser," an after-dinner drink.

poverty line

poverty-stricken

POW Abbreviation for *prisoner of war*.

powder blue

powder-puff As adjective.

powder puff As noun.

-power Compounds ending in *-power* are written as one word (e.g., *waterpower*).

powerboat

power broker

powerhouse

power of attorney

powwow

pox; *pl.,* **pox** *or* **poxes**

p.p. Abbreviation for *past participle*.

ppd. *or* **P.P.** Abbreviations for *postpaid; prepaid*.

PPS Abbreviation for *post postscriptum*, "a later postscript."

pr. Abbreviation for *pair*.

practicable Feasible, usable. (Compare **practical, practically**.)

practical Reasonable, realistic, useful. (Compare **practicable, practically**.)

practically Reasonably or almost, nearly. (Compare **practicable, practical**.)

pragmatic *or* **pragmatical**

pragmatics The study of signs and linguistic expressions. (Compare **pragmatism**.)

pragmatism A philosophy of care,

balance, reasonability. (Compare **pragmatics**.)

prairie dog

praline

pray To speak to a higher being. (Compare **prey**.)

prayer book

praying mantis

pre- Compounds formed with *pre-*, which means before, are usually written as one word unless the second word is a proper noun (e.g., *pre-Christian*, but *preexistent*, *preflight*, *premarital*, *preregister*, *preschooler*, *presoak*, *preview*).

precedence *or* **precedency**

preceding Immediately before. (Compare **previous, prior**.)

precept A principle, order. (Compare **preceptor**.)

preceptor Teacher. (Compare **precept**.)

precipitancy *or* **precipitance**

precipitant Speeding, rushing, happening quickly. (Compare **precipitate, precipitous**.)

precipitate Causing to occur abruptly; or, to condense and fall, as snow or rain. (Compare **precipitant, precipitous**.)

precipitous *or* **precipitate** Very steep or sheer. (Compare **precipitant, precipitate**.)

précis French; a concise summary.

precise

precocious Showing premature development.

pred. Abbreviation for *predicate*, *predicative*.

predatory *or* **predaceous** *or* **predacious**

predecessor

predicable Able to be asserted or affirmed. (Compare **predictable**.)

predictable Able to be anticipated. (Compare **predicable**.)

predilection Favoring, strong liking. (Compare **predisposition**.)

predisposition Susceptibility or inclination toward something. (Compare **predilection**.)

predominance *or* **predominancy**

predominant *or* **predominate**

preemie *or* **premie** A prematurely born baby.

preeminent

preempt

preemptory Exclusively or privileged. (Compare **peremptory, perfunctory**.)

pre-engineered

pref. Abbreviation for *preface*, *prefatory; preferred, preference*.

prefab As adjective and noun.

prefabricate As verb.

preface

preferred stock

prefix

pregnable Vulnerable.

pregnant

prehensile Able to be used for grabbing and holding, or being perceptive.

prehistoric *or* **prehistorical**

prejudicial *or* **prejudicious**

prelection A public lecture.

prelude

prem. Abbreviation for *premium; premier*.

premedical *or* **premed**

premenstrual syndrome *or* **PMS**

premier *or* **premiere** First, earliest.

premiere *or* **premier**   As verb.

premise   Proposition, presupposition. (Compare **premises**.)

premises   Building, property. (Compare **premise**.)

pre-owned *or* **secondhand**

prep school

prep.   Abbreviation for *preposition; prepare, preparatory, preparation.*

prepd.   Abbreviation for *prepared.*

preponderance *or* **preponderancy**

prepossess   To take, influence early. (Compare **prepossessing**.)

prepossessing   Attractive, impressive. (Compare **prepossess**.)

preppy *or* **preppie**; *pl.,* **preppies**

prereq.   Abbreviation for *prerequisite.*

prerequisite

prerogative

pres.   Abbreviation for *present; president.*

prescience   Foresight.

prescribe   To order, dictate, specify with authority. (Compare **proscribe**.)

presence of mind

presentiment   A feeling that something is going to happen. (Compare **presentment**.)

presentment   The act of giving, setting forth something. (Compare **presentiment**.)

president   Capitalize only if part of formal title preceding name or proper noun: *President Thomas Jefferson.*

president-elect; *pl.,* **presidents-elect**

Presidents' Day

Presidents of the United States of America

1. *George Washington*
   1732–1799
2. *John Adams*
   1735–1826
3. *Thomas Jefferson*
   1743–1826
4. *James Madison*
   1751–1836
5. *James Monroe*
   1758–1831
6. *John Quincy Adams*
   1767–1848
7. *Andrew Jackson*
   1767–1845
8. *Martin Van Buren*
   1782–1862
9. *William Henry Harrison*
   1773–1841
10. *John Tyler*
    1790–1862
11. *James K. Polk*
    1795–1849
12. *Zachary Taylor*
    1784–1850
13. *Millard Fillmore*
    1800–1874
14. *Franklin Pierce*
    1804–1869
15. *James Buchanan*
    1791–1868
16. *Abraham Lincoln*
    1809–1865
17. *Andrew Johnson*
    1808–1875
18. *Ulysses S. Grant*
    1822–1885
19. *Rutherford B. Hayes*
    1822–1893

20. *James Garfield*
    1831–1881
21. *Chester A. Arthur*
    1829–1886
22. *Grover Cleveland*
    1837–1908
23. *Benjamin Harrison*
    1833–1901
24. *Grover Cleveland*
    1837–1908
25. *William McKinley*
    1843–1901
26. *Theodore Roosevelt*
    1858–1919
27. *William H. Taft*
    1857–1930
28. *Woodrow Wilson*
    1856–1924
29. *Warren G. Harding*
    1865–1923
30. *Calvin Coolidge*
    1872–1933
31. *Herbert C. Hoover*
    1874–1964
32. *Franklin D. Roosevelt*
    1882–1945
33. *Harry S Truman*
    1844–1972
34. *Dwight D. Eisenhower*
    1890–1969
35. *John F. Kennedy*
    1917–1963
36. *Lyndon B. Johnson*
    1908–1973
37. *Richard M. Nixon*
    1913–
38. *Gerald R. Ford*
    1913–
39. *Jimmy Carter*
    1924–
40. *Ronald Reagan*
    1911–

41. *George Bush*
    1924–
42. *William Clinton*
    1946–

presidio; *pl.,* **presidios**
press agent
pressboard
press box
press conference
press release
pressroom
pressrun
press secretary
pressure cooker
pressure group
prestidigitation Sleight of hand.
prestige
presto
presume To take for granted not
   having proof to the contrary.
   (Compare **presumptuous**.)
presumptuous Overstepping
   reasonable bounds. (Compare
   presume.)
preteen
pretense *or* **pretence** A claim no
   supported by facts, a false show
   (Compare **pretext**.)
pretermission An omission.
preternatural Extraordinary.
pretext *or* **pretension** A pretend
   purpose that hides the real inten
   or state. (Compare **pretense**.)
pretzel
prev. Abbreviation for *previous,*
   previously.
preventable *or* **preventible**
preventive *or* **preventative**
previous Existing or occurring
   earlier. (Compare **preceding,**
   prior.)

172

prey A victim, something that is being stalked. (Compare **pray**.)

price-earnings ratio

price tag

pricey or **pricy**

prie-dieu; pl., **prie-dieux** A piece of furniture designed for a person to kneel upon with a prayer book resting at reading height.

prima ballerina The leading female dancer in a ballet company.

prima facie Latin; at first glance.

primal scream therapy

primary First, principal, basic. (Compare **primitive**.)

prime minister Capitalize only if part of formal title preceding a name. Abbreviation is *P.M.*: *Prime Minister Margaret Thatcher.*

prime mover

primer

prime rate

prime time

primeval Primitive, ancient. (Compare **primordial**.)

primitive Original, primary. (Compare **primary**.)

primo First.

primogenitor; primogeniture

primordial First created, earliest; fundamental. (Compare **primeval**.)

primrose path

prin. Abbreviation for *principal, principally.*

prince, princess

principal The most important thing; an authority. (Compare **principle**.)

principle A fundamental

assumption or rule. (Compare **principal**.)

printer's ink

printout As noun.

prior Existing or occurring earlier. (Compare **preceding, previous**.)

prism A crystal.

prison A penitentiary or correctional institution. Capitalize if part of proper noun. (Compare **jail**.)

prisoner of war or **POW;** pl., **prisoners of war** or **POWs**

priv. Abbreviation for *private, privately.*

private investigator or **private eye** or **private detective**

privy Secret, special.

prix fixe French; literally, "fixed price," a meal served by an establishment to all guests at a set price, with no substitutions or other choices from a menu.

prizefight

prize money

prizewinner

pro forma Latin; standard, prescribed in advance.

pro; pl., **pros**

prob. Abbreviation for *probable, probably.*

probate court

probation officer

probative or **probatory**

probity Uprightness.

problematic or **problematical**

proboscis; pl., **proboscises** or **proboscides**

proc. Abbreviation for *proceedings; procedures; process.*

proceed To come forth, move along. (Compare **proceeds**.)

proceedings

proceeds Money made after deductions. (Compare **proceed**.)

process cheese or **processed cheese**

processible or **processable**

procès-verbal

pro-choice

proclivity Bent, predisposition.

procure

procurement or **procurance** To get posssession; achieve.

prod. Abbreviation for *produce, produced, producer, product, production*.

prodigal Extravagant, luxurious.

prodigious Strange, amazing.

prodigy An omen, or something amazing.

prof. Abbreviation for *profession, professional*.

Prof. Abbreviation for *professor*. Capitalize only when directly preceding a name.

proffer To present for acceptance.

profit and loss

profiteer

profit-sharing As adjective.

profit sharing As noun.

profligate Very extravagant.

prog. or **pgm.** Abbreviations for *program*.

progenitor An ancestor in direct line. (Compare **progeny**.)

progeny Children. (Compare **progenitor**.)

program, programmed or **programed**

prohibitive or **prohibitory**

projectile

projection booth or **projection room**

proletariat The workers or wage laborers in an industrial society.

pro-life

prolific Fruitful, productive.

prolix Too long, wordy.

prologue or **prolog**

promenade

promisor or **promiser**

promised land

promissory note

pron. or **pr.** Abbreviations for *pronounced, pronunciation*.

pron. or **pro.** Abbreviations for *pronoun*.

prone Lying facedown. (Compare **supine**.)

pronoun A word used to substitute for a noun, which refers to the noun but does not name it specifically (e.g., *him, it*).

The possessive of indefinite pronouns is often formed by adding *'s* (e.g., *somebody's*). Other indefinite pronouns take the word *of* before them to show possession (e.g., *the duties of each*).

Possessive pronouns have no apostrophes (e.g., *hers, his, its, mine, ours, theirs, yours*).

pronto Right away.

-proof Compounds ending in *-proof* are written as one word (e.g., *foolproof*).

proofread

propaganda Information disseminated with the intent of influencing public opinion.

propellant or **propellent**

propeller or **propellor**

proper name or **proper noun** A noun that designates a particular being, group, place, or thing and

174

is capitalized (e.g., *Pam Smith, Canada*).

proper name plurals Plurals of proper names are usually formed by adding *s* or *es* (e.g., *the Smiths, the Wellses*) and those ending in *y* usually retain the *y* and add *s* (e.g., *the winners of Grammys*).

property tax

prophecy or **prophesy;** *pl.,* **prophecies** or **prophesies**

prophesy As verb.

prophetic or **prophetical**

prophylactic

propinquity Kinship, proximity.

propitiate To appease, pacify. (Compare **propitious**.)

propitious Auspicious, favorable. (Compare **propitiate**.)

propjet engine

propone To argue in favor of something. (Compare **propound**.)

proportion or **proportionate** As verb.

proportionate or **proportionable**

propound To put up for discussion. (Compare **propone**.)

proprietary Exclusive, by rights. (Compare **propriety**.)

propriety Appropriateness, politeness. (Compare **proprietary**.)

propylene glycol

prorate To distribute proportionately.

prorogue or **prorogate** To postpone.

prosaic Ordinary, dull.

proscenium

prosciutto; *pl.,* **prosciuttos**

proscribe To prohibit, restrain. (Compare **prescribe**.)

prose Ordinary form of written or spoken language, without rhyme or meter, as opposed to poetry.

prosecutor Capitalize only if part of a formal title preceding a name.

proselyte A converted person. (Compare **proselytize**.)

proselytize To convert or recruit. (Compare **proselyte**.)

prosodic or **prosodical**

prosody The study of versification.

prospective Anticipated, expected, likely.

prospectus; *pl.,* **prospectuses**

prostate A muscular gland surrounding the urethra in most male animals. (Compare **prostrate**.)

prosthesis; *pl.,* **prostheses** An artificial limb.

prostrate Lying flat. (Compare **prostate**.)

prostrating Moving into a position of lying flat, or humbling oneself. (Compare **prostration**.)

prostration Exhaustion. (Compare **prostrating**.)

protagonist A leading character, the main actor in a situation.

protean Versatile, changeable.

protégé *(male),* **protegée** *(female)* French; someone under the protection of a person of higher knowledge, authority, or prestige.

protein

protester or **protestor**

proto- Compounds formed with *proto-*, which means first in time, original, or primitive, are written as one word (e.g., *prototype*).

protocol

prototypical *or* **prototypal**

protozoon; *pl.,* **protozoa**

Proust, Marcel (1871–1922) French novelist. Author of *Remembrances of Things Past.*

prove, proved *or* **proven**

provender Food. (Compare **provenience**.)

provenience *or* **provenance** Origin, source. (Compare **provender**.)

proverbial

provident Frugal, careful. (Compare **providential**.)

providential Lucky. (Compare **provident**.)

province Capitalize only if part of proper noun.

proving ground

provisional Temporary.

proviso; *pl.,* **provisos** *or* **provisoes**

provocateur *or* **agent provocateur**

provolone cheese

prox. Abbreviation for Latin, *proximo,* "in the next month."

proximate *or* **proximal**

proxy; *pl.,* **proxies** A stand-in.

pr.p. Abbreviation for *present participle.*

prudent Discreet, wise. (Compare **prurient**.)

prurience *or* **pruriency**

prurient Unhealthily interested in something. (Compare **prudent**.)

P.S. Abbreviation for *post scriptum, postscript.*

psalm

pseud-, pseudo- Compounds of this combining form, which means fictitious or counterfeit, are written as one word (e.g., *pseudomorpha, pseudoscience*).

pseud. Abbreviation for *pseudonym, pseudonymous.*

psoriasis

PST Abbreviation for *Pacific Standard Time.*

psych *or* **psyche** As verb.

psych-, psycho- Compounds of this combining form, which means mind or mental process, are written as one word (e.g., *psychoanalysis, psychosomatic, psychotherapy*).

psych. *or* **psychol.** Abbreviations for *psychological, psychology, psychologist.*

psychedelic

psychiatry

psychic *or* **psychical**

psycho; *pl.,* **psychos**

psychological *or* **psychologic**

psychosis; *pl.,* **phychoses**

p.t. Abbreviation for *past tense.*

pt. Abbreviation for *part; pint.*

PT boat

ptomaine poisoning

pub. *or* **publ.** Abbreviations for *published, publisher, publishing.*

pub crawler

public-address system *or* **PA system**

puddle jumper

pueblo Spanish; a village or community of Indians in the southwestern United States.

puerile Childish. (Compare **puerperal**.)

puerperal Relating to childbirth. (Compare **puerile**.)

puffball

pugnacious Belligerent.

pug nose

pug-nosed

puisne Inferior in rank. (Compare puny.)

puissant Powerful.

Pulitzer prize

pulley; *pl.,* **pulleys**

Pullman

pullout As noun.

pullover As noun.

pulmonary

pulverizable *or* **pulverable**

pumice stone

pummel, pummeled *or* **pummelled**

pumpernickel

punch bowl

punch-drunk

punching bag

punctilio; *pl.,* **punctilios**

punctilious Careful, exact.

puncture To poke a hole in.

pungent

punk rock

puny Weak or tiny. (Compare puisne.)

pupa; *pl.,* **pupae** *or* **pupas**

puppy dog

puppy love

pup tent

pureblood As noun.

pure-blooded *or* **pure-blood** As adjective.

purebred

puree, pureed

purgatory

puritanical

purlieu Neighborhood.

purloin

Purple Heart

purposely *or* **purposeful** *or* **purposive**

purr

purse strings

pursuant to Following upon, in accordance with.

push-button As adjective.

push button As noun.

pushcart

pushover As noun.

push-pull

push-up As noun.

pusillanimous Cowardly.

pussycat

pussyfoot

putative Generally considered or reputed.

put-down As noun.

put-on As adjective or noun.

putout As noun.

putrefy

putrescent

putting green

put-upon

Pygmalion

pyr-, pyro- Compounds of this combining form, which means fire or heat, are written as one word (e.g., *pyromania*).

pyramid

python

Q. and A. *or* **Q&A** *or* **Q-A**
Abbreviations for *question and
answer*.

Q.E.D. Abbreviation for Latin,
quod erat demonstrandum,
"which was to be demonstrated."

Q-Tips A trademark name for a
cotton swab.

qty. Abbreviation for *quantity*.

qua Latin; as, in the capacity of
(e.g., *Politicians, qua politicians,
tend toward insincerity*).

Quaalude A trademark name for a
sedative drug.

quadrennial Lasting four years or
happening every four years.

quadrennium; *pl.,* **quadrenniums**
or **quadrennia**

quadri, quadr-, quadru- Compounds of these combining forms,
which mean four times or
fourfold, are written as one word
(e.g., *quadrilateral, quadrupled*).

quadrille Decorated with squares
or rectangles.

quaff

quagmire

quahog *or* **quahaug**

quail; *pl.,* **quail** *or* **quails**

Quaker

qual. *or* **qlty.** Abbreviations for
quality.

qualify

quality control

quandary

quantify

quantum; *pl.,* **quanta**

quarantine

quarrel, quarreled *or* **quarrelled**

quarry; *pl.,* **quarries**

quart *or* **qt.**

quart. Abbreviation for *quarterly*.

quarterfinal

quarter horse

quarter hour

quartet *or* **quartette**

quarto; *pl.,* **quartos**

quartz battery

quasar

quasi This word, which means
seemingly, or in part, combined
with an adjective is hyphenated
(e.g., *quasi-judicial*). If directly
modifying a noun, it is not
hyphenated (e.g., *quasi student*).

quatrain

quay A landing place at water's
edge.

queen-size

quencher

querulous Complaining, whining.

query; *pl.,* **queries**

quesadilla

question mark

questionnaire

queue To get in a waiting line.

queuing *or* **queueing**

quiche lorraine *or* **quiche Lorraine**

quick bread

quick fix

quick-freeze, quick-froze

quickie

quick-lunch

quickset

quicksilver

quick-tempered

quick-witted

quidnunc A busybody, a nosy
person.

quid pro quo Latin; literally,
"something for something," an
equal trade.

quietude Silence, peace. (Compare **quietus**.)

quietus Settlement, or death. (Compare **quietude**.)

quinine water

quintet *or* **quintette**

quire Twenty-four or twenty-five sheets of paper, one twentieth of a ream.

quit, quit *or* **quitted**

quitclaim

quittance Paying off of a debt.

qui vive French; used as *on the qui vive*, on the alert.

quixotic *or* **quixotical**

quiz show

quondam Latin; former (e.g., *a quondam criminal, now reformed*).

quorum; *pl.*, quorums The minimum number of people required to conduct business or make decisions.

quot. Abbreviation for *quotation*.

quota

quotation mark

quotidian Everyday, ordinary.

quotient

q.v. Abbreviation for Latin, *quod vide*, "which see."

rabbet A groove, recess. (Compare **rabbit**.)

rabbet joint

rabbi

rabbit The long-eared small mammal. (Compare **rabbet**.)

rabbit punch

rabble-rouser

rabies; *pl.*, **rabies**

raccoon *or* **racoon**

racecourse *or* **raceway**

racehorse

race riot

racetrack

racket *or* **racquet**

raclette A Swiss cheese and potato dish.

raconteur A storyteller.

racquetball

radar A word derived from *radio detecting and ranging*, a system of using radio waves to detect and locate the position of an object.

radi-, radio- Most compounds are written as one word (e.g., *radioactive, radioisotope*).

radial tire

radiance *or* **radiancy**

radical

radicle Part of plant or root.

radio, radioed

radio; *pl.*, **radios**

radio beacon

radiobroadcast As verb.

radio car

radio frequency

radio spectrum

radio telescope

radio wave

radius; *pl.*, **radii** *or* **radiuses**

radix; *pl.*, **radices** *or* **radixes** A root, or a primary source.

radon A radioactive gas formed by the disintegration of radium.

raffia

ragamuffin

ragbag

rag doll

ragged *or* **raggedy**

raglan sleeve

ragout

ragtag

ragtime

ragtop

ragweed

rah-rah

railcar

raillery Ridicule.

railroad *or* **railway** Capitalize if part of proper noun.

raiment Clothing.

rain Precipitation. (Compare **reign, rein**.)

rain- Compounds written as one word include *raincoat, raindrop, rainfall, rainmaker, rainmaking, rainproof, rainspout, rainsquall, rainstorm, rainwash, rainwater, rainwear*.

rainbow trout

rain check

rain forest

raisin bread

raison d'être French; reason for being, justification for existence.

rake-off As noun.

Raleigh, Sir Walter (1554–1618) English courtier, navigator, historian, and poet.

rally; *pl.*, **rallies**

RAM Abbreviation for *random access memory*.

ramekin or **ramequin**

ramie The fiber, fabric.

ramjet engine

ramrod

ramshackle

rancher or **ranchero**

ranch house

rancid Foul in smell or taste. (Compare **rancor**.)

rancor Hate, ill will. (Compare **rancid**.)

R&B Abbreviation for *rhythm and blues*.

R and D or **R&D** Abbreviation for *research and development*.

R&R Abbreviation for *rest and recreation, rest and relaxation, rest and recuperation, rest and rehabilitation*.

random-access

randy Lecherous.

range finder

rank and file

ransacker

rap To hit, or (slang) to talk; or a type of popular music in which rhyming song lyrics are meant to be spoken to the accompaniment of a heavily rhythmic beat.

rapacious Greedy, preying.

rapid eye movement or **REM**

rapid-fire

rapid transit

rapier A two-edged sword.

rapporteur Someone who gives the report at a meeting.

rapprochement Reconciliation.

rapscallion

rapt Engrossed.

rapturous Inducing passion, ecstasy.

rara avis; *pl.*, **rara avises** or **rarae aves** Latin; literally, "rare bird," a unique person or thing, a rarity.

rarebit or **Welsh rarebit** or **Welsh rabbit** A dish made with melted cheese over crackers or toast.

rare earth

rarefy or **rarify**

raring Enthusiastic (e.g., *raring to go dancing*).

rasher A slice of bacon or ham.

raspberry

ratable or **rateable**

rat-a-tat or **rat-a-tat-tat**

ratatouille

ratchet

rat fink

rathskeller German; a basement alehouse.

ratio; *pl.*, **ratios**

ratiocinate To think, reason.

rational Using reason.

rat race

rattail

rattan

rattlebrained

rattlesnake

rattletrap

rattrap

raucous

ravage To cause severe damage. (Compare **ravish**.)

ravel, raveled or **ravelled** Variant of *unravel*.

ravine A narrow, deep valley.

ravioli; *pl.*, **ravioli** or **raviolis**

ravish To violate, rape, or plunder. (Compare **ravage**, **ravishing**.)

ravishing Very beautiful, striking. (Compare **ravish**.)

rawboned

raw deal

rawhide

raw material

rayon

razor A shaving tool.

razorback

razor blade

razzle-dazzle

razzmatazz

RBI; *pl.,* **RBIs** *or* **RBI** Abbreviation for *run batted in;* pl., *runs batted in.*

re- Compounds beginning with the prefix *re-* are usually written as one word when meaning "again" or "back" (e.g., *realignment, rebuild*).

read-only memory *or* **ROM** A computer memory that contains a special-purpose program and cannot be changed by the computer.

reading room

readout As noun.

ready-made

ready-to-wear

reagent A chemically or biologically active substance.

real estate *or* **realty**

real-life

real-time As adjective.

realm

realpolitik German; politics based on expedience rather than ethics.

realtor *or* **real estate agent** *or* **realty broker**

rear end

rearguard

rearview mirror

rearward *or* **rearwards**

rebel yell

rebel, rebelled

rebound To spring back, get back.

rebut To argue back. (Compare **refute.**)

recalcitrance *or* **recalcitrancy**

recapitulate *or* **recap**

recd. *or* **rcd.** Abbreviations for *received.*

receipt

receivable *or* **receptible**

Received Pronunciation *or* **RP** *or* **Received Standard** English as spoken by the upper-class English.

receiving blanket A lightweight baby blanket.

recension A critical revision, as of religious writing.

rechauffé French; warmed over.

recherché French; intensely sought after; or overblown, forced.

recidivist A repeat offender, such as a criminal.

recipe

reclaim To take back or subdue. (Compare **re-claim.**)

re-claim To claim again. (Compare **reclaim.**)

recognizance An obligation, pledge. (Compare **reconnaissance.**)

recollect To remember. (Compare **re-collect.**)

re-collect To gather again. (Compare **recollect.**)

recompense Compensation.

recondite Hidden, obscure.

reconnaissance A survey, exploration. (Compare **recognizance.**)

reconnoiter *or* **reconnoitre** To make a reconnaissance.

record player

recover To recuperate. (Compare re-cover.)

re-cover To cover again. (Compare recover.)

recpt. *or* **rec.** Abbreviations for *receipt*.

recreant Cowardly (adjective), coward (noun). (Compare recreate.)

recreate To refresh or to enjoy sports or exercise. (Compare re-create, recreant.)

re-create To create or form again, anew. (Compare recreate.)

re-form To form again. (Compare reform.)

recreational vehicle *or* **RV**

recreation room

recrudesce To become active; renew.

rectory A religious leader's residence.

recursion A return.

recyclable

red alert

redbird

redbrick As adjective.

red-blooded

red-carpet As adjective.

red carpet As noun.

redcoat

Red Cross

red dog *or* **blitz** A football term.

red-eye An overnight plane flight.

redeye gravy

red flag

red-handed

redheaded *or* **red-haired**

red herring A false or deceptive clue.

red-hot

red ink

red-letter

red light

redline

redolent Fragrant, aromatic.

redoubtable Formidable, awesome.

redound To overflow or accrue, to have a result or effect to the credit or discredit of something, or to come back or react upon something.

red-pencil

redress Compensation, remedy.

redshirt

red tape

redux Brought back.

red wine

red-winged blackbird

redwood

reecho *or* **re-echo**

reed organ

reefer Slang for marijuana.

reel-to-reel

ref.; *pl.,* **reff.** Abbreviation for *reference, references*.

refer To mention specifically. (Compare allude.)

referendum; *pl.,* **referenda** *or* **referendums**

refinery; *pl.,* **refineries**

refl. Abbreviation for *reflexive*.

reflex arc

reform school

reform To amend, improve, change for the better. (Compare re-form.)

re-form To form again. (Compare reform.)

reformative *or* **reformatory**

refried beans

refugee

refulgent Brilliant, shining.

refute To deny and prove wrong.
(Compare **rebut**.)

reg. Abbreviation for *regular,
regularly; regulate, regulation,
regulator.*

regalia

regatta

reggae

regime A political system or a
form or manner of government
rule. (Compare **regimen,
regimental**.)

regimen A plan, course, rule.
(Compare **regime, regimental**.)

regimental Authoritative.
(Compare **regime, regimen**.)

regnant Reigning (as royalty, e.g.,
the regnant king).

regnum; *pl.,* **regna** Latin;
kingdom.

regress A privilege of reentry, a
return, or to return to an earlier
state.

regret, regretted

rehabilitation *or* **rehab**

reign To rule, control. (Compare
rain, rein.)

rein Straps of leather attached to a
horse's bit and used to control the
animal; or, to control, check, or
restrain. (Compare **rain, reign**.)

reindeer; *pl.,* **reindeer**

rejecter *or* **rejector**

rejoinder A reply.

rel. Abbreviation for *related,
relating, relative, relatively.*

relative humidity

relay, relaid To put down again.

relay, relayed To pass along.

released time

released-time capsules

relevance *or* **relevancy**

relic

relief map

relief pitcher

religion Capitalize the names of
organizations and adherents:
Judaism, Episcopalians.

reluctance *or* **reluctancy**

reluctant Hesitant, unwilling to
act.

remake, remade

remand To send or order back.

Rembrandt van Rijn (1606–1669)
Dutch painter and etcher. Painted
Anatomy Lesson of Dr. Tulp and
The Nightwatch.

remediable Able to be fixed.
(Compare **remedial**.)

remedial Fixing, helpful.
(Compare **remediable**.)

reminisce

remiss Negligent, careless.
(Compare **remissible**.)

remissible Capable of being
forgiven. (Compare **remiss**.)

remodel

removable *or* **removeable**

remunerate

renaissance A revival or rebirth.

Renaissance The revival and
flourishing of art, literature, and
the sciences that began in Italy in
the 14th century and spread
through Europe.

Renaissance person A person who
has a wide variety of talent and
cultural interest.

rencontre A conflict or meeting.

rend To split, tear apart. The past
tense is *rent.*

rendezvous; *pl.,* **rendezvous**

rendezvous, rendezvoused As
verb

renege To go back on a promise.

Renoir, Pierre Auguste (1841–1919) French Impressionist painter.

renown Acclaim, fame.

rent-a-car

rent-controlled As adjective.

rep. *or* **repr.** Abbreviations for *representative*.

repairable *or* **reparable**

repartee A witty reply or conversation.

repast A meal.

repay, repaid

repel, repelled

repellent *or* **repellant**

repertoire The list or stock of things that a person or group is able to perform.

repertory An adjective referring to a theater company.

replete Complete, full.

replica A close reproduction, copy.

replicate To duplicate.

reportage Journalistic documentation of events.

report card

repose A noun or verb meaning "rest."

repoussé Adjective describing metalwork ornamented in relief.

repr. Abbreviation for *reprint, reprinted*.

reprehend To censure.

representative As a politician's title, capitalize only if part of formal title preceding a name (e.g., *U.S. Representative Tom Andrews*, but *Tom Andrews, the representative from Maine*).

repress To hold back; check.

reprieve Relief.

reprisal Retaliation.

repro; *pl.,* **repros**

reprobate Condemned, worthless.

reproof Criticism. (Compare **reprove**.)

reprove To scold. (Compare **reproof**.)

republic Capitalize only if part of proper noun: *People's Republic of China*.

republican Capitalize if referring to the political party or member.

repudiate To refuse to accept. (Compare **reputable**.)

repugnance *or* **repugnancy**

reputable *or* **reputed** Esteemed. (Compare **repudiate**.)

requester *or* **requestor**

requiem mass A religious service or musical work honoring the dead.

requisite Necessary. (Compare **requisition, requite**.)

requisition A request, something requested. (Compare **requisite, requite**.)

requite To repay, avenge. (Compare **requisite, requisition**.)

rerun

res. Abbreviation for *residence, residency, resident*.

rescind To cancel.

rescision *or* **recision** Cancellation.

resentment Very deep resentment.

reservation Capitalize only if part of proper noun.

reserve(s) Capitalize only if part of proper noun: *U.S. Army Reserves*.

reservoir

residence *or* **residency** A place for

living, or a period of activity, dwelling.

residue Something that is left over. (Compare **residuum**.)

residuum; *pl.*, **residua** A word meaning "residue," used in technical contexts.

resilience *or* **resiliency**

resin An organic substance, especially that formed from plant secretion. (Compare **rosin**.)

resister One who resists. (Compare **resistor**.)

resistor An electrical control. (Compare **resister**.)

resolute Steady, faithful.

resolve Decidedness of purpose.

resort To end up having to do.

respectable Worthy of esteem; decent.

respectful Showing regard, deference.

respecting Concerning.

respective Particular.

respire To breathe.

respite A pause, relief.

resplendence *or* **resplendency**

restaurateur *or* **restauranteur**

rest home

restive Contrary, uncontrollable. (Compare **restless**.)

restless Moving constantly; changeful. (Compare **restive**.)

rest room

resume To take up again. (Compare **résumé**.)

résumé *or* **resume** *or* **resumé** A career summary. (Compare **resume**.)

retake, retook

retch To vomit. (Compare **wretch**.)

retell, retold

rethink, rethought

reticence *or* **reticency**

reticent Reluctant, hesitant, especially to speak.

reticulate *or* **reticular** Having veins, fibers.

retina; *pl.*, **retinas** *or* **retinae**

retiring Shy.

retractable *or* **retractile**

retro- Compounds of this combining form, which refers to back, backward, or behind, are written as one word (e.g., *retroactive, retrofit*).

retro-engine

retroflexion *or* **retroflection**

retrograde Contradictory.

retrogress To revert to earlier state.

retro-rocket

retroussé An adjective (French) meaning "turned up."

retsina A Greek wine.

Reuben sandwich

rev, revved

rev. Abbreviation for *reverse, reversed; review, reviewed; revise, revised.*

revaluate *or* **reevaluate**

revealer *or* **revelator**

reveille A bugle call at dawn.

reveler *or* **reveller**

revenant A person who returns after extended absence; or, a ghost.

revenge To get back at for a wrong or injury to oneself. (Compare **avenge**.)

reverberant *or* **reverberative**

reverend Capitalize only if part of formal title preceding a name. The abbreviation *Rev.* is acceptable when referring to the minister of a church and should be preceded by *the* (e.g., *The Rev. Janet Ford*).

reverent *or* **reverential**

reverie *or* **revery;** *pl.,* **reveries**

Revised Standard Version *or* **RSV** A modern revision of the American Standard Version of the English Bible.

reviser *or* **revisor**

revision *or* **revisal**

revocable *or* **revokable**

revolutions per minute *or* **rpm**

revue Theatrical production.

reward Compensation or profit.

rewind, rewound

Reye's syndrome *or* **Reye syndrome**

RF Abbreviation for *radio frequency*.

rhapsody; *pl.,* **rhapsodies**

rhetorical *or* **rhetoric**

rheumatism

Rh factor

rhinestone

Rhine wine

rhinitis

rhinoceros; *pl.,* **rhinoceroses** *or* **rhinoceros** *or* **rhinoceri**

rhiz-, rhizo- Compounds made from this combining form, which means root, are written as one word (e.g., *rhizogenic*).

rhizome

Rh-negative

Rhode Island Red

Rhode Island White

Rhodes scholar

rhododendron

rhombic

rhombus; *pl.,* **rhombuses** *or* **rhombi**

Rh-positive

rhubarb

rhyme

rhythm and blues

rhythmic *or* **rhythmical**

ribald Indulging in coarse humor.

rib cage

rib eye

riboflavin

rib roast

rice paper

Richter scale

rickrack *or* **ricrac**

ricochet, ricocheted *or* **ricochetted**

ricotta cheese

rid, rid *or* **ridded**

Riesling wine

riffraff

riflery

rigatoni

righteous

right-hand, right-handed Adjectives.

right hand, right-hander Nouns.

right-minded

right-of-way; *pl.,* **rights-of-way** *or* **right-of-ways**

right-to-life

right-to-work

right wing

right-winger

rigmarole *or* **rigamarole**

rigor mortis

rile To upset someone.

Rilke, Rainer Maria (1875–1926) German poet. Author of *Die Aufzeichnungen des Malte Laurids Brigge*.

ring, rang

ring-around-a-rosy or **ring-around-the-rosy**

ring binder

ring finger

ringleader

ringtoss

rinky-dink

riot act An emphatic warning or reproach, often used in the construction *to read the riot act (to someone)*.

riotous

R.I.P. Abbreviation for Latin, *requiescat in pace*, "may he/she rest in peace."

rip cord

rip current

rip-off As adjective and noun.

riposte A retort or swift response.

ripple effect

rip-roaring

rise, rose

risible Funny, able to laugh.

risqué

rite of passage

ritzy

rival, rivaled or **rivalled**

river Capitalize only if part of proper noun (e.g., *the river was half a mile wide*, but *the Ohio River*).

riverbank

riverbed

riverboat

riverfront

Riviera The resort area in southeastern France and northwestern Italy.

rivulet A small stream.

RN or **R.N.** Abbreviation for *registered nurse*.

road Capitalize if part of proper

noun or address. Abbreviation is *Rd.*.

roadblock

road hog

roadhouse

road racing

roadrunner

road show

road test

roadwork

rock and roll or **rock 'n' roll** or **rock music**

rock and roller or **rock 'n' roller** or **rocker**

rock-bottom As adjective.

rock bottom As noun.

rock candy

rock crystal

rocket ship

rocking chair

rocking horse

rock salt

rococo Elaborate, florid; used especially to describe a style of art.

rodeo; *pl.,* **rodeos**

rodomontade Blustering boastfulness.

roentgen A noun. A unit of quantity used to measure radiation, such as X rays.

rogue

role model

role-play

roll call

roller coaster

roller skate As noun.

roller-skate As verb.

roller skater

rollicking

rolling pin

roll-on As adjective and noun.

rollout   As noun.

rollover   As noun.

rolltop desk

roly-poly

ROM   Abbreviation for *read-only memory*.

romaine lettuce

roman à clef   French; literally, "a novel with a key," a novel where real people are portrayed under fictional names.

Roman candle

Roman Catholic

Romanesque

roman-fleuve; *pl.*, **romans-fleuves**   French; a novel that chronicles the saga of several generations of a family or community.

Roman holiday

Roman numeral   See Part 2, Roman numerals.

Romano cheese

romanticize

roman type *or* **roman typeface**

Romeo and Juliet

rondeau; *pl.*, **rondeaux**   French; a type of verse or song with a fixed form.

rondel *or* **rondelle** *or* **roundel**   A type of rondeau.

roof; *pl.*, **roofs**

roof garden

rooftop

-room   Compounds ending in *-room* are usually written as one word (e.g., *elbowroom, bathroom*).

room and board

rooming house

roommate

room service

Roosevelt, Eleanor   (1884–1962) American author, diplomat, and humanitarian. Author of *On My Own*. Niece of Theodore Roosevelt; wife of Franklin D. Roosevelt.

root beer

root canal

Roquefort cheese

Rorschach test   A psychological exam in which the person being tested tells what is suggested to him or her by a series of inkblot designs. The responses are then analyzed and interpreted.

rosary; *pl.*, **rosaries**

roseate   Pink.

rosebud

rosebush

rose-colored

roseola   A deep pink skin rash.

Rosetta stone

rosewater   As adjective.

rose water   As noun.

Rosh Hashanah

rosin   A resin for making varnish.

rostrum; *pl.*, **rostrums** *or* **rostra**   A platform for public speaking.

ROTC   Abbreviation for *Reserve Officers' Training Corps*.

rote   Routine.

rotisserie

rotogravure   A type of printing press.

rotorcraft

Rottweiler

rotunda

roué

rouge

roughage

rough-and-ready

rough-and-tumble

rough cut

rough-hewn   As adjective.

roughhouse

roughneck

roughrider

roughshod

roulade

rouleau; *pl.,* **rouleaux**   A small roll of something, such as coins in a wrapper.

roulette

roundabout

roundelay   A song with a regularly repeated refrain.

round-robin

round steak

round table

round-the-clock

round-trip

roundup   As noun.

roundworm

rouse   To awaken from sleep.

roustabout

rout   A big crowd or disturbance. (Compare **route**.)

route   A course of travel. (Compare **rout**.) Capitalize only if part of proper noun or address.

router   A machine for milling wood.

routine

rowboat

rowdy; *pl.,* **rowdies**

row house

royal blue

RR   Abbreviation for *railroad* or *rural route*.

R.S.V.P.   Abbreviation for French, *répondez s'il vous plait,* "please reply."

rubber band

rubber cement

rubberneck   To gawk.

rubber-stamp   As verb.

rubber stamp   As noun.

rubber tree

rubbing alcohol

rubdown   As noun.

rubella   German measles. (Compare **rubeola**.)

rubeola   Measles (Compare **rubella**.)

rubicund   Rosy-complected, ruddy.

rubric   A category.

ruby-throated hummingbird

rucksack

ruction   An uproar.

rudimentary

ruffed grouse

ruffian

rule of the road

rule of thumb

rumaki   An appetizer made with pieces of marinated chicken liver.

rumba *or* **rhumba**

rumble seat

rummage sale

rumormonger

rumpus room

runabout   As noun.

runaround   As noun.

runaway   As adjective or noun.

runcible spoon

rundown   As noun.

run-down   As adjective.

rune

runic

run-in; *pl.,* **run-ins**

runner-up; *pl.,* **runners-up** *or* **runner-ups**

running mate

running start

runoff   As noun.

run-of-the-mill
run-on As adjective or noun.
runover As noun.
run-over As adjective.
run-through As noun.
runway
rush hour
russet
Russian dressing

Russian roulette
rustic *or* **rustical**
rusticate To live in the country or take on countrified mannerisms.
rustler
rustproof
rutabaga
Rx
rye bread

s/a Abbreviation for *subject to approval*.

Sabbath

sabbatical *or* **sabbatic** As adjective.

saber *or* **sabre**

saber-toothed

sable Black, very dark.

sabotage

saboteur

sac An animal or plant pouch. (Compare **sack**.)

facchar-, facchari-, faccharo- Compounds of these combining forms, which mean sugar, are written as one word (e.g., *saccharometer*).

saccharin A calorie-free sweetener. (Compare **saccharine**.)

saccharine Sugary, sweet. (Compare **saccharin**.)

sacerdotal Concerning priests.

sachem The chief of a Native American tribe.

Sacher torte German; chocolate cake layered with apricot jam.

sachet A potpourri package.

sack A bag used for toting objects. (Compare **sac**.)

sackcloth

sack coat

sack race

sacred cow

sacrifice fly *or* **SF**

sacrifice hit *or* **SH**

sacrilege

sacroiliac

sacrosanct

saddlebag

saddle shoe

sadism

sadomasochism

sad sack

SAE Abbreviation for *self-addressed envelope* or *stamped, addressed envelope*. (Compare **SASE**.)

safari jacket

safe-conduct

safecracker

safe-deposit box

safeguard

safe house

safekeeping

safety pin

safflower

saffron

saga; *pl.,* **sagas**

sagacious Keen, perceptive.

sagebrush

sage cheese

saggital

Sagittarius (see **Zodiac Signs**).

sailboat

sailcloth

sailor

sailplane

Saint Bernard *or* **St. Bernard**

Saint-John's-wort

Saint Patrick's Day

Saint Valentine's Day

Saint Vitus' dance *or* **Saint Vitus's dance** Chorea, a nervous disorder that causes twitching of the arms, legs, and face.

sake *or* **saki** A Japanese alcoholic beverage made from fermented rice.

salaam Arabic; a very deep bow made in obeisance.

salable *or* **saleable**

salacious

salad bar

salad days A time of greenness in one's life, a time of youth and inexperience.

salami

sales check

salesclerk

salespeople

sales slip

sales tax

salience or saliency

saline

Salisbury steak

Salk vaccine

salmagundi An assortment, or potpourri.

salmon; pl., salmon or salmons

salon A living room or place for entertaining; also a hair-styling business. (Compare saloon.)

saloon A bar. (Compare salon.)

salsa

SALT Abbreviation for Strategic Arms Limitation Treaty.

salt-and-pepper As adjective.

saltbox

saltine cracker

salt marsh

saltpeter

saltshaker

saltwater As adjective.

salt water As noun.

salubrious Healthy, healthful. (Compare salutary, salutatory.)

saluki A Middle Eastern hunting dog.

salutary or salutiferous Curative, remedial. (Compare salubrious, salutatory.)

salutatory Welcoming. (Compare salubrious, salutary.)

salvageable or salvable

Salvation Army

salve A healing ointment. (Compare salver, salvo.)

salver A serving tray. (Compare salve, salvo.)

salvo; pl., salvos or salvoes A discharge or attack from a number of weapons at once.

salvo; pl., salvos A dishonest mental hesitation, a quibbling evasion.

Samaritan

samba

samovar Russian; a large metal urn for boiling tea.

Samoyed or Samoyede

samurai

sanatorium; pl., sanatoriums or sanatoria

sanctimonious Hypocritical, pretending piousness.

sanctuary; pl., sanctuaries

sanctum; pl., sanctums or sancta

sandalwood

sandbagger

sandbar

sandblaster

sandbox

sand-cast As verb.

sand casting As noun.

sand dollar

S and L or S&L Abbreviation for savings and loan association.

sandlot

S&M or S-M or S/M Abbreviations for sadism and masochism, sadomasochism.

sandman

sandpapery

sandpiper

sandstone

sandstorm

sand trap

sandwich

Sanforized Trademark for a type of preshrunk fabric.

Sanger, Margaret H. (1879–1966) American leader of birth control movement.

sangfroid French; composure, self-possession.

sanguine Bloody or red.

sanitarium; *pl.*, **sanitariums** *or* **sanitaria**

sanitary napkin

San Jacinto Day A Texas holiday celebrating the battle by which independence from Mexico was won.

sans French; without.

Sanskrit

sans serif *or* **sanserif**

Santa Claus

Santayana, George (1863–1952) Spanish-American poet and philosopher.

sapid Agreeable, flavorful.

sapiens Relating to human beings. (Compare **sapient**.)

sapient Wise. (Compare **sapiens**.)

sapodilla A tropical evergreen tree that bears an edible russet fruit.

sapphire

sapsucker

saran wrap

sarcolemma

sarcoma; *pl.*, **sarcomas** *or* **sarcomata**

sarcophagus; *pl.*, **sarcophagi** *or* **sarcophaguses**

sarcoplasm

sari *or* **saree** A wrapped Indian garment. (Compare **sarong**.)

sarong A wrapped skirt. (Compare **sari**.)

sarsaparilla

sartorial Relating to clothing, especially tailored.

Sartre, Jean-Paul (1905–1980) French Existential writer and philosopher. Author of *L'Etre et le neant* and *La Nausée*.

SASE Abbreviation for *self-addressed, stamped envelope*. (Compare **SAE**.)

sashay

sassafras

SAT Abbreviation for *Scholastic Aptitude Test*.

Satan

satanic

satanism

satchel

sateen A cotton fabric with a lustrous, satiny finish.

satellite dish

satiny

satiric *or* **satirical**

Saturday night special A small, inexpensive handgun (usually homemade).

saturnalia Unrestrained revelry.

saturnine Taciturn.

satyr A lecherous person.

sauceboat

saucepan

saucy

sauerbraten German; a marinated pot roast.

sauerkraut German; cabbage that has been chopped, salted, and fermented in its juice.

sauté, sautéd *or* **sautéed** To panfry in oil or butter.

sauternes *or* **sauterne** A type of sweet white wine.

sauvignon blanc A wine of dry, white California wine.

savanna *or* **savannah**

savable *or* **saveable**

savant A knowledgeable person.

save-all

saving grace

savings account

savior *or* **saviour**

savoir faire French; adroitness in dealing with any situation tactfully.

savor *or* **savour**

savory *or* **savoury**

savvy

saw, sawed *or* **sawn**

sawbones

sawbuck

sawdust

sawed-off

sawhorse

sawmill

sawtooth *or* **saw-toothed** As adjective.

saxophone

say-so

s.c. *or* **sm. cap.** Abbreviations for *small capitals*.

scabrous Rough or indecent.

scalawag *or* **scallywag**

scaloppine *or* **scallopini**

scampi

scandalmonger

scandal sheet

scapegoat

scapula; *pl.,* **scapulae** *or* **scapulas**

scaramouch *or* **scaramouche** A buffoon.

scarecrow

scaredy-cat

scarf; *pl.,* **scarves** *or* **scarfs**

scarify To make small marks or loosen up a surface.

scarlet fever *or* **scarlatina**

scarlet letter

scathe

scatological

scatterbrained

scene-stealer

scenic

scent A smell, an odor. (Compare cent.)

scepter

Scheherazade

schema; *pl.,* **schemata** *or* **schemas**

scherzando Playful; used as a direction in music.

schismatic *or* **schismatical**

schiz-, schizo- Compounds of this combining form, which means split or division, are written as one word (e.g., *schizocarp*, *schizophrenia*).

schlemiel *or* **schlemiehl** Yiddish; chump.

schlepp *or* **schlep** *or* **shlep** *or* **shlepp** Yiddish, to drag or haul.

schlock *or* **shlock** Yiddish, indicating something of shoddy quality.

schmaltz *or* **schmalz** Yiddish, indicating something overly sentimental.

schmear *or* **schmeer** Yiddish; the whole works.

schmo *or* **schmoe** Yiddish; a dolt.

schmooze *or* **shmooze** Yiddish; to gab or gossip.

schmuck Yiddish; a jerk.

schnauzer

schnitzel

schnook Yiddish; a pitifully meek person.

schnorrer Yiddish; a person who wheedles to get something. (Compare **snorer**.)

schnozzle Yiddish; nose.

schola cantorum Latin; literally, "school of singers," a church-choir school.

school Capitalize only if part of proper noun (e.g., *Brooklyn Technical High School,* but *the first day of school*).

school- Compounds written as one word include *schoolbag, schoolbook, schoolboy, schoolchild, schoolchildren, schoolgirl, schoolhouse, schoolmate, schoolroom, schoolteacher, schoolwork, schoolyard.*

school-age As adjective.

school board

school bus

school year

schuss To ski fast and straight down a very steep slope.

schwa A symbol (ə) designating an indistinct vowel sound.

sciatic nerve

science fiction *or* **sci-fi** *or* **SF**

scientific terms The New Latin names of phylum, class, order, and family (and sub or intermediate groupings)—which are more general than genus terms—are capitalized and not italicized (e.g., *the class* Arachnida).

Adjectives and nouns derived from Latin names but used in a general sense are not capitalized (e.g., *amoeba*).

All generic and specific Latin names of plants and animals are italicized. Genus terms are capitalized; species, subspecies, races, and varieties are lowercased (e.g., *Acer rubrum*). A genus name's first letter may be abbreviated (with a period) in a second reference (e.g., *A. rubrum*)

Chemical elements and compounds are lowercased. (See **chemical elements and compounds**.)

Computer languages, data bases, and services that are trademarked or copyrighted are capitalized (e.g., *COBOL, FORTRAN*).

See individual entries for spellings of particular computer languages.

The names of planets are capitalized (e.g., *Venus, Mars*); *earth, moon,* and *sun* are generally lowercased unless they are being written about in the context of other planets. Other meteorological terms are lowercased (e.g., aurora borealis).

scilicet *or* **ss** Latin; namely, or to wit.

scimitar

scion A twig from a woody plant used in grafting; or, a descendant, offspring.

scissors *or* **scissor**

scissors kick

scler-, sclero- Compounds of this combining form, which means

196

hard, are written as one word
(e.g., *sclerosis*).

scofflaw

sconce A candleholder affixed to
wall; or, a small fort. (Compare
scone.)

scone A pastry. (Compare **sconce**.)

scoopful

-scope A combining form, usually
not hyphenated, that indicates an
instrument for observing (e.g.,
stethoscope).

-scopy A combining form, not
hyphenated, that indicates
observation (e.g., *laparoscopy*).

scoreboard

scorecard

scorekeeper

Scorpio (see **Zodiac Signs**).

Scotch egg

Scotch tape A trademark name for
cellulose adhesive tape.

Scotch whisky *or* **Scotch**

scot-free

Scottish terrier

scour To clean roughly. (Compare
scourge.)

scourge Affliction, pain. (Compare
scour.)

scowl

scraggly Rough, unkempt.
(Compare **scraggy**.)

scraggy Rough, jagged. (Compare
scraggly.)

scrapbook

scrap heap

scrap iron

scratch pad

scratch paper

scratch test

screaming meemies

screech owl

screed

screenplay

screen test As noun.

screen-test As verb.

screenwriter

screwball

screwdriver

screwup As noun.

scrimshaw Elaborate decoration on
a bone or ivory article.

scriptorium A room in a
monastery for viewing or writing
manuscripts.

scripture Capitalize when referring
to the Bible (e.g., *Holy
Scriptures*).

scriptwriter

scrivener

scrod

scrollwork

scrub brush

scrutable Understandable.

scuba Self-contained underwater
breathing apparatus.

scuba diver

scull An oar. (Compare **skull**.)

scurrilous *or* **scurrile** *or* **scur-
ril** Given to using vulgar,
abusive language.

scuttlebutt

scythe

s.d. Abbreviation for *same day* or
Latin *sine dato*, "without date."

sea- Compounds written as one
word include *seabed, seabird,
seaboard, seacoast, seafarer,
seafaring, seafood, seafloor,
seagoing, seaplane, seaport,
seascape, seashell, seashore,
seasick, seawall, seaway,
seaweed*.

sea gull

sea horse

sea level

sealskin

séance A gathering of people who are attempting to receive messages from the spirits of the dead.

searchlight

search warrant

seasonable Appropriate, timely. (Compare **seasonal**.)

seasonal Occurring or related to a time of year. (Compare **seasonable**.)

seasoning *or* **seasoner**

seasons Lowercase the names of seasons of the year: *autumn, fall, spring, summer, winter*.

season ticket

seat belt

seat-of-the-pants

seaward *or* **seawards**

sebaceous gland

seborrhea; seborrheic

sec. *or* **s.** Abbreviation for *second; secondary*.

secede To leave an organization. (Compare **succeed**.)

second base The abbreviation is *2b*.

second-best As adjective.

second best As noun.

second-class As adjective.

second class As noun.

second-degree burn

second-guess

secondhand As adjective or adverb.

second-rate

second sight

second-string As adjective.

second string As noun.

second thought

secretary-general; *pl.*, **secretaries-general** Capitalize only if part of a formal title preceding a name.

secretary of state; *pl.*, **secretaries of state** Capitalize only if part of a formal title preceding a name (e.g., *Secretary of State James Dugan*).

secretary-treasurer; *pl.*, **secretary-treasurers** *or* **secretaries-treasurers** Capitalize only if part of a formal title preceding a name.

secrete To give off, or to hide.

secty. *or* **sec'y.** *or* **sec.** Abbreviations for *secretary*.

securityholder

sedan

sedentary

seder *or* **Seder** Jewish Passover feast.

sedition Resistance to authority.

sedulous Very careful, diligent.

see Abbreviations for *see* are *s.* and *vid.* (from Latin, *vide*).

see above The abbreviation is *v.s.* (*vide supra*).

see below The abbreviation is *v.i.* (*vide infra*).

seed- Compounds formed with *seed-* that are written as one word include *seedbed, seedling, seedpod, seedtime*.

Seeing Eye dog

seek, sought

seersucker

seesaw

seethe

see-through

segue To slide gracefully from one thing to another, as in music or conversation.

seism-, seismo- Compounds of this combining form, which means earthquake, are written as one word (e.g., *seismic, seismologist*).

sel. Abbreviation for *select, selected, selection, selector.*

self; *pl.,* **selves**

self- Compounds formed with *self-* are hyphenated (e.g., *self-addressed, self-confidence, self-conscious, self-defense, self-employed, self-important, self-respect, self-sufficient*).

selfsame

sell, sold

seller's market

selling point

sellout As noun.

seltzer

selvage *or* **selvedge** Edging, border, or outside part, especially in reference to fabric.

semantic *or* **semantical**

semaphore

semasiology Semantics.

semblance

semen

semi- Compounds formed with *semi-*, which means partly, or twice in a specific period, are written as one word, unless the second word is a proper noun or begins with *i* (e.g., *semiautobiographical, semicircle, semicolon, semifinal, semiprecious, semiretired, semisoft, semisweet,* but *semi-informed*).

semiannual *or* **biannual** *or* **semiyearly** Twice a year.

semimonthly *or* **bimonthly** Twice a month.

semiotic *or* **semiotics**

semiotics *or* **semiology**

semiprofessional *or* **semipro**

Semitic

semiweekly Twice a week. (Compare **biweekly**.)

sen. Abbreviation for *senator, senate.*

senator Capitalize only if part of a formal title preceding a name (e.g., *Senator Gillian Cole*, but *the senator from Maryland*).

send, sent

send-off As noun.

send-up As noun.

senescent Old, or in old age.

senior citizen

senor *or* **señor;** *pl.,* **senors** *or* **señores** Spanish courtesy title for a man.

senora *or* **señora** Spanish courtesy title for a married or older woman.

senorita *or* **señorita** Spanish courtesy title for a young, unmarried woman.

sensible Reasonable, practical, having good judgment. (Compare **sensitive**.)

sensitive Responding or feeling readily and acutely, receptive, attuned. (Compare **sensible**.)

sensorium; *pl.,* **sensoriums** *or* **sensoria** The sensory system.

sensual Indulgent of the bodily senses, especially in a sexual way. (Compare **sensuous**.)

sensuous Appealing or gratifying to the senses. (Compare **sensual**.)

sententious Expressing much in few words; or, trite and moralizing. (Compare **sentient**.)

sentient Aware. (Compare **sententious**.)

septicemia Variant for *blood poisoning* or *sepsis*.

septic tank

septuagenarian A person in his or her seventies.

septum; *pl.*, **septa** A partition between two cavities in a living thing, as in the human nose.

sepulcher or **sepulchre**

seq. Abbreviation for *sequel; sequence;* (Latin, *sequitur;* "it follows") or *sequens, sequentes, sequentia* (Latin, "the following").

sequined or **sequinned**

sequoia

ser. Abbreviation for *series*.

serape or **sarape** A woolen cloak worn in Latin America.

seraphim or **seraph**; *pl.*, **seraphim** or **seraphs**

Serbo-Croatian

sergeant at arms; *pl.*, **sergeants at arms** Capitalize only if part of a formal title preceding a name.

sergeant major; *pl.*, **sergeants major** or **sergeant majors** Capitalize only if part of a formal title preceding a name. Abbreviation is *Sgt. Maj.*

serial Occurring as a series. (Compare **cereal**.)

serial number

seriatim Arranged in a series.

serifed or **seriffed**

seriocomic

serious-minded

Sermon on the Mount

sero- Compounds formed with *sero-*, which means serum, are

written as one word (e.g., *serotype*).

serous Related to serum.

serum; *pl.*, **serums** or **sera** The watery part of blood or other animal fluid.

service-connected disability

serviette A table napkin (British usage).

sesame oil

sesqui- Compounds formed with *sesqui-* ("one and a half times") are written as one word (e.g., *sesquicentennial*).

session A meeting, or a planned part of an event. (Compare **cession**.)

setback As noun.

set-in As adjective and noun.

setout As noun.

set-piece As adjective.

set piece As noun.

setscrew

settee

settle A wooden bench with high back.

set-to; *pl.*, **set-tos**

setup As noun.

seventeen

seventh

Seventh-Day Adventist

seventy; *pl.*, **seventies**

Seven-Up or **7Up** Trademark for a type of soft drink.

Seven Wonders of the World

sew, sewn or **sewed** To repair or make using thread, needle, and fabric.

sewage Waste in a sewer or sewerage.

sexagenarian A person in his or her sixties.

sextet

sextuplet

SF Abbreviation for *square foot; science fiction.*

s/h Abbreviation for *shipping and handling.*

shade tree

shadowbox As verb.

shadow dance

shaggy-dog story A long, drawn-out story or joke that ultimately has no point.

shah Lowercase as descriptive noun, but capitalize when used as a name for a sovereign of Iran (i.e., *the Shah of Iran*).

shakedown As noun.

shakeout As noun.

Shakespeare, William (1564–1616) English dramatist and poet.

Shakespearean *or* **Shakespearian** *or* **Shakesperean** *or* **Shaksperian**

shake-up As noun.

shall, should

shalom Hebrew; a greeting meaning ''peace,'' or used as a greeting or farewell.

shamefaced

shampoo, shampooed

shamrock

shanghai, shanghaied To kidnap someone and force him or her into service.

Shangri-la An earthly paradise, a utopia.

shantytown

shapable *or* **shapeable**

-shaped Compounds ending in *-shaped* are hyphenated.

shape-up As noun.

shard *or* **sherd**

shareable *or* **sharable**

sharecropper

shareholder

sharkskin

sharper *or* **sharpie** *or* **sharpy** A person who cheats.

sharp practice

sharpshooter

sharp-sighted

sharp-tongued

shatterproof

shave, shaved *or* **shaven**

Shaw, George Bernard (1856–1950) Irish playwright and critic. Author of *Pygmalion.*

shawl collar

Shawnee; *pl.,* **Shawnee** *or* **Shawnees**

sheaf; *pl.,* **sheaves**

shear, sheared *or* **shorn** To cut, or to cut across. (Compare **sheer**.)

sheath; *pl.,* **sheaths**

sheathe *or* **sheath** As verb.

sheath knife

shebang Used in the phrase *the whole shebang* to mean the entire situation or a complete set of things.

sheepdog

sheepherder

sheepshead

sheepskin

sheer Utter; pure or transparent. (Compare **shear**.)

sheet glass

sheet music

Sheetrock Trademark for a type of plasterboard.

sheikh *or* **sheik** An Arab leader. (Compare **chic**.)

shelf; *pl.,* **shelves**

shelfful

shelf life
shelflike
shellac, shellacked
shellback
Shelley, Percy Bysshe
(1792–1822) English Romantic
poet and dramatist.
shellfish
shell game
shell-shocked
shenanigan
shepherd's pie
sherbet *or* sherbert
sheriff   Capitalize only if part of a
formal title preceding a name.
Shetland wool
shiatsu *or* shiatzu   Japanese; a type
of massage where finger pressure
is applied to acupuncture points.
shibboleth   Hebrew; a feature,
custom, idea, or saying that
distinguishes a particular group.
shift key
shillelagh *or* shillalah   Irish; a club
or cudgel.
shilling
shilly-shally
shinbone
shindig
shine, shone *or* shined
shinsplints
shipboard
shipbuilder
shipload
shipmate
shipshape
shipwrecked
shipyard
shirtdress
shirt jacket
shirt-sleeve *or* shirt-sleeves *or*
shirt-sleeved

shirttail
shirtwaist
shish kebab *or* shish kabob
shivaree *or* charivari
shock absorber
shocking pink
shockproof
shock wave
shoe, shod *or* shoed
shoehorn
shoelace
shoemaker
shoeshine
shoestring
shoe tree
shogun   An extremely powerful
Japanese military leader.
shoofly pie   A Pennsylvania Dutch
pie with a filling of either
molasses or brown sugar.
shoo-in
shook-up   Agitated.
shoot, shot
shoot-'em-up   A Western movie or
television show with a great deal
of gunfighting.
shoot-out   As noun.
-shop   Compounds ending in *-shop*
are written as one word (e.g.,
bakeshop).
shopkeeper *or* storekeeper
shoplifter
shopping center
shopping mall
shoptalk
shorefront
shoreline
short-   Compounds formed with
short- that are written as one word
include *shortbread, shortcake,
shortchange* (verb), *shortcoming,
shortcut, shortfall, shorthaired*

(adjective), shorthair (noun),
shorthand, shorthanded, shortlist
(noun), *shortsighted, shortstop,*
shortwave.

short-circuit As verb.

short circuit As noun.

short-haul As adjective.

short-list As verb.

short-lived

short-order As adjective.

short order As noun.

short-range

short ribs

short story

short subject

short-tempered

short-term

shorty *or* **shortie**; *pl.*, **shorties**

shotgun wedding

shot put

shot-putter

shoulder bag

shoulder blade

should not *or* **shouldn't**

shovel, shoveled *or* **shovelled**

shovelful; *pl.*, **shovelfuls** *or*
  shovelsful

show, shown *or* **showed**

show-and-tell

showboat

show business *or* **show biz**

showcase

showdown

show-off As noun.

showpiece

showplace

showroom

showstopper

shpmt. *or* **shipt.** *or* **ship.** *or*
  shipt. Abbreviations for
  shipment.

shredded wheat

shrift Confession.

shrimp; *pl.*, **shrimps** *or* **shrimp**

shrink, shrank *or* **shrunk**

shrinking violet

shrink-wrap

shrive, shrived *or* **shrove**

shrivel, shriveled *or* **shrivelled**

Shropshire sheep

Shrove Tuesday The Tuesday
  preceding Ash Wednesday, set
  aside as a day to go to confession
  and be shriven from sin.

shtick *or* **shtik** *or* **schtick** Yiddish;
  a method of doing something, or
  an idiosyncratic attribute or talent.

shuffleboard

shunpike A secondary road taken
  to avoid tolls on a major highway.

shush

shutdown As noun.

shut-eye

shut-in As adjective and noun.

shutoff As noun.

shutout As noun.

shutterbug An enthusiastic
  amateur photographer.

shuttlecock

shuttle diplomacy

shut up

shy; **shier** *or* **shyer**

shylock A loan shark, a creditor
  who loans money at extortionate
  rates.

shyster An unscrupulous lawyer.

Siamese twins

sibilant An *s* or *sh* sound.

sibling

sic *or* **sick, sicced** *or* **sicked** To
  chase or to set upon.

sic Latin; so, or thus. Used after a
  word (in printed material) to
  indicate that the word is intended

to appear exactly as it does. **Sic** is usually put in parentheses and italicized.

sick and tired

sickbed

sickie or **sicko**

sick leave

sickle-cell anemia

sick-out

sick pay

sickroom

SID, SIDS Abbreviations for *sudden infant death, sudden infant death syndrome.*

side-by-side As adjective.

side by side As adverb.

sidearm As adjective, adverb, and verb.

side arm As noun.

sidebar

sideboard

sideburns

sidecar

side dish

side effect

side-glance

sidekick

sidelight

sideline

sidelong

sidereal Relating to the stars.

sidesaddle

sideshow

sidesplitting

sidestep As verb.

side step As noun.

side street

sideswipe

sidetrack

sidewalk

sideward or **sidewards**

sideways or **sidewise** or **sideling**

sidewinder

sienna

sierra

sightboard

sight gag

sight-read

sight reader

sightseer

sight-seeing

signal, signaled or **signalled**

signer or **signee**

signet ring

significance or **significancy**

sign language

sign-off As noun.

signor or **signior** or **signore**; *pl.,* **signors** or **signori** or **signiors** Italian courtesy title for a man, men.

signora; *pl.,* **signoras** or **signore** Italian courtesy title for a married or older woman.

signorina; *pl.,* **signorinas** or **signorine** Italian courtesy title for an unmarried woman.

signpost

sign-up As adjective and noun.

Sikh An adherent of a monotheistic Hindu religion.

silence or **silentness**

silent partner

silhouette

silicon A naturally abundant nonmetallic chemical element. (Compare **silicone**.)

silicone A polymeric silicon compound. (Compare **silicon**.)

silk screen As noun.

silk-screen As verb.

silk-stocking As adjective.

silk stocking As noun.

silkworm

silo; *pl.,* silos
silverfish
silver screen
silver-tongued
silverware
simile   A phrase using *like* or *as* to make a comparison. (Compare **metaphor**.)
similitude   A likeness or image; a comparison. (Compare **simile**.)
simon-pure
simpatico
simpleminded
simpleton
simplex; *pl.,* **simplexes** *or* **simplices** *or* **simplicia**
simulacrum; *pl.,* **simulacra** *or* **simulacrums**
simulcast
simultaneousness *or* simultaneity
sincereness *or* sincerity
sinecure
sine die   Latin; without a date set or indefinitely.
sine qua non   Latin; essential item.
sing, sang *or* sung
sing. *or* sg.   Abbreviations for *singular.*
sing-along
single   Abbreviations include *sing., sgl., S.,* or *s.* In baseball, the abbreviation is *1b.*
single-action
single-breasted
single-handedly
single-hearted
single-minded
single-space   As verb.
singleton
single-track
singsong
sinistral   Left, or left-handed.

sink, sank *or* sunk
sinkhole
sinuous
sinus   Nasal cavity.
sinusitis
Sioux; *pl.,* Sioux
siphon *or* syphon
siren song
-sis   A suffix meaning "process," or "action" (e.g., *metamorphosis*).
sisal bag   A bag made from a type of hemp native to Mexico.
sister-in-law; *pl.,* sisters-in-law
Sistine chapel
sit-down   As adjective and noun.
site   A location or place (noun) or to locate, place in position (verb). (Compare **cite**.)
sit-in   As noun.
Sitting Bull   (c.1831–1890) American Indian leader.
sitting duck
sitting room
situation comedy *or* sitcom
sit-up   As noun.
sitz bath
six-gun *or* six-shooter
six-pack
sixteenth
sixth sense
sixty; *pl.,* sixties
sizable *or* sizeable
skateboard
skedaddle
skeg *or* skag
skein   A wound bundle of yarn.
skeleton key
sketchbook
skew lines
ski boot
skid row

skiddoo or skidoo To depart.
ski jump
ski lift
skillful or skilful
skill-less or skilless
skim milk
skin-deep
skin-dive As verb.
skin diver
skin diving
skinflint
skinhead
skinny-dipping
skin test
skintight
skirr To move by fast or skim.
skirt steak
skiwear
Skt. Abbreviation for *Sanskrit*.
skulduggery or skullduggery
skull The skeleton of the head.
   (Compare **scull**.)
skull and crossbones
sky blue
skycap
sky diver
skydiving
sky-high
skyjack
skylark
skylight
skyline
skyrocket
skyscraper
skywalk
skyway
skywrite
SL Abbreviation for *sea level*.
slab-sided
slalom
slam-bang
slander Spoken or indicated

defamation or misrepresentation.
   (Compare **libel**.)
slantways or slantwise
slapdash
slaphappy
slap shot
slapstick
slash-and-burn
slash pocket
slate black
slave driver
slaver To drool. (Compare
   slavery, slavish.)
slavery The owning or keeping of
   slaves; domination; hard work.
   (Compare **slaver, slavish**.)
slavish Subservient; laborious;
   imitative. (Compare **slaver,
   slavery**.)
slay, slew
sled dog
sledgehammer
sleep, slept
sleep-in As adjective.
sleeping bag
sleepwalker
sleepwear
sleepyhead
sleigh bell
sleight of hand
slenderize
slew A large number.
slice-of-life
slide rule
sliding scale
slime Mud, or a sticky substance.
slingshot or slungshot
slink, slunk or slinked
slipcover
slipknot
slip-on As noun.
slipover or pullover

slipped disk

slipper   A lightweight shoe for indoor wear.

slipshod

slip stitch

slipup   As noun.

slit, slitted or slit

sliver   A splinter, or a scrap.

sloe-eyed   Having almond-shaped, dark eyes.

sloe gin

slog   To move along trudgingly. (Compare slough.)

slogan

sloshed   Drunk.

slotback

slot machine

slough   To sluff, shed. (Compare slog.)

slowdown   As noun.

slow-motion   As adjective.

slow motion   As noun.

slow-pitch or slo-pitch

slowpoke

slow-witted

SLP   Abbreviation for super long play.

sluiceway

slumberous or slumbrous

slumber party

slush fund

sly, slier or slyer

sm. or sml. or S or s   Abbreviations for small.

smack-dab

small-claims court

small-fry

small-minded

smallmouth bass

smallpox

small-scale

small talk

small-time

smarmy

smart aleck or smart alec

smart-alecky or smart-aleck

smart money

smarty or smartie; pl., smarties

smarty-pants

smashup   As noun.

smegma

smell, smelled or smelt

smelling salts

smidgen or smidgeon or smidgin

smirch   To dirty, or to discredit. (Compare smirk.)

smirk   To smile smugly. (Compare smirch.)

smite, smote

smithereens

Smithfield ham

smokable or smokeable

smoke bomb

smoke detector

smoke-filled room

smokehouse

smoke screen

smokestack

smoky or smokey

smolder or smoulder

smoothy or smoothie; pl., smoothies

smorgasbord

SMV   Abbreviation for slow-moving vehicle.

SN   Abbreviation for serial number.

snack bar

snafu

snaggletooth

snaillike

snail-paced

snakebite

snake charmer

snake-dance   As verb.

snake dance   As noun.

snake in the grass

snakelike

snake pit

snakeskin

snaky *or* snakey

snap bean

snapdragon

snapshot

snare drum

sneak, sneaked *or* snuck

sneaker   A casual shoe, a shoe
worn for athletic activity.

sneak preview

snicker *or* snigger   To laugh in a
sly and partly stifled manner.

snip   To cut. (Compare **snipe**.)

snipe   To shoot at, or to attack.
(Compare **snip**.)

snivel, sniveled *or* snivelled

snob appeal

snorer   A person who wheezes
during sleep. (Compare
schnorrer.)

snow-   Compounds formed with
snow- that are written as one word
include *snowball, snowbank,
snowbelt, snowbird, snowblower,
snowbound, snowdrift, snowdrop,
snowfall, snowfield, snowflake,
snowmaker, snowman, snowplow,
snowscape, snowshoe, snowshoer,
snowstorm, snowsuit.*

snow-blind *or* snow-blinded

snow cone *or* sno-cone

snow fence

snow job

snowmobiler *or* snowmobilist

snow pea

snow-white

snub-nosed

so-and-so; *pl.,* so-and-sos *or* so-
and-so's

soapbox

soap bubble

soap opera

soapsuds

soar   To move up or along very
fast, to glide high in the air.

Soave wine

so be it   Then let it be so.
(Compare **sobeit**.)

sobeit   Provided that, if it should
be that. (Compare **so be it**.)

sobriquet *or* soubriquet   French; a
nickname.

sob story

soc. *or* socy.   Abbreviation for
society.

so-called

sociability *or* sociality

socialist, socialism   Capitalize
socialist if referring to the
political party or one of its
members.

social security   Can be capitalized
when referring to the U.S.
government program.

social worker

society   Capitalize only if part of
proper noun (e.g., *Society of
Friends*).

socio-   Compounds formed with
socio-, which means social,
society, or sociological, are
written as one word (e.g.,
socioeconomic).

sociol.   Abbreviation for *sociology*.

socket wrench

Socrates   (c.470–399 B.C.) Greek
philosopher. Worked with Plato to
establish a philosophy of ideas on
the foundation of Western culture.

Socratic

soda jerk

soda pop

soda water

sofa bed

softball

soft-boiled

soft-core

softcover or **softbound**   Used to describe a paperback book.

soft-focus

softheaded

softhearted

soft-pedal   As verb.

soft-shell or **soft-shelled**

soft-shoe

soft-soap   As verb.

soft-spoken

software   Computer programs, or programmable or interchangeable recording components used with hardware. (Compare **hardware**.)

softy or **softie**; *pl.,* **softies**

soigné or **soignée**   French; carefully maintained or first-rate.

soiree or **soirée**   An evening party or reception.

sojourner

solder   To melt metals together; unite.

soldering iron

soldier of fortune

sold-out

solecism   A blunder in speaking.

solicitation or **solicitude**

solicitor general; *pl.,* **solicitors general**   Capitalize only if part of a formal title preceding a name.

solidarity   Unity. (Compare **solidity**.)

solidity   Hardness, compactness. (Compare **solidarity**.)

solid-state

solitaire

soluble   Dissolvable.

solvable   Explainable.

solvent   Able to pay, financially stable.

soma; *pl.,* **somata** or **somas**

somat-, somato-   Compounds of this combining form, which means body, are written as one word (e.g., *somatoplasm*).

somber or **sombre**

some-   Compounds formed with *some-* that are written as one word include *somebody, someday, somehow, someone, someplace, something, sometime, sometimes, someway, somewhat, somewhere.*

somersault or **summersault**

sometimes   At times.

sommelier; *pl.,* **sommeliers**   French; wine steward.

somnambulate   To sleepwalk.

somnolence or **somnolency**

sonar   Sound, navigation, and ranging.

song and dance

songbird

songbook

song titles   (See Part 2, **Titles of works**.)

songwriter

sonic boom

son-in-law; *pl.,* **sons-in-law**

son of God   Capitalize as *Son of God* when referring to Jesus Christ.

son of man   Capitalize as *Son of Man* when referring to Jesus Christ.

sooner or later

soothsayer

SOP Abbreviation for *standard operating procedure*.

sopaipilla *or* **sopapilla** Spanish; sweetened, deep-fried dough.

sophistic *or* **sophistical**

sophistry *or* **sophism**

Sophocles (c.496–406 B.C.) Greek tragic playwright. Author of *Antigone* and *Oedipus Rex*.

sophomore *or* **soph**

-sophy A combining form meaning "knowledge," or "science" (e.g., *theosophy*).

soporific *or* **soporiferous**

soprano; *pl.,* **sopranos**

sorbet Fruit-flavored ice.

sorehead

sore throat

sorghum

sorority; *pl.,* **sororities**

sorrowful

sortie A military raid.

SOS A signal of distress.

so-so

soufflé *or* **souffléed** French; a fluffy baked dish made with beaten egg whites, egg yolks, and a flavorful purée.

soul kiss *or* **French kiss**

soul mate

soul music

soul-searching

sound barrier

sound bite

soundproof

soundstage

sound track

sound truck

soupçon French; a tiny amount, a trace.

soup du jour Soup of the day.

soup kitchen

soupspoon

sour ball

source language

sourcebook

sour cream

sourdough

sour grapes

sour mash

sourpuss

sousaphone

Southeast Asia

southerner

southmost *or* **southernmost**

South Pole

souvenir

souvlakia *or* **souvlaki** Greek; shish kebab.

sow, sown *or* **sowed**

soybean

soy sauce

sp. Abbreviation for *spell, spelled, spelling*.

space-age

spacecraft

spaced-out *or* **spaced**

spaceflight

space heater

spaceship

space shuttle

space suit

space-time

space walk

spacey *or* **spacy**

spacious Roomy.

spackle

spaghetti western A movie about cowboys in the western U.S. made by Italians.

spandex

spaniel

Spanish rice

spar To box, fight. (Compare **spare**.)

spare To refrain. (Compare **spar**.)

spareribs

sparkling wine

spark plug

sparring partner

Spartan

spate A flood, or a bunch.

speakeasy

speakerphone

spearhead

spearmint

spec, specced or **spec'd**

spec. or **sp.** or **spl.** Abbreviation for *special*.

special or **especial**

special delivery

specially or **especially**

specialty or **speciality** Distinctive feature, point, activity, or characteristic.

species; *pl.,* **species**

specif. or **spec.** Abbreviations for *specific, specifically, specification*.

specious Deceptively attractive.

spectacles or **specs**

specter or **spectre**

spectro- Compounds formed with *spectro-*, which means of radiant energy (as exhibited in a spectrum), are written as one word (e.g., *spectroscopy*).

spectrum; *pl.,* **spectra** or **spectrums**

speech and lecture titles (See Part 2, **Titles of works**.)

speechwriter

speed, sped or **speeded**

speedball

speedboat

speedometer

speed-read

speed trap

speedup As noun.

speedway

speedwriting

spelling bee

spelunker Someone who explores caves.

spendthrift

sperm-, spermo-, sperma-, spermi-, spermat-, spermato- Compounds of these combining forms, all of which mean seed, are written as one word (e.g., *spermatic, spermatozoic*).

sperm whale

SPF Abbreviation for *sun protection factor*, used as a guide to the strength of sunblocks and tanning lotions.

sphere of influence

sphincter

sphinx; *pl.,* **sphinxes** or **sphinges**

spick-and-span or **spic-and-span**

spiderweb

spiel German; to talk at length extravagantly, to persuade, or to give a sales pitch.

spill, spilled or **spilt**

spillover As noun.

spill the beans

spinnaker

spin-off As noun.

spin off As verb.

spinout As noun.

Spinoza, Benedict (1632–1677) Dutch philosopher of rational pantheism. Author of *Tractatus Theologico-Politicus*.

spin the bottle

spiral binding

spiral-bound

spiraled *or* **spiralled**

spirits Alcohol.

spirituous *or* **spiritous** Containing alcohol.

spit, spit *or* **spat**

spit and polish

spitball

spit curl

spiteful

spitfire

spitting image

splashdown As noun.

splash guard

splay To spread out.

splendent Shiny.

splendid *or* **splendiferous**

splendorous *or* **splendrous**

splenetic Spiteful.

split-brain

split decision

split end

split-level

split-up

spoil, spoiled *or* **spoilt**

spoilsport

spokesperson

spoliate To plunder.

sponge bath

sponge cake

spoon bread

spoon-feed, spoon-fed

spoonful; *pl.,* **spoonfuls** *or* **spoonsful**

spor-, spori-, sporo- Compounds of these combining forms, which refer to seeds or spores, are written as one word: *sporogenesis.*

sport *or* **sports** As adjective.

sport fish As verb.

sportfisherman

sportive Playful.

sports car

sportscaster

sportswear

sportswriter

spot-check

spotlight

spot test

spray gun

spread-eagle As adjective or verb.

sprier *or* **spryer**

spring, sprang *or* **sprung**

springboard

spring chicken A young, inexperienced person.

spring-cleaning

springer spaniel

spring fever

springform pan

spring-load

springtime *or* **springtide**

springwater

spruce pine

spumoni *or* **spumone** An Italian ice-cream dessert.

spun glass

spun sugar

spurious Falsified, deceitful.

spur-of-the-moment

sputnik Russian; literally, ''traveling companion'' (of the Earth), a satellite.

spy; *pl.,* **spies**

spyglass

sq. *or* **sqr.** Abbreviations for *square.*

squad car

squalid Sordid, dirty.

square Capitalize only if part of address or proper noun (e.g., *Harvard Square*).

square dance

square one

square root

square shooter

squash; *pl.*, squashes *or* squash

squash racquets Singles or doubles game played with rubber ball.

squash tennis Singles game played with inflated ball.

squeegee

squeeze bottle

squeeze play

squirrel, squirreled *or* squirrelled

squirt gun

Sr. Abbreviation for *senior* in a family name; follows surname (e.g., *Harold Pope, Sr.*).

SRO Abbreviation for *standing room only* or *single room occupancy*.

SS Abbreviation for *shortstop; Social Security.*

SST Abbreviation for *supersonic transport.*

staccato

staff; *pl.*, staffs *or* staves Club, stick.

staff; *pl.*, staff Personnel.

Staffordshire terrier

stagecoach

stage fright

stagehand

stage-manage

stage manager

stage set

stagestruck

stagflation

staid Serious.

stained glass As noun.

stained-glass As adjective.

stainless steel

staircase

stairway

stairwell

stakeholder

stakeout As noun.

stalactite Calcium carbonate, hanging down.

stalagmite Calcium carbonate, pointing up.

stalemate

Stalin, Joseph (1879–1953) Soviet political leader; close associate of V. I. Lenin.

stamen; *pl.*, stamens *or* stamina

stamina Endurance, energy.

stamping ground

stand, stood

stand-alone

standard of living

standard time

standard-bearer

standby As adjective, adverb, or noun.

stand-in As noun.

standoff As adjective and noun.

standoffish

standout As noun.

standpat As adjective.

stand pat As verb.

standpoint

standstill

stand-up comedian

Stanford-Binet test A test designed to measure intelligence.

staphylococcal *or* staphylococcic

starboard

star-crossed

stardom

stardust

starfish

starflower

stargazer

starlight

star-of-Bethlehem A type of lily.

star of Bethlehem In the Christian

tradition, the star that guided the Magi to the newborn Jesus.

Star of David or **Magen David** A six-sided star that is a symbol for Judaism.

starry-eyed

Stars and Stripes The flag of the United States of America.

star sapphire

star-spangled or **star-studded**

starting block

start-up As noun.

stasis; *pl.*, **stases** Equilibrium, or stagnation.

statable or **stateable**

state Capitalize only if referring to a specific state (e.g., *the State of New Hampshire*, but *the Middle Atlantic* states).

statehouse

state line

state-of-the-art As adjective.

state of the art As noun.

stateroom

state's attorney

state's evidence

states' rights

stateside

statewide

static or **statical**

station Capitalize if part of proper noun (e.g., *Grand Central Station*), but not when referring to media (e.g., *radio station WPLR, station WTNH*).

stationary Immobile, fixed. (Compare **stationery**.)

station break

stationer A seller of paper goods.

stationery Paper goods for writing or typing. (Compare **stationary**.)

station house

station wagon

statue, statuary, statuette Representative sculpture.

Statue of Liberty

statuesque

stature Height or status. (Compare **statute**.)

status; *pl.*, **statuses**

status quo Latin; the existing situation.

statute A law. (Compare **stature**.)

statute mile The standard measurement of the mile, 5,280 feet.

statutory or **statutable**

stave, staved or **stove**

stay, stayed or **staid**

stay-at-home

staying power

std. or **stan.** Abbreviation for *standard*.

steadfast

steady; *pl.*, **steadies**

steak knife

steak tartare

steamboat

steam engine

steamer trunk

steamfitter

steam fitting

steamroller As noun.

steamroller or **steamroll** As verb.

steamship

steam table

steel-trap

steel wool

steelworker

steelyard

steeplechase

steering committee

steering wheel

stein A large mug.

Stein, Gertrude (1874–1946) American writer who experimented in using Cubist theories in literature. Author of *Tender Buttons*.

stellar Relating to the stars, or very important, outstanding.

stemware

sten-, steno- Compounds of this combining form, which means narrow, thin, or small, are written as one word (e.g., *stenographer*).

stencil, stenciled *or* **stencilled**

step Compounds with *step-* designating family are written as one word: *stepbrother*, *stepchild*, *stepdaughter*, *stepfather*, *stepmother*, *stepparent*, *stepsister*, *stepson*.

step-by-step

step-down As noun.

step-in As noun.

stepladder

stepped-up

stepping-off place

stepping-place

stepping-stone

step-up As noun.

-ster A combining form that indicates a person who does or uses (e.g., *trickster*).

stere-, stereo- Compounds of this combining form, which means solid, firm, or three-dimensional, are written as one word (e.g., *stereophonic*).

stereo; *pl.,* **stereos**

stereotypical *or* **sterotypic**

sterling silver

sternum; *pl.,* **sternums** *or* **sterna**

stern-wheeler

stet Latin; literally, "let it stand," leave as is.

stethoscope

Stetson

stevedore

Stevens, Wallace (1879–1955) American poet. Author of *The Blue Guitar*.

Stevenson, Adlai (1835–1914) American politician. Vice-president of the United States.

Stevenson, Adlai (1900–1965) American politician. Democratic candidate for U.S. president. Grandson of Adlai Stevenson.

Stevenson, Robert Louis (1850–1894) Scottish writer. Author of *Dr. Jekyll and Mr. Hyde*.

stickball

stick-in-the-mud

stickpin

stick shift A manual transmission.

stick-to-itiveness

stickum

stickup As noun.

Stieglitz, Alfred (1864–1946) American photographer, editor, and founder of the Photo-Secession Group. Georgia O'Keefe's spouse.

stiff-arm *or* **straight-arm**

stiff-necked

stiff upper lip

stigma; *pl.,* **stigmas**

stigmata Marks on the body corresponding to and resembling the wounds of the crucified Christ, sometimes associated with religious ecstasy.

stiletto; *pl.,* **stilettos** *or* **stilettoes**

stillborn

still life; *pl.*, still lifes
Stilton cheese
stimulus; *pl.*, stimuli
sting, stung
stingray
stink, stank *or* stunk
stir-crazy
stir-fry
stirrup
stochastic Random, chance.
stockbroker
stock car
stockholder
stocking cap
stock-in-trade
stockpiler
stockroom
stock-still
stocktaking
stockyard
stogie *or* stogy; *pl.*, stogies
stoic *or* stoical
stopwatch
store-bought
storefront
storehouse
storekeeper
storeroom
storied *or* storeyed
storm door
storm window
story *or* storey; *pl.*, stories *or*
    storeys A floor or a level of a
    building.
story; *pl.*, stories An account, or
    narrative. (See also Part 2, **Titles
    of works.**)
storyboard
storybook
story line
storyteller
stouthearted

stovepipe
stowaway As noun.
Stowe, Harriet Beecher
    (1811–1896) American author and
    antislavery abolitionist. Author of
    Uncle Tom's Cabin.
stolid Unemotional.
stoma; *pl.*, stomata *or* stomas
stomachache
stomat-, stomato- Compounds of
    this combining form, which means
    of, like, or relating to the mouth,
    are written as one word (e.g.,
    stomatitis).
Stone Age
stone-blind
stone-broke
stone-cold
stonecutter
stone-deaf
stone's throw
stone wall As noun.
stonewaller
stoneware
stony *or* stoney
stool pigeon *or* stoolie
stop-and-go
stopgap
stoplight
stopover As noun.
stop payment
stop sign
-storm Compounds formed with
    -storm are usually written as one
    word (e.g., *snowstorm*).
Stradivarius A violin made by
    Antonio Stradivari (1644–1737).
straight As *or* straight A's
straight and narrow
straight-arrow As adjective.
straightaway
straightedge

straightforward

straight-line As adjective.

straight-out

straight razor

strait A narrow passageway, or a bad situation. Capitalize if part of proper noun (e.g., *the Bosphorus Strait*).

straitjacket *or* **straightjacket**

straitlaced *or* **straightlaced**

stranglehold

straphanger A regular subway rider.

strapless

stratagem A trick, deception. (Compare **strategy**.)

strategic *or* **strategical**

strategy A plan. (Compare **stratagem**.)

stratosphere

stratum; *pl.,* **strata** A layer.

Stravinsky, Igor (1882–1971) American composer. Composed the ballet *Rite of Spring*.

strawberry

straw boss

strawflower

straw vote

streamline

stream of consciousness

street Capitalize only if part of address (e.g., *5 Water Street*, but *a tree-lined street*). Abbreviation is *St.*

streetcar

street-length

streetlight

strength; *pl.,* **strengths**

strep throat *or* **septic sore throat**

strew, strewed *or* **strewn**

striate

stricture A narrowing, a restriction, or a criticism.

stridence *or* **stridency**

strident Harsh, loud. (Compare **stridulous**.)

stridulous Shrill-sounding. (Compare **strident**.)

strife; *pl.,* **strifes**

strike, struck *or* **stricken**

strikebreaker

strikeout As noun. The abbreviation is *K* (*SO* for "strikeouts").

strikeover As noun.

strike zone

string bean

stringent Tight, strict.

string quartet

strip-cropping

stripe To make lines on.

strip mine As noun.

strip-mine As verb.

stripped-down

strive, strove *or* **strived**

strobe *or* **strobe light**

strong-arm

strongbox

stronghold

strong-minded

strong point *or* **strong suit**

struct. *or* **struc.** Abbreviation for *structure*.

strudel German; a pastry made by rolling dough around a filling.

strychnine

stucco; *pl.,* **stuccos** *or* **stuccoes**

stuck-up

stud. Abbreviation for *student*.

studhorse

studio; *pl.,* **studios**

study; *pl.,* **studies**

stuffed shirt

stumblebum

stumbling block

stupendous Tremendous, amazing. (Compare **stuporous**.)

stuporous In a dull state. (Compare **stupendous**.)

sturgeon A type of fish.

Sturm und Drang German; literally, "storm and stress," a literary movement celebrating the individual's struggle against society. Individual turmoil, volatility. (See **Nietzsche**.)

stylebook

stylus; *pl.*, **styli** *or* **styluses**

styptic pencil

Styrofoam A trade name for a type of polystyrene plastic.

suasion Persuasion.

sub- Compounds formed with *sub-*, which means under, beneath, or inferior, are written as one word (e.g., *subcommittee, subconscious, subcontractor, subculture, subdivide, subhuman, subnormal, subordinate, subplot, subservient, subset, substructure, subtotal, subzero*).

subj. Abbreviation for *subject; subjective, subjectively; subjunctive.*

subjacent Lying under; lower. (Compare **subjugate**.)

subject matter

subjugate To control, conquer. (Compare **subjacent**.)

sublate To deny.

sublease *or* **sublet**

sublime Exalted, grand.

submachine gun

subpoena

sub-rosa As adjective.

sub rosa As adverb.

subs. *or* **sub.** Abbreviations for *subscriber, subscription; subsidiary.*

subs. *or* **subst.** Abbreviation for *substitute; substantive.*

subscript Symbol written below and adjacent to another. (Compare **superscript**.)

subsequent Following, succeeding.

subservience *or* **subserviency**

substand. *or* **substd.** Abbreviations for *substandard.*

substantive Essential, enduring, or a considerable amount (as adjective), or a group of words used as a noun (as noun).

substitute To put something in the place of.

substratum; *pl.*, **substrata**

subsume To encompass or include in a larger group.

subterranean *or* **subterraneous**

subtile Cunning, discerning. (Compare **subtle**.)

subtitle An explanatory title appended to the main title.

subtle Delicate, obscure or keen, ingenious. (Compare **subtile**.)

subvert To corrupt or ruin.

succeed To achieve or attain a goal. (Compare **secede**.)

succor Help.

such and such

sudden infant death syndrome *or* **crib death**

suede *or* **suède**

suff Abbreviation for *sufficient; suffix.*

suffuse To fill, spread.

sugarcane

sugarcoat

sugarhouse

sugar-loaf As adjective.

sugarloaf As noun.

sugar maple

sugarplum

sugg. *or* **sug.** Abbreviations for *suggested, suggestion*.

sui generis Latin; one of a kind.

sui juris Latin; literally, "of one's own right," having full ability to manage one's own legal affairs.

suitcase

suitor A person who courts another.

sukiyaki A Japanese dish of meat and vegetables cooked quickly in soy sauce, sake, and sugar.

sulfur *or* **sulphur**

sulfuric acid

sumac *or* **sumach**

summa cum laude Distinguishes a university degree as being of the highest honors.

summerhouse

summer school

summertime

summing-up

summit meeting

sumo wrestler

sump pump

sumptuous Excessive, expensive, extravagant.

sunbaked

sunbather

sunbeam

Sunbelt The southern and southwestern United States.

sunburn, sunburned *or* **sunburnt**

sundae

Sunday school

sun deck

sundial

sundown

sundries Various items. (Compare **sundry**.)

sundry Various. (Compare **sundries**.)

sunflower

sunglasses

sunlamp

sunlight

sunny-side up

sunroof

sunscreen

sunset

sunshine

sunspot

suntanned

sunup

sup. Abbreviation for *supra*, "above".

super- Compounds formed with *super-* are written as one word (e.g., *superannuated, superego, superhighway, superhuman, supermarket, supernatural, superpower, superstar, superstructure*).

super. *or* **sup.** Abbreviations for *superior*.

superciliary Relating to eyebrows. (Compare **supercilious**.)

supercilious Cool, haughty. (Compare **superciliary**.)

super-duper

supererogatory Not needed; extra. (Compare **supernumerary**.)

superfluous Wasteful, extra.

superintendence *or* **superintendency**

superintendent Capitalize *superintendent* if part of formal title or proper noun.

superior court

superjacent Lying above.

superlative Unsurpassed, excellent or excessive (as adjective), or the utmost degree (as noun).

supernumerary Exceeding, numerous. (Compare **supererogatory**.)

superscript Symbol written above and adjacent to another, as when indicating a footnote. (Compare **subscript**.)

supersede To take the place of or force out.

supine Lying on one's back, face up. (Compare **prone**.)

supper club or **nightclub**

suppertime

suppl. or **supp.** or **sup.** Abbreviations for *supplement, supplementary.*

suppliant or **supplicant**

supplicate To be humble or ask humbly.

supposititious or **suppositious** Spurious, counterfeit, or hypothetical. (Compare **suppository**.)

suppository Medicine inserted into a body cavity such as the rectum, where it is melted or diffused by the body temperature. (Compare **supposititious**.)

supr. or **sup.** Abbreviations for *supreme.*

supra- Compounds formed with *supra-*, which means above or over, are written as one word, unless the second word begins with an *a* (e.g., *supramolecular*).

supreme court Capitalize if part of proper noun or formal title and in any references to the Supreme Court of the United States.

Supreme Court Justices Members of the court should be addressed as *Mr./Madam Justice _____.* Justices who have served the court (an * denotes *chief justice*):

*John Jay
   1789–95
John Blair
   1789–96
William Cushing
   1789–1810
Robert H. Harrison
   1789–90
John Rutledge
   1789–91
James Wilson
   1789–98
James Iredell
   1790–99
Thomas Johnson
   1791–93
William Paterson
   1793–1806
*John Rutledge
   1795 (Congress rejected appointment)
*Oliver Ellsworth
   1796–99
Samuel Chase
   1796–1811
Bushrod Washington
   1798–1829
Alfred Moore
   1799–1804
*John Marshall
   1801–35
William Johnson
   1804–34
Brockolst Livingston
   1806–23

Thomas Todd
1807–26

Joseph Story
1811–45

Gabriel Duval
1812–35

Smith Thompson
1823–43

Robert Trimble
1826–28

John McLean
1829–61

Henry Baldwin
1830–44

James M. Wayne
1835–67

*Roger B. Taney
1836–64

Philip P. Barbour
1836–41

John Catron
1837–65

John McKinley
1837–52

Peter V. Daniel
1841–60

Samuel Nelson
1845–72

Levi Woodbury
1845–51

Robert C. Grier
1846–70

Benjamin R. Curtis
1851–57

John A. Campbell
1853–61

Nathan Clifford
1858–81

David Davis
1862–77

Samuel F. Miller
1862–90

Noah H. Swayne
1862–81

Stephen J. Field
1863–97

*Salmon P. Chase
1864–73

Joseph P. Bradley
1870–92

Wiliam Strong
1870–80

Ward Hunt
1873–82

*Morrison R. Waite
1874–88

John M. Harlan
1877–1911

Stanley Matthews
1881–89

William B. Woods
1881–87

Samuel Blatchford
1882–1903

Horace Gray
1882–1902

*Melville W. Fuller
1888–1910

Lucius Q. C. Lamar
1888–93

David J. Brewer
1890–1910

Henry B. Brown
1891–1906

George Shiras, Jr.
1892–1903

Howell E. Jackson
1893–95

Edward D. White
1894–1910

Rufus W. Peckham
1896–1909

Joseph McKenna
1898–1925

Oliver W. Holmes
1902–32

William R. Day
1903–22

William H. Moody
1906–10

*Edward D. White
1910–21

Charles E. Hughes
1910–16

Horace H. Lurton
1910–14

Joseph R. Lamar
1911–16

Willis Van Devanter
1911–37

Mahlon Pitney
1912–22

James C. McReynolds
1914–41

Louis D. Brandeis
1916–39

John H. Clarke
1916–22

*William H. Taft
1921–30

Pierce Butler
1922–39

George Sutherland
1922–38

Edward T. Sanford
1923–30

Harlan F. Stone
1925–41

*Charles E. Hughes
1930–41

Owen J. Roberts
1930–45

Benjamin N. Cardozo
1932–38

Hugo L. Black
1937–71

Stanley F. Reed
1938–57

William O. Douglas
1939–75

Felix Frankfurter
1939–62

Frank Murphy
1940–49

*Harlan F. Stone
1941–46

James F. Byrnes
1941–42

Robert H. Jackson
1941–54

Wiley B. Rutledge
1943–49

Harold H. Burton
1945–58

*Fred M. Vinson
1946–53

Tom C. Clark
1949–67

Sherman Minton
1949–56

*Earl Warren
1953–69

John Marshall Harlan
1955–71

William H. Brennan, Jr.
1956–

Charles E. Whittaker
1957–62

Potter Stewart
1958–81

Arthur J. Goldberg
1962–65

Byron R. White
1962–

Abe Fortas
1965–69

Thurgood Marshall
1967–91

*Warren E. Burger
1969–86
Harry A. Blackmun
1970–
Lewis F. Powell, Jr.
1972–87
*William H. Renquist
1972–
John Paul Stevens, III
1975–
Sandra Day O'Connor
1981–
Antonin Scalia
1986–
Anthony Kennedy
1988–
Clarence Thomas
1992–

supt. *or* **supr.** Abbreviations for for *superintendent*.

supvr. *or* **super.** Abbreviation for *supervisor*.

sur- Compounds formed with this prefix, which means above, over, or up, are written as one word (e.g., *surcharge, surtax*).

surcease To discontinue.

sure-enough As adjective.

sure enough As adverb.

surefire

surefooted

sure-handed

sure thing

surety A guarantee.

surface structure

surface-to-air missile

surfboard

surfeit An excess.

surg. Abbreviation for *surgeon, surgery, surgical*.

surgeon general; *pl.*, **surgeons general** Capitalize only if part of

a formal title preceding a name: *Surgeon General Antonia Novello*.

surplus

surreptitious Clandestine.

surv. *or* **svy.** Abbreviations for *survey*.

survivor *or* **survivalist**

sushi A Japanese dish made by rolling flavored cold rice in raw fish or seaweed.

suspendable *or* **suspensible**

suspended animation

susurrous Whispering.

s.v. Abbreviation for *sub verbo* or *sub voce*, ''under the word.''

svelte Slim-figured.

Svengali

svgs. *or* **savs.** Abbreviations for *savings*.

swaddling clothes

swag curtain

Swahili; *pl.*, **Swahili** *or* **Swahilis**

SWAK Abbreviation for *sealed with a kiss*.

swami

swampland

swan dive

swank *or* **swanky**

swan song

swastika

SWAT Abbreviation for *Special Weapons and Tactics*.

swath *or* **swathe** A cut row.

swayback As noun.

swearword

sweat, sweat *or* **sweated**

sweatband

sweatpants

sweatshirt

sweatshop

sweat suit

sweep, swept

sweepstakes
sweet-and-sour
sweetbrier
sweet corn
sweetheart
sweetie pie
sweet-talk   As verb.
sweet talk   As noun.
sweet tooth
swelled head
swept-back
swim, swam
swimmer's itch
swimmingly   Easily and with success.
swimming pool
swimsuit
swingby   As noun.
swing shift
Swiss cheese
Swiss steak
switchblade
switchboard
switcheroo; *pl.*, switcheroos
switch-hit
swivel, swiveled *or* swivelled
swivel chair
swivel-hipped
swizzle stick
swordfish
swordplay
SY   Abbreviation for *square yard.*
sybarite   A sensuous person.
sycophantic *or* sycophantish
syllabication *or* syllabification
syllabus; *pl.*, syllabi *or* syllabuses

sym.   Abbreviation for *symbol, symbolic.*
symbiosis; *pl.*, symbioses
symbol   Something that represents another thing. (Compare cymbal.)
symbolic *or* symbolical
symmetrical *or* symmetric
symposium; *pl.*, symposia *or* symposiums
syn-, sym-   Compounds of these prefixes, which mean with, or at the same time, are written as one word (e.g., *synchronize*).
syn.   Abbreviation for *synonym, synonymous, synonymy.*
synagogue *or* synagog   A meeting place, or a congregation of people gathered for Jewish worship.
sync *or* synch
sync. *or* synch. *or* syn.   Abbreviations for *synchronize* and variants.
synchronic *or* synchronous *or* synchronical
synd.   Abbreviation for *syndicate.*
synecdochic *or* synecdochical
synodal *or* synodic *or* synodical
synoptic *or* synoptical
syrup *or* sirup
sys. *or* syst.   Abbreviations for *system.*
systaltic   Pulsing.
systematic *or* systematical
systemic   Relating to the body's system.
systems analysis

T

t. *or* **tn.** Abbreviations for *ton*.

TA Abbreviation for *teaching assistant*.

Tabasco sauce

table d'hôte French; a communal meal served to all guests within given hours and at a fixed price.

table-hopper

table linen

table talk

table tennis *or* **Ping-Pong**

tableau; *pl.,* **tableaux** *or* **tableaus**

tablecloth

tablemate

tablespoonful; *pl.,* **tablespoonfuls** *or* **tablespoonsful**

tabletop

tableware

taboo *or* **tabu**

tabor *or* **tabour** A small drum played by a fifer as an accompaniment to his or her fife.

taboret *or* **tabouret** French; a low stool.

tabula rasa; *pl.,* **tabulae rasae** Latin; a state of the mind as a hypothetical "blank state," before receiving any outside impressions or experience.

tachy- Compounds formed with *tachy-*, which means rapid or swift, are written as one word (e.g., *tachycardia*).

tacit Implied, indicated.

taco; *pl.,* **tacos**

tadpole

tae kwon do *or* **Tae Kwon Do** A Korean martial art.

taedium vitae Latin; an exhaustion or despising of life.

tagalong As noun.

tag sale

Tahitian

tailback

tail end

tail fin

tailgater

taillight

taillike

tailor-made

tail pipe

tailspin

tail wind

take, took

takedown As adjective, noun.

take-home pay

take-in As noun.

takeout As noun.

take-out As adjective.

take-up As noun.

takeoff As noun.

takeover As noun.

talcum powder

talisman; *pl.,* **talismans**

talking-to

talk show

tallyho

Talmud

tamable *or* **tameable**

tamale A hot, highly seasoned Mexican dish.

tambourine

tam-o'-shanter

tamperproof

tandem bicycle

Tao Mandarin Chinese; literally, "the Way," a philosophical and religious principle that is the basis of the teachings of Lao-tse, dating from the sixth century B.C.

tap dance As noun.

tap-dance As verb.

tap dancer
tap dancing
tape deck
tape measure
tape player
tapestry *or* tapis
tapeworm
tapioca
tap pants
taproom
tarantula; *pl.*, tarantulas *or* tarantulae
tarmac *or* Tarmac   Short for *tarmacadam*, a pavement often used on airport runways.
tarot cards
tar paper
tarpaulin *or* tarp
tarpon   A type of fish.
tarsus; *pl.*, tarsi
tartar sauce *or* tartare sauce
task force
tasseled *or* tasselled
tatami   Japanese; a straw floor mat.
tattersall
tattletale
tattoo; *pl.*, tattoos
Taurus   (see Zodiac Signs).
tax-exempt
taxi, taxis *or* taxies, taxiing *or* taxying
taxicab
taxi stand
taxon.   Abbreviation for *taxonomy, taxonomic*.
taxpayer
tax shelter
Tay-Sachs disease
TB   Abbreviation for *tuberculosis*.
TBA   Abbreviation for *to be announced*.
T-bone steak

tbsp. *or* T *or* tbs. *or* tb.   Abbreviations for *tablespoon, tablespoonful*.
tea bag
tea cake
teach, taught
teachers college
teacher's pet
teacup
teahouse
teak *or* teakwood
teakettle
teammate
teamster   Capitalize only when used to refer to the Teamsters labor union.
teamwork
teapot
tear, tore
teardrop
tear gas
tearjerker
tear-jerking
tearoom
tear sheet
tearstain
teaspoonful; *pl.*, teaspoonfuls *or* teaspoonsful
teatime
tech.   Abbreviation for *technical, technically; technician*.
tech. *or* technol.   Abbreviations for *technology, technological*.
technical knockout *or* TKO
Technicolor   A trademark for a motion-picture-coloring process.
technological *or* technologic
teddy bear
teenage *or* teenaged
teenager *or* teen
teensy-weensy *or* teeny-weeny
teenybopper

teeter-totter

teething ring

teetotaler or **teetotaller**

TEFL Abbreviation for *teaching English as a foreign language.*

Teflon Trade name for a type of non-stick cooking surface.

tel. Abbreviation for *telephone.*

tele-, tel-, telo- Compounds of these combining forms, which mean at, over, from, or to a distance, are written as one word, (e.g., *telecommunications, teleconferencing, telegram, telekinesis, telepathy, telescope, telethon*).

telecast To broadcast via television. (Compare **televise**.)

Telecopier

telegrapher or **telegraphist**

telephoto A camera lens that magnifies the photographed image of a distant object.

Telephoto A brand name for a machine that transmits photos electrically.

TelePrompTer A trademark for a type of cuing device that displays magnified script.

telesis, *pl.,* **teleses**

Teletype

televise To electronically pick up and broadcast on television. (Compare **telecast**.)

television show titles (See Part 2, **Titles of works**.)

telex or **Telex**

tell, told

telltale

temblor Earthquake.

temerity Rashness. (Compare **timorous**.)

temp. or **tmp.** Abbreviations for *temperature.*

temp. Abbreviation for *temporary; temporal; template.*

tempera paint Poster paint. (Compare **tempura**.)

temperate Mild; restrained.

tempo; *pl.,* **tempi** or **tempos**

tempura A Japanese method of preparing food, in which fish and vegetables are dipped in batter and deep fried. (Compare **tempera paint**.)

tenable Reasonable, maintainable. (Compare **tenebrific**.)

tenacious Adhering, cohesive. (Compare **tendentious**.)

tenant A person who rents or occupies a habitat. (Compare **tenet**.)

ten-cent store

Ten Commandments

tendentious or **tendencious** Biased. (Compare **tenacious**.)

tender loving care or **TLC**

tenderfoot; *pl.,* **tenderfeet** or **tenderfoots**

tenderhearted

tenderloin

tendinitis or **tendonitis**

tendriled or **tendrilled**

tenebrific or **tenebrous** Gloomy, obscure. (Compare **tenable**.)

tenement house

tenet Doctrine, principle. (Compare **tenant**.)

ten-gallon hat

tennis elbow

tennis shoe

Tennyson, Alfred Lord (1809–1892) English poet. Author of "Lady of Shallot."

tenpin

tensile Ductile, stressed.

ten-speed

tentative Temporary, uncertain.

tenterhooks

tepee *or* **teepee**

tepid Lukewarm.

tequila

tergiversate To equivocate, to desert a cause or party.

teriyaki A Japanese dish of meat or fish marinated in soy sauce and then broiled or grilled.

term. *or* **trml.** *or*
trm. Abbreviations for *terminal*.

terminal Station for travel arrivals and departures (noun), or the end or conclusion of something (adj).

terminus; *pl.*, **termini** *or*
terminuses

term paper

terpsichorean Pertaining to dancing.

terra-cotta

terra firma

terrain Land, ground.

terrarium; *pl.*, **terraria** *or*
terrariums

terrazzo

terrestrial Earthly.

terrier

territory Capitalize *territory* only if it is part of a proper noun (e.g., *the Northwest Territory*). The abbreviation is *terr.* or *ter.*

terror-stricken

tertiary Third.

TESL Abbreviation for *teaching English as a second language*.

test ban

test case

test-drive

test pilot

test tube As noun.

test-tube As adjective.

tête-à-tête French; literally, "head to head," a face-to-face meeting held in private.

tetherball

tetra-, tetr- Compounds with this combining form (meaning "four") are written as one word (e.g., *tetrapod*).

Texas leaguer

Tex-Mex Having to do with Mexican-American culture, as exemplified in southern Texas on the Mexican border.

textbook

T formation

TGIF Abbreviation for *thank God it's Friday*.

Thackeray, William Makepeace (1811–1863) English novelist, journalist, and humorist.

Thanksgiving Day

thank-you As noun.

that is Sometimes replaced in scholarly writing with the Latin abbreviation *i.e.* (*id est*).

thaumaturgist *or* **thaumaturge**

the-, theo- Compounds with this prefix, meaning "God," are written as one word (e.g., *theology*).

theat. Abbreviation for *theater, theatrical*.

theater *or* **theatre**

theatergoer

theatergoing

theater-in-the-round

the following Sometimes replaced in scholarly writing with the Latin abbreviations *seq.* or *sq.* (*sequens* or *sequentes* or *sequentia*).

themselves

then and there

thenceforth

thenceforward or **thenceforwards**

theol. Abbreviation for *theology, theologian, theological.*

theological or **theologic**

theoretical or **theoretic**

theoretician or **theorist**

there- Compounds written as one word include *thereabouts* or *thereabout, thereafter, thereat, thereby, therefrom, therein, thereinafter, thereinto, thereof, thereon, thereto, theretofore, thereunder, thereunto, thereupon, therewith.*

therefor In return; for it. (Compare **therefore**.)

therefore For that reason; because of; consequently; hence. (Compare **therefor**.)

therm-, thermo- Compounds of this combining form, which means heat, are written as one word (e.g., *thermometer, thermostat*).

-therm Compounds formed with *-therm* indicate an animal with a certain body heat (e.g., *poikilotherm*).

thermal blanket

thermos or **vacuum bottle**

the same Sometimes replaced in scholarly writing with the Latin abbreviations *id.* (*idem*) or *ead.* (*eadem*).

the same as Sometimes replaced in scholarly writing with the Latin abbreviation *i.q.* (*idem quod*).

thesis; *pl.*, **theses**

thespian

the work already cited Sometimes replaced in scholarly writing with the Latin abbreviation *op. cit.* (*opus citatum*).

THI Abbreviation for *temperature-humidity index.*

thi-, thio- Compounds with this prefix meaning "sulfur" or "sulfuric" are written as one word (e.g., *thiocyanate*).

thickheaded

thickset

thick-skinned

thief; *pl.*, **thieves**

thimbleful; *pl.*, **thimblefuls**

thingamabob

thingamajig or **thingumajig**

thing-in-itself; *pl.*, **things-in-themselves**

think tank

think, thought

thinking cap

thin-skinned

third or **thirdly** As adverb.

third base The abbreviation is *3b*.

third-class As adjective or adverb.

third class As noun.

third-degree burn

third-rate

thirdhand

third world or **Third World**

thirteenth

thirty; *pl.*, **thirties**

thirty-three

Thomas, Dylan (1914–1953) Welsh poet.

Thoreau, Henry David (1817–1862) American Transcendentalist writer. Author of *Walden* and "Civil Disobedience."

thoroughbred
thoroughfare
thoroughgoing
thoughtfulness
thought-out
thought-provoking
thousand; *pl.,* thousands *or* thousand   The abbreviations are K and *thou.*
Thousand Island dressing
thrash   To beat, flail at, or defeat soundly. (Compare **thresh.**)
threadbare
three-bagger *or* triple   A hit in baseball that allows the batter to reach third base.
3-D *or* three-dimensional
three-decker
three-legged race
three-mile limit
three of a kind
three-piece suit
three-point landing
three-quarter
three-ring circus
three R's   Reading, writing, and arithmetic.
threesome
thresh   To harvest grain or strike repeatedly. (Compare **thrash.**)
threshold
thrice   Three times.
thromb-, thrombo-   Compounds of this combining form, which means blood clot, are written as one word (e.g., *thrombosis*).
through   Sometimes shortened to *thru* in informal writing.
through and through
throughout
throughput   Output of a machine.
through street

throw rug
throw, threw
throwaway   As adjective and noun.
throwback   As noun.
throw-in   As noun.
thruway *or* throughway   Capitalize only if part of an address.
thumbhole
thumb index
thumbnail
thumbprint
thumbs-down; thumbs-up
thumbtack
thunderbolt
thundershower
thunderstorm
thunderstruck
thyme   The spice.
thyr-, thyro-   Compounds with the prefix meaning "thyroid" or "thyroidal" are written as one word (e.g., *thyrotoxicosis*).
thyself
ticker tape   As noun.
ticker-tape   As adjective.
tick off
ticky-tacky *or* ticky-tack; *pl.,* ticky-tackies *or* tick-tacks
tic-tac-toe *or* ticktacktoe
tidal wave
tidbit
tiddledywinks *or* tiddlywinks
tidewater
tieback   As noun.
tiebreaker
tie-dye
tie-in   As noun.
tiepin
tiered
tie silk
tie tack *or* tie tac

tie-up As noun.
tiger cat
tiger lily
tight end
tightfisted
tight-lipped or **tight-mouthed**
tightrope or **tightwire**
tightwad
timber Wood, woodland. (Compare **timbre**.)
Timberland
timberline
timbre or **timber** An overtone in sound.
time- Most compounds formed with time are written as two words (e.g., *time sheet, time warp, time zone*). Compounds written as one word include *timekeeper, timekeeping, timepiece, timesaver, timesaving, timetable, timeworn*.
time-consuming
time-honored
time immemorial or **time out of mind**
time-lapse
time-out
time-sharing
time-tested
time zones Abbreviations are usually uppercase, unpunctuated, and unspaced: *Pacific standard time (PST), mountain standard time (MST), central standard time (CST), eastern standard time (EST)*.
timorous Fearful. (Compare **temerity**.)
timpani A set of kettledrums of different pitches
tin can

tinderbox
tin ear
tinfoil
tinge To slightly change the color or character of.
tinker's damn or **tinker's dam** Something of no value or hardly worth noting.
Tinkertoy
Tin Pan Alley
tinplate As noun.
tin-plate As verb.
tintinnabulary Pertaining to bells or their sounds.
tip-in As noun.
tip-off As noun.
tip of the iceberg
tip-top
tissue paper
tit for tat
title page
titleholder or **titlist**
titmouse; *pl.*, **titmice**
titular In name only.
TM Abbreviation for *transcendental meditation*.
TNT Abbreviation for *trinitrotoluene*, used as an explosive.
-to-be
toadstool
to-and-fro
tobacco road or **Tobacco Road**
Tocqueville, Alexis de (1805–1859) French writer and politician.
today
to-do; *pl.*, **to-dos**
toehold
toenail
toffee or **toffy**

tofu A soybean curd rich in protein used in cooking.

toggle switch

toilet paper

toilette Related to grooming.

toilet water

toilsome

to infinity Sometimes replaced in scholarly writing with the Latin abbreviation *ad inf.* (*ad infinitum*).

Tolkien, J. R. R. (1892–1973) British fantasy writer. Author of *The Lord of the Rings*.

tollbooth

toll bridge

toll call

tollhouse cookies

tollway

Tolstoy, Leo (1828–1910) Russian novelist and philosopher. Author of *Anna Karenina* and *War and Peace*.

tomahawk

tomato; *pl.,* **tomatoes**

tombstone *or* **gravestone**

tomfoolery

tomorrow

tom-tom

tonearm

tone-deaf

tone deafness

tongue and groove Lumber milled so that the edges of the boards can overlap.

tongue-in-cheek As adjective.

tongue in cheek As adverb.

tongue-lashing

tongue-tied

tongue twister

tonight Sometimes spelled *tonite* in informal writing.

tonneau; *pl.,* **tonneaus** French; the rearmost seating area in an automobile.

tonsorial Related to barbering.

tool- Compounds formed with *tool-* that are written as one word include *toolbox, toolholder, toolmaker, toolmaking, toolroom, toolshed.*

tooth; *pl.,* **teeth**

toothache

tooth and nail

toothbrush

toothpaste

toothpick

toothsome

too-too

top-, topo- Compounds with this prefix, which means "location" or "place," are written as one word (e.g., *topographical*).

top banana

top billing

topcoat

top dog

top-down

top drawer

top flight

topflight As adjective.

Top 40 As adjective or noun. Refers to the forty best-selling songs of a given period.

top hat

top-heavy

topknot

top-notch

toponym A place-name.

topsail

top secret

topspin

topstitch

topsy-turvy

Torah

torchlight

torch song

toric lens

tormentor or **tormenter**

tornado; *pl.,* **tornadoes** or **tornados** A rapidly rotating column of air extending downward as a funnel, which usually destroys everything in its narrow path. (Compare **tournedo.**)

torpor Numbness, dullness.

torrid Hot, steamy.

torsion The process of twisting around an axis.

torso; *pl.,* **torsos** or **torsi**

torte; *pl.,* **tortes** or **torten** German; a type of rich cake.

tortellini Italian; ring-shaped or round pasta filled with meat or vegetables.

tortilla A Mexican flatbread made of cornmeal.

tortoiseshell

tortoni An Italian ice-cream dessert.

tortuous Twisted, winding. (Compare **torturous.**)

torturous Causing torture. (Compare **tortuous.**)

toss-up As noun.

tostada or **tostado** A deep-fried tortilla.

total, totaled or **totalled**

total eclipse

total recall

tote bag

totem pole

touch and go

touchback As noun.

touchdown As noun.

touch-me-not

touchstone

touch-type

touch-up As noun.

toughie or **toughy;** *pl.,* **toughies**

toupee; *pl.,* **toupees**

tour de force French; a great feat.

touring car

tourist class

tournament or **tourney**

tournedo; *pl.,* **tournedos** French; strips of beef tenderloin. (Compare **tornado.**)

toward or **towards**

towboat

towel, toweled or **towelled**

towelette

towheaded

to wit Namely.

town car

town hall

town house

townie or **towny;** *pl.,* **townies**

townsfolk

township Capitalize if part of proper noun or address (e.g., *Township 30,* but *an unorganized township*). Abbreviation is *twp.*

townspeople

towrope

tow truck

toxemia

trache-, tracheo- Compounds of this combining form, which means of the trachea or windpipe, are written as one word (e.g., *tracheid*).

tracing paper

track-and-field

track record

tractable Easily taken care of; malleable, or docile.

233

tractional *or* tractive

tractor pull

tradable *or* tradeable

trade-in   As noun.

trade-off   As noun.

trademark *or* TM

tradespeople

trade union *or* trades union

trading stamp

tragedian   An actor in or a writer of tragedies.

tragic *or* tragical

tragicomic *or* tragicomical

trail bike

trailblazer

trailer park

train case

training camp

trainload

tram *or* tramcar

trammeled *or* trammelled

trampolier *or* trampolinist

trancelike

tranquillity *or* tranquility

tranquilize *or* tranquillize

trans-   Compounds formed with *trans-*, which means across, above and beyond, or on the other side of, are written as one word unless the second word is a proper noun (e.g., *transcontinental, transcribe, transformation, transfusion, transmigration, transplant, transsexual,* but *trans-Siberian journey*).

trans. *or* tr.   Abbreviations for *transitive; translator, translation.*

trans. *or* transp.   Abbreviations for *transport, transportation; transparent.*

transatlantic

transcendence *or* transcendency

transduce   To convert to another form.

transf. *or* trans. *or* tr.   Abbreviations for *transfer, transferred.*

transferable *or* transferrable

transfusible *or* transfusable

transgress   To go beyond limits.

transitory   Temporary.

translucence *or* translucency

translucent   Allows some light through, like frosted glass. (Compare **transparent**.)

transmittable *or* transmissible

transparent   Allows all light through, like glass. (Compare **translucent**.)

trapdoor

trapshooting

trapunto; *pl.*, trapuntos   A quilted design.

trash can

trauma; *pl.*, traumata *or* traumas

travel, traveled *or* travelled

traveler's check

travelogue *or* travelog

traverse rod

tread, trod *or* treaded, trodden *or* trod

treadmill

treas. *or* treasr.   Abbreviations for *treasurer.*

treasonable *or* treasonous

treasure hunt

treasury note *or* Treasury note

treasury   Capitalize only if part of proper noun.

treaty   Capitalize only if part of proper noun: *Treaty of Versailles.*

treble clef

tree farm

tree house

treetop

trefoil A type of plant whose leaves are divided into three leaflets.

tremulous *or* **tremulant**

trench coat

trenchant Clear, sharp.

trendsetter

tri- Compounds formed with *tri-* (meaning "three") are written as one word (e.g., *triad, triangular, tricolor, tricot, tricycle, triennial, trilateral, trimester, tripartite, triplex, tristate, triweekly*).

trial and error

trick-or-treat As verb.

trickle-down

tried-and-true

trigger-happy

triple-header

triple jump

triple-space

troche A small medicinal lozenge.

troglodyte A cave dweller, or, a recluse.

troika Russian; a triumvirate.

Trojan horse

trolley car

trolley *or* **trolly**; *pl.*, **trolleys** *or* **trollies**

trompe l'oeil From French, meaning "to deceive the eye," a painting or a painted surface that reproduces an image or texture with photographic realism.

troop An organized group, as soldiers. (Compare **troupe**.)

trop-, tropo- Compounds with the prefix meaning "turn," "change" or "reflex" are written as one word (e.g., *troposphere*).

Trotsky, Leon (1879–1940) Russian Communist leader. Organized Bolshevik seizure of power in October Revolution of 1917. Was associated with V. I. Lenin.

troubadour

troublemaker

troubleshoot

troublesome *or* **troublous**

troupe A group of entertainers. (Compare **troop**.)

trousseau; *pl.*, **trousseaux** *or* **trousseaus** French; the wardrobe that a bride assembles for her marriage.

trove Treasured collection.

truant officer

truancy *or* **truantry**

truckload

truculence *or* **truculency**

truculent Cruel.

true-blue As adjective.

true-false

truehearted

true-life

truelove

trump card

trumped-up

trundle bed

trunk line

truth; *pl.*, **truths**

tryout As noun.

tsetse fly

T-shirt *or* **t-shirt** *or* **tee shirt**

tsp. *or* **tspn.** Abbreviations for *teaspoon, teaspoonful.*

T square

tubaist *or* **tubist**

Tudor house

tugboat

tug-of-war

tulip tree

tulle A stiff netting used for special clothing such as veils or ballet costumes.

tumbledown

tumbleweed

tundra The treeless, level plains of the Arctic where the subsoil is permanently frozen.

tuned-in

tune-up As noun.

tungsten A metallic chemical element used in electric contact points and lamp filaments.

tuning fork

tunnel, tunneled *or* **tunnelled**

turban A wrapped head covering. (Compare **turbine**.)

turbid Muddy, dense, or confused. (Compare **turgid**.)

turbine A rotary engine. (Compare **turban**.)

turbojet

turbo-propeller *or* **turboprop**

turbulence *or* **turbulency**

turgid Swollen. (Compare **turbid**.)

Turkish bath

Turkish towel

turnabout

turnaround As noun.

turncoat A traitor.

turndown As noun.

turned-on

turning point

turnkey; *pl.,* **turnkeys** The person in charge of the keys of a prison.

turnoff As noun.

turn-on As noun.

turnout As noun.

turnover As noun.

turnpike Capitalize as part of a proper name (e.g., *the*

Pennsylvania Turnpike). Abbreviations are *tpke.* or *tnpk.* or *tpk.*

turnstile

turntable

turquoise *or* **turquois**

turtleneck

tutti-frutti

tuxedo; *pl.,* **tuxedos** *or* **tuxedoes**

TV

TV dinner

Twain, Mark (1835–1910) American writer. Author of *The Adventures of Tom Sawyer*.

Twelfth Night The evening of January 5, before the Epiphany (the twelfth day after Christmas).

Twelve Step

twenty; *pl.,* **twenties**

twice-told

twilight

TWIMC Abbreviation for *to whom it may concern*.

twin bed

twin-size

two-bagger *or* **double** A hit in baseball that allows the batter to reach second base.

two-bit As adjective.

two-by-four

two cents

two-faced

twofer Two things available for purchase at the price of one.

two-handed

two-piece

two-ply

two-step

two-time

two-tone

two-way street

tying *or* **tieing**
tyke A small child.
typeface
typeset

typewrite
typo; *pl.,* **typos**
tyrannical *or* **tyrannic**
tyro; *pl.,* **tyros** A novice.

U

Ubangi A river in central Africa.

U-boat A German submarine from World War I or World War II.

u.c. Abbreviation for *uppercase*.

UFO; pl., UFO's or UFOs Abbreviation for *unidentified flying object*.

ugh An interjection expressing displeasure or distaste.

ugly duckling

uh-huh

U/I Abbreviation for *unidentified*.

ukulele or ukelele

ultimatum; pl., ultimatums or ultimata

ultimo Latin; in the preceding month.

ultra- Compounds formed with *ultra-*, which means beyond or to an extreme degree, are written as one word unless the second word begins with an *a* or is a proper noun (e.g., *ultrasonic, ultrasound, ultraviolet,* but *ultra-acidic*).

ultrahigh frequency or UHF

ululate To howl.

umbilical cord

umlaut A type of diacritical mark placed over a vowel used especially in German (e.g., *ä, ö, ü*).

umpteen

un- Compounds formed with *un-*, which means not, lack of, or opposite of, are written as one word unless second word is a proper noun (e.g., *un-American,* but *unadulterated, unapproachable*). (Compare **in-**.)

unapt Unlikely or not suitable. (Compare **inapt, inept**.)

unaware As adjective.

unawares As adverb.

unbeknown or unbeknownst

unbeliever A person who does not hold something as true. (Compare **disbeliever**.)

uncalled-for

unchristian or un-Christian

Uncle Sam

unction An ointment, an anointing, or an exaggerated manner. (Compare **unctuous**.)

unctuous Oily, greasy, or exaggerated in manner, false. (Compare **unction**.)

under- Most compounds formed with *under-* are written as one word (e.g., *underage, underbelly, underclothing, underwrite*).

underhand or underhanded

under secretary or under-secretary Capitalize only if part of formal title preceding a name.

undersized or undersize

under-the-counter

under-the-table

underway As adjective.

under way As adverb.

undulate or undulated As adjective

uneconomic or uneconomical

unexceptionable Honorable, beyond reproach. (Compare **unexceptional**.)

unexceptional Common, ordinary. (Compare **unexceptionable**.)

unfocused or unfocussed

unguent An ointment.

unheard-of

UNICEF Abbreviation for *United*

Nations Children's Emergency Fund.

unidirectional

unilateral

uninterested Not wanting to pay attention. (Compare **disinterested**.)

unionized Organized by a labor union.

union shop

unisex

unitarian But *Unitarian* when referring to the church.

United Nations *or* **UN**

United States of America *or* **U.S.A.**

United States *or* **U.S.**

univ. Abbreviation for *university* (also *U.*); *universal, universally*.

universal joint

university Capitalize only if part of proper noun (e.g., *a university student;* but *New York University*).

unkn. *or* **unk.** Abbreviations for *unknown*.

Unknown Soldier

unwritten rule

up, upped *or* **up**

up-and-coming

up and down As adverb.

up-and-down As adjective.

up-and-up

upbeat

upcoming

update

upend To set, turn, or stand on end.

up-front

upgrade

uphill

upkeep

uppercase As adjective and verb.

uppercase *or* **upper case** As noun.

upper class As noun.

upper-class As adjective.

upper crust

upper hand

uprightness

uprise

ups and downs

upside down As adverb.

upside-down As adjective.

upstate

uptight

uptime

up-to-date

up-to-the-minute

uptown

upward *or* **upwards** As adverb.

upward (adjective)

urban Concerning a city. (Compare **urbane**.)

urbane Suave, polished. (Compare **urban**.)

usable *or* **useable**

USDA Abbreviation for *United States Department of Agriculture*.

user-friendly

USPS Abbreviation for *United States Postal Service*.

util. Abbreviation for *utility*.

utopia *or* **Utopia** A concept or a place (respectively) representing social or political perfection or both.

utopian

U-turn

V Abbreviation for *volt, voltage.*

v. *or* **vb.** Abbreviations for *verb.*
The abbreviation for an
intransitive verb (one that has no
direct object) is *v.i.* The
abbreviation for a transitive verb
is *v.t.*

VA Abbreviation for *Veterans
Administration.*

vacuity *or* **vacuousness**

vacuum; *pl.,* **vacuums** *or* **vacua**

vacuum bottle

vacuum cleaner

vacuum-packed

vade mecum; *pl.,* **vade mecums**
Latin; literally, ''go with me,'' a
handbook, or a useful thing that
one carries constantly.

vagina; *pl.,* **vaginae** *or* **vaginas**

vain Overly concerned with
appearance. (Compare **vane,
vein.**)

vainglorious

val. Abbreviation for *value,
valued.*

valance A short drape. (Compare
valence.)

vale A valley.

valence Degree or capacity of
elements to combine with other
elements and form molecules.
(Compare **valance.**)

valentine

Valentine's Day *or* **Valentine Day**

valet parking

valiance *or* **valiancy** *or* **valor**

Valium Trademark for a type of
tranquilizer.

valley Capitalize if part of proper
noun (e.g., *Death Valley*).

value judgment

value-added tax *or* **VAT**

Vandyke A closely-trimmed,
pointed beard.

vandyked As adjective.

vane An instrument indicating
wind direction. (Compare **vain,
vein.**)

vanguard

Van Gogh, Vincent (1853–1890)
Dutch post-impressionist painter.
Works include *The Potato Eaters*
and *Starry Night.*

vanilla

vanity plate A personalized
license plate.

vanpool People commuting to
work together in a van rather than
using separate vehicles.

vantage point

vapid Dull, uninteresting.

var. Abbreviation for *variable;
variant; variety, various.*

varicolored

varicose veins

varmint A pesty creature.
(Compare **vermin.**)

vas-, vaso- Compounds with the
prefix meaning ''blood vessel'' or
''vascular'' are written as one
word (e.g., *vasodilator*).

vas deferens; *pl.,* **vase deferentia**

Vaseline Brand name for
petroleum jelly.

Vatican

vaulted Arched.

vaunt To brag about, to boast of.

VCR *or* **videocassette recorder**

V-day Victory day (as in a war).

VDT Abbreviation for *video
display terminal* or *visual display
terminal,* the screen for visually

monitoring work being done on a computer.

veg. Abbreviation for *vegetable*.

V-8 A type of internal-combustion engine with two opposing rows of four cylinders, in which the rows are slanted toward each other to form a V-shape.

vein A blood vessel that carries blood toward the heart. (Compare **vain, vane**.)

Velcro Trademark for a nylon fastening material.

velleity An inclination that is not acted upon.

vellum A special strong paper or binding. (Compare **velum**.)

velodrome A cycling track.

velour *or* **velours**; *pl.,* **velours**

velum Animate membrane. (Compare **vellum**.)

vena cava; *pl.,* **venae cavae** The vein that returns blood to the heart.

venal Buyable, corruptible. (Compare **venial, venous**.)

vendible *or* **vendable** For sale.

vending machine

vendor *or* **vender**

venerate To regard highly.

venereal disease *or* **V.D.**

venetian blind

venetian glass *or* **Venetian glass**

venial Pardonable, excusable. (Compare **venal, venous**.)

venison Deer meat.

venomous Poisonous.

venous Relating to veins. (Compare **venal, venial**.)

ventr-, ventro- Compounds with this prefix meaning "belly" or "abdomen" are written as one word (e.g., *ventricle*).

ventral Abdominal

venture capital

venue The place where a cause of action or a crime occurs (in law); or, the scene of a local gathering (for a concert, sporting event, etc.)

Venus's-flytrap

ver.; *pl .,* **vss.** Abbreviation for *version; pl., versions*.

veracious Truthful.

veranda *or* **verandah**

verbal Relating to words or speech.

verbal noun A noun derived from a verb; in English, a gerund or an infinitive.

verbatim Word for word.

verbiage Wordiness..

verbose Wordy.

verboten German; forbidden.

verdant Green. (Compare **vernal**.)

veridical True, genuine.

verily Truly.

verisimilar Plausible, likely.

veritable Real, actual.

vérité French; realism, especially in visual art.

vermicelli

vermiculate *or* **vermiculated** *or* **vermicular** *or* **vermiform** Wormlike.

vermilion *or* **vermillion** *or* **vermeil** Bright red.

vermin An offensive animal. (Compare **varmint**.)

vermouth

vernacular Local dialect.

vernal Having to do with spring. (Compare **verdant**.)

verso; *pl.,* **versos** The lefthand page of an open book, or the back side of a single page.

versus Against. Abbreviation is *v.* (in legal context) or *vs.* (in general context).

vert. Abbreviation for *vertical.*

vertebra; *pl.,* **vertebrae** or **vertebras**

vertex; *pl.,* **vertices** or **vertexes** The summit, the topmost point, the apex.

vertiginous Inconstant, everchanging; dizzying; or spinning.

very high frequency or **VHF**

vespers In Christian religious, a prayer or service said in the evening.

vested interest

vest-pocket

vet. Abbreviation for *veterinary, veterinarian.*

veteran or **vet**

Veterans Day

VFR Abbreviation for *visual flight rules.*

VFW Abbreviation for *Veterans of Foreign Wars.*

VHF Abbreviation for *very high frequency.*

VHS Abbreviation for *video home system.*

v.i. Abbreviation for Latin *vide infra,* ''see below.''

via By way of.

viaduct

vibrancy or **vibrance**

vice An evil habit. (Compare **vise.**)

vice admiral Capitalize only if part of a formal title preceding a name.

vice chairperson Capitalize only if part of a formal title preceding a name.

vice-chancellor

vice-consul

vice president Capitalize only if part of a formal title preceding a name. If treatment is consistent, it may also be capitalized in references to the second highest executive in the U.S. government.

Vice Presidents of the United States of America

1. *John Adams*
   1735–1826
2. *Thomas Jefferson*
   1743–1826
3. *Aaron Burr*
   1756–1836
4. *George Clinton*
   1739–1812
5. *Elbridge Gerry*
   1744–1814
6. *Daniel D. Tompkins*
   1774–1825
7. *John C. Calhoun*
   1782–1850
8. *Martin Van Buren*
   1782–1862
9. *Richard M. Johnson*
   1780–1850
10. *John Tyler*
    1790–1862
11. *George M. Dallas*
    1792–1864
12. *Millard Fillmore*
    1800–1874
13. *William R. King*
    1786–1853
14. *John C. Breckinridge*
    1821–1875

15. *Hannibal Hamlin*
    1809–1891
16. *Andrew Johnson*
    1808–1875
17. *Schuyler Colfax*
    1823–1885
18. *Henry Wilson*
    1812–1875
19. *William A. Wheeler*
    1819–1887
20. *Chester A. Arthur*
    1829–1886
21. *Thomas A. Hendricks*
    1819–1885
22. *Levi P. Morton*
    1824–1920
23. *Adlai E. Stevenson*
    1835–1914
24. *Garret A. Hobart*
    1844–1899
25. *Theodore Roosevelt*
    1858–1919
26. *Charles W. Fairbanks*
    1852–1918
27. *James S. Sherman*
    1855–1912
28. *Thomas R. Marshall*
    1854–1925
29. *Calvin Coolidge*
    1872–1933
30. *Charles G. Dawes*
    1865–1951
31. *Charles Curtis*
    1860–1936
32. *John N. Garner*
    1868–1967
33. *Henry A. Wallace*
    1888–1965
34. *Harry S Truman*
    1884–1972
35. *Alben W. Barkley*
    1877–1956

36. *Richard M. Nixon*
    1913–
37. *Lyndon B. Johnson*
    1908–1973
38. *Hubert H. Humphrey*
    1911–1978
39. *Spiro T. Agnew*
    1918–
40. *Gerald R. Ford*
    1913–
41. *Nelson A. Rockefeller*
    1908–1979
42. *Walter F. Mondale*
    1928–
43. *George Bush*
    1924–
44. *J. Danforth Quayle*
    1947–
45. *Al Gore*
    1948–

vice squad

vice versa

vichyssoise   A French soup made with leeks, potatoes, and cream, and served cold.

vicious circle

Victorian

victual   Food.

videocassette recorder *or* **VCR**

videodisc *or* **videodisk**

video display terminal *or* **VDT**

video game

videotape

video tape recording

videotex *or* **videotext**

video vérité   A candidly filmed television documentary.

Vienna sausage

Vietnamese

viewfinder

viewpoint

VIN Abbreviation for *vehicle identification number*.

vincible Conquerable.

vindictive *or* **vindicative** Hateful, revengeful.

vintner A wine producer.

vinyl

violoncello *or* **cello**

VIP; *pl.,* **VIPs** Abbreviation for *very important person*.

viperous *or* **viperish** *or* **viperine**

virescent Greenish.

Virgil (70–19 B.C.) Roman poet. Author of the *Aeneid*.

Virgin Mary

virgin wool

Virgo (see **Zodiac Signs**).

virtually For all practical purposes. (Compare **figuratively, literally**.)

virtual reality

virtuoso; *pl.,* **virtuosos** *or* **virtuosi**

virulence *or* **virulency** Malignance, poisonousness.

vis-à-vis French; face to face, or compared to.

vis. Abbreviation for *visual*.

visage Appearance.

viscous *or* **viscid** Gummy, sticky. (Compare **viscus**.)

viscus An organ within one's body trunk. (Compare **viscous**.) The plural is *viscera*.

vise A type of tool used to hold the object being worked on in place. (Compare **vice**.)

visual acuity

vital signs

vital statistics

vitamins Complex organic substances found in most foods that are essential, in small amounts, for the normal growth and functioning of the human body. They are A, B (thiamine), B complex, B_6, B_{12}, B_2 (riboflavin), C, D, E, G (riboflavin), H (biotin), K.

vitiate To impair, to make ineffective.

vitreous Like glass.

vituperate To abuse, berate. (Compare **vociferate**.)

viva voce Latin; orally, by word of mouth.

vivify To renew, animate.

viz. Abbreviation for *videlicet*, "namely."

V neck As noun.

V-necked As adjective.

voc. Abbreviation for *vocative*.

vocab. Abbreviation for *vocabulary*.

vocal cords

vocation An occupation, career. (Compare **avocation**.)

vociferate To shout, call out. (Compare **vituperate**.)

vodka

voice box *or* **larynx**

voice-over (As noun)

voilà *or* **voila** French; an exclamation meaning "here it is!"

voile A very sheer fabric.

vol.; *pl.,* **vols.** Abbreviation for *volume, volumes* (also *vv.*).

vol. Abbreviation for *volunteer; voluntary*.

vol-au-vent French; a pastry shell filled with fish or meat.

volition One's personal choice.

volleyball

Voltaire (1694–1778) French

writer and satirist. Author of *Le Siecle de Louis XIV*.

volte-face *or* **about-face**

voluble   Talkative, or rolling.

volume   Capitalize if part of document title.

voluminous   Long and winding, full, numerous.

volunteer *or* **voluntarist**

voodoo

VOR   Abbreviation for *very-high-frequency omnidirectional radio range*.

vortex; *pl*., vortices *or* vortexes   A whirlpool or whirlwind.

votary   Enthusiast, devout worshiper, or one bound by a solemn (as religious) vow.

vote-getter *or* **votegetter**

vouchsafe   To grant a favor.

vox populi   Latin, "the voice of the people," or a common sentiment.

vroom

v.s.   Abbreviation for Latin *vide supra*, "see above."

w. *or* **aq.** Abbreviations for *water*.

w Abbreviation for *watt*.

w. *or* **wdt.** *or* **wth.** Abbreviations for *width*.

w. Abbreviations for *with; within*.

wacko

wading pool

waffle iron

wage earner

waggish Playful clowning, mischievous.

wagon train

wainscoting *or* **wainscotting** Wood lining or paneling on the walls of a room.

waist The part of the body between the ribs and the hips. (Compare **waste**.)

waistband

waist-deep

waistline

waiting game

waiting list

waiting room

waive To forgo, put off.

wake, woke *or* **waked**

Waldorf salad A salad made with diced raw apples, celery, walnuts, and mayonnaise.

walk-in As adjective or noun.

walkie-talkie

walk-on As noun.

walkout As noun.

walkover As noun. An easily won victory.

walk-through As noun.

walk-up As adjective or noun.

walkway

wallboard A fibrous material made in thin slabs for making or covering walls and ceilings.

wallflower

wallpaper

Wall Street

wall-to-wall

wampum Money, taken from North American Indian usage.

wanderlust

want ad

war Capitalize only if part of proper noun (e.g., *World War I*).

war chest Money accumulated to fight a military or political campaign.

ward Capitalize only as part of a proper name for a geographical or political division (e.g., *the Fifth Ward School*, but *the psychiatric ward*).

war game

war horse

warhead

Warhol, Andy (1928?–1987) American founder and leader of Pop Art. Known especially for his paintings of Campbell soup cans.

warlock

warm-blooded

warmed-over

warmhearted

warmonger

warm-up As noun.

warpath

warplane

warrantor *or* **warranter**

warship

wartime

war zone

wash- Compounds formed with *wash-* that are written as one word include *washbasin, washboard,* *washbowl, washcloth, washhouse, washout* (noun), *washrag, washroom, washstand, washtub, washup* (noun).

wash-and-wear

washed-out

washed-up

washing machine

Washington, Booker T. (1856–1915) American educator. Chosen to establish and head the Tuskegee Institute, a school dedicated to the practical training of African Americans.

Washington's Birthday

WASP *or* **Wasp** White Anglo-Saxon Protestant.

waste To use carelessly or throw away without regard. (Compare **waist**.)

wastebasket

wasteland

wastepaper

wastewater *or* **sewage**

watchband

watchdog

watchmaker

watchtower

watchword A password or slogan.

water- Most compounds formed with *water-* are written as two words (e.g., *water bed, water glass, water meter*).

watercolor

watercooler

watercress

waterfall

waterfowl; *pl.,* **waterfowl**

watering hole

waterline

waterlogged

watermark

water moccasin

water-repellent *or* **water-resistant**

watershed The area drained by a river, or a crucial turning point affecting action or opinion.

water ski As noun.

water-ski As verb.

water-skier

waterskiing

waterspout

watertight

waterway

waterworks

WATS Abbreviation for *wide-area telecommunications service*.

watt-hour

Waugh, Evelyn (1903–1966) English satirical novelist. Author of *Brideshead Revisited*.

wave band

wavelength

wax bean

waxed paper *or* **wax paper**

waxwing A type of fruit-eating bird.

-way Most compounds formed with *-way* are written as one word (e.g., *roadway*).

wayfarer

waylay, waylaid

way-out As adjective.

ways and means

way station

wayward

wea. *or* **wthr.** Abbreviations for *weather*.

weak Not strong. (Compare **week**.)

weakhearted

weak-kneed

weakling

weak-minded

wear, wore
wear and tear
weather-beaten
weather bureau
weather map
weatherproof
weather station
weather strip   As noun.
weather-strip   As verb.
weather vane
weather-wise   Hyphenate as adjective meaning "skilled in predicting weather."
weave, wove *or* weaved
webfoot
Webster, Daniel   (1782–1852) American lawyer and statesman. Served as U.S. senator from Massachusetts and U.S. secretary of state.
Wedgwood   A trademark for a fine English pottery depicting neoclassical figures in relief against a colored background.
wedlock
week   Capitalize only if part of proper noun (e.g., *National Bike Safety Week*). (Compare **weak**.)
weekday
weekend
weeknight
weeping willow
weevil   A beetle that feeds upon fruits and grains.
weigh-in   As noun.
weight lifter
weight-watcher
weimaraner   A type of hunting dog with a smooth, gray coat.
weirdo; *pl.*, weirdos
welfare state
well-   Most compounds formed with *well-* are hyphenated (e.g., *well-advised, well-appointed, well-being, well-bred, well-conditioned, well-disposed, well-defined, well-done, well-founded, well-groomed, well-informed, well-intentioned, well-known, well-mannered, well-meaning, well-nigh, well-off, well-read, well-rounded, well-spoken, well-taken, well-thought-of, well-timed, well-to-do, well-wisher, well-wishing, well-worn*).
Wellington (boot) *or* Wellie
wellspring
Welsh rabbit *or* Welsh rarebit
welterweight
werewolf; *pl.*, werewolves
weskit   A waistcoat or vest.
western omelet
western saddle
westerner
westernize
wet bar
wet blanket
wet dream
wet suit
wet nurse   As noun.
wet-nurse   As verb.
wh.   Abbreviation for *which*.
whacked-out
whaleboat
wharf; *pl.*, wharves *or* wharfs
Wharton, Edith   (1862–1937) American novelist. Author of *Ethan Frome*.
whatever
whatnot
whatsoever
wheat bread
wheat germ
wheelbarrow

wheelbase The distance in inches from the center of the hub of a motor vehicle's front wheel to the center of the hub of the corresponding back wheel.

wheelchair

wheeler-dealer *or* **wheeler and dealer**

whenever

whensoever

where- Compounds formed with *where-* that are spelled as one word include *whereabouts* or *whereabout, whereat, whereas, whereby, whereof, wherever, wherefrom, wherein, whereinto, whereon, wheresoever, whereunto, whereupon, wherever, wherewith, wherewithal.*

wherefor For which. (Compare **wherefore**.)

wherefore Why. (Compare **why**.)

whew

whey Watery part of milk.

whichever *or* **whichsoever**

which is The abbreviation is *q.e.* (for Latin, *quod est*).

which see The abbreviation is *qq.v.* (for Latin, *quae vide*) or *q.v.* (for Latin, *quod vide*).

which was to be demonstrated The abbreviation is *Q.E.D.* (for Latin, *quod erat demonstrandum*).

whimsy *or* **whimsey**

whipcord

whiplash

whippersnapper

whipping boy

whippoorwill

whipstitch

whir *or* **whirr**

whirlpool bath

whirlwind

whirlybird A slang term for a helicopter.

whisk broom

whiskey *or* **whisky**; *pl.,* **whiskeys** *or* **whiskies**

whiskey sour

whistle-blower

Whistler, James Abbott McNeill (1834–1903) American painter and etcher.

white- Most compounds formed with *white-* are written as two words (e.g., *white hope, white lightning, white flag, white sale, white slave*).

whitecap

white-collar As adjective.

whitefish

Whitehead, Alfred North (1861–1947) English mathematician and philosopher.

white-hot

White House

whitening *or* **whiting**

whiteout As noun.

white-tie

whitewash

whither Where; to what place. (Compare **wither**.)

Whitman, Walt (1819–1892) American poet. Author of *Leaves of Grass.*

whiz *or* **whizz**

whizbang As noun.

whiz-bang As adjective.

whiz kid

whodunit *or* **whodunnit** A murder mystery.

whoever *or* **whosoever**

whole An entire entity. (Compare hole.)

wholehearted

whole hog As adverb or noun

whole-hog As adjective.

wholesaler

wholesome

whole wheat As noun.

whole-wheat As adjective.

wholly In its entirely. (Compare holey, holy.)

whomever *or* **whomsoever**

whoop-de-do *or* **whoop-de-doo**

whoopee

whooping cough

whoopla

whoosh

whsle. *or* **whol.** Abbreviations for *wholesale.*

wickerwork

-wide Compounds formed with *-wide* are written as one word (e.g., *citywide*).

wide-angle

wide-awake

wide-eyed

widemouthed

wide-open

wide receiver

widespread

wiener *or* **weiner** *or* **wienie**

Wiener schnitzel German; a breaded veal cutlet.

wigwam

wildcat

wildcatter One engaged in a risky business scheme.

Wilde, Oscar (1854–1900) Irish poet and dramatist. Author of *The Importance of Being Earnest.*

wild-eyed

wildfire

wildflower

wildlife

wild oats

wild pitch

wild rice

willful *or* **wilful**

Williams, Tennessee (1911–1983) American playwright. Author of *A Streetcar Named Desire.*

will not *or* **won't**

will-o'-the-wisp

willpower

willy-nilly

win, won

wind, wound

wind- Many compounds formed with *wind-* are spelled as one word (e.g., *windbag, windblown, windbreaker, windburn, windchill, windfall, windjammer, windmill, windpipe, windshield, windstorm, windswept*).

windchill factor

wind chime

window dressing

windowpane

window seat

window shade

window-shop

windowsill

wind sock *or* **wind sleeve** A long, cloth, cone-shaped instrument open at both ends and attached to a mast to show wind direction.

Windsor tie A wide necktie tied in a loose double bow.

windup As adjective and noun.

wine cellar

wine cooler

wineglass

wine taster

wingback

wingding
winglike
wingspan
wing tip
winner's circle
winter *or* wintertime *or* wintertide
wintry *or* wintery
wipeout   As noun.
wirehaired
wiretap
wisdom tooth
-wise   Compounds formed with
   -wise are written as one word
   (e.g., *clockwise*).
wiseacre
wisecrack
wishbone
wishful thinking
wishy-washy
wisteria *or* wistaria   A vine or
   shrub whose fruit is clusters of
   blue, pink, purple, or white
   flowers.
witchcraft
witch doctor
witch hazel   A disinfectant or
   lotion used to soothe bruises and
   cuts.
witch-hunt   As noun or verb.
wither   To droop or shrivel.
   (Compare **whither**.)
with expression   The abbreviation
   is *esp.* (*espressivo*) when used as
   a musical direction.
with-it
witness-box
witness stand
wk.   Abbreviation for *week*.
wkg.   Abbreviation for *working*.
wkly.   Abbreviation for *weekly*.
wkr.   Abbreviation for *worker*.
w/o   Abbreviations for *without*.

woebegone
wok   A bowl-shaped metal pan
   used in Chinese cooking.
wolf; *pl.*, wolves
wolf dog
wolfhound
wolf pack
woman; *pl.*, women
woman's rights *or* women's rights
women's liberation *or* women's lib
wonder drug
wonderland
wonder-worker
wood carving
woodchopper
woodcut
wood engraving
woodland
woodlot
woodpecker
woodpile
woodshed
woodwind
woodworking
woolen *or* woollen
Woolf, Virginia   (1882–1941)
   English "Bloomsbury Group"
   novelist. Author of *A Room of
   One's Own*.
wool-gather
woolgatherer
woolgathering
woolly *or* wooly
woolly-headed
Worcestershire sauce
word-association test
wordbook
word for word   As adverb.
word-for-word   As adjective.
wordlist
wordmonger
word-mongering

word of mouth As noun.

word-of-mouth As adjective.

wordplay

word processor The abbreviation is *WP*.

work- Compounds formed with *work-* that are written as one word include *workaday, workaholic, workbag, workbasket, workbench, workbook, workday, workhorse, workout* (noun), *workplace, workroom, workshop, workstation, worktable, workup* (noun), *workweek*.

-work, -worker Compounds of these combining forms are written as one word (e.g., *woodworker*).

worker's compensation

work ethic

work force

working class As noun.

working-class As adjective.

work load

work of art

work-study program

world-class

worldly-wise

World Series

World War; World War I; World War II

world-weary

worldwide

worm-eaten

wormwood A strong-smelling plant that yields a bitter-tasting oil used in making absinthe.

worn-out

worry beads

worrywart

worship, worshiped *or* **worshipped**

would-be

would have *or* **would've**

would not *or* **wouldn't**

WP Abbreviation for *word processor, word processing.*

wpm Abbreviation for *words per minute*, for instance as a measure of typing speed.

wraith; *pl.*, **wraiths** A ghost.

wraparound As adjective or noun.

wrap-up As noun.

wreak havoc

wretch A miserable person. (Compare **retch**.)

Wright, Frank Lloyd (1869–1959) American architect. Founded and practiced "Prairie school" architecture in such buildings as "Falling Water" in Pennsylvania. Also built the Guggenheim Museum in New York City.

wristband

wristwatch

write-in As noun.

write-off As noun.

writer's block

writer's cramp

write-up As noun.

wrongdoer

wrongdoing

wrongheaded Perverse.

wrought iron A kind of iron resistant to corrosion used in fences and gratings.

wt. *or* **wgt.** *or* **P** Abbreviations for *weight.*

wunderkind; *pl.*, **wunderkinder** German; literally, "wonder child," a child prodigy or a precocious talent.

X

X-C Abbreviation for *cross-country*.

X chromosome

x-coordinate

xenophobia Fear or hatred of people foreign to one's own culture.

xerography

Xerox Trade name of a type of photocopying machine.

xl *or* **XL** Abbreviations for *extra large; extra long*.

Xmas Variant for *Christmas*.

X-rated

X ray As noun.

x-ray *or* **X-ray** As verb.

X-ray As adjective.

xs *or* **XS** Abbreviations for *extra small*.

xxl *or* **XXL** Abbreviations for *extra, extra large*.

xylophone

Y

yacht club

yak *or* **yack, yakked** *or* **yacked**

Yankee *or* **Yankee-Doodle**

yard goods Material sold by the yard.

yard sale

yardstick

Y chromosome

yd. *or* **y.** Abbreviations for *yard*.

yea-sayer One who says "yes" to anything.

yeah *or* **yea** Variants for *yes*.

year Capitalize only if part of proper noun (e.g., *International Geophysical Year*).

yearbook

year-end

year-round

Yeats, William Butler (1865–1939) Irish poet and playwright.

yech *or* **yecch** An interjection used to express distate or repulsion.

yellow jacket

yellow pages

yest. *or* **yday.** Abbreviation for *yesterday*.

yesterday

yesteryear

YMCA Abbreviation for *Young Men's Christian Association*.

yodel, yodeled *or* **yodelled**

yoga

yogi *or* **yogin** A person who practices yoga.

yogurt *or* **yoghurt**

yoke A frame or bar for carrying a load. (Compare **yolk**.)

yolk The yellow of an egg. (Compare **yoke**.)

Yom Kippur A Jewish holy day also known as the Day of Atonement.

yoo-hoo

Yorkshire pudding A batter of flour, eggs, and milk baked in the drippings of roasting meat.

Yorkshire terrier

your A possessive adjective meaning "belonging to you."

you're A contraction of "you are." (Compare **your**.)

yourself; *pl.*, **yourselves**

youth; *pl.*, **youths**

yo-yo; *pl.*, **yo-yos**

yr. Abbreviation for *year*.

Yule log

yuletide *or* **Yuletide** The Christmas season.

yuppie A term derived from the abbreviation for *young, urban professional* or *young, upwardly mobile professional*.

YWCA Abbreviation for *Young Women's Christian Association*.

Z

zaftig *or* **zoftig** Yiddish; plump, having an ample figure.

Zen

zero; *pl.,* **zeros** *or* **zeroes**

zero gravity A condition in which weightlessness occurs.

zero hour The time set for the beginning of a military operation; or, any crucial moment.

zero-zero Having weather conditions in which ceiling and visibility are zero.

Zeus

zigzag, zigzagged

zilch Zero, none.

zinfandel A dry, red wine made in California.

zip code *or* **ZIP code** A postal delivery number; the name is derived from the 1963 *zone improvement plan.*

ziti; *pl.,* **ziti**

Zodiac Signs

Aries
The Ram
Mar. 21–Apr. 19

Taurus
The Bull

Apr. 20–May 20

Gemini
The Twins
May 21–June 21

Cancer
The Crab
June 22–July 22

Leo
The Lion
July 23–Aug. 22

Virgo
The Virgin
Aug. 23–Sept. 22

Libra
The Scales
Sept. 23–Oct. 23

Scorpio
The Scorpion
Oct. 24–Nov. 21

Sagittarius
The Archer
Nov. 22–Dec. 21

Capricorn
The Goat
Dec. 22–Jan. 19

Aquarius
The Water Carrier
Jan. 20–Feb. 18

Pisces
The Fishes
Feb. 19–Mar. 20

Zola, Emile (1840–1902) French naturalist writer. Author of *Les Rougon-Macquart.*

zombie *or* **zombi**

zone Capitalize only if part of a proper noun (e.g., *the Canal Zone in Panama*).

zookeeper

zoom lens

zoot suit A suit with high-waisted

baggy trousers and a long, draped coat.

zucchine; *pl.,* **zucchini** *or* **zucchinis**

zuppa inglese Italian; literally "English soup," a creamy rum-flavored dessert, a trifle.

zwieback German; literally, "twice-baked," a sweet, toasted bread.

zyg-, zygo- Compounds of this combining form, which means yoke or pair, are written as one word (e.g., *zygomorphic*).

2

DESCRIPTION

ACADEMIC DEGREES AND TITLES

Academic degrees are often abbreviated, and always capitalized and set off with a comma, when used following a person's name. The abbreviation is punctuated (e.g., *Barbara Hope, M.S.W.*).

When a degree is referred to generally (e.g., *bachelor's degree, master's degree, doctorate*), the terms are not capitalized.

The rules for academic degrees also apply to professional ratings, except that abbreviations of three or more letters are written with no punctuation. (e.g., *CPA*).

An academic title is capitalized if used as a formal title preceding a name (e.g., *Chairman Reinhard R. K. Hartmann*) and may be abbreviated. A title is spelled out and lowercased when used as a modifier (e.g., *linguistics professor Barbara Ann Kipfer*).

The following are some commonly encountered degrees and titles and their abbreviations:

Assistant Professor *or* Asst. Prof.
Associate in *or* A.
Associate in Applied Science *or* A.A.S.
Associate in Arts *or* A.A.
Associate in Science *or* A.S.
associate professor *or* Assoc. Prof.
baccalaureate
Bachelor in *or* B.
Bachelor of Arts in Education *or* B.A.E. *or* B.A.Ed.
Bachelor of Arts *or* B.A. *or* A.B. (*artium baccalaureus*)
Bachelor of Chemical Engineering *or* B.C.E. *or* B.Ch.E.
Bachelor of Divinity *or* B.D. *or* D.B. (*divinitatis baccalaureus*)
Bachelor of Education *or* B.E. *or* B.Ed. *or* Ed.B.
Bachelor of Engineering *or* B.E. *or* B. Engr.
Bachelor of Fine Arts *or* B.F.A.
Bachelor of Letters *or* B.L. *or* B.Lit. *or* B.Litt. *or* Lit.B. *or* Litt.B.
Bachelor of Literature *or* B.Lit. *or* B.Litt. *or* Lit.B. *or* Litt.B.
Bachelor of Medicine *or* B.M. *or* M.B.
Bachelor of Music Education *or* B.M.E. *or* B.M.Ed.
Bachelor of Philosophy *or* B.Ph. *or* B.Phil. *or* Ph.B. (*philosophiae baccalaureus*)
Bachelor of Sacred Theology *or* S.T.B.
Bachelor of Science in Nursing *or* B.Sc.N. *or* B.S.N.
Bachelor of Science *or* B.S. *or* B.Sc. *or* S.B. *or* Sc.B.
dean
Doctor of *or* D.
Doctor of Arts *or* D.A.
Doctor of Chiropractic *or* D.C.
Doctor of Dental Medicine *or* D.M.D.
Doctor of Dental Science *or* D.D.S. *or* D.D.Sc.
Doctor of Dental Surgery *or* D.D.S.
Doctor of Divinity *or* D.D. (*divinitatis doctor*)
Doctor of Education *or* D.Ed. *or* Ed.D.

259

Doctor of Humane Letters *or*
L.H.D.
Doctor of Humanities *or* D.H. *or*
H.H.D. *or* L.H.D. (*litterarum
humaniorum doctor*)
Doctor of Juridical Science *or*
J.S.D. *or* D.J.S. *or* S.J.D. *or*
D.Jur.Sc.
Doctor of Jurisprudence *or* D.J.
or D.Jur. *or* J.D. (*juris doctor*)
Doctor of Laws *or* Dr.LL. *or* J.D.
or LL.D. (*legum doctor*)
Doctor of Letters *or* D.Lit. *or*
D.Litt. *or* Lit.D. *or* Litt.D.
(*litterarum doctor*)
Doctor of Medicine *or* M.D.
Doctor of Music *or* Mus.D.
Doctor of Optometry *or* O.D. *or*
Opt.D.
Doctor of Osteopathy *or* D.O.
Doctor of Pharmacy *or* Phar.D. *or*
Pharm.D.
Doctor of Philosophy *or* D.Ph. *or*
D.Phil. *or* Ph.D. (*philosophiae
doctor*)
Doctor of Psychology *or* Psy.D.
Doctor of Public Health *or*
D.P.H. *or* Dr.P.H.
Doctor of Science *or* D.S. *or*
D.Sc. *or* Sc.D. *or* S.D.
Doctor of Veterinary Medicine *or*
D.V.M. *or* V.M.D.
Juris Doctor *or* J.D.
Master of *or* M.
Master of Arts in Education *or*
M.A.E. *or* M.A.Ed.
Master of Arts *or* A.M. *or* M.A.
(*artium magister*)
Master of Business Administration
or M.B.A.
Master of Education *or* Ed.M. *or*
M.Ed.

Master of Science *or* M.S. *or*
M.Sc. *or* Sc.M *or* S.M.
Master of Social Work *or* M.S.W.
Master of Theology *or* M.Th. *or*
Th.M.
Ph.D. *or* doctorate.
Professor (Prof.)
Professor Emeritus

ADDRESSES

Post office designations and
their abbreviations for street
addresses are: Alley (Aly), Arcade
(Arc), Avenue (Ave), Boulevard
(Blvd), Branch (Br), Bypass
(Byp), Causeway (Cswy), Center
(Ctr), Circle (Cir), Court (Ct),
Crescent (Cres), Drive (Dr),
Expressway (Expy), Extension
(Ext), Freeway (Fwy), Gardens
(Gdns);
Grove (Grv), Heights (Hts),
Highway (Hwy), Lane (Ln),
Manor (Mnr), Place (Pl), Plaza
(Plz), Point (Pt), Road (Rd),
Rural (R), Square (Sq), Street
(St), Terrace (Ter), Trail (Trl),
Turnpike (Tpke), Viaduct (Via),
Vista (Vis).
Compass points are abbreviated
when they come after street names
(e.g., *Hawthorne Blvd. SW*), but
are written out when used
internally in an address (e.g.,
South Allen St.).

AIRCRAFT NAMES

Capitalize names of planes
(e.g., *Air Force One, Boeing 747,*
and hyphenate between letters and
numbers (e.g., *DC-10, L-1011*).

Plurals are formed by adding an *s* to names of aircraft that end with a number (e.g., *Boeing 707s*); by adding *'s* to those that end with a letter (e.g., *C-5A's*).

ARABIC NUMERALS

Numbers formed using the symbols 0, 1, 2, 3, 4, 5, 6, 7, 8, 9. Used except for sequence of wars or family descendants, which use Roman numerals.

AUTOMOBILES

Capitalize brand names (e.g., *Mazda Miata*); lowercase generic references (e.g., a Montero jeep).

CABINET OF THE UNITED STATES

Capitalize names of cabinet departments serving a head of state (e.g., *Department of Defense, the State Department*).

The departments of the U.S. cabinet are:

Department of Agriculture (USDA)
Department of Commerce
Department of Defense (DOD)
Department of Education
Department of Energy (DOE)
Department of Health and Human Services
Department of Housing and Urban Development (HUD)
Department of the Interior
Department of Justice
Department of Labor
Department of State
Department of Transportation (DOT)
Department of the Treasury

COMPANIES

The names of companies and other institutions are capitalized and spelled out as proper nouns.

Abbreviations are sometimes used for *company* (*Co.*), *corporation* (*Corp.*), *incorporated* (*Inc.*), *limited* (*Ltd.*), and so forth.

Company names should be styled as they appear on official documents or company letterhead. Firms that capitalize *the* as the first word of their official name (e.g., *The Frankin Mint*) may therefore fall alphabetically under *T* in the following listing:

A&P (Great Atlantic & Pacific Tea Company Inc.)
A&W Restaurants
AAMCO Transmissions Incorporated
Abbott Laboratories
Adolph Coors Company
Aer Lingus
Aeroflot
AeroMexico
Aetna Life and Casualty Company
Air Canada
Air France
Air-India
Air Jamaica
Alberto-Culver Company
Alco Standard Corporation
Alitalia Airlines
Allied-Signal Incorporated
Allis-Chalmers Corporation

Allstate Insurance Company (a
subsidiary of Sears, Roebuck
and Company)
Aluminum Company of America
or ALCOA
Amax Incorporated
American Airlines, Incorporated
(a subsidiary of AMR
Corporation)
American Brands, Incorporated
American Cyanamid Company
American Express Company
American Financial Corporation
American Home Products
Corporation
American International Group,
Incorporated
American Stores Company
American Telephone & Telegraph
Company *or* AT&T
Ameritech Corporation
Amoco Corporation
AMR Corporation
Amtrak (stands for *American
travel by track* and is the rail
line operated by the National
Railroad Passenger Corporation)
Anheuser-Busch Companies,
Incorporated
Apple Computer, Incorporated
Arby's Incorporated
Archer-Daniels-Midland Company
Armco Incorporated
Armstrong World Industries
Incorporated
Asarco Incorporated
Athlete's Foot Group Incorporated
(a subsidiary of General Sports
Ventures Enterprises
Incorporated)
Atlantic Richfield Company *or*
Arco

Avianca-Colombian Airlines
Avon Products, Incorporated
Baby Bells *or* Bell Operating
Companies (They are
Ameritech, Bell Atlantic, Bell
South, NYNEX, Pacific
Telesis, Southwestern Bell, and
US West.)
Baker Hughes Incorporated
BankAmerica Corporation
Bantam Doubleday Dell
Publishing Group, Inc.
BASF Corporation (a subsidiary
of Basfin Corporation)
Baskin-Robbins Incorporated
Bausch & Lomb
Baxter International Incorporated
Bayer AG
Beatrice/Hunt-Wesson Foods (a
subsidiary of Beatrice
Company)
Becton, Dickinson & Company
Beech Aircraft Corporation (a
subsidiary of Raytheon
Company)
Bell & Howell Company
Bell Atlantic Corporation
Bell South Corporation
Bergdorf Goodman Incorporated
(a subsidiary of Neiman
Marcus)
Bergen Brunswig Corporation
Berkshire Hathaway Incorporated
Bethlehem Steel Corporation
Bic Corporation
Big Boy Family Restaurants
Black & Decker Corporation
Blue Cross & Blue Shield
Association
Boise Cascade Corporation
Bonanza Restaurants
Borden, Incorporated

Borg-Warner Corporation
Bristol-Myers Squibb Company
British Airways PLC
British Broadcasting Corporation
  or BBC
British Petroleum Company p.l.c.
Budget Rent-A-Car Corporation
Burlington Holdings Incorporated
Campbell Soup Company
Campeau Corporation
Capital Cities/ABC Incorporated
Carson Pirie Scott & Company
Carvel Corporation
Caterpillar Incorporated
CBS Incorporated
Century 21 Real Estate
  Corporation
Champion International
  Corporation
Chem-Dry Cleaning
Chevron Corporation
Chrysler Corporation
Church's Fried Chicken,
  Incorporated (a subsidiary of A.
  Copland Enterprises
  Incorporated)
CIGNA Corporation
Citibank N.A.
Citicorp
City University of New York *or*
  CUNY
Clorox Company
Colgate-Palmolive Company
Communications Satellite
  Corporation *or* Comsat
Compaq Computer Corporation
CompuServe Incorporated (a
  subsidiary of H&R Block,
  Incorporated)
ComputerLand Corporation
ConAgra, Incorporated
Connecticut General Corporation

(a subsidiary of CIGNA
  Holdings, Incorporated)
Consolidated Edison Company of
  New York, Incorporated *or* Con
  Ed *or* Con Edison
Consolidated Rail Corporation *or*
  Conrail
Continental Airlines Holdings
  Incorporated
Control Data Corporation
Corning Incorporated
Cosmair, Incorporated
CSX Corporation
Cummins Engine Company,
  Incorporated
Dairy Queen
Dayton-Hudson Corporation
Deere & Company
Delta Air Lines, Incorporated
Diet Center Incorporated
Digital Equipment Corporation
Diners Club
Dollar Rent A Car Systems
  Incorporated
Dominion Resources, Incorporated
Domino's Pizza Incorporated
Dow Jones & Company,
  Incorporated
Dresser Industries, Incorporated
Dr Pepper/Seven-Up Company
Dunkin' Donuts Incorporated
Eastman Kodak Company
Eaton Corporation
Econo-Lodges of America
  Incorporated
E.I. du Pont de Nemours &
  Company
El Al Israel Airlines
Eli Lilly and Company
Emerson Electric Company
Equitable Life Assurance Society
  of the United States

263   *COMPANIES*

ESPN Incorporated
Exxon Corporation
Faberg, Incorporated
Federal Deposit Insurance
    Corporation *or* FDIC
Federal National Mortgage
    Association *or* Fannie Mae
Fieldcrest Cannon, Incorporated
Fleming Companies, Incorporated
Fluor Corporation
Ford Motor Company
Fruehauf Trailer Operations (a
    subsidiary of Terex
    Corporation)
Fruit of the Loom, Incorporated
Gannett Company, Incorporated
Genentech, Incorporated (a
    subsidiary of Roche Holdings
    Incorporated)
General Dynamics Corporation
General Electric Company *or* GE
General Mills, Incorporated
General Motors Corporation *or*
    GMC
Georgia-Pacific Corporation
Gillette Company
Grand Metropolitan PLC
Great Atlantic & Pacific Tea
    Company Incorporated *or* A&P
Greyhound Dial Corporation
Grumman Corporation
GTE Corporation (formerly the
    General Telephone and
    Electronics Corporation)
Halliburton Company
Hallmark Cards Incorporated
Hammacher Schlemmer
H&R Block, Incorporated
Harcourt Brace Jovanovich,
    Incorporated
Hardee's Food Systems
    Incorporated
Harley-Davidson, Incorporated

Hartmarx Corporation
Hasbro, Incorporated
Hershey Foods Corporation
Hewlett-Packard Company
H. J. Heinz Company
Hoechst Celanese Corporation (a
    subsidiary of Hoechst AG)
Holiday Inns, Incorporated (a
    subsidiary of Bass PLC)
Home Box Office Incorporated
Honda Motor Company, Ltd.
Honeywell Incorporated
Hospital Corporation of America
Houghton Mifflin Company
Hyundai Group
Icelandair
Ingersoll-Rand Company
Inland Steel Industries,
    Incorporated
International Business Machines
    Corporation *or* IBM
International Paper Company
ITT Corporation
James River Corporation of
    Virginia
Jazzercise Incorporated
J.C. Penney Company,
    Incorporated
Jiffy Lube International
    Incorporated
John Hancock Mutual Life
    Insurance Company
Johns Hopkins University
Johnson & Johnson
Johnson Controls Incorporated
J. P. Morgan & Company
    Incorporated
Kellogg Company
Kellwood Company
Kentucky Fried Chicken
    Corporation (a subsidiary of
    Pepsico Incorporated)
Kimberly-Clark Corporation

KLM Royal Dutch Airlines
K mart Corporation
Knight-Ridder, Incorporated
Kwik-Kopy Corporation
Lafarge Corporation
La-Z-Boy Chair Company
Little Caesar's Enterprises
 Incorporated
Litton Industries, Incorporated
Liz Claiborne, Incorporated
Lloyd's Bank Plc
Lloyd's of London
Lockheed Corporation
Loews Corporation
Lord & Taylor (a subsidiary of
 The May Department Stores
 Company)
LTV Corporation
Lufthansa German Airlines
Mack Trucks, Incorporated
Mail Boxes Etc.
Manpower PLC
Manufacturers Hanover
 Corporation
Manville Corporation
Marine Midland Banks,
 Incorporated
Mars Stores, Incorporated
Martin Marietta Corporation
Massachusetts Institute of
 Technology *or* MIT
Mattel Incorporated
Mazda Motor Corporation
MCA Incorporated
McDonald's Corporation
McDonnell Douglas Corporation
McGraw-Hill, Incorporated
MCI Telecommunications
 Corporation
McKesson Corporation
Mead Data Central, Incorporated
 (a subsidiary of The Mead
 Corporation)

Meineke Discount Muffler Shops
 Incorporated
Merck & Company Incorporated
Merrill Lynch & Company,
 Incorporated
Metropolitan Life Insurance
 Company
Midas International Corporation
Minuteman Press International
 Incorporated
Mister Donut of America
Mobil Corporation
Monsanto Company
Morgan Stanley Group
 Incorporated
Motorola, Incorporated
Mutual Broadcasting System
 Incorporated (a subsidiary of
 Westwood One, Incorporated)
Nabisco Brands, Incorporated (a
 subsidiary of RJR Nabisco,
 Incorporated)
National Broadcasting Company,
 Incorporated (a subsidiary of
 General Electric Company) *or*
 NBC
National Steel Corporation
Navistar International Corporation
NCR Corporation
Neiman Marcus (a subsidiary of
 General Cinema Corporation)
New York Life Insurance
 Company
North American Philips
 Corporation
Northrop Corporation
Northwestern Mutual Life
 Insurance Company
Nutri/System, Incorporated
NWA Incorporated (a subsidiary
 of the Alfred Checci Group)
NYNEX Corporation
Occidental Petroleum Corporation

Olsten Corporation
1 Hour Martinizing Dry Cleaners
Orange Julius of America
Outboard Marine Corporation
Owens-Corning Fiberglas
Corporation
Pacific Telesis Group
Pan Am Corporation
Paramount Communications
Incorporated
Parker Hannifin Corporation
Pearle, Incorporated (a subsidiary
of Grandmet USA Incorporated)
Pennzoil Company
Pepsico, Incorporated
Pfizer Incorporated
Phelps Dodge Corporation
Philip Morris Companies
Incorporated
Phillips Petroleum Company
Phillips–Van Heusen Corporation
Pillsbury Company (a subsidiary
of Gramet Holdings
Corporation)
PIP Printing Corporation
Pitney Bowes Incorporated
Polaroid Corporation
Popeye's Famous Fried Chicken
& Biscuits Incorporated
PPG Industries, Incorporated
Premark International Incorporated
Procter & Gamble Company
Public Broadcasting Service *or*
PBS
Qantas Airways
Quaker Oats Company
Ralston Purina Company
Ramada Incorporated (a subsidiary
of New World Hotels [USA],
Incorporated)
RAND Corporation
Raytheon Company

Realty World/Metro Group
Reebok International Ltd.
RE/MAX International
Incorporated
Reuters Holdings P.L.C.
Revlon Group Incorporated (a
subsidiary of the MacAndrews
& Forbes Group, Incorporated)
Reynolds Metals Company
R.H. Macy & Company,
Incorporated
Ringling Brothers–Barnum &
Bailey Combined Shows, Inc.
(a subsidiary of Irvin Feld &
Kenneth Feld Productions,
Incorporated)
Rite Aid Corporation
RJR Nabisco Incorporated
Rockwell International
Corporation
Roto-Rooter, Incorporated (a
subsidiary of Chemed
Corporation)
Royal Dutch/Shell Group
R.R. Donnelly & Sons Company
Rubbermaid Incorporated
Ryder System, Incorporated
Saatchi & Saatchi Company p.l.c.
Sabena Belgian World Airlines
Safeway Incorporated
Salomon Incorporated
Sara Lee Corporation
Scandinavian Airlines System *or*
SAS
Schering-Plough Corporation
Scott Paper Company
Sears, Roebuck and Company
ServiceMaster Limited Partnership
7-Eleven Stores
Shell Oil Company (a subsidiary
of Shell Petroleum
Incorporated)

Sherwin-Williams Company
Sir Speedy, Incorporated (a subsidiary of KOA Holdings Corporation)
Sizzler Restaurants International Incorporated (a subsidiary of Collins Foods International Incorporated)
SmithKline Beecham p.l.c.
Southland Corporation
Southwestern Bell Corporation
Subaru of America, Incorporated (a subsidiary of Fuji Heavy Industries, Incorporated)
Subway World Headquarters
Super 8 Motels Incorporated
Super Valu Stores, Incorporated
Swissair Transport Company Ltd.
Sysco Corporation
Taco Bell Corporation
Tandy Corporation
TCBY Enterprises Incorporated
Teachers Insurance & Annuity Association of America
Textronix, Incorporated
Teledyne, Incorporated
Tenneco Incorporated
Texaco Incorporated
Texas Instruments Incorporated
Textron Incorporated
The Associated Press or AP
The Atchison Topeka and Santa Fe Railway Company
The B.F. Goodrich Company
The Boeing Company
The Chase Manhattan Corporation
The Coca-Cola Company
The Dow Chemical Company
The Dun & Bradstreet Corporation
The Franklin Mint
The Goodyear Tire & Rubber Company

The Henley Group, Incorporated
The Hertz Corporation (a subsidiary of Park Ridge Corporation)
The Kroger Company
The Leslie Fay Companies (a subsidiary of New LEFCO Corporation & Goldome)
The May Department Stores Company
The Mead Corporation
The New York Times Company
The Prudential Insurance Company of America
The Seagram Company Ltd.
The Stanley Works
The Stride Rite Corporation
The Stroh Brewery Company (a subsidiary of The Stroh Companies, Incorporated)
The Times Mirror Company
The Travelers Corporation
The Walt Disney Company
3M Company or Minnesota Mining & Manufacturing Company
Thrifty Rent-A-Car System, Incorporated (a subsidiary of Chrysler Motors Corporation)
Time Warner Incorporated
Tootsie Roll Industries, Incorporated
Toys Я Us Incorporated
Trans World Airlines or TWA
Tribune Company TRW Incorporated
20th Century Fox
UAL Corporation
Unilever United States, Incorporated
Union Carbide Corporation
Union Pacific Corporation

Uniroyal Goodrich Tire Company
Unisys Corporation
United Parcel Service of America,
  Incorporated
United Press International *or* UPI
United Technologies Corporation
United Telecommunications,
  Incorporated
Unocal Corporation
Upjohn Company
USAIR Group Incorporated (owns
  USAir)
USF&G Corporation
US West, Incorporated
USX Corporation
Volkswagen A.G.
Waldenbook Company
  Incorporated
Walgreen Company
Wal-Mart Stores, Incorporated (a
  subsidiary of Walton
  Enterprises, Incorporated)
Wang Laboratories, Incorporated
Warnaco Incorporated
Warner-Lambert Company
Waste Management, Incorporated
Weight Watchers International
  Incorporated (a subsidiary of
  H.J. Heinz Company)
Wells Fargo & Company
Wendy's International
  Incorporated
Westinghouse Electric Corporation
West Point–Pepperell,
  Incorporated
Wetterau Incorporated
Weyerhaeuser Company
Whirlpool Corporation
William Wrigley Jr. Company
Winn-Dixie Stores, Incorporated
Winnebago Industries,
  Incorporated
Woolworth Company

W.R. Grace & Company
Xerox Corporation
Young & Rubicam Incorporated
Zenith Electronics Corporation

COURTESY TITLES

These include *Ms., Miss,
Mrs.,* and *Mr.*

Ms. is the preferred form of
address for women, equivalent to
Mr. for men. *Miss,* the traditional
courtesy title for unmarried
women, should no longer be used
unless it is the known preference
of a specific individual. Girls and
young women may also be
addressed as *Ms.*

Mrs. is the traditional courtesy
title for married women. Unless
an individual's preference is
known, use *Ms.*

A courtesy title is dropped if
another title, such as *Jr.* or an
academic degree, is used.

FORMAL TITLES

Military, nobility,
organizational, religious, and
other formal designations of
position are capitalized when used
as a title before a person's name.
But when used in apposition—that
is, along with the name in an
explanatory sense (e.g., *the
American president Thomas
Jefferson* or *Ann Miller, chief of
staff*), the title is lowercased.

In formal usage, as in an
acknowledgment or introduction,
a title following a name and set
off by commas is capitalized
(e.g., *I wish to thank R.R.K.*

Hartmann, Professor of Linguistics, University of Exeter). Titles used in direct address are also capitalized (e.g., *Your table is ready, Professor*).

FRATERNAL ORGANIZATIONS

Capitalize the proper nouns referring to fraternal organizations, service clubs, and their members (e.g., *American Legion, Legionnaire, Kiwanis Club, Kiwanian*).

GEOGRAPHIC TERMS

Words or phrases that identify distinct areas, regions, places, divisions, or districts of continents and countries are capitalized when used as proper nouns or in an address. Derivatives are also capitalized.

Other guidelines are:

Names of mountains, rivers, oceans, islands, and other geographic features are capitalized, including generic terms when used as part of a proper noun (e.g., *Pacific Ocean, Hudson River*). Generic terms are also capitalized when preceding a proper noun (e.g., *Lakes Michigan and Huron*). Generic terms used in the plural following the names of more than one geographical place (e.g., *the Allegheny, Monongahela, and Ohio rivers*) and generic terms used alone are lowercased.

Buildings, public places (as monuments, parks, landmarks), and names of streets are capitalized when used as proper nouns or in an address (e.g., *the Washington Monument, Prospect Park*).

Popular and legendary names of places are capitalized (e.g., *Windy City,* or *the Street* for Wall Street).

Compass points and directions are capitalized when they refer to a specific region (e.g., *the American South*) or are part of an address. But a descriptive term used to denote direction or position is not a proper noun and is not capitalized (e.g., *western Connecticut*). Derivative nouns and adjectives of compass points that refer to a particular region are usually capitalized (e.g., *the Western Hemisphere*).

Words or phrases that designate political divisions are capitalized when used as proper nouns or in an address (e.g., *Washington State, Third Congressional District*).

The word *Saint* is often abbreviated in geographic names (e.g., *St. Louis*).

See Appendix 7 for state abbreviations, capitals, and resident names, and Appendix 5 for a listing of nations with their capitals and resident names. Names of countries are usually abbreviated only in closely set material such as tables, but *United States* is often abbreviated when used as an adjective (e.g., *U.S. military action*). Countries whose abbreviations are formed by the initial letters of the constituent words may be unpunctuated (e.g., *USA*).

The following list is an extensive sampling of place names:

Aberdeen, Scotland
Abidjan, Ivory Coast
Abu Dhabi, United Arab Emirates
Acapulco de Juarez, Mexico
Addis Ababa, Ethiopia
Adelaide, Australia
Adirondack Mountains
Adriatic Sea
Aegean Sea
Afghanistan
Ahmedabad, India
Akron, Ohio
Alamo
Albania
Alberta   A Canadian province.
Albuquerque, New Mexico
Aleutian Islands
Alexandria, Egypt
Algeria
Allegany County, Maryland
Allegany County, New York
Alleghany County, Virginia
Allegheny Mountains
Amarillo, Texas
Amazon River
Amman, Jordan
Amsterdam, the Netherlands
Andes Mountains
Andorra
Anguilla
Ankara, Turkey
Antarctica, Antarctic Ocean, Antarctic Circle
Antigua and Barbuda
Antigua, Guatemala
Appalachia
Appalachian Mountains

Appian Way
Appomàttox, Virginia
Arc de Triomphe
Arctic Circle
Arctic Ocean
Arlington National Cemetery
Armenia
Aruba
Asia Minor
Atchison, Kansas
Athabasca, Canada
Athens, Greece
Atlantic City, New Jersey
Atlantic Ocean
Auckland, New Zealand
Auschwitz, Poland
Avenue of the Americas *or* Sixth Avenue
Azores
Baghdad, Iraq
Baku, Azerbaijan
Balkans *or* Balkan States   The nations on the Balkan Peninsula in southeastern Europe: Romania, Bulgaria, Greece, Albania, the former Yugoslavia, and part of Turkey.
Baltic States   Nations on the eastern coast of the Baltic Sea: Latvia, Lithuania, Estonia.
Baltimore, Maryland
Bandung, Indonesia
Bangalore, India
Bangkok, Thailand
Bangladesh
Barbados
Barcelona, Spain
Barranquilla, Colombia
Beijing, China   Formerly Peking.
Beirut, Lebanon
Belgrade, Yugoslavia
Belize

Belo Horizonte, Brazil

Benelux   Refers to the economic
union formed in 1947
comprising Belgium, the
Netherlands, and Luxembourg.

Bering Sea

Berlin, Germany

Bern, Switzerland

Birmingham, England

Bogalusa, Louisiana

Bogotá, Colombia

Bombay, India

Bophuthatswana

Botswana

Brainerd, Minnesota

Brisbane, Australia

British Columbia   A Canadian
province.

British Virgin Islands

Brussels, Belgium

Bucharest, Romania

Buckhannon, West Virginia

Budapest, Hungary

Buenos Aires, Argentina

Cairo, Egypt

Calcutta, India

Calgary, Alberta, Canada

Cali, Colombia

Cambodia or Kampuchea

Cameroon

Canal Zone or Panama Canal
Zone

Cannes, France

Canton, China

Cape Breton, Nova Scotia,
Canada

Cape Canaveral or the John F.
Kennedy Space Center

Cape Town, South Africa

Caracas, Venezuela

Caribbean Sea

Caribbean   The ocean islands
between the southern end of
Florida to the northern part of
South America, including
Antigua and Barbuda, the
Bahamas, Barbados, Belize,
Cuba, Dominican Republic,
French Guinea, Grenada,
(Grenadines), Guyana, Haiti,
Jamaica, (Montserrat), (Puerto
Rico), St. Kitts and Nevis,
Suriname, Trinidad and
Tobago, (West Indies islands).

Casablanca, Morocco

Casper, Wyoming

Central America   The region
between Mexico and Colombia
including Belize, Costa Rica, El
Salvador, Guatemala,
Honduras, Nicaragua, and
Panama.

Champaign, Illinois

Champs-Elysées

Charleston, South Carolina

Charleston, West Virginia

Chattanooga, Tennessee

Chicago, Illinois

Chicopee, Massachusetts

Chile

Chillicothe, Ohio

China

Chittagong, Bangladesh

Christmas Island

Chungking, China

Cincinnati, Ohio

Cleveland, Ohio

Cocos (or Keeling) Islands

Cologne, West Germany

Congo River

Continental Divide   The
watershed of North America
formed by the crests of the
Rocky Mountains.

Copenhagen, Denmark
Córdoba, Argentina
Corsica
Corvallis, Oregon
Costa Rica
Court of St. James's *or* St. James's Palace   The royal court of Britain.
Curaçao
Dairy Belt
Dakar, Senegal
Dallas, Texas
Damascus, Syria
Dardanelles
Dark Continent Africa   Described as such by Europeans because it was largely uncharted until late in the 19th century.
Dayton, Ohio
Deauville, France
Deep South   The region of the United States encompassing Alabama, Georgia, Mississippi, and South Carolina, sometimes also used to mean the entire southeast including Florida and Louisiana.
Delhi, India
Des Moines, Iowa
Detroit, Michigan
Dhaka, Bangladesh
Dien Bien Phu, Vietnam
District of Columbia (D.C.)
Djibouti *or* Jibuti
Djkarta *or* Jakarta, Indonesia
Dnepropetrovsk, Ukraine
Donetsk, Ukraine
Down Under   The Australia and New Zealand area.
Dresden, Germany
Dublin, Ireland
Duluth, Minnesota
Düsseldorf, Germany

Eastern Hemisphere   Africa, Asia, Australia, and Europe.
Eastern Shore   The Chesapeake Bay region of Maryland, Virginia, and Delaware.
East Germany *or* German Democratic Republic   Now incorporated in united Germany.
East North Central states   Indiana, Illinois, Michigan, Ohio, and Wisconsin.
East South Central states   Alabama, Kentucky, Mississippi, and Tennessee.
Edinburgh, Scotland
Edmonton, Alberta, Canada
Eglin Air Force Base
El Salvador   Central American country whose capital is San Salvador.
Elkhart, Indiana
England
Essen, Germany
Euphrates River
Faeroe Islands   Part of Denmark.
Faneuil Hall   In Boston Massachusetts.
Far East   The easternmost part of Asia: Burma, Cambodia, China, Hong Kong, Indonesia, Japan, Laos, Malaysia, North Korea, Philippines, Siberia, South Korea, Taiwan, Vietnam.
Fiji Islands
Florida Keys
Flushing Meadows, New York
Fontainebleau, France
Fort Lauderdale, Florida
Fort Wayne, Indiana
Frankfort, Kentucky
Frankfurt, West Germany
Fredericksburg, Virginia

Fribourg, Switzerland
Fuji or Fujiyama or Mount Fuji or
    Fuji-no-Yama
Fukuoka, Japan
Galápagos Islands   Part of
    Ecuador.
Gallipoli, Turkey
Genoa, Italy
Glasgow, Scotland
Gloucester, Massachusetts
Gloucestershire, England
Gorky, Russia
Governors Island, Massachusetts
Governors Island, New York
Grand Rapids, Michigan
Great Britain   England, Scotland,
    and Wales.
Great Lakes   Lake Superior,
    Lake Huron, Lake Michigan,
    Lake Erie, and Lake Ontario.
Great Plains   The region of the
    United States from North
    Dakota south to Texas and from
    the Missouri River west to the
    Rocky Mountains.
Greenwich Village   In New York
    City.
Guadalajara   A city in Mexico; a
    province in Spain.
Guadalupe, Mexico
Guadeloupe, West Indies
Guam
Guantánamo, Cuba
Guatemala City, Guatemala
Guayaquil, Ecuador
Guiana   The region of South
    America including Surinam,
    Guyana, French Guiana, and
    parts of Brazil and Venezuela.
Hague (The), the Netherlands
Haifa, Israel
Hamburg, Germany
Harbin, China

Hattiesburg, Mississippi
Havana, Cuba
Hawaii   Main islands are Hawaii,
    Kahoolawe, Kauai, Lanai,
    Maui, Molokai, Niihau, and
    Oahu.
Himalaya Mountains
Hiroshima, Japan
Hispaniola   The island in the
    West Indies comprised of Haiti
    and the Dominican Republic.
Ho Chi Minh City, Vietnam
Hollywood   Part of Los Angeles,
    California.
Holy See, Vatican City
Hong Kong
Honolulu, Hawaii
Houston, Texas
Hyannis Port, Massachusetts
Hyderabad, Pakistan
Indianapolis, Indiana
Indochina   Cambodia, Laos, and
    Vietnam.
Istanbul, Turkey   Formerly called
    Constantinople.
Jerusalem
Johannesburg, South Africa
John F. Kennedy Space Center
    At Cape Canaveral, Florida.
Kanpur, India
Kansas City   The name of cities
    in Kansas and Missouri.
Karachi, Pakistan
Ketchikan, Alaska
Kharkov, Ukraine
Kiev, Ukraine
Kinshasa, Zaire
Kobe, Japan
Kuala Lumpur, Malaysia
Kuibyshev, Russia
Kuril Islands
Kuwait
Labrador, Newfoundland, Canada

La Guardia Airport   In New York City.
Lagos, Nigeria
Lahore, Pakistan
La Jolla, California
La Paz, Bolivia
La Porte, Indiana
Laredo, Texas
Latin America   The region in the Western Hemisphere south of the United States where Romance (Latin-based) languages are primarily spoken including: Argentina, Bolivia, Brazil, Chile, Colombia, Costa Rica, Cuba, Dominican Republic, Ecuador, El Salvador, Guatemala, Haiti, Honduras, Mexico, Nicaragua, Panama, Paraguay, Peru, Puerto Rico, Uruguay, Venezuela, and the French West Indies.
Leaning Tower of Pisa
Leicester, England
Leipzig, Germany
Leningrad, USSR   Now St. Petersburg, Russia.
Liechtenstein
Lige, Belgium
Lima, Peru
Lisbon, Portugal
Liverpool, England
Lodz, Poland
London, England
Los Angeles, California
Low Countries   Belgium, Luxembourg, and the Netherlands.
Lyndon B. Johnson Space Center   At Houston, Texas.
Macao
Mackinac Island, Michigan
Madagascar

Madras, India
Madrid, Spain
Majorca, Spain
Maldive Islands
Managua, Nicaragua
Manasquan, New Jersey
Manila, Philippines
Manitoba   A Canadian province.
Maritime Provinces or the Maritimes   New Brunswick, Nova Scotia, and Prince Edward Island, provinces in Atlantic Canada.
Marrakech or Marrakesh or Marakesh, Morocco
Marseilles, France
Marshall Islands
Mason-Dixon Line or Mason and Dixon's Line   The southern boundary of Pennsylvania, separating it from Maryland; sometimes regarded as the division between the North and the South.
Matawan, New Jersey
Mayotte Island   In the Indian Ocean.
Mecca, Saudi Arabia
Medellin, Colombia
Mediterranean Sea
Melbourne, Australia
Memphis, Tennessee
Meriden, Connecticut
Middle Atlantic states   New Jersey, New York, and Pennsylvania. Part of Northeast region of the United States.
Middle East   Southwest Asia and northeast Africa, including Cyprus, Egypt, Iran, Iraq, Israel, Kuwait, Jordan, Lebanon, Oman, Qatar, Saudi Arabia, Sudan, Syria, Turkey,

United Arab Emirates, and
Yemen.

Middle West *or* Midwest *or* North
  Central states   Indiana, Illinois,
  Iowa, Kansas, Michigan,
  Minnesota, Missouri, Nebraska,
  North Dakota, Ohio, South
  Dakota, and Wisconsin.

Milan, Italy

Milwaukee, Wisconsin

Minneapolis, Minnesota

Minsk, Byelorussia

Missoula, Montana

Mogadishu, Somalia

Monterey, California

Monterrey, Mexico

Montevideo, Uruguay

Montpelier, Vermont

Montreal, Quebec, Canada

Moscow, Russia

Mountain states   Arizona,
  Colorado, Idaho, Montana,
  Nevada, New Mexico, Utah,
  Wyoming.

Mozambique

Munich, West Germany

Muscle Shoals, Alabama

Muskegon, Michigan

Muskogee, Oklahoma

Mykonos, Greece

Nagoya, Japan

Nanking, China

Naples, Italy

Nashville, Tennessee

N'Djamena, Chad

Nepal

Netherlands, the (Holland)

Netherlands Antilles

New Brunswick   A Canadian
  province.

New England   Connecticut,
  Maine, Massachusetts, New
  Hampshire, Rhode Island, and

Vermont. Part of Northeast
  region of the United States.

Newfoundland   A Canadian
  province comprising the island
  of Newfoundland and part of
  Labrador.

New Orleans, Louisiana

New South Wales, Australia

New York City, New York

Norfolk Island

North America   The continent
  including Canada, Central
  America, Greenland, Mexico,
  the United States, and the
  islands surrounding these
  countries, such as Bermuda, the
  West Indies, and the Caribbean
  islands.

North Central region   Indiana,
  Illinois, Michigan, Ohio,
  eastern Wisconsin, Iowa,
  Kansas, Minnesota, Missouri,
  Nebraska, North Dakota, and
  western South Dakota.

Northeast region   New England
  and the Middle Atlantic states.

North Pole

Northwest Territories, Canada

Nova Scotia   A Canadian
  province.

Novosibrisk, Russia

Nuremberg, Germany

Oahu, Hawaii

Oakland, California

Odessa, Ukraine

Okinawa, Japan

Omaha, Nebraska

Ontario, Canada

Orient

Osaka, Japan

Oskaloosa, Iowa

Ottawa, Ontario, Canada

Ozark Mountains

Pacific Ocean
Pacific states   Alaska, Hawaii,
    Oregon, and Washington.
Paducah, Kentucky
Palermo, Sicily
Panama City, Panama
Paraguay
Paris, France
Paterson, New Jersey
Peking, China   Now called
    Beijing.
Penobscot Bay
Persian Gulf
Perth, Australia
Petaluma, California
Phenix City, Alabama
Philadelphia, Pennsylvania
Phnom Penh, Cambodia
Phoenix, Arizona
Pikes Peak   A mountain peak in
    central Colorado.
Pittsburgh, Pennsylvania
Plattsburgh, New York
Pocatello, Idaho
Port-au-Prince, Haiti
Pôrto Alegre, Brazil
Portobelo *or* Porto Bello *or* Puerto
    Bello, Panama
Poughkeepsie, New York
Prague, Czechoslovakia
Pretoria, South Africa
Prince Edward Island
    A Canadian province.
Pusan, South Korea
Pyongyang, North Korea
Quad Cities   Davenport, Iowa,
    and Rock Island, Moline, and
    East Moline, Illinois.
Quebec City, Quebec, Canada
Quezon City, Philippines
Quito, Ecuador
Recife, Brazil
Rensselaer, New York

Reykjavík, Iceland
Rhodesia
Rio de Janeiro, Brazil
Rio Grande
Riyadh, Saudi Arabia
Rocky Mountains *or* the Rockies
Romania
Rome, Italy
Rosario, Argentina
Rotterdam, the Netherlands
Saarbrücken, Germany
Sahara Desert
St. John, New Brunswick, Canada
St. John's, Newfoundland,
    Canada
Saint-Moritz, Switzerland
St. Petersburg, Russia   Formerly
    Leningrad, USSR.
St. Pierre and Miquelon
Salt Lake City, Utah
Salvador, Brazil
Salzburg, Austria
Samoa
San Diego, California
San Francisco, California
San Jose, California
Santiago, Chile
Santo Domingo, Dominican
    Republic
São Paulo, Brazil
Sapporo, Japan
Sarajevo, Bosnia and Herzegovina
    Formerly Sarajevo, Yugoslavia.
Sardinia, Italy
Sarh, Chad
Saskatchewan   A Canadian
    province.
Sault Sainte Marie *or* Sault Ste.
    Marie, Ontario, Canada
Savannah, Georgia
Scandinavia   Denmark, Norway,
    and Sweden, and sometimes
    Finland and Iceland.

Schenectady, New York

Schuylkill, the

Scranton, Pennsylvania

Seattle, Washington

Sedalia, Missouri

Seoul, South Korea

Seven Seas   The Arabian Sea, Atlantic Ocean, Bay of Bengal, Mediterranean Sea, Persian Gulf, Red Sea, and South China Sea.

Seven Wonders of the World   The Egyptian pyramids, the hanging gardens of Babylon, the mausoleum at Halicarnassus, the temple of Artemis at Ephesus, the Colossus of Rhodes, the statue of Zeus by Phidias at Olympia, and the *pharos* (lighthouse) at Alexandria.

Seville, Spain

Seychelles

Shanghai, China

Sheboygan, Wisconsin

Shenyang *or* Mukden, China   The major city of Manchuria.

Sicily, Italy

Sierra Leone

Sierra Nevada, the

Sinai Peninsula

Singapore, Singapore

Sioux City, Iowa

Smolensk, Russia

Smyrna, Delaware

Sofia, Bulgaria

South   In the United States this refers to the sixteen states of the East South Central, South Atlantic, and West South Central regions.

South America   The continent including Argentina, Bolivia, Brazil, Chile, Colombia, Ecuador, French Guinea, Guyana, Paraguay, Peru, Suriname, Uruguay, Venezuela.

South Atlantic states   Delaware, Florida, Georgia, Maryland, North Carolina, South Carolina, Virginia, and West Virginia.

Southeast Asia   Burma, Cambodia, Indonesia, Laos, Malaysia, Papua New Guinea, Philippines, Singapore, Thailand, and Vietnam.

Soviet Union *or* USSR   Refers to the former Union of Soviet Socialist Republics (see entry at USSR).

Spartanburg, South Carolina

Spokane, Washington

Stamford, Connecticut

Staten Island   Borough in New York City.

Stockholm, Sweden

Strait of Gibraltar

Strasbourg, France

Stratford-upon-Avon, England

Stuttgart, Germany

Suez Canal

Surabaja, Indonesia

Surinam

Suriname River

Susquehanna River

Svalbard Islands

Sverdlovsk, Russia

Sydney, Australia

Tacoma, Washington

Taipei, Taiwan

Tallahassee, Florida

Tallahatchie River

Tampa, Florida

Tangier, Morocco

Tbilisi, Georgia   The capital of

the former Soviet socialist republic, and the new republic.

Teheran, Iran

Tel Aviv, Israel

Terre Haute, Indiana

Throgs Neck, New York

Tianjin, China

Timbuktu *or* Tombouctou, Mali

Tippecanoe River

Tokelau Islands

Tokyo, Japan

Toledo, Ohio

Toms River, New Jersey

Tooele, Utah

Toronto, Ontario, Canada

Trinidad and Tobago

Tripoli, Libya

Tucson, Arizona

Tulsa, Oklahoma

Tunis, Tunisia

Turin, Italy

Twin Cities   Minneapolis and St. Paul, Minnesota.

USSR *or* Union of Soviet Socialist Republics   The former Soviet Socialist Republics are the now-independent states of Armenia, Azerbaijan, Byelorussia (or Belorussia), Estonia, Georgia, Kazakhstan, Kirgizia, Latvia, Lithuania, Moldavia, Russia, Tadzhikistan, Turkmenistan, Ukraine, Uzbekistan.

Valencia, Spain

Vancouver, British Columbia, Canada

Vermillion, South Dakota

Vienna, Austria

Wahpeton, North Dakota

Waikiki Beach, Hawaii

Wailuku, Hawaii

Walla Walla, Washington

Warsaw, Poland

Washington, D.C.

Waukegan, Illinois

Wellington, New Zealand

Wenatchee, Washington

West   In United States, refers to the thirteen states making up the Mountain and Pacific regions.

West Germany *or* Federal Republic of Germany   Now incorporated in united Germany.

West Indies   The region of islands in an arc from Florida's tip to Venezuela including Anguilla, Antigua and Barbuda, Antilles, Bahamas, Barbados, Cuba, Dominica, Jamaica, Grenada, Guadeloupe, Hispaniola, Leeward and Windward Islands, Martinique, Netherlands Antilles, Puerto Rico, St. Lucia, St. Vincent and the Grenadines, St. Kitts and Nevis, Trinidad and Tobago, Virgin Islands.

West North Central states   Iowa, Kansas, Minnesota, Missouri, Nebraska, North Dakota, and South Dakota.

West Point, New York

West South Central states   Arkansas, Louisiana, Oklahoma, and Texas.

White House   The residence and office of the President of the United States.

Wichita, Kansas

Wichita Falls, Texas

Wiesbaden, Germany

Wilkes-Barre, Pennsylvania

Williamsburg, Virginia

Woonsocket, Rhode Island
Worcester, Massachusetts
Yerevan, Armenia
Yokohama, Japan
Ypsilanti, Michigan
Yucatán, Mexico
Yukon Territory, Canada

GOVERNMENT ORGANIZATIONS

Capitalize proper nouns referring to government agencies, departments, offices for nations, states, counties, cities, and so forth. Capitalize proper nouns that refer to foreign governmental or legislative bodies and departments.

In the following list of examples for styling and abbreviating the names of governmental organizations, those not identified by country are U.S. organizations:

Air National Guard
Arab League *or* League of Arab States   Includes Algeria, Bahrain, Djibouti, Egypt, Iraq, Jordan, Kuwait, Lebanon, Libya, Mauritania, Morocco, Oman, Palestine Liberation Organization (PLO), Qatar, Saudi Arabia, Somalia, Sudan, Syria, Tunisia, United Arab Emirates, and Yemen.
Association of Southeast Asian Nations (ASEAN)   Members are Brunei, Indonesia, Malaysia, Philippines, Singapore, and Thailand.
Bureau of Labor Statistics (BLS)

Bureau of Land Management (BLM)
Caribbean Community *or* Caricom   Members are Antigua, Bahamas, Barbados, Belize, Dominica, Grenada, Guyana, Jamaica, Montserrat, St. Kitts, St. Lucia, St. Vincent, and Trinidad and Tobago.
Centers for Disease Control
Central Intelligence Agency (CIA)
Civil Aeronautics Board (CAB)
Commission on Civil Rights (CCR)
Common Market *or* European Economic Community (EEC) *or* European Community (EC)   Members are Belguim, Denmark, France, Germany, Greece, Ireland, Italy, Luxembourg, the Netherlands, Portugal, Spain, and the United Kingdom.
Commonwealth of Nations   Originally the British Commonwealth. States recognizing England as symbolic head: Antigua and Barbuda, Australia, Bahamas, Bangladesh, Barbados, Belize, Botswana, Brunei, Canada, Cyprus, Dominica, Gambia, Ghana, Grenada, Guyana, India, Jamaica, Kenya, Kiribati, Lesotho, Malawi, Malaysia, Maldives, Malta, Mauritius, Namibia, Nauru, New Zealand, Nigeria, Northern Ireland, Pakistan, Papua New Guinea, St. Kitts and Nevis, St. Lucia, St. Vincent and the Grenadines, Samoa, Seychelles, Sierra Leone, Singapore, Solomon

Islands, Sri Lanka, Swaziland, Tanzania, Tonga, Trinidad and Tobago, Tuvalu, Uganda, United Kingdom, Vanatu, Western Samoa, Zambia, and Zimbabwe.

Consumer Product Safety Commission (CPSC)

Council of Economic Advisers

Drug Enforcement Administration (DEA)

Energy Research and Development Administration (ERDA)

Environmental Protection Agency (EPA)

Equal Employment Opportunity Commission (EEOC)

European Economic Community (EEC) *or* Common Market *or* European Communities (EC) See the entry at Common Market.

European Free Trade Association (EFTA) Members are Austria, Finland, Great Britain, Iceland, Norway, Portugal, Sweden, and Switzerland.

Export-Import Bank of the United States

Federal Aviation Administration (FAA)

Federal Bureau of Investigation (FBI)

Federal Communications Commission (FCC)

Federal Deposit Insurance Corporation (FDIC)

Federal Election Commission (FEC)

Federal Emergency Management Agency (FEMA)

Federal Energy Regulatory Commission (FERC)

Federal Highway Administration (FHA)

Federal Housing Administration (FHA)

Federal Labor Relations Authority (FLRA)

Federal Mediation and Conciliation Service

Federal Reserve System (FRS) *or* Federal Reserve Board (FRB)

Federal Savings and Loan Insurance Corporation (FSLIC)

Federal Trade Commission (FTC)

Food and Agriculture Organization (FAO) An agency of the United Nations.

Food and Drug Administration (FDA)

Foreign Service (Department of State)

French Foreign Legion

General Accounting Office (GAO)

General Assembly The principal body of the United Nations.

General Services Administration (GSA)

Government Printing Office (GPO)

House of Commons Part of the English Parliament.

House of Lords Part of the English Parliament.

House of Representatives Part of the U.S. Congress.

Immigration and Naturalization Service (INS)

Internal Revenue Service (IRS)

International Court of Justice *or* the World Court Under the auspices of the United Nations

International Criminal Police Organization *or* Interpol

Interpol *or* International Criminal Police Organization

Interstate Commerce Commission (ICC)

Joint Chiefs of Staff

Judicial Conference of the United States

KGB   The former Soviet Union's secret police and intelligence agency; the abbreviation stands for "Committee for State Security" in Russian. Has been reorganized as the NSB (see entry).

Law Enforcement Assistant Administration (LEAA)

Library of Congress

National Aeronautics and Space Administration (NASA)

National Archives and Records Administration

National Bureau of Standards (NBS)

National Foundation on the Arts and the Humanities

National Governors' Association

National Highway Traffic Safety Administration

National Institutes of Health

National Labor Relations Board (NLRB)

National League of Cities

National Mediation Board

National Oceanic and Atmospheric Administration (NOAA)

National Park Service (NPS)

National Science Foundation (NSF)

National Security Council (NSC)

National Transportation Safety Board

National Weather Service

North Atlantic Treaty Organization (NATO)   Members of the NATO alliance are Belgium, Canada, Denmark, France, Germany, Greece, Iceland, Italy, Luxembourg, the Netherlands, Norway, Portugal, Spain, Turkey, the United Kingdom, and the United States.

NSB   The Inter-Republican Council for Security.   The former Soviet KGB, which coordinates and assists security organization in the now-sovereign republics of the former USSR.

Nuclear Regulatory Commission (NRC)

Occupational Safety and Health Administration (OSHA)

Office of Administration

Office of Management and Budget (OMB)

Office of Personnel Management

Office of Policy Development (OPD)

Office of Science and Technology Policy

Office of the United States Trade Representative

Organization for Economic Cooperation and Development (OECD)   Members are Australia, Austria, Belgium, Canada, Denmark, Finland, France, Germany, Greece, Iceland, Ireland, Italy, Japan, Luxembourg, Netherlands, New Zealand, Norway, Portugal, Spain, Sweden, Switzerland,

Turkey, United Kingdom, United States, and the former Yugoslavia.

Organization of American States (OAS)   Members are Antigua and Barbuda, Argentina, Bahamas, Barbados, Bolivia, Brazil, Chile, Colombia, Costa Rica, Cuba, Dominica, Dominican Republic, Ecuador, El Salvador, Grenada, Guatemala, Haiti, Honduras, Jamaica, Mexico, Nicaragua, Panama, Paraguay, Peru, St. Kitts and Nevis, St. Lucia, St. Vincent and the Grenadines, Suriname, Trinidad and Tobago, United States, Uruguay, Venezuela.

Organization of Petroleum Exporting Countries (OPEC)   Members are Algeria, Ecuador, Gabon, Indonesia, Iran, Iraq, Kuwait, Libya, Nigeria, Qatar, Saudi Arabia, United Arab Emirates, and Venezuela.

Palestine Liberation Organization (PLO)

Patent and Trademark Office

Peace Corps

Politburo or Political Bureau of the Communist Party   The policy-making committee of a Communist party. Was the executive committee of the former Soviet Union, when Communism was the state's single party.

Reserve Officers' Training Corps (ROTC)

Securities and Exchange Commission

Selective Service System (SSS)

Small Business Administration (SBA)

Smithsonian Institution

Social Security Administration (SSA)

Southeast Asia Treaty Organization (SEATO)

Strategic Air Command (SAC)

Tennessee Valley Authority (TVA)

United Nations (UN)   Members are Afghanistan, Albania, Algeria, Angola, Antigua and Barbuda, Argentina, Australia, Austria, Bahamas, Bahrain, Bangladesh, Barbados, Belgium, Belize, Benin, Bhutan, Bolivia, Botswana, Brazil, Brunei, Bulgaria, Burkina Faso, Burundi, Byelorussia;

Cambodia, Cameroon, Canada, Cape Verde, Central African Republic, Chad, Chile, China, Colombia, Comoros, Congo, Costa Rica, Croatia, Cuba, Cyprus, Czechoslovakia, Denmark, Djibouti, Dominica, Dominican Republic, Germany, Ecuador, Egypt, El Salvador, Equatorial Guinea, Ethiopia, Fiji, Finland, France;

Gabon, Gambia, Ghana, Greece, Grenada, Guatemala, Guinea, Guinea-Bissau, Guyana, Haiti, Honduras, Hungary, Iceland, India, Indonesia, Iran, Iraq, Ireland, Israel, Italy, Ivory Coast, Jamaica, Japan, Jordan, Kenya, Kuwait, Laos, Lebanon, Lesotho, Liberia, Libya, Luxembourg;

Malagasy, Malawi, Malaysia, Maldives, Mali, Malta, Mauritania, Mauritius, Mexico, Mongolia, Morocco, Mozambique, Myanmar, Namibia, Nepal, Netherlands, New Zealand, Nicaragua, Niger, Nigeria, Norway, Oman, Pakistan, Panama, Papua New Guinea, Paraguay, Peru, Philippines, Poland, Portugal; Qatar, Romania, Russia, Rwanda, St. Christopher and Nevis, St. Lucia, St. Vincent and the Grenadines, São Tome and Principe, Saudi Arabia, Senegal, Seychelles, Sierra Leone, Singapore, Slovenia Solomon Islands, Somalia, South Africa, Spain, Sri Lanka, Sudan, Suriname, Swaziland, Sweden, Syria; Tanzania, Thailand, Togo, Trinidad and Tobago, Tunisia, Turkey, Uganda, Ukraine, United Arab Emirates, United Kingdom, United States, Uruguay, Vanuatu, Venezuela, Vietnam, Western Samoa, Yemen, Zaire, Zambia, Zimbabwe.

United Nations Children's Emergency Fund (UNICEF)

United Nations Educational, Scientific, and Cultural Organization (UNESCO)

United Nations Security Council

United States Air Force (USAF)

United States Air Force Academy At Colorado Springs, Colorado

United States Army

United States Coast Guard

United States Coast Guard Academy At New London, Connecticut

United States Conference of Mayors

United States Court of Appeals

United States Customs Service

United States Department of Agriculture *or* USDA

United States District Courts

United States Information Agency (USIA)

United States International Trade Commission

United States Marine Corps (USMC)

United States Merchant Marine Academy At Kings Point, New York

United States Military Academy At West Point, New York

United States Mint

United States National Guard

United States Naval Academy At Annapolis, Maryland

United States Naval Reserve (USNR)

United States Navy (USN)

United States Postal Service (USPS)

United States Secret Service

United States Supreme Court *or* Supreme Court of the United States

Veterans Affairs (VA)

Warsaw Pact Members were Bulgaria, Czechoslovakia, Hungary, Poland, Romania, and the USSR until the treaty was abolished and the alliance disbanded in July 1991.

Women's Army Corps (WAC)

World Health Organization (WHO)

HISTORICAL EVENTS AND PERIODS

Proper nouns for names of specific notable cultural and historical events are capitalized (e.g., *Seattle World's Fair, Great Depression, the Crash*).

Historical and cultural periods and movements that are widely recognized in archaeology, anthropology, geology, or other technical fields are capitalized (e.g., *Middle Ages, Dark Ages, Iron Age*).

The Earth's geological periods are *Early Precambrian (Archean), Late Precambrian (Algonkian), Cambrian, Ordovician, Silurian, Devonian, Mississippian, Pennsylvanian, Permian, Triassic, Jurassic, Cretaceous, Tertiary (Paleocene, Eocene, Oligocene, Miocene, Pliocene)*, and *Quaternary (Pleistocene, Holocene)*.

Popular contemporary terms such as *nuclear age* are lowercased.

Proper nouns that numerically describe a historical period are capitalized (e.g., *Roaring Twenties, the Third Reich*).

Proper nouns for names of wars are capitalized (e.g., *the American Revolution, the Gulf War*).

In addition to the list that follows, many specific examples appear throughout Part 1.

Age of Man
Age of Reason
American Revolution 1775–1783.

Arab-Israeli Wars
Atomic Age   Began December 2, 1942.
Bronze Age   Approximately 3500–1000 B.C., between the Stone Age and the Iron Age.
Christian Era
Civil War 1861–1865.
Crusades   Approximately the 11th through the 13th centuries.
Dark Ages *or* Middle Ages Approximately the 5th through the 15th centuries.
Depression *or* the Great Depression   Began October 28 and 29, 1929; continued through the 1930s.
Elizabethan Age
Fall of Rome
Gilded Age   Approximately 1875–1900.
Ice Age
Industrial Revolution Approximately 1750–1850, in England.
Iron Age   Began approximately 1350 B.C., through 800–500 B.C.
Jazz Age   Began in 1920's.
Korean War   1950–1953.
Lent   Means the forty days from Ash Wednesday through Holy Saturday, the day before Easter, excluding Sundays.
Louisiana Purchase   1803.
Mardi Gras
Middle Ages *or* Dark Ages Approximately the 5th through the 15th centuries.
Norman Conquest Approximately 1066–1070.
Peloponnesian War   431–404 B.C.

Reconstruction Following the American Civil War, 1865–1877

Reformation Began in the 16th century.

Reign of Terror 1792–1994.

Renaissance Approximately 1400–1600 in Italy; in Europe to the mid 17th century.

Restoration Approximately 1660–1688.

Roaring Twenties 1920–1929.

Space Age Began October 4, 1957, with the Soviet Union's launching of Sputnik 1.

Spanish-American War 1898.

Stone Age Earliest human development, beginning approximately two million years ago.

Thirty Years War 1618–1648.

V-E Day May 8, 1945.

V-J Day September 2, 1945.

Victorian Age Approximately 1837–1901.

Vietnam War 1954–1975.

War of 1812 1812–1815.

World War I 1914–1918.

World War II 1939–1945.

LABOR ORGANIZATIONS

Names of labor organizations are capitalized.

Actors' Equity Association

Air Line Pilots Association

Aluminum, Brick & Glass Workers International Union (ABG–WIU)

Amalgamated Clothing and Textile Workers Union of America (ACTWU)

Amalgamated Transit Union (ATU)

American Association of University Professors (AAUP)

American Civil Liberties Union (ACLU)

American Federation of Government Employees (AFGE)

American Federation of Grain Millers (AFGM)

American Federation of Labor and Congress of Industrial Organizations (AFL–CIO)

American Federation of Musicians (AF of M)

American Federation of State, County and Municipal Employees (AFSCME)

American Federation of Teachers (AFT)

American Federation of Television and Radio Artists (AFTRA)

American Nurses Association

American Postal Workers Union (APWU)

Associated Actors and Artistes of America (AAAA)

Bakery and Confectionery Workers' International Union of America

Bricklayers, Masons and Plasterers' International Union of America

Brotherhood of Locomotive Engineers (BLE)

Brotherhood of Maintenance of Way Employes (BMWE)

Brotherhood of Railway, Airline and Steamship Clerks, Freight Handlers, Express and Station Employees

Communications Workers of America (CWA)

Distillery, Wine & Allied Workers International Union (DWU)

Fraternal Order of Police (FOP)

Glass, Molders, Pottery, Plastics & Allied Workers International Union (GMP)

Graphic Communications International Union (GCIU)

Hotel and Restaurant Employees and Bartenders International Union

Industrial Union of Marine & Shipbuilding Workers of America (IUMSWA)

International Alliance of Theatrical Stage Employes and Moving Picture Machine Operators of the United States and Canada (IATSE)

International Association of Bridge, Structural and Ornamental Iron Workers

International Association of Fire Fighters

International Association of Machinists and Aerospace Workers (IAM)

International Brotherhood of Boilermakers, Iron Shipbuilders, Blacksmiths, Forgers and Helpers (IBBISB/BF&H)

International Brotherhood of Electrical Workers (IBEW)

International Brotherhood of Firemen and Oilers

International Brotherhood of Painters and Allied Trades of the United States and Canada (IBPAT)

International Brotherhood of

Teamsters, Chauffeurs, Warehousemen and Helpers of America (IBT) *or* Teamsters

International Chemical Workers Union (ICWU)

International Labor Organization (ILO)

International Ladies' Garment Workers Union (ILGWU)

International Longshoremen's and Warehousemen's Union (ILWU)

International Telecommunication Union

International Typographical Union

International Union of Allied Industrial Workers of America (AIW)

International Union of Bricklayers and Allied Craftsmen

International Union of Electronic, Electrical, Salaried, Machine and Furniture Workers (IUE)

International Union of Novelty & Production Workers

International Union of Operating Engineers (IUOE)

International Union of United Automobile, Aerospace and Agricultural Implement Workers of America *or* United Auto Workers (UAW)

International Union of United Plant Guard Workers of America

International Woodworkers of America–U.S. (IWA–U.S.)

Laborers' International Union of North America (LIUNA)

Marine Engineer Beneficial Association/National Maritime Union (MEBA/NMU)

National Association of Letter
Carriers (NALC)
National Association of Postal
Supervisors
National Education Association
(NEA)
National Federation of Federal
Employees (NFFE)
National Rural Letter Carriers'
Association
National Treasury Employees
Union (NTEU)
Newspaper Guild, The (TNG)
Office and Professional Employees
International Union (OPEIU)
Oil, Chemical and Atomic
Workers International Union
(OCAW)
Plasterers' and Cement Mason's
International Association of the
United States & Canada
Retail, Wholesale and Department
Store Union
Seafarers International Union of
North America (SIUNA)
Service Employees International
Union (SEIU)
Sheet Metal Workers International
Association (SMWIA)
Transport Workers Union of
America (TWUA)
Transportation Communications
International Union (TCU)
United Association of Journeymen
and Apprentices of the
Plumbing and Pipe Fitting
Industry of the United States
and Canada
United Automobile, Aerospace
and Agricultural Implement
Workers of America
United Brotherhood of Carpenters
and Joiners of America

United Electrical, Radio and
Machine Workers of America
United Farm Workers of America
(UFW)
United Food and Commercial
Workers International Union
(UFCW)
United Garment Workers of
America (UGWA)
United Mine Workers of America
(UMWA)
United Rubber, Cork, Linoleum
and Plastic Workers of America
(URW)
United Steelworkers of America
(USWA)
United Textile Workers of
America (UTWA)
United Transportation Union
(UTU)
United Union of Roofers,
Waterproofers & Allied
Workers
Upholsterers' International Union
of North America (UIU)
Utility Workers Union of America
(UWUA)

LANGUAGES

Always capitalize the names of
languages and dialects.

Afrikaans
Amharic
Arabic
Armenian
Assamese
Azerbaijani
Bengali
Burmese
Byelorussian
Cantonese
Cebuano

Czech
Dutch-Flemish
English
Estonian
French
Fula
Georgian
German
Greek
Gujarati
Hakka
Hausa
Hindi
Hungarian
Igbo *or* Ibo
Italian
Japanese
Javanese
Kannada
Kazakh
Khmer *or* Cambodian
Kirghiz
Korean
Latvian
Lithuanian
Madurese
Malagasy
Malay-Indonesian
Malayalam
Mandarin
Marathi
Min
Moldavian
Nepali
Oriya
Oromo
Pashtu
Persian
Polish
Portuguese
Punjabi
Romanian

Russian
Serbo-Croatian
Sindhi
Sinhalese
Spanish
Sundanese
Swahili
Tagalog
Tamil
Telugu
Turkoman *or* Turkmen
Thai
Turkish
Ukrainian
Urdu
Uzbek
Vietnamese
Wu
Yoruba
Zhuang

MILITARY TITLES AND ORGANIZATIONS

The proper nouns for the armed forces of the United States (and their branches and units) are capitalized, as are short forms referring to specific organizations. But terms such as *army* and *navy* are lowercased when standing alone or used collectively and not part of a proper noun.

Military titles of rank are capitalized only when they are part of a formal title preceding a name. Military titles of rank are abbreviated as indicated in the list below. In most contexts, abbreviations are only used when given with the full name of a person and the abbreviation is punctuated and written with initial letters capitalized. (See Appendix 6 for a table of forms of address.)

Abbreviations for military branches and units (e.g., *the 7th Fleet*) are capitalized and unpunctuated.

Military medals and awards are capitalized (e.g., *Purple Heart*).

adjutant general; *pl.*, adjutants general (Adj. Gen. *or* AG)
admiral (Adm. *or* Adml. *or* ADM)
airman (Amn. *or* AN)
airman basic (AB)
airman first class (A1c. *or* A/1C)
air marshal (AM)
brevet (Bvt. *or* Bt.)
brigadier general (Brig. Gen. *or* B.Gen. *or* BG)
captain (Capt. *or* Cpt. *or* CPT)
captain general (CG)
chief petty officer (CPO)
chief warrant officer (CWO)
colonel (Col. *or* COL)
commander (Cmdr. *or* Comdr. *or* Cdr. *or* CDR)
commander in chief; *pl.*, commanders in chief
commanding general (CG)
commanding officer (CO)
command sergeant major (CSM *or* Command Sgt. Maj.)
corporal (Cpl.)
ensign (Ens. *or* ENS)
first lieutenant (1st Lt.)
first sergeant (1st Sgt.)
fleet admiral (FADM)
flight lieutenant (FL)
general (Gen.)
generalissimo; *pl.*, generalissimos
general of the armies

gunnery sergeant (Gy. Sgt. *or* Gunnery Sgt.)
inspector general; *pl.*, inspectors general (Insp. Gen.)
lance corporal (LC *or* LCpl *or* Lance Cpl.)
lieutenant (Lt. *or* Lieut.)
lieutenant colonel (Lt. Col. *or* LTC)
lieutenant commander (Lt. Cmdr. *or* Lt. Comdr. *or* LCDR)
lieutenant general (Lt. Gen. *or* LTG)
lieutenant, junior grade (Lt. [jg] *or* LTJG *or* Lt. j.g.)
major (Maj.)
major general (Maj. Gen. *or* MG)
master chief petty officer (CPOM *or* MCPO)
master gunnery sergeant (M. Gy. Sgt. *or* Master Gunnery Sgt.)
master sergeant (M. Sgt. *or* MSG *or* Master Sgt.)
petty officer (PO)
petty officer first class
petty officer second class
petty officer third class
platoon sergeant (Platoon Sgt.)
private (Pvt. *or* Pte.)
private 1 (Pvt. 1)
private 2 (Pvt. 2)
private first class (Pfc. *or* PFC)
rear admiral (Rear Adm. *or* R.Adm. *or* RA *or* RADM)
rear admiral lower half (Rear Adm.)
rear admiral upper half (Rear Adm.)
seaman (Sea.)
seaman apprentice (SA)
seaman first class (S1c.)
seaman recruit (SR)

second lieutenant (2d Lt.)
senior airman
senior chief petty officer (CPOS
   or SCPO)
senior master sergeant (S. M. Sgt.
   or Senior Master Sgt.)
senior naval officer (SNO)
sergeant (Sgt. *or* Serg. *or* Sergt.
   or SG)
sergeant at arms; *pl.*, sergeants at
   arms
sergeant first class (Sgt. 1st Class
   or Sfc. *or* SFC)
sergeant major; *pl.*, sergeants
   major *or* sergeant majors (Sgt.
   Maj. *or* S.Maj. *or* SM)
sergeant major of the Army (SMA
   or Army Sgt. Maj.)
specialist (Spc.)
specialist third class (Sp3c.)
staff sergeant (Staff Sgt.)
staff sergeant major (Staff Sgt.
   Maj.)
surgeon general; *pl.*, surgeons
   general (Surg. Gen. *or* SG)
technical sergeant (T. Sgt. *or*
   Tech. Sgt.)
technician second grade (T2g.)
vice admiral (Vice Adm. *or*
   V.Adm. *or* VA *or* VADM)
warrant officer (WO)
warrant officer junior grade
   (WOJG)

NOBILITY TITLES

Titles of royalty are capitalized
when used as a formal title (e.g.,
Prince Charles of England).
Some British titles are also
capitalized when standing alone
(e.g., *Prince of Wales*) because
nobility are frequently known by
their titles rather than their given
or family names.

Honorific titles and forms of
address are capitalized (e.g., *Your
Majesty, His Eminence, Your
Grace*).

The royalty of Britain are, in
order of rank: king, queen, prince,
princess, duke, marquess or
marquis, earl, viscount, and
baron. Honorary titles are baronet
and knight.

See Appendix 6 for a table of
forms of address.

Titles of nobility are rarely
abbreviated, although
abbreviations are given for some
of the examples in the following
list.

archduke (Archd. *or* AD)
baron (Bn.)
baroness (Bnss.)
baronet (Bt. *or* Bart.)
count (Ct.)
countess (Ctss.)
duchess (D.)
duke (D. *or* Du.)
earl
emperor (Emp.)
her *or* his majesty (HM)
king
knight (Kt.)
lady
lord
marchioness *or* marquise (March.)
marquess *or* marquis (Marq.)
prince
princess
queen
queen mother
viscount (Vis. *or* Visc.)
viscountess (Vis. *or* Visc.)

ORGANIZATIONAL AND TEAM NAMES

Administrative, legislative, judicial, educational, political, and special interest groups' names (including departments, bureaus, and offices) and abbreviations are capitalized when they are used as proper nouns.

Generic terms such as *agency, bureau,* or *department* are not capitalized. Derivative adjectives and shortened or incomplete designations are lowercased.

Political parties' (and other national and international organizations') names (e.g., *the Green Party*) and designations of members are capitalized, though *party, movement,* and similar terms need not be. Political factions are usually lowercased (e.g., *conservative, right-winger*), except for *the Right* and *the Left*.

Philosophies are capitalized only if derived from a proper noun (e.g., *Marxism*).

Derivatives referring to organizations' members are capitalized (e.g., *Kiwanian*).

Names of associations, societies, meetings, and conferences are capitalized when used as proper nouns (e.g., *LaPorte Historical Society*).

Abbreviations and nicknames of organizations are capitalized, (e.g., *Big Brother* for the U.S. government, *Big Blue* for IBM).

Academy of Motion Picture Arts & Sciences
Administration   Capitalized when referring to a specific body serving a U.S. president.
Agency for International Development (AID)
Aircraft Owners and Pilots Association
Al-Anon Family Groups
Alcoholics Anonymous (AA)
Alzheimer's Disease and Related Disorders Association
Amateur Athletic Union of the United States
American Academy of Arts & Sciences
American Association for the Advancement of Science (AAAS)
American Automobile Association *or* AAA
American Bar Association (ABA)
American Booksellers Association
American Hospital Association (AHA)
American Legion   Members are called *Legionnaires*.
American Medical Association *or* AMA
American National Red Cross *or* the Red Cross
American Newspaper Publishers Association
American Society for Testing Materials (ASTM)
American Society for the Prevention of Cruelty to Animals (ASPCA)
American Society of Composers, Authors and Publishers (ASCAP)
American Society of Mechanical Engineers (ASME)
American Stock Exchange *or* Amex

American Veterans of World War II, Korea and Vietnam *or* AMVETS

Amnesty International (AI)

Association of American Indian Affairs

Atlanta Braves Baseball team.

Atlanta Falcons Football team.

Atlanta Hawks Basketball team.

Axis, the Alliance between Germany, Italy, and Japan in World War II.

B'nai B'rith

Baltimore Orioles Baseball team.

Black Panther Party

Blue Angels Association

Boston Bruins Hockey team.

Boston Celtics Basketball team.

Boston Red Sox Baseball team.

Boy Scouts of America

Boys' Clubs of America

Buffalo Bills Football team.

Buffalo Sabres Hockey team.

Calgary Flames Hockey team.

California Angels Baseball team.

Cooperative for American Relief Everywhere Inc. (CARE)

Chamber of Commerce of the U.S.A.

Charlotte Hornets Basketball team.

Chicago Bears Football team.

Chicago Black Hawks Hockey team.

Chicago Bulls Basketball team.

Chicago Cubs Baseball team.

Chicago White Sox Baseball team.

Cincinnati Bengals Football team.

Cincinnati Reds Baseball team.

Cleveland Browns Football team.

Cleveland Cavaliers Basketball team.

Cleveland Indians Baseball team.

Confederate States of America *or* the Confederacy

Council of Better Business Bureaus

Courts Names of higher courts are capitalized in all but very general writing, and any reference to the Supreme Court is always capitalized. References to lower courts, even when specific, are lowercased (e.g., *traffic court*).

Cub Scouts

4-H Club *or* Four-H Club

Dallas Cowboys Football team.

Dallas Mavericks Basketball team.

Daughters of the American Revolution (DAR)

Democratic National Committee

Democratic party

Denver Broncos Football team.

Denver Nuggets Basketball team.

Detroit Lions Football team.

Detroit Pistons Basketball team.

Detroit Red Wings Hockey team.

Detroit Tigers Baseball team.

Edmonton Oilers Hockey team.

Elks of the U.S.A., Benevolent and Protective Order of

Girl Scouts of the United States of America

Golden State Warriors Basketball team.

GOP *or* Grand Old Party   The
    Republican party.
Green Bay Packers   Football team.
Hartford Whalers   Hockey team.
Houston Astros   Baseball team.
Houston Oilers   Football team.
Houston Rockets   Basketball
    team.
Humane Society of the U.S.
Indiana Pacers   Basketball team.
Indianapolis Colts   Football team.
International Bank for
    Reconstruction and
    Development *or* World Bank
International Monetary Fund
    (IMF)
International Telecommunications
    Satellite Organization *or* Intelsat
Irish Republican Army (IRA)
Ivy League   Brown University,
    Columbia University, Cornell
    University, Dartmouth College,
    Harvard University, Princeton
    University, the University of
    Pennsylvania, and Yale
    University.
Jaycees International
John Birch Society
Juilliard School
Junior Achievement
Kansas City Chiefs   Football
    team.
Kansas City Royals   Baseball
    team.
Kiwanis International
Knights of Columbus *or* K. of C.
Ku Klux Klan *or* Klan in America
    or KKK
Ladies' Professional Golf
    Association *or* LPGA
Los Angeles Clippers   Basketball
    team.

Los Angeles Dodgers   Baseball
    team.
Los Angeles Kings   Hockey
    team.
Los Angeles Lakers   Basketball
    team.
Los Angeles Raiders   Football
    team.
Los Angeles Rams   Football
    team.
Mafia
Mensa
Miami Dolphins   Football team.
Miami Heat   Basketball team.
Midwest Stock Exchange
Milwaukee Brewers   Baseball
    team.
Milwaukee Bucks   Basketball
    team.
Minnesota North Stars   Hockey
    team.
Minnesota Timberwolves
    Basketball team.
Minnesota Twins   Baseball team.
Minnesota Vikings   Football
    team.
Montreal Canadiens   Hockey
    team.
Montreal Expos   Baseball team.
Moose, Loyal Order of
Muscular Dystrophy Association
National Association for Stock
    Car Auto Racing (NASCAR)
National Association for the
    Advancement of Colored
    People (NAACP)
National Association of
    Intercollegiate Athletics (NAIA)
National Association of Securities
    Dealers Automated Quotations
    (NASDAQ)
National Association of Securities
    Dealers (NASD)

National Audubon Society
National Basketball Association (NBA)
National Collegiate Athletic Association (NCAA)
National Easter Seal Society
National Geographic Society
National Organization for Women (NOW)
National Parents and Teachers Association *or* PTA *or* National Congress of Parents and Teachers
National Rifle Association (NRA)
New England Patriots Football team.
New Jersey Devils Hockey team.
New Jersey Nets Basketball team.
New Orleans Saints Football team.
New York Giants Football team.
New York Islanders Hockey team.
New York Jets Football team.
New York Knickerbockers Basketball team.
New York Mets Baseball team.
New York Rangers Hockey team.
New York Stock Exchange (NYSE)
New York Yankees Baseball team.
Oakland A's Baseball team.
Orlando Magic Basketball team.
Overeaters Anonymous
Philadelphia Eagles Football team.
Philadelphia Flyers Hockey team.

Philadelphia Phillies Baseball team.
Philadelphia 76ers Basketball team.
Phoenix Cardinals Football team.
Phoenix Suns Basketball team.
Pittsburgh Penguins Hockey team.
Pittsburgh Pirates Baseball team.
Pittsburgh Steelers Football team.
Portland Trail Blazers Basketball team.
Professional Golfers' Association (PGA)
Quebec Nordiques Hockey team.
Radio Free Europe *or* Radio Liberty
Republican Governors Association
Republican National Committee
Sacramento Kings Basketball team.
St. Louis Blues Hockey team.
St. Louis Cardinals Baseball team.
San Antonio Spurs Basketball team.
San Diego Chargers Football team.
San Diego Padres Baseball team.
San Francisco 49ers Football team.
San Francisco Giants Baseball team.
Screen Actors Guild
Seattle Mariners Baseball team.
Seattle Seahawks Football team.
Seattle SuperSonics Basketball team.
Securities and Exchange Commission (SEC)

Sierra Club
Smithsonian Institution
Society for the Prevention of
    Cruelty to Animals (SPCA)
Tampa Bay Buccaneers   Football
    team.
Texas Rangers   Baseball team.
Toronto Blue Jays   Baseball
    team.
Toronto Maple Leafs   Hockey
    team.
United Service Organizations
    (USO)
Utah Jazz   Basketball team.
Vancouver Canucks   Hockey
    team.
Veterans of Foreign Wars (VFW)
Volunteers in Service to America
    (VISTA)
Washington Bullets   Basketball
    team.
Washington Capitals   Hockey
    team.
Washington Redskins   Football
    team.
Winnipeg Jets   Hockey team.
Woman's Christian Temperance
    Union (WCTU)
Young Men's Christian
    Association (YMCA)
Young Women's Christian
    Association (YWCA)

ORGANIZATIONAL TITLES

Words or phrases used as
proper nouns that serve as formal
professional, corporate, or
governmental titles are capitalized
when they precede a name. When
such a title is used as a descriptive
phrase, set in commas after a
name), it is lowercased.

The word *president* is
sometimes capitalized even when
used alone, when referring to the
highest elected officer of the U.S.
government.

adjutant general; *pl.*, adjutants
    general
administrative law judge (ALJ)
administrator (Adm. *or* Admr. *or*
    Adms. *or* Admstr.)
alderman (Ald. *or* Aldm.)
ambassador (Amb.)
ambassador at large
assemblyman *or* assemblywoman
associate justice (AJ)
attorney general; *pl.*, attorneys
    general *or* attorney generals
    (Atty. Gen. *or* Att. Gen. *or*
    AG)
borough president
chairman/chairwoman *or* chair
    (Chmn. *or* Chm.)
chairman of the joint chiefs of
    staff
chancellor (Chanc.)
chaplain (Chap.)
chargé d'affaires; *pl.*, chargés
    d'affaires
chief judge (CJ)
chief justice (CJ)
chief of staff; *pl.*, chiefs of staff
    (C. of S. *or* CS *or* COS)
commissioner (Comm. *or* Commr.
    or Com.)
committeeman/committeewoman
comptroller (Comp.)
congressman/congresswoman *or*
    congressperson; *pl.*,
    congresspeople
constable (Cons.)
consul (Con.)
consul general (CG)

councilman/councilwoman
county clerk
district attorney, (Dist. Atty. or DA)
emperor
esquire (Esq.)
foreign minister or foreign secretary
foreign service officer (FSO)
führer
generalissimo
governor (Gov.)
governor general; pl., governors general (CG)
high commissioner (HC)
inspector (insp. or ins.)
judge (jud.)
judge advocate general; pl., judge advocate generals (JAG)
judge advocate (JA)
justice (just. or jus.)
justice of the peace (JP)
kaiser
king
lieutenant governor (Lt. Gov.)
magistrate
major general
mayor
member of Parliament (MP)
postmaster general; pl., postmasters general (PMG)
president (Pres.)
prime minister (PM)
queen mother
registered nurse (RN)
representative (Rep. or Repr.)
secretary (Sec. or Secty.)
secretary-general; pl., secretaries-general (SG)
secretary of agriculture
secretary of commerce and labor
secretary of defense
secretary of education

secretary of energy
secretary of health and human services
secretary of health, education, and welfare
secretary of housing and urban development
secretary of state (SS)
secretary of the interior
secretary of the treasury
secretary of transportation
secretary of war
secretary-treasurer; pl., secretary-treasurers or secretaries-treasurers
senator (Sen.)
shah
sheriff
solicitor general; pl., solicitors general (SG)
superintendent (Supt. or Supr.)
surgeon general; pl., surgeons general
treasurer (Treas. or Treasr.)
under secretary; pl., undersecretaries (US)
vice-chairman; pl., vice-chairmen (VC)
vice-chancellor (VC)
vice-consul (VC)
vice president (VP)

PERSONAL NAMES

People's names and nicknames, fictitious names, or epithets for specific people (e.g., *William the Conqueror*) are capitalized and usually not abbreviated.

If the first and middle names are abbreviated, they are spaced and punctuated (e.g., *I. F. Stone*).

If a nickname or epithet is used between the first and last names, it is often enclosed in quotation marks and/or parentheses (e.g., *Alexander ["Scotty"] Gordon*).

Family titles used as names are capitalized unless preceded by a modifier (e.g., "I know *Mother* was born in 1921," but "*His mother* is sweet.").

PROPER NOUNS AND THEIR DERIVATIVES

Proper nouns (that is, nouns designating by name a specific person or thing) are always capitalized, including common nouns or adjectives that are essential parts (e.g., *Yellow Birch Farm*). A common noun used alone as a substitute for the proper noun should not be capitalized unless it is a very well-known form (e.g., *the Capitol* for Washington, DC, or *the Channel* for the English Channel).

The plural of a common noun that is an essential part of a proper noun is also capitalized (e.g., *10th and I Streets, Lakes Erie and Superior*).

The article *the* is capitalized if it is part of a formal title, address, document title or part, or other proper noun. When the proper noun is used as an adjective (e.g., *the New York area*) or is used to refer to a proper noun (e.g., *the New York Times*) *the* is not capitalized.

Words or phrases that are derived from proper nouns are capitalized when their meaning directly refers to the proper noun

(e.g., *Victorian house, Roman architecture*).

If a derivative word or phrase has taken on its own meaning or a specialized meaning, it is usually not capitalized (e.g., *frankfurter, graham cracker*).

Words or phrases describing people based on a proper noun designating a country, race, or tribe are capitalized (e.g., *Italian, Cherokee, Caucasian*).

RELIGIOUS CONCEPTS, TITLES, AND ORGANIZATIONS

Religious concepts and events are often capitalized (e.g., *the Crucifixion, the Hegira*). References to the Christian Eucharistic rite may be capitalized (e.g., *High Mass, Holy Communion, the Sacrament*). Other services are lowercased (*bar mitzvah, confirmation*).

Proper nouns naming deities, saints, apostles, and prophets are capitalized (e.g., *Buddha, Shakti, Saint Cecilia, John the Baptist, Mohammed*).

Titles of people serving in positions of religious organizations and churches are capitalized when used as a formal title preceding a name. (See Appendix 6 for forms of address.)

archbishop (Arch. or Archbp. or Abp.)
archbishop of Canterbury
  Capitalize *Archbishop* if part of a formal title designating a specific person.

archdeacon (Archd.)
bishop (Bp. *or* Ep.)
bishopric
cardinal (Card.)
Dalai Lama
deacon
father (Fr.)
Holy Father   Variant for the pope
    or pontiff.
Mohammed *or* Muhammad
mother *or* mother superior
pope
rabbi (R.)
reverend (Rev. *or* Revd.)
right reverend (R.R. *or* Rt. Rev.)
sister

The names of religious
    organizations, churches, and
    their members, as well as
    adjective derivatives, are
    capitalized. Religious
    denominations, sects, and
    movements are capitalized. The
    word *church* standing alone is
    capitalized when referring to a
    specific body or place.

Advent Christian Church
African Methodist Episcopal Zion
    Church (AME Zion)
American Baptist Association
American Baptist Churches in
    U.S.A.
American Carpatho-Russian
    Orthodox Greek Catholic
    Church
Anglican Communion
Anglican Orthodox Church
Antiochian Orthodox Christian
    Archdiocese of North America
Apostolic Christian Churches of
    America

Armenian Church of America
Assemblies of God
Associate Reformed Presbyterian
    Church (General Synod)
Association of Free Lutheran
    Congregations
Baha'i Faith
Baptist Church
Baptist General Conference
Baptist Missionary Association of
    America
Beachy Amish Mennonite
    Churches
Bible Church of Christ
Bible Way Church of Our Lord
    Jesus Christ World Wide
Black Muslims
Brethren Church
Buddhist Churches of America
Bulgarian Eastern Orthodox
    Church
Catholic Church
Central Conference of American
    Rabbis
Christadelphians
Christian Church (Disciples of
    Christ)
Christian Churches and Churches
    of Christ
Christian Congregation
Christian Methodist Episcopal
    Church
Christian Reformed Church in
    North America
Christian Union
Churches of Christ
Churches of Christ in Christian
    Union
Churches of God, General
    Conference
Church of Christ, Scientist *or*
    Christian Science Church

Church of England *or* Anglican
Church
Church of God
Church of God of Prophecy
Church of Jesus Christ of Latter-
day Saints *or* Mormon Church
Church of the Lutheran Brethren
of America
Church of the Lutheran
Confession
Church of the Nazarene
Church of the United Brethren in
Christ
Congregational Holiness
Conservative Baptist Association
of America
Conservative Congregational
Christian Conference
Conservative Judaism
Coptic Orthodox Church
Cumberland Presbyterian Church
Diocese of the Armenian Church
of America
Eastern Orthodox Church
Eastern Rite Church
Episcopal Church
Evangelical Church of North
America
Evangelical Congregational
Church
Evangelical Free Church of
America
Evangelical Friends Alliance
Evangelical Lutheran Church in
America
Evangelical Lutheran Synod
Evangelical Methodist Church
Evangelical Presbyterian Church
Fellowship of Grace Brethren
Free Methodist Church of North
America
Free Will Baptists

Friends General Conference
Friends United Meeting
General Association of Regular
Baptist Churches
General Conference of Mennonite
Brethren Churches
General Council, Christian Church
of North America
Greek Orthodox Archdiocese of
North and South America
Greek Orthodox Church
Hinduism
Hungarian Reformed Church in
America
Independent Fundamental
Churches of America
International Church of the
Foursquare Gospel
Islam   Members are Moslem (or
Muslim).
Jehovah's Witnesses
Latvian Evangelical Lutheran
Church in America
Lutheran Church in America
Lutheran Church–Missouri Synod
Maronite Church
Melkite Church
Mennonite Church
Methodist Church
Moravian Church (Unitas
Fratrum), Northern Province
Moravian Church in America
(Unitas Fratum), Southern
Province
Mormon Church *or* Church of
Jesus Christ of Latter-day Saints
Moslems   Adherents of Islam.
National Association of
Evangelicals
National Baptist Convention of
America
National Baptist Convention
U.S.A. Incorporated

National Conference of Catholic Bishops

National Council of the Churches of Christ in the United States of America

National Primitive Baptist Convention

New Apostolic Church of North America

North American Baptist Conference

North American Old Roman Catholic Church

Old Order Amish Church

Old Order (Wister) Mennonite Church

Open Bible Standard Churches

Orthodox Church in America

Orthodox Judaism

Orthodox Presbyterian Church

Patriarchal Parishes of the Russian Orthodox Church in the U.S.A.

Pentecostal Church of God

Pentecostal Free-Will Baptist Church

Pentecostal Holiness Church

Polish National Catholic Church of America

Presbyterian Church (U.S.A.)

Presbyterian Church in America

Primitive Methodist Church U.S.A.

Protestant Episcopal Church

Rabbinical Assembly

Rabbinical Council of America

Reformed Church in America

Reform Judaism

Religious Society of Friends

Reorganized Church of Jesus Christ of Latter Day Saints

Roman Catholic Church Clergy, in order of rank, are: pope, cardinal, archbishop, bishop, monsignor, priest, and deacon.

Romanian Orthodox Church

Romanian Orthodox Episcopate of America

Russian Orthodox Church

Serbian Eastern Orthodox Church

Seventh-day Adventist Church

Seventh Day Baptist General Conference

Southern Baptist Convention

Southern Methodist Church

Synagogue Council of America

Syrian Catholic Church

Syrian Orthodox Church of Antioch (Archdiocese of the U.S.A. and Canada)

The Christian and Missionary Alliance

The Episcopal Church in the U.S.A.

The Evangelical Covenant Church of America

The General Conference Mennonite Church

The Salvation Army

The Wesleyan Church

Ukrainian Catholic Church

Ukrainian Orthodox Church in the U.S.A.

Union of American Hebrew Congregations

Union of Orthodox Jewish Congregations of America

Unitarian Universalist Association

United Church of Christ

United Methodist Church

United Pentecostal Church International

United Presbyterian Church in the U.S.A.

United Synagogue of America

Universal Fellowship of
   Metropolitan Community
   Churches
Volunteers of America
Wisconsin Evangelical Lutheran
   Synod
World Council of Churches

RELIGIOUS WRITINGS

Titles of religious texts and
sacred documents are capitalized,
including well-known passages
and prayers from the bible.

Apocrypha (Apoc.)
Bible, American Beatitudes
   Revised Version (ARV)
Bible, American Translation (AT)
Bible, Authorized (King James)
   Version (AV)
Bible, English Revised Version
   (ERV)
Bible, Revised Standard Version
   (RSV)
Book of Common Prayer
Book of the Dead
Codex Sinaiticus
Complutensian Polyglot Bible
Dead Sea Scrolls
Decalogue
Douay Bible or Douay Version
Epistles
Gloria Patri
Gospels
Haggadah
Hagiographa
Jerusalem Bible
King James Version
Kaddish
Koran
Litany of the Saints
Miserere

Mishnah
New American Bible (NAB)
New English Bible (NEB)
Oxford Annotated Bible (OAB)
Pentateuch
Peshitta
Revised Standard Version
Septuagint
Sermon on the Mount
Shema
Talmud
Ten Commandments
Tripitaka
Upanishads
Vedas
Vinegar Bible
Vulgate

The books of the Bible are
capitalized, and may be
abbreviated in references to
specific passages. The following
list is based on the Revised
Standard Version:

OLD TESTAMENT

Genesis (Gen./Gen)
Exodus (Exod./Ex)
Leviticus (Lev./Lev)
Numbers (Num./Num)
Deuteronomy (Deut./Deut)
Joshua (Josh./Josh)
Judges (Judg./Judg)
Ruth
1 Samuel (1 Sam./1 Sam)
2 Samuel (2 Sam./2 Sam)
1 Kings
2 Kings
1 Chronicles (1 Chron./1 Chron)
2 Chronicles (2 Chron./2 Chron)
Ezra
Nehemiah (Neh./Neh)

Esther
Job
Psalms (Ps./Ps)
Proverbs (Prov./Prov)
Ecclesiastes (Eccles./Eccles)
Song of Solomon (Song of Sol./
    Song)
Isiah (Isa./Is)
Jeremiah (Jer./Jer)
Lamentations (Lam./Lam)
Ezekiel (Ezek./Ezek)
Daniel (Dan./Dan)
Hosea (Hos./Hos)
Joel
Amos
Obadiah (Obad./Obad)
Jonah (Jon./Jon)
Micah (Mic./Mic)
Nahum (Nah./Nahum)
Habakkuk (Hab./Hab)
Zephaniah (Zeph./Zeph)
Haggai (Hag./Hag)
Zechariah (Zech./Zech)
Malachi (Mal./Mal)

NEW TESTAMENT

Matthew (Matt./Mt)
Mark (Mark/Mk)
Luke (Luke/Lk)
John (John/Jn)
Acts of the Apostles (Acts)
Romans (Rom./Rom)
1 Corinthians (1 Cor./1 Cor)
2 Corinthians (2 Cor./2 Cor)
Galatians (Gal./Gal)
Ephesians (Eph./Eph)
Philippians (Phil./Phil)
Colossians (Col./Col)
1 Thessalonians (1 Thess./1
    Thess)
2 Thessalonians (2 Thess./2
    Thess)
1 Timothy (1 Tim./1 Tim)

2 Timothy (2 Tim./2 Tim)
Titus (Titus/Tit)
Philemon (Philem./Philem)
Hebrews (Heb./Heb)
James (James/Jas)
1 Peter (1 Pet./1 Pet)
2 Peter (2 Pet./2 Pet)
1 John
2 John
3 John
Jude
Revelation (Rev./Rev)

ROMAN NUMERALS

Roman numerals are written in capital letters to designate succession of wars, monarchs, popes, family members, and musical chords. Lowercase roman numerals are used for the page numbers of prefatory matter in a book to distinguish it from the rest of the book.

Roman numerals may also be used in formal contexts such as dates on monuments or documents, or in numeration of parts of dramatic works (e.g., *Act II, scene iii*).

1	I	14	XIX
2	II	15	XV
3	III	20	XX
4	IV	21	XXI
5	V	29	XXIX
6	VI	30	XXX
7	VII	40	XL
8	VIII	50	L
9	IX	60	LX
10	X	70	LXX
11	XI	90	XC
12	XII	99	IC
13	XIII	100	C

101	CI	600	DC
200	CC	900	CM
400	CD	1,000	M
500	D	2,000	MM

TITLES OF WORKS

The titles of published and publicly available books, magazines newspapers, poems, movies, operas, plays, documents, speeches, musical compositions, and works of art are capitalized (except for articles, conjunctions, prepositions of four letters or more, and *to* in an infinitive, unless they are the first or last word of the title). An initial article is capitalized when included (e.g., *The Sun Also Rises*). The first word following a colon in a title is capitalized (e.g., *WordPerfect 5.1: The Complete Reference*).

The titles of works of art, published books, periodicals, movies, plays, and long musical compositions (such as whole operas or other performances), are italicized or underlined.

The titles of stories, chapters and sections of books, essays, speeches or lectures, articles, dissertations (unpublished), radio and television shows, and songs are enclosed in quotation marks.

The titles of legal and government agreements, documents, and programs, as well as acts, pacts, plans, policies, or treaties, are capitalized when used as proper nouns, but do not take italics or quotation marks.

The names of legal cases are

italicized and the abbreviation *vs.* or *v.* used for *versus*. Legal writings or documents may not use italicization.

Some examples:

Bill of Rights
Congressional Directory
Congressional Record
Constitution of the United States
Declaration of Independence
Emancipation Proclamation
Equal Rights Amendment *or* ERA
Federal Insurance Contributions
   Act *or* FICA
Federal Register
G.I. Bill of Rights *or* the G.I. Bill
''Good Morning, America''
Hemingway's ''The Killers''
Ladies' Home Journal
Magna Charta *or* Magna Carta
Monet's *Water Lilies*
Monroe Doctrine
Mozart's *The Marriage of Figaro*
Pledge of Allegiance
Roe *v.* Wade
Singin' in the Rain
State of the Union address
''The Star-Spangled Banner''
Who's Afraid of Virginia Woolf?

TRADEMARKS AND TRADE NAMES

Trade and brand names, registered trademarks, and service marks are capitalized.

Academy Award
Ace bandage
Addressograph
Adidas
Adrenalin
Ajax

Alfa Romeo
Alka-Seltzer
Anacin
Aqua-Lung
Armour meats
Aston Martin
Astroturf
Aubusson carpet
Audi
Baggies
Bakelite
Band-Aid
Beech Nut
Ben-Gay
Benzedrine
Betty Crocker
Birds Eye foods
BMW (Bayerische Motoren
    Werke)
Brylcreem
Budweiser
Bufferin
Cadillac
Cap'n Crunch cereal
Caterpillar
Cessna
ChapStick
Charmin toilet tissue
Cheerios cereal
Chee-tos
Chef Boy-ar-dee
Chemical Mace
Chevrolet or Chevy
Chock Full o'Nuts
Citroën
Clairol
Clorox
Coca-Cola or Coke
Concorde
Contac
Cracker Jack
Crisco
Cutex

Cyclone fence
Dacron
Datsun
Deepfreeze freezer
Demerol
Dexedrine
Dictaphone
Disposall garbage disposer
Doritos chips
Dramamine
Drambuie liqueur
Drano
Dr Pepper
Dumpster bins
Duncan Hines
Easy-Off oven cleaner
Efferdent dental cleanser
Ekco
Electrolux
Eveready batteries
Excedrin
Ex-Lax
Fannie May candy
Fiat
Fiberglas (Owens-Corning)
Fig Newtons
Folger coffee
Formica
Franco-American foods
Frigidaire refrigerator
Frisbee
Fuller Brush
Gatorade drink
Gold Medal flour
Gore-Tex
Handi Wipes
Hawaiian Punch
Head and Shoulders shampoo
Heinz 57
Hi-C drinks
Hovercraft
Hula-Hoop
Hush Puppies shoes

Jacuzzi
Jaguar
Jell-O
Jujyfruits
Keds shoes
Kellogg cereals
Ken-L-Ration pet foods
Kleenex tissue
Knorr
Kodak photographic products
Kool-Aid
Kotex
9-Lives cat food
Laetrile
Land-Rover
Laundromat
Lay's potato chips
Lego and Duplo blocks
Leica camera
Lenox china
Lestoil cleaner
Letraset
Levi's
Life Savers candy
Lifebuoy
Linotype
Listerine mouthwash
Lucite
Maalox
Mace
Mailgram
Maserati
Masonite
Max Factor
Maxwell House coffee
Mazola
Mercedes-Benz
Mercurochrome
MG (Morris Garages)
Michelob
Milk of Magnesia
Milton Bradley games
Minolta

Mitsubishi
Muzak
Nabisco
Naugahyde
Nescafé
Nikon
Novocain
NutraSweet
Oldsmobile
Ore-Ida frozen foods
Oreo cookies
Orlon
Ouija board
Ovaltine
Oxydol
Pablum
Paper Mate pens
Pepperidge Farm foods
Pepsi Cola *or* Pepsi
Pepto-Bismol medication
Peugeot
Photostat
Ping-Pong
Playskool toys
Playtex
Plexiglas
Polaroid
Popsicle
Porsche
Post-It stickers
Pyrex dishes
Q-Tips
Raisinets
Reddi-Wip
Reese's candy
Revlon
Right Guard deodorant
Rolaids medication
Rolex
Rolls-Royce
Sanforized
Sanka coffee
Saran Wrap

Schweppes
Scotch tape
Scrabble game
Seconal
Seven-Up *or* 7Up
Sheetrock
Simoniz
Smithfield Ham
Spam
Spic and Span
Styrofoam
Sugartwin
Suzuki
Sweet 'n Low
Tabasco
Tampax
Tarmac
Technicolor
Teflon
TelePrompTer
Teletype
Thermos
Thom McAn shoes
Timex

Tinkertoy
Tiparillo
Tupperware
Turtle Wax
Ty-D-bol
V-8 drink
Valium
Vaseline petroleum jelly
Velcro
Velveeta cheese
Volvo
Wash 'n Dri
Windbreaker
Xerox
Zipper

VEHICLE NAMES

The names of specific ships, submarines, airplanes, and spacecraft are capitalized and italicized (e.g., *Air Force One*, the *Titanic*). Abbreviations preceding the names (e.g., *H.M.S* or *HMS*, *S.S.* or *SS*) are not italicized.

3

RULES OF
PUNCTUATION

APOSTROPHE

The apostrophe (') is used when leaving out a letter or letters in a contraction and is used in forming most possessives and certain plurals.

Plurals of letter abbreviations with periods and single letters may take an *'s* (e.g., *p's and q's*). Other plurals do not take an apostrophe.

The possessive of singular nouns end in *'s*, including nouns ending in the sibilants *s*, *x*, *z*, *ch*, or *sh* (e.g., *fox's*). An apostrophe alone is used to form the possessive of a word with two sibilant sounds (e.g., *Kansas'*, *Moses'*). The apostrophe follows the *s* to form the possessive of plural nouns (e.g., *neighbors'*) except for plurals that do not end in *s* (e.g., *people's*).

No apostrophe is used for the possessive of personal pronouns such as *hers*, *its*, *theirs*. The possessive of indefinite pronouns requires an apostrophe (e.g., *one's classmate*).

Joint possession is shown by adding *'s* to the last word of a series (e.g., Francis and Kucera's book).

BRACE

Braces ({ }) are used to show the relationship of elements in a group; a brace may be used to connect printed lines (as in a table) and is used in mathematical equations inside square brackets that are inside parentheses.

BRACKET

Brackets ([]) are used to insert letters or words in quoted matter, for explanatory, correctionary, or commentary reasons. Brackets indicate that the insertion takes the place of or slightly alters the original text.

Brackets are used as parentheses within parentheses.

Brackets are used in mathematical expressions (to show matter to be treated as a unit), chemical formulas, and for phonetic symbols.

COLON

The colon (:) follows the salutation of a business letter (e.g., *Dear Ms. Hollingsworth:*); it divides hours and minutes in notating clock time (e.g., *2:15*), it divides volume and issue number in notating a periodical reference (e.g., *4:3*); and it distinguishes a book title from a book subtitle (e.g., *Dictionaries: The Art and Craft of Lexicography*).

A colon is used to introduce material that explains or amplifies the first part of a sentence (e.g., *There are four food groups: meats and fish, dairy, breads and grains, fruits and vegetables*).

A colon introduces a series, list, or summarizing statement (e.g., *The following is on our list of places to go: grocery store, video store, dry cleaners; He had one great passion: sailing*).

A colon is used in proportions

(e.g., *2:1*), and as a ratio sign (e.g., *1:2::3:6*).

A colon may introduce a quotation, especially a long one.

A colon is used in dialogue text (e.g., *Kyle: Do you want to have lunch? Holly: Yes*).

A colon is used in correspondence for headings and introductory terms (e.g., *To:*, *From:*, *Re:*).

COMMA

The comma (,) is most commonly used to separate items that might otherwise be misread; it separates items in a series joined by *and*, *or*, or *nor* (e.g., *The dish called for celery, carrots, potatoes, and scallions*); it separates main clauses or provides a pause before the conjunction in a compound sentence (e.g., *They drove for miles, and then they gave up and checked into a motel*).

The comma may be used to separate two verb phrases in a sentence; to set off subordinate clauses or phrases within sentence; or to set off an apposite—a noun referring to previous noun (e.g., *my sister, Nancy*) or contrasting words or phrases (e.g., *I prefer orange juice, not lemonade*).

The comma sets off a direct address (e.g., *"Sir, can you tell me the correct time?"*); introductory phrases (e.g., *In essence, we felt the whole experience was a good one*); and interrupting or parenthetic items.

Use a comma before a quotation following an introductory phrase (e.g., *The taxi driver said, "The fare is three dollars"*) and inside a closing quotation mark (e.g., *I said "floor," not "drawer"*).

A comma replaces the word *and* between compound qualifiers (e.g., *The rabbit had large, floppy ears*).

Use a comma between name and title, title and organization, surname and degree, or surname and the words *Junior* (or *Jr.*) or *Senior* (or *Sr.*). Use a comma to clarify an inverted name (e.g., Kipfer, Barbara Ann).

A comma separates thousands, millions, and so on in a number of four or more digits (e.g., *2,000,000*); it separates the day of the month from the year in dates (e.g., *They got together on May 30, 1987, for the first time*); and sets off elements of an address (e.g., *Write to him at The Language Centre, University of Exeter, Exeter, England EX4 4QH*).

Use a comma after the salutation in informal correspondence (e.g., *Dear T.B.,*) and after the complimentary close in all correspondence (e.g., *Respectfully,*).

DASH

The dash (—), also called an em dash, is used to denote a sudden change or break in a sentence (e.g., *He disappeared—*

mysteriously—for over an hour).
No spaces are used before or after a dash. Do not combine a dash with a colon, comma, or semicolon.

The dash is also commonly used as a substitute for parentheses or commas to clarify meaning or place emphasis (e.g., *The primary colors—red, yellow, and blue—are used to make all the other colors)*

A dash may be used before an amplification, definition, explanation, or summary statement (e.g., *The news article was brief, clear, and precise—just the essentials to get the point across).*

Use a dash to show interruption of a word or sentence (e.g., *The story went on to say that—).*

Precede an author's credit for a quotation with a dash.

The en dash is used in typeset material and is shorter than the em dash, which is represented in typewritten material by two hyphens. The en dash is used as a replacement for a hyphen when the meaning intended is "through" or "up to and including" (e.g., *1987–91,* or *Monday–Saturday).*

DIVISION OF WORDS

Guidelines for dividing words at the end of lines are:

Pay attention to the units in the way the word is pronounced (syllables) and do not break the word so that it would be mispronounced or misunderstood.

Divide syllables between doubled consonants, except when that would divide a simple base form (e.g., *re-com-men-da-tion,* but *sell-ing, buzz-er).* When the doubled consonant comes before *-ing,* the second consonant stays with the *-ing.*

Do not divide a one-syllable word, even if there is an inflected ending such as *-ed* (e.g., *spelled, bummed).*

Do not divide a word if only one letter would be left either at the end of one line or the beginning of another (e.g., *a-bate* should not be divided between lines). Division after a prefix of more than one letter, putting it at the end of a line, is permissible (e.g., *re-direct).*

Do not divide words of six letters or less.

Divided hyphenated words at the hyphen.

Do not divide before the following suffixes (they should not be at the beginning of a line alone), nor should they be divided themselves: *-able, -ceous, -cial, -cion, -cious, -geous, -gion, -gious, -ible, -sial, -sion, -tial, -tion, -tious.*

When a vowel alone forms a syllable in the middle of a word, keep it with the previous syllable (e.g., *physi-cal).*

A liquid or silent *l* syllable at the end of a word or as part of an inflected ending should not be put on the next line alone (e.g., *read-able, twin-kling*).

Numerals and abbreviations should not be divided, and avoid dividing proper nouns whenever possible.

ELLIPSIS POINTS *OR* ELLIPSES

Ellipsis points (. . .), also called suspension points, are used when words are omitted. If the material omitted is the end of a sentence, the ellipses are followed by whatever punctuation ended the sentence—a period, a question mark (e.g., *Who said that . . . ?*), or an exclamation point (e.g., They always . . . !).

Ellipses may also indicate a trailing off or suspension in speech. Punctuation that normally falls before or after the ellipsis points can be retained for clarity. A space precedes and follows ellipses.

EXCLAMATION POINT

An exclamation point (!) is used to show surprise, incredulity, or praise, or to emphasize a command—to show extreme force in statement.

An exclamation point may replace a question mark when irony or an emphatic tone is meant (e.g., *How could you!*).

If the exclamation point ends a sentence in a quotation, no comma or period is used (e.g., *"Get lost!" she exploded*).

HYPHEN

The hyphen (-) is used to connect the elements of some compound words, especially ones of three or more words (e.g., *a know-it-all*), and to divide a word at the end of a line.

Use a hyphen in some fractions and compound numbers; in measurements with numbers and unit (e.g., *12-inch disk*); in ages with number and unit (e.g., *12,000-year-old fossil*).

A hyphen is used in prefixed words when a vowel is doubled (e.g., *anti-inflammatory*) or consonant is tripled (e.g., *bell-like*); for certain prefixes such as *ex-*; for certain suffixes such as *-elect*; or to make a word clear from its homonym (e.g., *recover* and *re-cover*).

Use a hyphen between a prefix and the second word if it is a proper noun (e.g., *pre-Columbian*) and between proper noun compounds (e.g., *Arab-Israeli*).

Compounds that begin with a single capital letter take a hyphen (e.g., *H-bomb*).

Use a hyphen for compound adjectives (e.g., *a bluish-green tint*), but not for compound modifiers that include an adverb and an adjective (e.g., *widely known author*).

Hyphens connect directions (e.g., *north-northwest*); show words spelled out letter by letter (e.g., *y-e-s*); and demonstrate stuttering speech.

NUMBERS

Written-out numbers between twenty-one and ninety-nine are hyphenated (e.g., *Fifty-three*).

Figures of four digits may be written with or without a comma between the hundreds place and the thousands place (e.g., *1,521* or *1521*).

Numbers of checks, contracts, military hours, pages, policies, rooms or suites, streets, telephone numbers, and years are written without commas. Check, telephone, and serial numbers may contain hyphens.

A fractional number spelled out and used as a modifier is hyphenated (e.g., *three-quarter time*). A fraction used with a whole number is written as a figure, (e.g., *5¼*), *as are measurements that are fractions (e.g., ¼ mile)*. A measurement as a modifier is hyphenated (e.g., *nine-pound boy*).

Inclusive year and page numbers are joined by a dash and may omit hundreds (e.g., *1989–90, pp. 140–50*).

If an abbreviation or symbol is used with a number, it should be written as a figure (e.g., *$1 million, 3 lbs.*).

A number should not be divided at the end of a line.

PARENTHESES

Parentheses (()) are used to enclose supplementary matter that is not essential to the statement.

At the end of a sentence, the period or other punctuation follows the closing parenthesis. A complete sentence within parentheses is punctuated like regular text, but the period at the end of the sentence should be omitted (retain exclamation points and question marks). Parentheses may indicate important material, but their use is interruptive.

Parenthesis are used to set off explanation, definitions, translations, or alternatives, to indicate abbreviation of the spelled-out word or to provide the spelled-out form of an abbreviation.

Bibliographical data, cross-references, or comments about a text may be offered in parenthesis.

Numbers or letters indicating an item in a series are enclosed in parentheses (e.g., *(1), (2), (3)* and *(a), (b), (c)*), and parentheses may be used for setting of numeric data, including Arabic numerals confirming a spelled-out number, and for other mathematical expressions.

PERIOD

The period (.) is used at the end of a declarative sentence and after a question that does not require an answer, after a letter or number indicating an item in a series, as part of an ellipsis, in some abbreviations, or after a person's initials.

Periods are also used in

numbers with integers and decimals.

QUESTION MARK

The question mark (?) is used after a direct interrogative or a statement expressing doubt (e.g. *Why do you ask?*). It is used after each element of an interrogative series when the series is not enumerated or lettered (e.g., *I've been asking myself, when did they arrive? Why did they leave?*).

Do not put a comma after a question mark that falls within quotation marks.

QUOTATION MARKS

Quotation marks (",") are used for direct quotations. Each part of an interrupted quotation begins and ends with quotation marks (e.g., *"I am convinced," the defense lawyer told the jury, "my client is innocent"*).

Quotation marks identify expressions following introductory terms such as *titled, the word, the term, marked, designated, classified, named, cited as, referred to as, signed*, and the like, which indicate a borrowing or special use.

Quotation marks may be used around mottos, slang, misnomers, coined words, proverbs and maxims, ironical reference, unspoken dialogue, around words referred to as words (e.g., *I said "tomato," not "potato"*), and around sentences referred to as sentences (e.g., *An example of an interrogative is, "Where are they?"*).

Quotation marks may be set around translations of foreign terms or around single letters within a sentence (e.g., *His name begins with a "C"*).

A period or comma always falls inside quotation marks (e.g., *"The buck stops here," he joked*), whether or not it belongs to the quotation or the sentence as a whole. The dash, question mark, and exclamation point fall inside quotation marks if they belong with the quoted matter but outside if they punctuate the sentence as a whole. A colon or a semicolon goes outside the quotation marks.

For quotations that extend beyond one paragraph, a quotation mark begins each paragraph, but a closing quotation mark appears only at the end of the last paragraph.

Single quotation marks (',') are used to enclose a quotation within a quotation (e.g., *We told him, "Martina said, 'Ask Ivan to do it.' "*).

SEMICOLON

The semicolon (;) is sometimes regarded as a weak period or a strong comma and is used in ways similar to periods and commas. A semicolon can mark the end of a clause and indicate that a clause following is closely related to it; a semicolon can also divide a sentence to make meaning clearer.

A semicolon is placed outside quotation marks and parentheses.

More specifically, a semicolon separates independent clauses in place of a coordinating conjunction such as *and, because, for,* and the like. It also separates independent clauses when the second clause begins with a conjunctive adverb; that is, it can precede words such as *accordingly, all the same, also, as a result, besides, by the same token, consequently, furthermore, hence, however, indeed, in that case, likewise, moreover, nevertheless, on the other hand, otherwise, still, then, therefore, and thus.* These usually explain or summarize preceding matter.

The semicolon clarifies meaning by providing a long pause in long sentences and in sentences with several commas. It may be used before explanatory phrases and clauses such as *for example, for instance, i.e., namely, that is.* The semicolon also separates lists or phrases in a series when the phrases themselves have commas.

SLASH

The slash (/) is also called the virgule, diagonal, solidus, oblique, or slant.

A slash represents *or* or *and/or* in alternatives such as *yours/mine.*

A slash may represent *and,* (e.g., *1990/91, Minneapolis/St. Paul*).

A slash may represent abbreviation of some prepositions (e.g., *c/o addressee, w/ dressing, w/o reference*).

A slash represents *per* or *to* in measures and ratios (e.g., *2 ft./ min., price/earnings ratio*).

A slash is used to separate numbers in dates (e.g., *2/14/93*), fractions, and sometimes telephone numbers. A slash used to divide lines of poetry when written as continuous text.

A slash is used in representing pronunciations (phonemic transcriptions).

APPENDICES

1. ABBREVIATIONS

ABBREVIATIONS OFTEN IN ENTYMOLOGIES

A.D. anno Domini
AF Anglo-French
Afr Afrika
Afrik Afrikaans
Alb Albanian, Albania
alter alteration
Am, Amer America, American
AmerF American French
AmerInd American Indian
AmerSp American Spanish
AN Anglo-Norman
angl anglicized
Ar Arabic
Arab Arabian, Arabic
Aram Aramaic
Argen Argentine
Arm Armenian
AS Anglo-Saxon
Assyr Assyrian
attrib attributive, attributively
Austral Australian
AV Authorized Version
AV Avestan
Bab Babylonian
B.C. before Christ; British Columbia
Belg Belgian, Belgium
Beng Bengali
Braz Brazilian
Bret Breton
Brit Britain, British
Bulg Bulgarian, Bulgaria
c century
ca, c circa
Canad, Can Canadian, Canada
CanF Canadian French
Cant Cantonese
Catal Catalan

Celt Celtic
Chin Chinese
Col Columbia, Colossians
Confed Confederate
Copt Coptic
Corn Cornish
Croat Croatian
D, Du Dutch
Dan Danish; Daniel
Den Denmark
deriv derivative
Dom Rep Dominican Republic
Dor Doric
E east, eastern; English
EE Early English
EGmc East Germanic
Egypt Egyptian
Eng England, English
Esk Eskimo
Eth Ethiopic
F French; Fahrenheit
Fin Finland
Finn Finnish
Flem, Fl Flemish
Fr France, French
fr from
Fris Frisian
G German
Gael Gaelic
Ger German, Germany
Gk, Gr Greek
Gmc Germanic
Goth Gothic
Gr Brit Great Britain
Heb Hebrew
Hind Hindustani
Hitt Hittite
Hon Honduras
Hung Hungarian, Hungary
I Indian
Icel Icelandic
IE Indo-European
imit imitative

Ind India, Indian
Ion Ionic
Ir Irish
Ire Ireland
IrGael Irish Gaelic
ISV International Scientific
  Vocabulary
It, Ital Italian, Italy
Jav Javanese
Jp Japanese, Japan
L Latin
LaF Louisiana French
Lat Latin
LG Low German
LGk Late Greek
LHeb Late Hebrew
Lith Lithuanian, Lithuania
LL Late Latin
MBret Middle Breton
MD Middle Dutch
ME Middle English
Medit Mediterranean
Mex Mexican, Mexico
MexSp Mexican Spanish
MF Middle French
MFlem Middle Flemish
MGk Middle Greek
MHG Middle High German
MIr Middle Irish
ML Medieval Latin
MLG Middle Low German
ModE Modern English
Mongol Mongolian
MPer Middle Persian
MW Middle Welsh
NE New England
Neth Netherlands
NewEng New England
NewZeal New Zealand
NGk New Greek
NGmc North Germanic
NHeb New Hebrew
NL New Latin
Norw Norwegian, Norway

NZ New Zealand
OCatal Old Catalan
OE Old English
OF Old French
OFris Old Frisian
OGael Old Gaelic
OHG Old High German
OIr Old Irish
OIt Old Italian
OL Old Latin
ON Old Norse
ONF Old North French
Ont Ontario
OPer Old Persian
OPg Old Portuguese
OProv Old Provençal
OPruss Old Prussian
orig original, originally
ORuss Old Russian
OS Old Saxon
OSlav Old Slavic
OSp Old Spanish
OW Old Welsh
PaG Pennsylvania German
Pek Pekingese
Per, Pers Persian
Pg Portuguese
Phil Philippines
PhilSp Philippine Spanish
Pol Polish, Poland
Port Portuguese, Portugal
PR Puerto Rico
Prov Provençal
Pruss Prussian
Rom Roman; Romanian, Romania
Rum Rumanian
Russ Russian
S Afr South Africa, South African
S Amer South America, South
  American
Sc Scotch, Scots
Scand, Scan Scandinavian
ScGael Scottish Gaelic
Scot, Sc Scotland, Scottish

Scrip Scripture
Sem Seminary; Semitic
Serb Serbian
Shak Shakespeare
Skt Sanskrit
Slav Slavic
So Afr South Africa, South African
Sp, Span Spanish
Sw, Swed Swedish
Switz Switzerland
Syr Syriac
Tag Tagalog
Tasm Tasmania
Toch Tocharian
trans translation
Turk Turkish
UK United Kingdom
Ukrain Ukrainian
US United States
USA United States of America
USSR Union of Soviet Socialist Republics
Ven Venezuela
VL Vulgar Latin
W Welsh; west, western
WGmc West Germanic

COMMON ABBREVIATIONS

ab about
abbr abbreviation
abl ablative
absol absolute, absolutely
Acad Academy
acc accusative
act active
adj adjective
adv adverb
AFB Air Force Base
Agric Agriculture
alt altitude
A&M Agricultural and Mechanical
anat anatomy

anc ancient
ant antonym
anthropol,
anthrop anthropologist, anthropology
aor aorist
apos apostrophe
approx approximate, approximately
arch archaic
archaeol archaeologist
archit architecture
art article
Assoc Association
astron, astr astronomer, astronomy
atty attorney
aug augmentative
av average
b born
bacteriol bacteriologist
bef before
bet between
bib biblical
bibliog bibliography
biochem biochemist
biol biologist
bot botany
bro brother
C centigrade; College
cap capital, capitalized
caus causative
cen center, central
cent century
Ch Church
chem chemistry, chemical
class classical
co(s) county (counties)
coll college
collect collective, collectively
colloq colloquial, colloquially
comb combining, combination
Comm Community
compar comparative

conj conjugation; conjunction
constr construction
contr contraction
cook cookery
criminol criminologist
cu cubic
d died
dat dative
dau daughter
def definite
dept department
derog derogatory
dial dialect
dim diminutive
disc discovered
dist district
div division
dram dramatist
dyn dynamics
E east, eastern
e.g. *exempli gratia* ("for example")
eccl ecclesiastical
econ economist
Ed Education
elec electrical
emp emperor
equiv equivalent
esp especially
est estimated, estimate
estab established
et al. *et alii* ("and others")
etc *et cetera* ("and so forth")
ethnol ethnologist
exc except
excl excludes, excluding, exclusive
exclam exclamation
f founded
Fahr Fahrenheit
fam family
fed federation
fem, f feminine
ff following
fig figurative, figuratively

fl flourished
form former, formerly
fr from
freq frequentative
ft feet, foot
fut future
gen general; genitive
geog geography
geol geology
geom geometry
gov governor
govt government
gram grammar
her heraldry
hist historian, history
hort horticulture
I island
i.e. *id est* ("that is")
imper imperative
in inch
incho inchoative
incl included, includes, including
incorp incorporated
indef indefinite
indep independent
indic indicative
infin infinitive
inst institute, institution
instr instrumental
intens intensive
interj interjection
interrog interrogative
irreg irregular
ital italic
joc jocular, jocularly
lat latitude
lit literally; literary
liturg liturgical, liturgy
long longitude
m meters; mile; masculine
manuf manufacturer
masc masculine
math mathematician
max maximum

Mech Mechanical
mech mechanics
Med Medical
med medicine
met metropolitan
meteor meteorology
mfr manufacture
mi miles
mil military
min minister
mod modern
modif modification
MS (S) manuscript (s)
MT Mount, Mountain
munic municipal
mus music
myth mythology
n pl noun plural
N north, northern
n noun
naut nautical
neut, n neuter
nom nominative
nonstand nonstandard
nov novelist
nr near
obs obsolete
occas occasionally, occasional
off official
opp opposite
org organized
ornith ornithology
p page
part, partic participle
pass passive
path pathology
perf perfect
perh perhaps
pers person
philos philosopher
photog photography
phys physics, physical
physiol physiologist
pl plural

poet poetical
polit political, politician
pop population
pp past participle; pages
prec preceding
predic predictive, predicatively
prep preposition
pres present; president
prob probably
pron pronoun; pronunciation, pronounced
pronunc pronunciation
propr proprietary
prp present participle
pseud pseudonym
psychol, psych psychologist
pub published
qqv, qv *quod vide* (''which see'')
redupl reduplication
refl reflexive
rel relative
relig religion
resp respectively
rev revolution
rhet rhetoric, rhetorical
riv river
S south, southern
Sch School
sci science
secy secretary
sig signature
sing singular
sociol sociologist
specif, spec specifically
spp species
St Saint
Ste Sainte
subj subjunctive
substand substandard
superl superlative
syn synonym, synonymy
Tech Technology
techn technical
theat theatre

theol theologian, theology, theological

treas treasury

U University

univ university

usu usually, usual

v, vb verb

var variant

vi verb intransitive

voc vocative

vt verb transitive

W west, western

zool zoologist

2. AFFIXES

PREFIXES

a- From, away from (e.g., *awake*); at, in, on (e.g., *aboard*); in such a manner, state, or condition (e.g., *afoot*); not, without, lacking (e.g., *amoral*).

ab- From, away from (e.g., *abnormal*).

abs- From, away from (e.g., *abstract*).

acanth-, acantho- Spiny, thorny (e.g., *acanthoid*).

acous- Hearing (e.g., *acoustics*).

acr-, acro- Top; extremity, end (e.g., *acromegaly*).

ad- To, toward, near (e.g., *adsorb, adjacent*).

aden-, adeno- Gland (e.g., *adenoma*).

adren-, adreno- Adrenal gland.

aer-, aero- Air, gas (e.g., *aerodynamic*).

af- To, toward, near (e.g., *affix*).

ag- To, toward, near (e.g., *aggress*).

al- To, toward, near (e.g., *allure*).

all-, allo- Other, different (e.g., *allopathic*).

alti-, alto- High (e.g., *altimeter*).

am-, amb-, ambi-, amphi- Both, both sides (e.g., *ambivalence*); round (e.g., *amphitheater*); about (e.g., *ambience*).

amyl-, amylo- Starch (e.g., *amylopsin*).

an- Not, without, lacking (e.g., *anaerobe*).

ana- Again; thorough, thoroughly (e.g., *anaphylaxis*); up, upward; back, backward (e.g., *anapest*).

andr-, andro- Man; male (e.g., *androgen*).

anem-, anemo- Wind (e.g., *anemology*).

ant-, ante- Before, prior, earlier; in front of (e.g., *anteroom*).

anthrop-, anthropo- Man (e.g., *anthropomorphize*).

anti-, ant-, anth- Against, opposite (e.g., *antihero*); combating, defending (e.g., *antigovernment*).

ap- To, toward, near (e.g., *appoint*).

api- Bee (e.g., *apiary*).

apo-, ap- Away (e.g., *apologue*); from; related.

aqui-, aqua- Water (e.g., *aquiculture*).

arbor-, arbori- Tree (e.g., *arboreal*).

arch-, archi- Chief, principal, supreme (e.g., *archenemy*).

arche-, archeo-, archae-, archaeo- Old, ancient (e.g., *archaeology*).

arteri-, arterio- Artery (e.g., *arteriosclerosis*).

arthr-, arthro- Joint (e.g., *arthritis*).

as- To, toward, near (e.g., *assimilate*).

astr-, astro-, aster- Star (e.g., *asteroid*).

at- To, toward, near (e.g., *attribute*).

atmo- Vapor (e.g., *atmosphere*).

audio- Hearing, sound (e.g., *audiotape*).

auto- Self-moving (e.g., *autodidact*).

avi- Bird, flying (e.g., *aviary*).

az-, azo- Nitrogenous.

bacci- Berry.

bacteri-, bacterio- Bacteria.

bar-, baro- Weight, pressure (e.g., *barometer*).

bath-, batho-, bathy- Deep, depth.

be- To make, cause (e.g., *belittle*); to take from (e.g., *behead*); on, over; against, across; thoroughly, excessively (e.g., *beset*).

bi-, bio- Life, living (e.g., *biopsy*).

bi-, bis- Twice, two, double, in two (e.g., *biannual*).

biblio- Book (e.g., *bibliography*).

blephar-, blepharo- Eyelid, eyelash.

bracchio- Arm.

brachy- Short.

bronch-, broncho-, bronchi-, bronchio- Throat, lung.

caco- Evil, bad, incorrect (e.g., *cacoethes*).

calci- Lime (e.g., *calciferous*).

cardio- Heart (e.g., *cardiovascular*).

carpo- Fruit (e.g., *carpophageous*).

cat-, cata-, cath-, cato- Down, downward, under (e.g., *catastrophe*); against; completeness, thorough, thoroughly (e.g., *catachresis*).

centi- Hundred (e.g., *centigrade*).

cephal-, cephalo- Head (e.g., *cephalopod*).

cerebro- Brain.

cervic-, cervico-, cervici- Neck.

chiro- Hand (e.g., *chiropractor*).

chlor-, chloro- Green (e.g., *chloroplast*).

chol-, chole-, cholo- Bile (e.g., *cholera*).

chondr-, chondri-, chondro- Cartilage.

choreo- Dance (e.g., *choreography*).

choro- Country (e.g., *chorographer*).

chrom-, chromo-, chromato- Color, colored (e.g., *chromatic*).

chron-, chrono- Time (e.g., *chronological*).

chrys-, chryso- Gold (e.g., *chrysolite*).

circum-, circu- Around, about (e.g., *circumnavigate*).

cirr-, cirri-, cirro- Curl (e.g., *cirrate*).

cis- On this side (e.g., *cisatlantic*).

cleisto- Closed (e.g., *cleistogamic*).

co- Together, with (e.g., *coauthor*).

cog- Together, with (e.g., *cognate*).

col- Together, with (e.g., *collateral*).

com- Together, with (e.g., *commingle*); thorough, thoroughly (e.g., *commination*).

con- Together, with (e.g., *concomitant*).

contra- Against, in opposition, contrasting, contrary (e.g., *contradistinction*).

cor- Together, with (e.g., *correlation*); thorough, thoroughly (e.g., *corroborate*).

cosmo- Universe (e.g., *cosmopolitan*).

counter- Against, in opposition (e.g., *countersink*); substitute.

cranio- Skull.

cruci- Cross (e.g., *cruciform*).

cry-, cryo- Cold (e.g., *cryoplankton*).

crypt-, crypto- Hidden (e.g., *cryptogram*).

cupr- Copper (e.g., *cupreous*); bronze.

cyst-, cysti-, cysto- Bladder, sac.

cyt-, cyto- Cell (e.g., *cytogenetics*).

dactyl-, dactylo- Finger, toe (e.g., *dactylology*).

de- Down, from, separation (e.g., *decease*); not; reverse (e.g., *debrief*); *remove* (e.g., *debar*); get off (e.g., *debark*); derived.

deca-, deci-, dec-, deka-, dek- Ten (e.g., *decathalon*).

demi- Half, part of (e.g., *demimonde*).

dent-, denti-, dento- Tooth (e.g., *denture*).

derm-, derma-, dermo- Skin (e.g., *dermatitis*).

deut-, deuto-, deutero- Second (e.g., *deuterogamy*).

dextr-, dextro- Right side (e.g., *dextrorotary*).

di- Two (e.g., *diclinous*).

dia-, di- Through, across (e.g., *diachronic*); not, opposite; apart.

dif- Not, opposite (e.g., *difficulty*); two, apart (e.g., *diffuse*).

digit-, digiti- Finger or toe (e.g., *digitigrade*).

dipl-, diplo- Double, twofold (e.g., *diplopia*).

dis- Exclude, remove (e.g., *disenfranchise*); do opposite.

dis- Not, opposite (e.g., *disingenuous*); apart; two.

dodeca-, dodec- Twelve (e.g., *dodecaphonic*).

dors-, dorsi-, dorso- Back of body.

dyna-, dynamo- Force, power (e.g., *dynamic*).

dys-, dis- Badly, difficult, hard; evil; abnormal (e.g., *dysfunctional*).

e- Out, not, absent (e.g., *ebracteate*).

ec- Out, not, absent (e.g., *ectopic*).

echin-, echino- Spine (e.g., *echinate*).

ect-, ecto- Outside, external (e.g., *ectoparasite*).

ef- Out, not, absent (e.g., *effluent*).

el- In, into, on, within.

en-, em- Cause to be, to make (e.g., *envision*); to surround, cover (e.g., *enmesh*); in, into, on, within.

encephal-, encephalo- Brain (e.g., *encephaloma*).

end-, endo- Inside, within (e.g., *endometrium*).

ennea- Nine (e.g., *ennead*).

ent-, ento- Inside, within (e.g., *entozoa*).

enter-, entero- Intestine (e.g., *enterotoxemia*).

entomo- Insect (e.g., *entomology*).

eo- Early, old (e.g., *eolith*).

epi-, ep- on, upon, beside, above (e.g., *epigraph*); out, on the outside (e.g., *epicardium*); during.

equi- Equal, alike (e.g., *equidistant*).

erg-, ergo- Work (e.g., *ergonomics*).

erythr-, erythro- Red (e.g., *erythrema*).

ethno- Race, nation (e.g., *ethnocentric*).

eu- Good, well (e.g., *eulogize*); true.

ex-, exo- From; out, out of, outside, external (e.g., *exoskeleton*); without; former (e.g., *ex-lover*).

extra- on the outside, external; beyond, in excess, additional, exceptionally (e.g., *extrasensory*).

febri- Fever (e.g., *febricity*).

ferri-, ferro- Iron.

fibr-, fibro- Threadlike, fibrous (e.g., *fibrovascular*).

fissi- Split (e.g., *fissipalmate*).

fluvio- River (e.g., *fluviomarine*).

for- Not; against, forth; away; prohibitive (e.g., *forbidden*).

fore- before, early (e.g., *foretell*); in front of, front part of (e.g., *foreskin*).

gain- Against (e.g., *gainsay*).

galact-, galacto- Milk (e.g., *galactose*).

gam-, gamo- Together, copulation (e.g., *gamete*).

gastr-, gastro-, gastri- Stomach, eating (e.g., *gastronome*).

ge-, geo- Earth, land (e.g., *geography*).

gem-, gemmi- Bud (e.g., *gemmulation*).

geront-, geronto- Old age (e.g., *gerontologist*).

gloss-, glosso- Tongue; language (e.g., *glossary*).

gluc-, gluco-, glyc- Sweet (e.g., *glucose*).

glypto-, glyph- Carving (e.g., *glyptographic*).

gon-, gono- Reproduction (e.g., *gonads*).

grapho- Writing (e.g., *grapheme*).

gymn-, gymno- Naked (e.g., *gymnasium*).

gynec-, gyneco-, gynaec-, gynaeco- Woman (e.g., *gynarchy*).

hagi-, hagio- Holy (e.g., *hagiography*).

hapl-, haplo- Simple, single (e.g., *haplosis*).

hect-, hecto- Hundred (e.g., *hectare*).

heli-, helio- Sun (e.g., *heliotherapy*).

helic-, helico- Spiral (e.g., *helicopter*).

hem-, hemo-, haem-, haemo-, haemato-, hema- Blood (e.g., *hematoma*).

hemi- Half (e.g., *hemisphere*).

hepat-, hepato- Liver (e.g., *hepatitis*).

hepta-, hept- Seven (e.g., *heptarchy*).

hetero-, heter- Different, opposite, another (e.g., *heterosexual*).

hexa-, hex- Six (e.g., *hexagon*).

hist-, histo- Tissue (e.g., *histolysis*).

hol-, holo- Whole, complete, total (e.g., *holohedral*).

hom-, homo-, homeo- Similar, same, alike (e.g., *homoerotic*).

hydr-, hydro- Water, liquid (e.g., *hydroelectric*).

hygr-, hygro- Wet (e.g., *hygroscopic*).

hyp-, hypo- Under, beneath; deficient, less than (e.g., *hypoglycemia*).

hyper- Above, over, beyond, extreme (e.g., *hyperactive*); beyond three dimensions (e.g., *hyperspace*).

hypn-, hypno- Sleep (e.g., *hypnotic*).

hypso- High, height (e.g., *hypsometry*).

hyster-, hystero- Womb; hysteria.

iatro- Medicine (e.g., *iatrogenic*).

ichthy-, ichthyo- Fish (e.g., *ichthyology*).

ig- Used to form adjectives meaning not, opposite (e.g., *ignoble*).

igni- Fire (e.g., *ignition*).

il- Used to form adjectives meaning not, opposite (e.g., *illogical*); used to form nouns or verbs indicating in, into, on (e.g., *illuminate*).

ile-, ileo- End of small intestine (e.g., *ileostomy*).

ilio- Upper hip bone, flank (e.g., *iliolumbar*).

in-, im-, ir- Used to form adjectives meaning not, opposite (e.g., *inapt, impotent, irregular*); used to form nouns or verbs indicating in, into, on.

infra- under, beneath (e.g., *infrastructure*); within

inter- Between (e.g., *interstate*); among, in the midst.

intra- Within, interior, between (e.g., *intramural*); on the outside; during.

intro- Within (e.g., *introspective*); into, in.

is-, iso- Equal, uniform, (e.g., *isometrics*).

juxta- Close to, near to, beside (e.g., *juxtaposition*).

kine-, kineto- Movement (e.g., *kinematics*).

labio- Lip.

lact-, lacti-, lacto- Milk.

laryng-, laryngo- Larynx, voice box (e.g., *laryngectomy*).

lepto- Slender (e.g., *leptocephalus*).

leuk-, leuko-, leuc-, leuco- White (e.g., *leukemia*).

lign-, ligni-, ligno- Wood (e.g., *lignocellulose*).

litho- Stone (e.g., *lithophyte*).

log-, logo- Word, oral (e.g., *logotype*).

luni- Moon (e.g., *lunitidal*).

lyo-, lysi- Dissolving, dispersed (e.g., *lyophilic*).

macr-, macro- Large (e.g., *macrocosm*); long.

magni- Great (e.g., *magnify*).

mal-, male- Bad, badly; ill; evil (e.g., *malevolent*); abnormal, inadequate (e.g., *malformed*).

mega-, megalo-, meg- great, large (e.g., *megalomaniac*); million.

melan-, melano- Black, dark (e.g., *melanotic*).

mero- Part (e.g., *meropia*).

mes-, meso- Middle, intermediate (e.g., *meso-America*).

meta-, met- Beyond (e.g., *metanovel*); after; over; changed, transferred, substituted (e.g., *metamorphosis*).

metr- Measure (e.g., *metrication*).

metr-, metro- Uterus (e.g., *metrorrhagia*).

micr-, micro- Very small (e.g., *microfilm*).

mid- Middle, mean (e.g., *midline*).

mini- Very small, short (e.g., *miniskirt*).

mis- Degrading, less, lack of (e.g., *mistrust*); defect (e.g., *misprint*); in error, wrong, badly (e.g., *misdirection*).

mis-, miso- Hatred, aversion (e.g., *misanthropic*).

mon-, mono- One, alone, solitary, single (e.g., *monotone*).

morph-, morpho- Shape, form (e.g., *morphosis*).

multi-, mult- Many, much (e.g., *multiply*).

my-, myo- Muscle (e.g., *myotonia*).

myc-, myco- Fungus (e.g., *mycelium*).

myel-, myelo- Spinal cord, marrow (e.g., *myelencephalon*).

naso- Nose (e.g., *nasopharynx*).

nati- Birth (e.g., *nativity*).

ne-, n- No, not (e.g., *nether, neuter*).

ne-, neo- New, recent; revived (e.g., *neoclassical*).

necr-, necro- Dead body (e.g., *necrotic*).

nephr-, nephro- Kidney (e.g., *nephrotomy*).

neur-, neuro- Nerve (e.g., *neuralgia*).

noct-, nocti- Night (e.g., *nocturnal*).

non- Not (e.g., *nonissue*); reverse; unimportant, lacking (e.g., *nonage*).

noso- Sickness (e.g., *nosology*).

not-, noto- Back of body (e.g., *notochord*).

ob- In the way of, against (e.g., *obstacle*); out (e.g., *obliterate*); inverse (e.g., *obovate*).

octa-, octo-, oct- Eight (e.g., *octagenarian*).

ocul-, oculo- Eye (e.g., *oculist*).

odont-, odonto- Tooth (e.g., *odontophore*).

oleo- Oil (e.g., *oleomargarine*).

olig-, oligo- Few (e.g., *oligarchy*).

omni- All (e.g., *omnipotent*).

oneiro- Dream (e.g., *oneiromancy*).

ont-, onto- Being, organism (e.g., *ontological*).

oo-, o- Egg (e.g., *oogenesis*).

op- In the way of; against (e.g., *oppose*); out, inverse.

ophthalm-, ophthalmo- Eye (e.g., *ophthalmologist*).

ornith-, ornitho- Bird (e.g., *ornithology*).

oro- Mountain (e.g., *orthography*).

orth-, ortho- Straight (e.g., *orthopedic*).

oste-, osteo-, ossi- Bone (e.g., *ossify*).

oto- Ear (e.g., *otolith*).

out- Beyond, exceeding, surpassing (e.g., *outrun*).

ov-, ovi-, ovo- Egg.

over- above, beyond, too much, excessive (e.g., *overpriced*).

oxy- Sharp; oxygen.

pachy- Thick (e.g., *pachyderm*).

pale-, paleo-, palae-, palaeo- Ancient, old (e.g., *paleobotany*).

pan-, panto- All, everything, group, whole (e.g., *pan-American*); worldwide.

para-, par- Close, beside; like, alike (e.g., *paralegal*).

para-, par- Unlike, contrary (e.g., *paranormal*); abnormal, faulty.

pari- Equal (e.g., *parity*).

path-, patho- Suffering, disease (e.g., *pathogen*).

ped-, pedo- Child (e.g., *pediatrics*).

penta-, pente-, pent- Five (e.g., *pentagon*).

per-, pel- Through (e.g., *pellucid*); thoroughly; by; for (e.g., *percent*).

peri- round; about, enclosing (e.g., *perimeter*).

petr-, petri-, petro- stone (e.g., *petroglyph*); petroleum.

phago- Eating (e.g., *phagocytosis*).

phleb-, phlebo- Vein (e.g., *phlebotomy*).

phon-, phono- Sound, speech (e.g., *phonetics*).

phot-, photo- Light; photograph (e.g., *photorealism*).

phren-, phreno- Brain (e.g., *phrenology*); diaphragm.

phyll-, phyllo- Leaf (e.g., *phylloclade*).

picr-, picro- Bitter (e.g., *picrotoxin*).

piezo- Pressure (e.g., *piezoelectrical*).

pisci- Fish (e.g., *piscivorous*).

plan-, plano- Flat (e.g., *planoconvex*); moving.

pleur-, pleuro- Side of body, lateral (e.g., *pleurodont*).

pluto- Wealth (e.g., *plutocracy*).

pluvio- Rain (e.g., *pluviose*).

pneum-, pneumo-, pneumat-, pneumato- Respiration, lungs (e.g., *pneumonia*); air, gas, breath, vapor.

poly- Many (e.g., *polysyllabic*); excessive.

post- later, afterward (e.g., *postprandial*); behind, following (e.g., *postorbital*).

pre-, prae- Before, earlier, in advance, preparatory (e.g., *predawn*); priority.

preter- Beyond, more than (e.g., *preternatural*).

primi-, prim- First (e.g., *primogeniture*).

pro- Taking the place of, favoring, on the side of (e.g., *prorebel*); front, forward, forth (e.g., *proactive*); before, earlier.

pros- to, towards, near (e.g., *prospect*); in front of.

prot-, proto- First, original (e.g., *protozoa*); lowest.

pseud-, pseudo- False, spurious (e.g., *pseudonym*).

psycho-, psycho- Mental; mind, spirit, soul (e.g., *psychotherapy*).

ptero- Wing (e.g., *pterosaur*).

pulmo- Lung (e.g., *pulmonic*).

pur- For, on the side of; front, forward, forth (e.g., *pursue*); before, earlier (e.g., *purvey*).

pyr-, pyro- Fire, heat (e.g., *pyrotechnics*).

quadri-, quadr-, quadru- Four (e.g., *quadruped*).

quinque- Five (e.g., *quinquennium*).

re- Again, back; anew, a second time (e.g., *rebirth*).

recti- Straight (e.g., *rectilinear*).

retro- Backward, back (e.g., *retrofit*).

rheo- Flow (e.g., *rheotaxis*).

rhin-, rhino- Nose (e.g., *rhinitis*).

rhiz-, rhizo- Root (e.g., *rhizomorph*).

racchar-, sacchari-, sacchro- Sugar.

sacr-, sacro- Pelvic; above tailbone (e.g., *sacroiliac*).

sangui- Blood (e.g., *sanguineous*).

sapr-, sapro- Dead, rotten; decaying (e.g., *saprozoic*).

sarc-, sarco- Flesh, muscle (e.g., *sarcophagus*).

schisto-, shiz-, schizo- Split (e.g., *schizophrenic*).

sclero- Hard (e.g., *scleroderma*).

se- Aside, apart; separating (e.g., *sedition*).

seba-, sebo- Fatty (e.g., *sebaceous*).

selen-, seleno- Moon (e.g., *selenography*).

semi- Half; in part, incomplete (e.g., *semicooked*).

septi- Seven (e.g., *septilateral*).

sero- Serum, blood (e.g., *serotonin*).

sex-, sexi- Six (e.g., *sextan*).

sider-, sidero- Star (e.g., *sidereal*); iron.

sine- Without (e.g., *sinecure*).

somat-, somato- Body (e.g., *somato type*).

somn- Sleep (e.g., *somnolence*).

sperm-, spermo-, sperma-, spermi-, spermat-, spermato- Seed (e.g., *spermicide*).

spiro- Breath (e.g., *spirograph*).

stato- Resting position, equilibrium (e.g., *statoblast*).

stell- Star (e.g., *stellar*).

sten-, steno- Short, narrow, close (e.g., *stenothermal*).

stere-, stereo- Solid; multidimensional (e.g., *stereophonic*).

stom-, stomo- Mouth (e.g., *stomodeum*).

styl-, styli-, stylo- Style.

styl-, stylo- Pillar.

sub- Below, beneath (e.g., *subterranean*); less, nearly, almost (e.g., *substandard*); secondary (e.g., *subplot*).

subter- Beneath, under (e.g., *subterfuge*).

suc- Below, beneath (e.g., *succor*); less, nearly, almost; secondary.

suf- Below, beneath (e.g., *suffix*); less, nearly, almost; secondary (e.g., *suffice*).

sug- Below, beneath (e.g., *suggest*); less, nearly, almost; secondary.

sup- Below, beneath (e.g., *supplant*); less, nearly, almost; secondary.

super-, supra-, sur- Above, over, higher, in excess (e.g., *surcharge*); very special, superior.

sus- Below, beneath, less, nearly, almost secondary (e.g., *suspire*).

sy-, syl-, sym-, syn- With, together, at the same time (e.g., *synchronized*).

tachy- Rapid (e.g., *tachycardia*).

taut-, tauto- Same (e.g., *tautology*).

tele-, tel-, telo- Distant; electronic communication (e.g., *teletype*).

teleo- Final, purpose (e.g., *teleology*).

terra- Land, earth (e.g., *terrarium*).

the-, theo- God (e.g., *theologian*).

therm-, thermo- Heat (e.g., *thermostat*).

thromb-, thrombo- Blood clot (e.g., *thromboembolism*).

topo- Place, point (e.g., *topography*).

tox-, toxi-, toxo- Poison (e.g., *toxin*).

trache-, tracheo- Windpipe (e.g., *tracheotomy*).

trans-, tra- Through; across, over, beyond, on the far side (e.g., *transcontinental*); from one place to another; change (e.g., *transform*).

tri-, tris- Three (e.g., *trio*).

ultra- Beyond; on the other side; extreme (e.g., *ultraconservative*).

un- Used to form verbs indicating to do the opposite or reverse; to release, remove (e.g., *unfasten*).

un- Used to form adjectives with the meaning of not; the opposite of (e.g., *unavailable*, *unelectable*).

undec- Eleven.

under- Lower, beneath (e.g., *underline*); too little (e.g., *undercooked*).

uni- One, single (e.g., *unilateral*).

up- Aloft, on high, upward (e.g., *upstairs*).

uter-, utero- Uterus, womb (e.g., *uterine*).

vari-, vario- Different, diverse (e.g., *variegated*).

vas-, vaso- Blood vessel (e.g., *vasodilation*).

ventr-, ventro- Abdominal, belly (e.g., *ventriculus*).

vice- Assisting, substituting, deputy (e.g., *vice-president*).

with- From, opposing (e.g., *withhold*).

xen-, xeno- Foreign, strange (e.g., *xenophobic*).

zo-, zoo- Living, animal (e.g., *zoophile*).

zyg-, zygo- Double, pair, union (e.g., *zygodactyl*); egg yolk.

zym-, zymo- Enzyme, fermentation (e.g., *zymurgy*).

SUFFIXES

-able Used to form adjectives meaning able to, fit to, worthy, or capable; apt to (e.g., *reasonable*).

-ac One affected with (e.g., *insomniac*).

-aceae Families of plants (e.g., *Rosaceae*).

-aceous, -ous Having resemblance to a substance; full of (e.g., *sebaceous*).

-acy Used to form nouns meaning state, condition, or quality of being (e.g., *literacy*); result.

-ade Product; action (e.g., *blockade*).

-age Place of; house (e.g., *parsonage*).

-age Used to form nouns meaning state, condition, or quality of being (e.g., *dotage*); nouns meaning an act of (e.g., *brokerage*); nouns indicating persons or things collectively; measure of (e.g., *poundage*); collection of, rate of, charge (e.g., *postage*).

-al Action or result of the verb stem (e.g., *denial*).

-al Like, of, or pertaining to (e.g., *chromosomal*); characterized by.

-algia Pain.

-an, -ean, -ian Adherent to; citizen of; language of; relating to, characteristic of; one who acts; one who is.

-ana, -iana A collection.

-ance, -ancy A state or quality of being; action, process; degree.

-androus Man.

-ant, -ent Used to form adjectives meaning being, belonging to;

performing. Used to form nouns indicating one who acts; one who is.

-ar Like, of, or pertaining to; characterized by (e.g., *titular*, *molecular*).

-ar, -ard, -art Used to form nouns indicating one who acts, one who is (e.g., *liar*, *braggart*).

-archy Government (e.g., *monarchy*).

-ary Related, connected, or pertaining to; characterized by (e.g., *parliamentary*); also used to form nouns indicating one who acts, one who is (e.g., *functionary*), a thing which.

-asm Used to form nouns meaning state, condition, or quality of being; result.

-aster Used to form nouns indicating one who acts; one who is.

-ate Used to form adjectives meaning full of, abundant; having (e.g., *sensate*).

-ate Used to form nouns indicating rank, office, jurisdiction, or dominion (e.g., *doctorate*); indicating one who acts, one who is.

-ate Used to form verbs meaning to make (e.g., *salivate*); to put; to take; to cause.

-ation Process, action (e.g., *liberation*); state of.

-ative Related to, connected to, or tending to (e.g., *demonstrative*).

-biosis Life (e.g., *symbiosis*).

-blast Bud, germ, cell.

-carpous Fruit.

-cele Hollow, tumor.

-celli, -cello Little.

-cephalic, -cephalous Head.

-chrome Color, colored (e.g., *monochrome*).

-cide, -cidal Kill, killing (e.g., *fratricide*).

-cle Used to form nouns indicating little, diminutive (e.g., *particle*).

-coccus Berry-shaped.

-coele, -coel Cavity.

-cracy *or* **-ocracy; -crat** *or* **-ocrat** Government, rule; ruler.

-cule Used to form nouns indicating little, diminutive.

-dendron Tree.

-derm, -derma, -dermo Skin, covering.

-dom Domain, office, jurisdiction, or rank (e.g., *dukedom*).

-dom Used to form nouns meaning state, condition, or quality of being (e.g., *freedom*); result.

-drome Large place (e.g., *airdrome*); racing place.

-dromous Running.

-eae Names of suborders in botany.

-ed Used to form adjectives from nouns to indicate having (e.g., *antennaed*).

-ed Past, past participle of regular verbs

-ee One who is object of the verb (e.g., *payee*); one who is (e.g., *trainee*).

-ee A small version of the stem word (e.g., *bootee*); something suggestive of the stem word (e.g., *goatee*).

-eer One skilled, engaged in (e.g., *auctioneer*).

-el Used to form nouns indicating little, diminutive.

-emia, -aemia, -hemia, -haemia Blood.

-en Used to form verbs meaning to cause to, to become, to make (e.g., *Waken*).

-en Used to form adjectives meaning made of or belonging to (e.g., *earthen*).

-en Plural form of some nouns (e.g., *oxen*).

-ence, -ency Used to form nouns indicating state, condition, or quality of being (e.g., *despondence*); result.

-ene Belonging to; carbon-related.

-er Comparative form of adjective (e.g., *higher*).

-er Inhabitant of, native (e.g., *New Yorker, easterner*).

-er, -or Producer, agent; one that acts or is (e.g., *teacher*).

-erel Little (e.g., *cockerel*).

-erly Used to form adverbs indicating direction (e.g., *easterly*).

-ern Use to form adjectives indicating direction (e.g., *Western*).

-ery Condition or behavior of (e.g., *bribery*); location of (e.g., *eatery*); aggregate.

-escence Used to form nouns indicating incipient state, beginning.

-escent Used to form adjectives indicating growing, becoming; reflecting light.

-ese Forms noun indicating member, native, style, language of (e.g., *computerese*); forms adjectives indicating origin in the place designated by the stem (e.g., *Japanese*).

-esque Used to form adjectives meaning belonging to; like, having the properties, manner of (e.g., *Daliesque*).

-ess Used to feminize a noun (e.g., *lioness*).

-est Superlative form of adjective (e.g., *highest*); second-person singular present of some irregular verbs.

-et Used to form nouns indicating diminution (e.g., *spinneret*).

-eth Third person singular of some irregular verbs.

-ette Compact (e.g., *Kitchenette*); imitation; feminine; diminutive.

-fid Split.

-fuge, -fugal making flee, run away from.

-ful Holding all it can, full of; amount that fill (e.g., *spoonful*).

-ful Providing (e.g., *healthful*); characterized by; tending to (e.g., *spiteful*).

-gamy Marriage; possession.

-gen, -genous, -geny, -gony Bearing, producing, giving birth; producer

-gnomy, -gnosis Knowledge.

-gon angled (e.g., *tetragon*).

-fy Used to form verbs indicating a making or forming into (e.g., *fancify*).

-gonium Seed.

-grade Indicates progression or movement (e.g., *retrograde*).

-gram, -graph, -graphy Writing (e.g., *monograph*); record.

-hedral, -hedron Side, many-sided (e.g., *polyhedron*).

-hood Period of a condition, state (e.g., *babyhood*); membership.

-ia Things belonging to; territory.

-ia, -iasis Disease (e.g., *neuralgia, psoriasis*).

-ia, -ious Class, order, or genus of plants and animals.

-iatrics, -iatry Medical treatment (e.g., *pediatrics*).

-ible, Used to form adjectives meaning able to, fit to, worthy, or capable; apt to (e.g., *sensible*).

-ic One having the nature of (e.g., *psychic*); producer.

-ic Used to form adjectives meaning having the properties of, related, in the manner of (e.g., *Hellenic, organic*); using (e.g., *analgesic*); affected with (e.g., *arthritic*).

-ical Like, of, pertaining to; characterized by (e.g., *paradoxical*).

-ics A thing relating to a system, practice, art, science (e.g., *athletics, poetics*).

-idae, -adae, -ides Descendent.

-ide; *pl.*, -ides Chemical combination.

-ie Used to form nouns in the diminutive.

-iff Used to form nouns meaning one who acts, one who is (e.g., *bailiff*).

-ify, -fy Used to form verbs meaning to make or make similar to (e.g., *falsify, liquify*).

-ile Used to form adjectives meaning like, pertaining to, able to, fit to, worthy, or capable; apt to (e.g., *servile*); characterized by (e.g., *infantile*

-ine Chemical compound.

-ine Like, made of, pertaining to; characterized by (e.g., *saturnine*).

-ing Present participle ending of regular verbs.

-ing Something made of such

material (e.g., *blanketing*); activity or process; noun referring to verb (e.g., *feeding*).

-ious Having the properties of; full of (e.g., *furious*).

-ish Used to form adjectives meaning somewhat like, becoming (e.g., *childish, countryish*); relating to, person of, language of (e.g., *Spanish*).

-isk Little.

-ism Practice of; doctrine of, theory (e.g., *feminism*); act, process (e.g., *heroism*); state, condition, quality of being.

-ist One skilled in, a specialist; practicing (e.g., *communist*), believer; one who acts; one who is.

-ite One who acts or is; adherent, member, inhabitant (e.g., *Manhattanite*); that which.

-ite Stone, mineral.

-itious Having the characteristic of (e.g., *superstitious*).

-itis Inflammation of an organ, disease (e.g., *phlebitis*); excessive enthusiasm (e.g., *travel-itis*).

-ity State, condition, quality of being (e.g., *anxiety, captivity*); degree.

-ive Able to do, capable; doing, tending (e.g., *disruptive*); one who acts or is.

-ization Action, result of making (e.g., *feminization*).

-ize, -ise Used to form verbs meaning to make (e.g., *sanitize*), to subject to (e.g., *brutalize*); cause to be, be like; become, adopt manner (e.g., *Europeanize*).

-kin Littleness (e.g., *catkin*).

-kind Of one type or race (e.g., *humankind*).

-kinesis Division; movement (e.g., *telekinesis*).

-lepsy Seizure, fit (e.g., *epilepsy*).

-less Without, deprived (e.g., *odorless*); unable.

-let Small, unimportant; thing worn as described by the stem word (e.g., *anklet*).

-like Like, resembling (e.g., *catlike*).

-ling Minor, smaller, offspring, one having quality of (e.g., *duckling, yearling*).

-lite, -lith Stone, mineral.

-logy Science of, study of, theory (e.g., *zoology*); list.

-ly In a manner of, having the qualities of, like (e.g., *lovingly*); to a degree (e.g., *overly*).

-ly Recurring regularly (e.g., *weekly*).

-lysis, -lyte Dissolving; disintegration.

-mancy, -mantic Foretelling, divination (e.g., *necromancy*).

-mania, -maniac Craving (e.g., *pyromania*).

-ment Used to form nouns indicating state, condition, quality of being (e.g., *confinement*); a result; an act of (e.g., *statement*); a thing done, a process (e.g., *appeasement*).

-mere, -merous Part (e.g., *blastomere*).

-meter Measuring instrument (e.g., *odometer*).

-metry Measuring (e.g., *geometry*).

-mony Used to form nouns indicating state, condition, or quality of being (e.g., *matrimony*).

-morphic, -morphous Shape (e.g., *geomorphic, amorphous*).

-most Superlative form of adjective (e.g., *topmost*).

-mycete Fungus.

-ness Used to form nouns indicating state, condition, or quality of being (e.g., *stubbornness*).

-nomy Science of, law of (e.g., *taxonomy*).

-ock Used to form nouns indicating smallness (e.g., *hillock*).

-odont A tooth of certain nature (e.g., *acrodont*).

-odynia Pain.

-oecium, -oecious Botanical suffixes relating to flowers' stamens and pistils.

-oid Like, resembling (e.g., *humanoid*).

-oma Tumor (e.g., *lymphoma*).

-on Unit, particle (e.g., *micron*).

-on, -one, -oon Used to form nouns, indicating largeness.

-opia Eye, sight condition (e.g., *myopia*).

-opsia Sight.

-opsis Appearance; thing resembling.

-or, -er Used to form nouns meaning producer, agent; one who acts; one who is (e.g., *communicator, operator*).

-ory Like, of, or pertaining to; characterized by (e.g., *sensory*); a place where; a thing which.

-ose Used to form adjectives indicating full of, abundant; having.

-ot Used to form nouns indicating little, diminutive.

-ous An acid compound with less

oxygen than an acid compound ending -*ic*.

-ous Having the properties of; full of (e.g., *odorous*).

-pathy Suffering, disease; type of medical treatment (e.g., *homeopathy*).

-phage, -phagous, -phagia, -phagy Eating, eater (e.g., *dysphagia*).

-phobe One fearing (e.g., *agoraphobe*).

-phobia fear of (e.g., *homophobia*).

-phobic Fearing; lacking affinity for (e.g., *xenophobic*).

-phone, -phony Sound, transmitting sound.

-phonia Speech disorder.

-phyllous Leafed, leaflike.

-phyte Plant; diseased growth (e.g., *thallophyte*).

-plasia, -plasy, -plasis Growth, formation (e.g., *dysplasia*).

-plasm Formed matter (e.g., *ectoplasm*).

-plast Cell.

-plegia Paralysis (e.g., *paraplegia*).

-ric Used to form nouns indicating rank, office, jurisdicition, or dominion (e.g., *bishopric*).

-rrhagia, -rrhagic, -rrhea Flow (e.g., *diarrhea*).

-ry Used to form nouns meaning state, condition, or quality of being (e.g., *savagery*); nouns indicating persons or things collectively (e.g., *citizenry*); measure of; collection of (e.g., *jewelry*).

-saur Lizard (e.g., *brontosaur*).

-scope, -scopy Observation; observing instrument (e.g., *periscope*).

-sect, -section Cut, divide (e.g., *bisect*); divided.

-ship State or condition of; rank, position; skill (e.g., *penmanship*); group participating in (e.g., *citizenship*).

-sion Used to form nouns meaning an act of (e.g., *cohesion*); a thing done, a process.

-soma, -some Body.

-some Used to form adjectives meaning full of, abundant; being or tending to be (e.g., *troublesmone*).

-sophy Wisdom, knowledge (e.g., *philosophy*).

-sperm, -spermous Seed.

-ster One who is involved in; one that is (e.g., *trickster*).

-stichous In a row.

-stome, -stomous Mouth.

-taxis, -taxy Order (e.g., *phyllotaxy*).

-teen Ten, to be added to (e.g., *nineteen*).

-th State, condition (e.g., *heighth*).

-tion Used to form nouns meaning an act of (e.g., *absolution*); a thing done, a process.

-tomy Cutting; section (e.g., *lumpectomy*).

-trophy Used to form nouns relating to type of nutrition (e.g., *ectotrophy*); growth.

-tropic Changing (e.g., *psychotropic*); attracted to.

-tropous Turned, curving (e.g., *amphitropous*).

-tropy Turning (e.g., *allotropy*).

-tude Used to form nouns indicating state, condition, or quality of being (e.g., *servitude*).

-ty   quality, degree; condition (e.g., *certainty*).

-ty   Ten, to be multiplied by (e.g., *ninety*).

-ule   Used to form nouns indicating smallness (e.g., *pustule*).

-ure   Used to form nouns indicating state, condition, or quality of being (e.g., *failure*); an act of (e.g., *erasure*); or

-vorous   Eating (e.g., *omnivorous*).

-ward, -wards   In the direction of (e.g., *skyward*)

-ways, -wise   In the manner of, in the direction of; way of being or acting.

-y, -ey   Full of, somewhat like, characterized by, tending toward (e.g., *snarly*).

-y   State, condition (e.g., *sleepy*); activity; group.

-y   Used to make a noun diminutive (e.g., *horsey*).

-yte   Used to form nouns indicating one who acts, one who is (e.g., *neophyte*).

3. ANIMALS

GROUP AND YOUNG NAMES

ant   colony

antelope   herd; calf

ape   shrewdness

ass   pace

badger   cete

bear   sleuth, sloth; cub, whelp

beaver   colony; kit, kitten, pup

bee   colony, grist, swarm

bird   dissimulation, flight, volery; fledgling, nestling

bison   herd, troop; calf

boar   singular, sounder

bovine   herd; calf

cat   clowder, clutter; kit, kitten, kitty, puss, pussy

caterpillar   army

cattle   herd, drove; calf, yearling

chicken   brood, clutch, flock, peep; chick, pullet, cockerel

clam   bed

cow   herd; calf, heifer

crane   sedge, siege

crow   murder

deer   herd; fawn

dog   kennel, pack; pup, whelp

duck   brace, flock, gaggle, paddling, team; duckling

eagle   eaglet, fledgling

elephant   herd, host; calf

elk   herd, gang; calf

falcon   passager; cast

fish   school, shoal; fingerling, fry

fox   leash, skulk; cub, kit, pup, whelp

frog   knot; polliwog, tadpole

giraffe   herd; cub, whelp

gnat   cloud, horde

goat   tribe, trip; kid

goldfinch   charm

goose   flock, gaggle, skein; gosling

gorilla   band

grouse   covey; cheeper, poult

hare   down, husk; leveret

hawk   cast; eyas

hen   brood; chick, pullet

heron   siege

hippopotamus   calf

hog   drift

horse   harras, herd, pair, stable, team; colt, filly, filt, foal, yearling

hound   cry, mute, pack

kangaroo   mob, troop; joey

kitten   kindle, kendle, litter

lark   ascension, exaltation

leopard   leap

lion pride; cub, whelp
locust host, plague
mallard sort
marten richness
mole labor
monkey troop; baby
moose cub, calf
mule barren, pack, span
nightingale watch
owl parliament; owlet
oxen yoke
oyster bed; spat
partridge covey; cheeper
peacock muster
pheasant bouquet, nest, nide, nye
pig drove, litter; piglet, shoat,
    farrow, suckling
pigeon flock; squab, squeaker
plover congregation, wing
pony string
porpoise school
quail bevy, covey; cheeper
rabbit colony, nest; bunny, kit,
    leveret
reindeer herd; fawn
rhinoceros crash; calf
rooster cockerel
seal pod, herd, school, trip harem,
    rookery; calf, pup
sea lion pup
shark cub
sheep drove, flock, herd; lamb,
    lambkin, cosset, hog, yearling
sparrow host
squirrel dray
starling murmuration
stork mustering
swan bevy; cygnet
swine drift, sounder; piglet, shoat,
    farrow
tiger cub, whelp
toad knot
turkey rafter; poult, chick

turtle bale, bevy
whale gam, herd, pod, shoal; calf
wolf pack, rout; cub, whelp
woodpecker descent
wolf pack; cub, whelp
zebra herd; colt, foal

4. MONTHS AND DAYS

April   Apr. or Ap
August   Aug. or Ag
December   Dec. or D
February   Feb. or F
Friday   Fri. or F
January   Jan. or Ja
July   July or Jl
June   June or Je
March   Mar. or Mr
May   May or My
Monday   Mon. or M
November   Nov. or N
October   Oct. or O
Saturday   Sat. or Sa
September   Sept. or S
Sunday   Sun. or Su
Thursday   Thurs. or Th or R
Tuesday   Tues. or Tu
Wednesday   Wed. or W

5. NATIONS OF THE WORLD

WITH CAPITAL,
RESIDENT NAME

Afghanistan   Kabul, Afghan
Albania   Tirana, Albanian
Algeria   Algiers/El Djazair,
    Algerian
Andorra   Andorra la Vella,
    Andorran

Angola Luanda, Angolan
Antigua and Barbuda St. John's, Antiguan
Argentina Buenos Aires, Argentine
Armenia Yerevan, Armenian
Australia Canberra, Australian
Austria Vienna, Austrian
Azerbaijan Baku, Azerbaijani
Bahamas Nassau, Bahamian
Bahrain Manama, Bahraini
Bangladesh Dhaka, Bangladeshi
Barbados Bridgetown, Barbadian
Belgium Brussels, Belgian
Belize Belmopan, Belizean
Benin Porto-Novo, Beninese
Bhutan Thimphu/Paro Dzong, Bhutanese
Bolivia Sucre/La Paz, Bolivian
Bosnia and
   Herzegovina Sarajevo, Bosnian
Botswana Gaborone, Motswana (singular)/Botswana (plural), President, National Assembly
Brazil Brasilia, Brazilian
Brunei Darussalam Bandar Seri Begawan, Bruneian
Bulgaria Sofia, Bulgarian
Burkina Faso Ouagadougou
Burundi Bujumbura, Burundian
Byelorussia Minsk, Byelorussian
Cambodia Phnom Penh, Cambodian/Khmer
Cameroon Yaounde, Cameroonian
Canada Ottawa, Canadian/Canadien
Cape Verde Praia, Cape Verdean
Central African Republic Bangui, Central African
Chad N'Djamena, Chadian
Chile Santiago, Chilean
China Beijing, Chinese
Colombia Bogotá, Colombian

Comoros Moroni, Comoran
Congo Brazzaville, Congolese
Costa Rica San Jose, Costa Rican
Côte d'Ivoire (Ivory
   Coast) Abidjan/Yamoussoukro, Ivorian
Croatia Zagreb, Croatian
Cuba Havana, Cuban
Cyprus Nicosia, Cypriot
Czechoslovakia Prague, Czechoslovak/Czech
Denmark Copenhagen, Dane
Djibouti Djibouti, Afar/Issa
Dominica Roseau, Dominican
Dominican Republic Santo Domingo, Dominican
Ecuador Quito, Ecuadorean
Egypt Cairo, Egyptian
El Salvador San Salvador, Salvadoran
Equatorial Guinea Malabo, Equatorial Guinean
Estonia Tallinn, Estonian
Ethiopia Addis Ababa, Ethiopian
Fiji Suva, Fijian
Finland Helsinki, Finn
France Paris, Frenchman, President
Gabon Libreville, Gabonese
Gambia Banjul, Gambian
Georgia Tbilisi, Georgian
Germany Bonn, German
Ghana Accra, Ghanaian
Greece Athens, Greek
Grenada St. George's, Grenadian
Guatemala Guatemala City, Guatemalan
Guinea Conakry, Guinean
Guinea-Bissau Bissau, Guinean
Guyana Georgetown, Guyanese
Haiti Port-au-Prince, Haitian
Honduras Tegucigalpa, Honduran
Hungary Budapest, Hungarian

Iceland   Reykjavík, Icelander
India   New Delhi, Indian
Indonesia   Jakarta, Indonesian
Iran   Teheran, Iranian
Iraq   Baghdad, Iraqi
Ireland   Dublin, Irishman
Israel   Jerusalem, Israeli
Italy   Rome, Italian
Jamaica   Kingston, Jamaican
Japan   Toyko, Japanese
Jordan   Amman, Jordanian
Kazakhstan   Alma-Ata, Kazakh
Kenya   Nairobi, Kenyan
Kirgizia   Pishpek, Kirgizian
Kiribati   Tarawa, Kiribatian
Kuwait   Kuwait, Kuwaiti
Laos   Vientiane, Laotian
Latvia   Riga, Latvian
Lebanon   Beirut, Lebanese
Lesotho   Maseru, Masotho
   (singular)/Basotho (plural)
Liberia   Monrovia, Liberian
Libya   Tripoli, Libyan
Liechtenstein   Vaduz,
   Liechtensteiner
Lithuania   Vilnius, Lithuanian
Luxembourg   Luxembourg,
   Luxembourger
Macedonia   Skopje, Macedonian
Madagascar   Antananarivo,
   Malagasy
Malawi   Lilongwe, Malawian
Malaysia   Kuala Lumpur,
   Malaysian
Maldives   Malé, Maldivian
Mali   Bamako, Malian
Malta   Valetta, Maltese
Marshall Islands   Majuro,
   Marshall Islander
Mauritania   Nouakchott,
   Mauritanian
Mauritius   Port Louis, Mauritian
Mexico   Mexico City, Mexican

Micronesia   Kolonia, Micronesian
Moldavia   Kishinyov, Moldavian
Monaco   Monaco-Ville, Monacan/
   Monégasque
Mongolia   Ulaanbaatar, Mongolian
Montenegro   Titograd,
   Montenegran
Morocco   Rabat, Moroccan
Mozambique   Maputo,
   Mozambican
Myanmar   Yangon, Burmese
Namibia   Windhoek, Namibian
Nauru   Yaren, Nauruan
Nepal   Kathmandu, Nepalese
Netherlands   Amsterdam,
   Netherlander
New Zealand   Wellington, New
   Zealander
Nicaragua   Managua, Nicaraguan
Niger   Niamey, Nigerois
Nigeria   Lagos, Nigeria
North Korea   P'yongyang, North
   Korean
Norway   Oslo, Norwegian
Oman   Muscat, Omani
Pakistan   Islamabad, Pakistani
Panama   Panama City, Panamanian
Papua New Guinea   Port Moresby,
   Papua New Guinean
Paraguay   Asunción, Paraguayan
Peru   Lima, Peruvian
Philippines   Quezon City/Manila,
   Filipino
Poland   Warsaw, Pole
Portugal   Lisbon, Portuguese
Qatar   Doha, Qatari
Romania   Bucharest, Romanian
Russia   Moscow, Russian
Rwanda   Kigali, Rwandan
Saint Kitts and Nevis   Basseterre,
   Kittsian/Nevisian
Saint Lucia   Castries, Saint Lucian
Saint Vincent and the

Grenadines Kingstown, Saint
Vincentian/Vincentian
San Marino San Marino,
Sanmarinese
São Tomé and Príncipe São
Tomé, São Toméan
Saudi Arabia Riyadh, Saudi
Senegal Dakar, Senegalese
Serbia Belgrade, Serbian
Seychelles Victoria, Setchellois
Sierra Leone Freetown, Sierra
Leonean
Singapore Singapore, Singaporean
Slovenia Ljubljana, Slovenian
Solomon Islands Honiara,
Solomon Islander
Somalia Mogadishu, Somali
South Africa Pretoria/Cape Town/
Bloemfontein, South African
South Korea Seoul, South Korean
Spain Madrid, Spaniard
Sri Lanka Colombo, Sri Lankan
Sudan Khartoum, Sudanese
Suriname Paramaribo, Surinamer
Swaziland Mbabane, Swazi
Sweden Stockholm, Swede
Switzerland Bern, Swiss
Syria Damascus, Syrian
Tadzhikistan Dushanbe, Tadzhik
Taiwan Taipei, Chinese
Tanzania Dar es Salaam,
Tanzanian
Thailand Bangkok, Thai
Togo Lomé, Togolese
Tonga Nuku'alofa, Tongan
Trinidad and Tobago Port-of-
Spain, Trinidadian/Tobagan
Tunisia Tunis, Tunisian
Turkey Ankara, Turk
Turkmenistan Ashkhabad,
Turkman
Uzbekistan Tashkent, Uzbekis
Ukraine Kiev, Ukrainian

Tuvalu Funafuti, Tuvaluan
Uganda Kampala, Ugandan
United Arab Emirates Abu
Dhabi, Emirian
**United Kingdom of Great Britain
and Northern Ireland** London,
Briton (singular)/British (plural)
**United States of
America** Washington, D.C.,
American
Uruguay Montevideo, Uruguayan
Vanuatu Port Vila, Vanuatuan
Vatican City Vatican City
Venezuela Caracas, Venezuelan
Vietnam Hanoi, Vietnamese
Western Samoa Apia, Western
Samoan
Yemen San'a', Yemeni
Yugoslavia See entries for former
republics.
Zaire Kinshasa, Zairian
Zambia Lusaka, Zambian
Zimbabwe Harare, Zimbabwean

6. OFFICIAL FORMS OF ADDRESS

LETTER ADDRESS, LETTER GREETING, FORMAL INTRODUCTION

Ambassador The Honorable —;
Dear M——. Ambassador; The
American Ambassador
Associate Justice M——.;
Justice —; M——. Justice —
baron/baroness The Right
Honorable Lord/Lady —;
My Lord/Madam *or* Dear Lord/
Lady —; Lord/Lady —
baronet Sir —, Bt.; Dear Sir *or*
Dear Sir —; Sir —

bishop/archbishop The Most Reverend —, Bishop/Archbishop of —; Your Excellency *or* Dear Bishop/Archbishop —; His Excellency *or* Bishop/Archbishop —

Brother Brother —; Dear Brother — *or* Dear Brother; Brother —

cabinet members The Honorable — *or* The Secretary of —; Dear M—. Secretary; The Secretary of —

cardinal His Eminence, —, Archbishop of —; Your Eminence *or* Dear Cardinal —; His Eminence, Cardinal —

Chief Justice The Chief Justice; Dear Mr./Madam Justice *or* Dear Mr. Chief Justice; The Chief Justice

Consul-General The Honorable —; Dear M—. —; M—. —

countess The Right Honorable the Countess of —; Madam *or* Dear Lady —; Lady —

duke/duchess His/Her Grace, the D— of —; My Lord Duke/Madam *or* Dear D— of; His/Her Grace, the D— of —

earl The Right Honorable the Earl of —; My Lord *or* Dear Lord —; Lord —

Episcopal bishop The Right Reverend —; Dear Bishop —; The Right Reverend —, Bishop of —

foreign ambassador His/Her Excellency —; Excellency *or* Dear M—. Ambassador; The Ambassador of —

former President The Honorable —; Dear Mr. —; The Honorable —

governor The Honorable —; Dear M—. —; M—. —

judge The Honorable —; Dear Judge —; The Honorable — *or* M—. Justice — *or* Judge —

king or queen His/Her Majesty King/Queen —

knight Sir —; Dear Sir *or* Dear Sir —; Sir —

Lady Dear Madam *or* Dear Lady —; Lady —

marquess/marchioness The Most Honorable the M— of —; My Lord/Madam *or* Dear Lord/Lady —; Lord/Lady —

mayor The Honorable —; Dear Mayor —; Mayor — *or* The Mayor

military personnel ''full title''; Dear Admiral/Chief/Colonel/Commander/General/Lieutenant/Private/Sail or/Sergeant/Soldier —; ''full title''

monsignor The Right Reverend Monsignor —; Right Reverend Monsignor *or* Dear Monsignor —; Monsignor —

Pope His Holiness, the Pope *or* His Holiness, Pope —; Your Holiness *or* Most Holy Father; His Holiness *or* the Holy Father *or* the Pope *or* the Pontiff

President of the United States The President; Dear Mr. President; The President *or* The President of the United States

priest The Reverend —; Reverend Father *or* Dear Father —; Father —

protestant minister The Reverend —; Dear Dr./M—. —; The Reverend/Dr. —

rabbi Rabbi —; Dear Rabbi/Dr. —; Rabbi/Dr. —

royalty His/Her Royal Highness, the —/— of —; Your Royal Highness; His/Her Royal Highness, the —/— of —

Secretary-General of the United Nations His/Her Excellency —; Dear M—. Secretary-General; The Secretary-General of the United Nations

Sister Sister —; Dear Sister — *or* Dear Sister; Sister —

Speaker of the House The Honorable —; Dear M—. Speaker; The Speaker of the House of Representatives

state legislator The Honorable —; Dear M—. —; M—. —

United Nations representative The Honorable —; Dear M—. Ambassador; The United States Representative to the United Nations

United States Representative The Honorable —; Dear M—. —; Representative — of —

United States Senator The Honorable —; Dear Senator —; Senator — from —

Vice President The Vice President; Dear Mr. Vice President; The Vice President *or* the Vice President of the United States

viscount/viscountess The Right Honorable the V— —; My Lord/Lady *or* Dear Lord/Lady —; Lord/Lady —

7. STATES AND TERRITORIES INFORMATION

STANDARD AND TWO-LETTER POSTAL ABBREVIATIONS, CAPITAL, RESIDENT NAME

Alabama Ala., AL, Montgomery, Alabamian

Alaska Alaska, AK, Juneau, Alaskan

American Samoa Amer. Samoa, AS, Pago Pago, Samoan

Arizona Ariz., AZ, Phoenix, Arizonan

Arkansas Ark, AR, Little Rock, Arkansan

California Calif., or Cal., CA, Sacramento, Californian

Canal Zone CZ

Colorado Colo., CO, Denver, Coloradan

Connecticut Conn., CT, Hartford, Connecticuter

Delaware Del., DE, Dover, Delawarean

District of Columbia D.C., DC, Washington

Florida Fla., FL, Tallahassee, Floridian

Georgia Ga., GA, Atlanta, Georgian

Guam GU

Hawaii HI, Honolulu, Hawaiian

Idaho Id., ID, Boise, Idahoan

Illinois Ill., IL, Springfield, Illinoisan

Indiana Ind., IN, Indianapolis, Indianian

Iowa Ia., IA, Des Moines, Iowan

Kansas Kans., KS, Topeka, Kansan

Kentucky Ky., KY, Frankfort, Kentuckian

Louisiana La., LA, Baton Rouge, Louisianian

Maine Me., ME, Augusta, Mainer

Maryland Md., MD, Annapolis, Marylander

Massachusetts Mass., MA, Boston, Massachusettsan

Michigan Mich., MI, Lansing, Michiganite

Minnesota Minn., MN, St. Paul, Minnesotan

Mississippi Miss., MS, Jackson, Mississippian

Missouri Mo., MO, Jefferson City, Missourian

Montana Mont., MT, Helena, Montanan

Nebraska Nebr., NE, Lincoln, Nebraskan

Nevada Nev., NV, Carson City, Nevadan

New Hampshire N.H., NH, Concord, New Hampshirite

New Jersey N.J., NJ, Trenton, New Jerseyite

New Mexico N. Mex., NM, Santa Fe, New Mexican

New York N.Y., NY, Albany, New Yorker

North Carolina N.C., NC, Raleigh, North Carolinian

North Dakota N.Dak., ND, Bismarck, North Dakotan

Northern Mariana Is CM

Ohio OH, Columbus, Ohioan

Oklahoma Okla., OK, Oklahoma City, Oklahoman

Oregon Oreg., OR, Salem, Oregonian

Pennsylvania Pa., PA, Harrisburg, Pennsylvanian

Puerto Rico PR, San Juan, Puerto Rican

Rhode Island R.I., RI, Providence, Rhode Islander

South Carolina S.C., SC, Columbia, South Carolinian

South Dakota S.Dak., SD, Pierre, South Dakotan

Tennessee Tenn., TN, Nashville, Tennessean

Texas Tex., TX, Austin, Texan

Trust Territories TT

Utah UT, Salt Lake City, Utahan

Vermont Vt., VT, Montpelier, Vermonter

Virginia Va., VA, Richmond, Virginian

Virgin Islands VI, Charlotte Amalie, Virgin Islander

Washington Wash., WA, Olympia, Washingtonian

West Virginia W.Va., WV, Charleston, West Virginian

Wisconsin Wis., WI, Madison, Wisconsinite

Wyoming Wyo., WY, Cheyenne, Wyomingite

8. WEIGHTS AND MEASURES

UNIT	U.S. WEIGHT/MEASURE	METRIC WEIGHT/ MEASURE
ton		
short ton	20 short hundredweight *or* 2000 pounds	0.907 metric ton
long ton	20 long hundredweight *or* 2240 pounds	1.016 metric ton
hundredweight (cwt.)		
short hundredweight	100 pounds *or* 0.05 short ton	45.359 kilograms
long hundredweight	112 pounds *or* 0.05 long ton	50.802 kilograms
pound (lb.)	16 ounces *or* 7000 grains	0.453 kilograms
ounce (oz.)	16 drams *or* 437.5 grains	28.349 grams
dram (dr.)	27.343 grains *or* 0.0625 ounce	1.771 grams
grain (gr.)	0.036 dram *or* 0.002285 ounce	0.0648 gram

CAPACITY
(U.S. Liquid Measure)

gallon (gal.)	4 quarts	3.785 liters
quart (qt.)	2 pints	0.946 liter
pint (pt.)	4 gills	0.473 liter
gill (gi.)	4 fluidounces	118.291 milliliters
fluidounce (fl. oz.)	8 fluidrams	29.573 milliliters
fluidram (fl. dr.)	60 minims	3.696 milliliters
minim (min.)	1/60 fluidram	0.061610 milliliter

(U.S. Dry Measure)

bushel (bu.)	4 pecks	35.238 liters
peck (pk.)	8 quarts	8.809 liters
quart (qt.)	2 pints	1.101 liters
pint (pt.)	1/2 quart	0.550 liters

LENGTH

mile (mi.)	5280 feet *or* 320 rods *or* 1760 yards	1.609 kilometers
rod (rd.)	5.50 yards *or* 16.5 feet	5.029 meters
yard (yd.)	3 feet *or* 36 inches	0.9144 meter
foot (ft.)	12 inches *or* 0.333 yard	30.480 centimeters
inch (in.)	0.083 foot *or* 0.027 yard	2.540 centimeters

UNIT	U.S. WEIGHT/MEASURE	METRIC WEIGHT/ MEASURE
	AREA	
square mile (sq. mi.)	640 acres *or* 102,400 square rods	2.590 square kilometers
acre	4840 square yards *or* 43,560 square feet	0.405 hectare *or* 4047 square meters
square rod (sq. rd.)	30.25 square yards *or* 0.006 acre	25.293 square meters
square yard (sq. yd.)	1296 square inches *or* 9 square feet	0.836 square meter
square foot (sq. ft.)	144 square inches *or* 0.111 square yard	0.093 square meter
square inch (sq. in.)	0.007 square foot *or* 0.00077 square yard	16.387 square centimeters
	VOLUME	
cubic yard (cu. yd.)	27 cubic feet *or* 46,656 cubic inches	0.765 cubic meter
cubic foot (cu. ft.)	1728 cubic inches *or* 0.0370 cubic yard	0.028 cubic meter
cubic inch (cu. in.)	0.00058 cubic foot *or* 0.000021 cubic yard	16.387 cubic centimeters

PROOFREADER'S SIGNS AND SYMBOLS

To denote:	Mark the text:
align	‖ straighten text
all capitals	all capitals
boldface	for emphasis b.f.
broken type	imperfection ✗
capitalize	United States of america
center	] Bantam Doubleday Dell [
close up	long time friends ⌒
delete	take out ~~out~~ of sentence ℘
delete and close up	philos⌢ophy
em dash	em—that is, long—dash

en dash	Picasso (1881–1973)
figures	(sixty-five years) fig.
flush right	move to right]
flush left	[move to left
indent em space	☐ insert here
insert apostrophe	here's the answer ⌄
insert brackets	introduction tk [/] ∥
insert colon	our ideas / new thoughts on ⌃
insert comma	apples, pears oranges ⌣
insert dash	the voters as a group declared ⅟M ∥
insert exclamation point	Absolutely authoritative ! /
insert hyphen	state of the art = ///
insert letter	accomodate m /
insert parentheses	footnote see page 82 (/) ∥
insert period	Barbara Ann Kipfer, Ph D ⊙
insert question mark	"Is that correct " they ?/ queried.
insert quote mark	"Yes, it is correct. ⌄ ⌄⌄
insert semicolon	raised the flag the veterans ⌃⌟
insert space	too close together #
italics	read The Great Gatsby ital.
lowercase	Twenty-First Avenue l.c.

new paragraph	the end. Now, begin ¶
no new paragraph	continue on. As we talked
reinstate or let stand	make ~~no~~ changes **stet**
roman	too (much) emphasis **rom.**
small caps	<u>small</u> capitals **sc**
space evenly	add equal ^ space ^ between **eq #**
spell out	NYC (sp)
substitute word	do it ~~correctly~~ **well /**
transpose	the (brightest student is) **tr.**